Originalism in American Law and Politics

The Johns Hopkins Series in Constitutional Thought
Sanford Levinson and Jeffrey K. Tulis, *Series Editors*

Originalism in American Law and Politics

A Constitutional History

Johnathan O'Neill

The Johns Hopkins University Press
Baltimore and London

The Johns Hopkins University Press
2715 North Charles Street
Baltimore, Maryland 21218-4363
www.press.jhu.edu

Library of Congress Cataloging-in-Publication Data

O'Neill, Johnathan G. (Johnathan George)
 Originalism in American law and politics : a constitutional history / Johnathan O'Neill.
 p. cm. — (Johns Hopkins series in constitutional thought)
 Includes bibliographical references and index.
 ISBN 0-8018-8111-0 (hardcover : alk. paper)
 1. Constitutional history—United States. 2. Law—United States—Interpretation and construction—History. I. Title. II. Series.
 KF4541.O54 2005
 342.7302⁄9—dc22
                                                                    2004023572

A catalog record for this book is available from the British Library.

For Rebecca

Contents

Preface

This book examines the originalist conception of constitutional authority and explains why it became a significant component of American political life after World War II. The core originalist idea—that "the intent of the law giver is the law"—is rooted in longstanding principles of Anglo-American constitutionalism. While the originalist idea embodies basic commitments from the nation's founding and the tradition that led to it, the reasons for the reappearance of originalism since the 1960s went beyond those deep roots. A variety of changes in the postwar period again made originalism attractive as a matter of both politics and constitutional jurisprudence, and this book traces the development and elaboration of originalism as both a political and a constitutional idea. This approach neither reduces law to politics nor denies the influence of politics on the law. As a history of constitutional thought in its political context, this work addresses a subject now more commonly treated by academic lawyers and political scientists. It is hoped that historians, who in the past accounted more carefully for constitutional issues, will also find this study a useful contribution to understanding twentieth-century America.

It is a pleasure to acknowledge the friends and colleagues who have aided me in the completion of this book. My greatest debt is to Herman Belz, scholar, teacher, and friend. His wisdom, generosity, and example have sustained me in innumerable ways, both professional and personal, and I will always be grateful that I was his student. Gary McDowell provided me with the crucial opportunity, encouragement, and welcoming friendship that enabled my ideas to mature. My understanding of originalism was deepened and clarified by his scholarship on the nature of a written constitution, as well as by his comments on an important early reading of the manuscript. I very much appreciate the interest that Sanford Levinson took in this volume. As with so many other works of constitutional scholarship over the years, this one could not have come about without him. Jeffrey K. Tulis gave the manuscript a thorough and encouraging reading, offering comments that prompted me to rethink important sections of the argument. At the Johns Hopkins University Press, Henry Tom was unfailingly professional and efficient, and the expert copyediting skills of Martin Schneider greatly improved the clarity and accuracy of the text. Over the years of research and writing, my brother Daniel I. O'Neill was always willing to take time away from his own work to console me or to celebrate with me—or just to argue with me about matters intellectual and political. After such conversations I returned to my study knowing I would always have a warm and faithful friend and with a renewed conviction that the scholarly life, despite its imperfections, is vastly better than others we both were destined to elude. I thank Tim Mahoney for his steadfast friendship, for a place to stay on my research trips to Cambridge, and for some last-minute citation checking. Finally, I am grateful for the generous support of the Earhart Foundation while I was a student and during the summer spent on the penultimate revision of the manuscript. Of course none of the people or institutions acknowledged here is in any way responsible for the interpretations in this book or any errors it may contain.

Chapter 5 is a slightly revised version of an article by the same title, which was first published in *Northwestern University Law Review* 96 (2001): 253–81. It is reprinted by special permission of the Northwestern University School of Law and the *Northwestern University Law Review*. I thank the editors of the *Review of Politics* for permission to use, in brief portions of chapters 2, 7, and 8, material that originally appeared in "Shaping Modern Constitutional Theory: Bickel and Bork Confront the Warren Court," *Review of Politics* 65 (2003): 325–51. I am grateful for the permission of Joanne Bickel and Robert H. Bork to publish material held in the Alexander Mordecai Bickel Papers, Manuscripts and Archives, Yale University Library and the permission of the Librarian of the Harvard Law School to publish material from the Papers of Henry M. Hart Jr. and the Papers of Raoul Berger.

My wife Rebecca gave me the support and understanding that ensured this book would be completed. Just as it was finished we welcomed into the world our daughter Anne, whose wonderful timing is but the smallest of her gifts to us.

Originalism in American Law and Politics

Introduction

Originalist jurisprudence, or "originalism," was one of the most vigorously debated topics in American constitutionalism in the last quarter of the twentieth century. What role the original meaning of the U.S. Constitution should have, if any, became a pressing question during the 1960s and 1970s under the Warren and Burger Courts. Originalism developed further during the administration of President Ronald Reagan and attracted perhaps the widest attention in the failed nomination of Robert H. Bork to the U.S. Supreme Court in 1987. Today opponents and defenders of originalism abound. It figures in important areas of Rehnquist Court jurisprudence and is a major component of professional constitutional commentary and theory. In this sense originalism is a relatively recent development, but it is old in that it draws on long-established components of Anglo-American constitutionalism. This book is the first historical examination of originalism as a defense of traditional understandings of legal interpretation, limited and consent-based government, and the rule of law.

This study explains how the originalist conception of legitimate constitutional authority became an increasingly cogent and systematic way of evaluating Supreme Court decisions and competing constitutional theories. The focus is on academic commentators, their ideas, and their criticism of the Court in the shifting political context of the twentieth century. Although many important judicial decisions prompted theoretical development, this study primarily investigates how constitutional commentators established limits for what could be considered legitimate Supreme Court decisions, rather than the jurisprudence of particular justices or the Court's decision-making process itself.

A brief working definition of the originalist idea is necessary to orient discussion of its development over time.[1] Originalism is best understood as several closely related claims about the authoritative source of American constitutional law, that is to say, what it means to interpret the Constitution and what evidence interpreters may legitimately consult to recover constitutional meaning. First, originalism holds that ratification was the formal, public, sovereign, and consent-conferring act which made the Constitution and subsequent amendments law. Second, originalism holds that interpretation of the Constitution is an attempt to discover the public meaning it had for those who made it law. Third, originalism holds that although interpretation begins with the text, including the structure and relationship of the institutions it creates, the meaning of the text can be further elucidated by extrinsic sources. This includes evidence from those who drafted the text in convention as well as from the public debates and commentary surrounding its ratification. Recourse to such evidence was rare before the twentieth century, but modern originalists have increasingly used it to contest the interpretations of their opponents. Finally, because originalism regards the sovereign act of lawmaking authority as having "fixed" the meaning of a constitution to be interpreted by ordinary legal methods, consultation of extrinsic evidence is usually limited to historical sources that might reveal the public meaning of the text at the time it became law. Any interpretation conceived as the application of a specific philosophical or moral theory is typically rejected. Thus, for example, although the Constitution emerged in the general context of modern natural rights theory, most originalists deny that the judiciary is therefore legitimately enabled to invoke such theory for creating rights beyond those enumerated in the document.[2] In sum, the originalist conception of constitutional authority aims to realize the overarching constitutionalist goal of defining and limiting official power before its exercise. It insists that interpreters be bound by the meaning the document had for those who gave it legal authority.

A brief sketch of the legal-political background of the founding is necessary to highlight the conceptions of constitutional authority and interpretative legitimacy that form the basis of originalism.[3] The American founders aimed to protect natural rights by creating a republican government with limited powers. The embodiment of this aim was a written constitution that enumerated official powers and a bill of rights that also constrained them. A written constitution was regarded as the culmination of the development of the concept of constitutionalism, which had evolved in both English and American thought and practice in the seventeenth and eighteenth centuries. By the time of the American founding, a constitution signified the principles, design, and structure of a government to which the members of a polity had given their consent. Additionally, the organization of colonial America under royal charters, religious covenants, and compacts encouraged Americans to regard a constitution as a written text and not merely a customary or traditional set of practices, as the term generally was understood in England. Equally important, Americans came to regard a written constitution as a higher or fundamental law whose principles and procedures normatively circumscribed the limits of routine political activity. The U.S. Constitution, as a law that was supreme over ordinary state and federal legislation, was enforceable in state and federal courts. The American founders hoped that legal enforcement of the written Constitution would make practicable a republican government that was limited, based on consent, and secured natural rights.

Considered from the perspective of Western political thought, the creation of the American Constitution was an effort to fulfill the ancient ideal of the rule of law. Government by a known set of principles, standards, and rules was thought preferable to the rule of personal desire, arbitrary will, or force. It was hoped that the new constitution would remedy chronic social instability, unaccountable official power, and ad hoc rule. The rule of law established by the Constitution would subordinate government power to principles, structures, and procedures outside of and anterior to the officers who exercised it. Officers could act legitimately only by constantly pointing to the source of their power in the Constitution. Thus, in an older formulation, the aim of the Constitution was to create a "government of laws and not of men" so that people might govern themselves by "reflection and choice" rather than by "accident and force."[4]

The American founders' attempt to secure the rule of law through a written constitution reflected not only their own experience with text-based self-government but also the emergence of modern social contract theory and its associated understanding of language. Following John Locke (and, more remotely, Thomas Hobbes), the founders' project regarded language as a medium capable of conveying thought from one mind to another with relative precision. Popular ratification of the written constitution signaled that the people (or the people as states) consented to the principles, structures, and procedures inscribed in it as the best protection of their rights. Government could now be held within the limits of the text that created it. Legalization of the text through this formal act of consent was thus a culmination of the fundamental contractarian idea: rights are best protected from arbitrary power by a lawful contract in which a limited government is compelled to exercise power through promulgated rules. Government would remain limited (and rights protected) by adherence to the terms of the contract; were the contract to be

misinterpreted or ignored, the limits would disappear and power would be illegitimate. Accordingly, proper interpretation would ascertain and apply the
parties' intent with regard to the contract. Hobbes, Locke, and the influential
popularization of social contract theory in *Cato's Letters* relied on this understanding of the relationship among language, consent, contract, the modern
philosophy of natural rights, and textual interpretation.[5]

Once the Constitution became law, interpretation would seek the intended,
ratified meaning of the text as the ultimate source of legitimate legal and political authority. Its words, though sometimes disputed, were understood to
have a real, limited meaning. This understanding of interpretation also incorporated historical knowledge: the American founding was a discernible
set of historical events and principles (evidence of which exists in a variety of
sources) that had produced the documentary Constitution. As social change
and unforeseen circumstances presented profound questions about application of the Constitution, the legitimacy of an interpretation could always be
measured against the meaning of the constitutional text as originally understood.[6]

Despite the close link between originalism and a regime based on a written
constitution, other methods of constitutional decision-making have long been
practiced and regarded as legitimate.[7] These methods ultimately differ from
originalism in their conceptions of legal and political authority. In practice,
though, these methods often complement and overlap one another as well as,
to some extent, originalism itself. "Textualism" decides cases by finding meaning in a close reading of the document and typically does not consult extrinsic historical evidence. There are three types of textualism: "clause-bound,"
which narrows its attention to particular pieces of the text; "structuralist,"
which considers individual clauses as part of the surrounding text; and "purposive," which seeks to identify the basic goals of the clauses and/or the text
as a whole. "Doctrinalism" decides cases by applying to new factual situations
rules or principles from previous interpretations of the Constitution, which
stand as precedents; it is the analogic method familiar to the common law.
"Structuralism" also has a second and wider meaning, as an appeal to the nature and relationship of the institutions created in the text or to the broader
political system surrounding the text. The "purposive" approach likewise has
a second and wider meaning, as an appeal to more abstract philosophical,

ethical, aspirational, or prudential theories which can supplement or override the text, its original meaning, or established doctrine.

In several of the approaches listed here, historical evidence may be consulted but usually in a fashion not allowed by originalism. In the helpful distinction of Charles A. Miller, originalists typically practice "intent" history, which ties the meaning of words in the text to the meaning they had for those who enacted them into law, as revealed in part by historical evidence contemporaneous with the enactment. Other methods of constitutional decision-making typically practice "ongoing" history. This use of history moves beyond evidence contemporaneous with the text to find meaning in the "currents and lessons of experience," as in precedents or historical developments outside of legal doctrine as such. "Ongoing history does not say 'this is what was expected,' but 'this is what the nation has become.'"[8] Thus, as noted above, the originalist view of the Constitution and the source of its legal authority defines tighter limits on the historical context that can be used to establish constitutional meaning than other methods of decision-making.

The originalist approach was present in American constitutional law and thought since the country's founding, but by the 1930s its conceptions of constitutional authority and legitimate interpretation had been marginalized. The first chapter of this book traces this shift. It begins with a historical survey of appeals to original intent and historical evidence in constitutional thought and judicial review and the limited scope of judicial power from the founding through the late nineteenth century. In this period the originalist approach directly implied by a written constitution was most often simply assumed as a principle of the regime and briefly acknowledged as an application of the common law approach to statutes. Interpreters typically expressed the originalist idea confidently and axiomatically, generally locating original meaning in the text. Accordingly, in this traditional period there was little drive to offer a detailed theoretical defense of originalism, and appeals to extrinsic historical evidence were rare. Chapter 1 then recounts the displacement of this axiomatic "textual originalist" understanding of the Constitution and interpretive practice as part of the early twentieth-century intellectual "revolt against formalism."[9] In jurisprudence this revolt was manifested in "legal realism," a watershed in the history of legal thought that drove theorists and, eventually, constitutional law to abandon the "economic substantive due process" jurisprudence of the pre–New Deal Court. With it went the inherited originalist understanding of interpretation as the application of legal categories established in the text, which by then had become tied to the rigidly formalist style of legal reasoning characteristic of what some scholars have labelled "classical legal thought."

Legal realism was the key development that paved the way for "modern judicial power" and, eventually, the plethora of theories about how best to constrain or justify the use of that power.[10] Following the realists, the modern understanding of constitutional judicial review was, first and most fundamentally, that constitutional judging was only another form of lawmaking. Adjudication in general and interpretation in particular were manipulated by judges to fashion political goals into law. Second, academic advocates and judicial practitioners of modern judicial power rejected older, text-based categorical and formalist legal reasoning in favor of quasi-legislative "balancing." Modern judges decided cases by identifying, comparing, and assigning values to supposedly abstract constitutional provisions or to competing interests, and then by balancing them in a fashion that had little discernible basis in the original Constitution.[11] Finally, modern judicial power was frequently defended by invoking the appealing metaphor of a "living Constitution" that the Court updated to the needs of the times.[12] As modern judicial power developed, it became common for courts and supportive commentators to restate constitutional language at a higher level of generality than it originally had for those who wrote and ratified the Constitution. Modern judicial power was institutionalized in the doctrinal and political sea change accompanying the New Deal and found support in the Democratic coalition that dominated national party politics from 1936 until 1968.

When modern judicial power defeated classical legal thought and economic substantive due process, it also displaced traditional axiomatic textual originalism and its associated but generally untheorized conceptions of constitutional authority and interpretation. However, as chapter 2 shows, after World War II theorists and the new Supreme Court were cautious. The Court practiced "self-restraint" in part because the Cold War political and ideological environment demanded that legislative choices be shielded from overly assertive judicial power. Further, the New Deal victory over economic substantive due process mandated judicial deference to the economic regulations of the Democrat-controlled Congress. At this time scholarship was dominated by a jurisprudential theory aimed at confining modern judicial power with appeals to "neutral principles" and the integrity of a "legal process" distinct from mere political preference. Process-restraint jurisprudence defended the rule of law and democracy with techniques for instilling neutrality in judicial decision-making and by fostering judicial deference to legislatures. Although the claims of original intent as a source of legitimate constitutional authority were too fundamental to be completely ignored, they were a subordinate concern in the process-restraint attempt to control modern judicial power. However, the process-restraint approach could not prevent the reassertion of that power.

Chapter 3 traces the growth of originalist thinking after the deployment of modern judicial power for liberal goals in *Brown v. Board of Education* (1954).[13] During the *Brown* litigation, and throughout the late 1950s and 1960s, critics and even some defenders of the Warren Court consulted history with renewed concern. Justices and commentators, including some in the process-restraint tradition, ever more stridently criticized the increasingly obvious gap between the received meaning of the Constitution and what the Court now said it meant. But despite some recognition of the legitimacy of originalist arguments, advocates of the process-restraint approach did not develop originalism as a positive response to the Warren Court's reassertion of modern judicial power, which their own approach had not forestalled. Thus, historically based criticisms of the Warren Court established a tendency toward modern originalism, but in doing so they carried forward the process-restraint insistence on neutrality in judicial decision-making and deference to legislatures in the absence of established constitutional authority.

Once historical analysis had become a major aspect of Supreme Court criticism in the late 1960s and early 1970s, as chapter 4 shows, additional jurisprudential and political developments constituted a "crossroads" that further encouraged the emergence of originalism. These developments were the liberal reformist rejection of the process-restraint approach, the character of the new liberal jurisprudence that replaced it, and the emergence of a conservative political challenge to modern American liberalism. The liberal-reformist abandonment of the process-restraint approach ended the suspicion of judicial power that had characterized liberalism since its resistance to "economic substantive due process" at the beginning of the twentieth century. In the 1960s a new generation insisted that liberal political goals were best achieved not by the moderating and braking tendencies of the older liberal process-restraint jurisprudence but rather by an active, reforming Court.

Originalism emerged in part to combat this new liberal embrace of modern judicial power, which has come to be known as "legal liberalism."[14] As used in this book, this term describes the common thrust of a number of complex, competing theories in which academics and judges sought to justify and elaborate modern judicial power and the landmark liberal decisions of the Warren and early Burger Courts. Legal liberals accepted the postrealist equation of judging and legislation and then offered theories that attempted to reconcile judicial review with the rule of law and consent-based democratic government.[15] Likewise, most legal liberals defended the closely related notion, sometimes expressed directly in the metaphor of a living Constitution, that judges should update the assertedly vague, abstract, or anachronistic fundamental law to contemporary values or needs.[16] At the doctrinal level, legal liberals, like the modern Court itself, typically advocated ad hoc, quasi-legislative "balancing" tests as the appropriate adjudicatory tool for the constitutional updating process.[17]

Amid the complex details of competing theories, the common direction of legal liberalism at the crossroads of the late 1960s and early 1970s was to encourage the Court to trump legislative judgments by discerning and protecting its own definition (that is, the theorist's preferred definition) of norms, values, or rights not clearly part of the Constitution as originally understood. Legal liberals called for the Court to get on with realizing the modern liberal program, through, for example, judicially created visions of "goodness" or "moral courage,"[18] judicially determined moral "conceptions" of constitutional "concepts,"[19] or judicially determined levels of participation in the political process.[20] But, as one theorist observed, the explosion in legal liberal justifications for the reformist use of modern judicial power was "plainly designed to protect the legacy of the Warren Court"[21] and usually constituted what another observer frankly called "advocacy scholarship—amicus briefs ultimately designed to persuade the Court to adopt our various notions of the public good."[22] Eventually in the 1980s originalists also faced theories derived from postmodernism and literary hermeneutics, some of which argued that the rule of law could be approximated only by a somewhat ambiguous ongoing "process" or "communal conversation."[23] More radical critics of this type sometimes claimed that constitutionalism and the rule of law were impossible.[24] These later developments aside, it was clear enough in the immediate aftermath of the Warren Court that constitutional theory had reached a crossroads, at which competing versions of "legal liberalism" superseded the process-restraint tradition.

At this crossroads the originalist idea stood as a fundamental and newly enlivened alternative to the reformist use and scholarly, legal liberal encouragement of modern judicial power. Led in the 1970s by Raoul Berger, Robert Bork, and William Rehnquist, originalism built on the persistent and now pressing historical component of constitutional decision-making and analysis, as well as the now embattled process-restraint insistence on judicial neutrality and deference. Further, originalists reasserted more strongly than had process-restraint theorists the original conception of constitutional authority and the nature of interpretation. Measuring by the standard of the original public meaning of the Constitution and demonstrating an increased willingness to consult extrinsic historical material as evidence of that meaning, originalists rejected the legal liberal embrace of modern judicial power as a threat to the rule of law, the separation of powers, and federalism. In challenging the legal liberal defense of modern judicial power, originalists often attacked the postrealist equation of judging and legislating. Likewise, they focused criticism on the highly generalized treatment of constitutional language and the creation of new rights that frequently characterized judicial updating of the living Constitution. The increasingly pervasive and complex practice of "balancing" received less sustained attention and consequently will receive less in this study.

Originalists criticized recent Supreme Court decisions that advanced liberal goals, although as a theoretical matter originalism is not inherently opposed to judicial review or decisions with liberal results. But given the historical context of the late 1960s and early 1970s, the emergence of originalism in constitutional theory was advanced by a related and simultaneous "crossroads" in American politics. The numerous contentious issues of the period, including the liberal policy results of many Warren and early Burger Court decisions, ended the political dominance enjoyed by the New Deal Democratic coalition since the 1930s. Key components of the coalition became alienated from one another; some moved into the emerging Republican majority, which eventually elected Ronald Reagan as president in 1980. The end of the New Deal order combined with the renaissance of political conservatism and the Republican Party to encourage originalism by decreasing support for legal liberalism. Originalism was politically attractive as a jurisprudentially traditional approach that, at least in the post–1960s atmosphere, implied conservative policy results as opposed to the prior wave of liberal Supreme Court decisions.

Chapters 5 through 8 show that as the New Deal coalition fragmented, originalism grew steadily in influence and reconfigured academic debate about judicial power. Originalism was galvanized by Raoul Berger, a New Deal liberal whose book on the Fourteenth Amendment rejected modern judicial power and struck at the heart of legal liberalism (chapter 5). In the 1980s originalism set the terms of jurisprudential debate and was further advanced by the political power conservatives achieved in the Reagan administration (chapter 6). In 1987 Robert Bork, one of originalism's earliest and most forceful defenders, was denied a seat on the Supreme Court in a spectacular public battle that put the doctrine on the defensive (chapter 7). However, in the 1990s originalism continued to develop. Its theoretical structure was elaborated and refined, and the output of originalist historical investigation also increased (chapter 8). Not all originalists advocated compatible versions of the theory, and a degree of fragmentation became apparent as the bases and implications of the doctrine were probed more widely and rigorously. Nevertheless, liberal theorists too had to take more account of originalist claims about the nature of interpretation as well as the relevance of historical evidence in constitutional adjudication. In these ways constitutional theory was marked by the growing influence and ongoing development of originalism. However, chapter 8 concludes by observing that despite the centrality of originalism to constitutional theory, there was no fundamental reorientation of Supreme Court jurisprudence. Originalism is now more of a factor on the Court than it once was, but as an empirical matter it does not predominate over other modes of decision-making.

Its limitations notwithstanding, the emergence and development of originalism must be understood in greater depth than it has been heretofore. Originalism remains relevant to constitutional politics because it will likely continue to influence the justices to some extent, especially if new originalists are added to the bench, as Republican politicians have suggested they might be. At a deeper level, "originalism" has entered the political and jurisprudential lexicon, and we learn something important about American history by assessing how and why there was traction for its claim that too frequently the Court had acted outside the limits of the Constitution as originally understood. Moreover, understanding the arrival and influence of originalism permits a fuller appreciation of how post–World War II constitutional history is connected to past eras. Originalism manifested much older fundamental concerns with limited government, consent, and the rule of law. It thus articulated the aims of the American experiment in written constitutionalism and showed that the nature of the regime could still call forth political and juris-prudential action amid modern developments.

Accordingly, originalism should not be dismissed, as too often it has been, just because the debate surrounding it includes difficult legal, constitutional, and historical issues or because in recent political settings originalist arguments frequently implied conservative policy results. Whatever its political thrust in particular cases and however remote it may appear, originalism raises issues of the utmost significance to citizens concerned with constitutional limitations on official power. It involves the nation's most basic ideals and concerns the proper ordering of its most important political institutions. At present it remains to be seen if originalism is the final manifestation of the characteristic American fidelity to a written fundamental law or perhaps the first step in returning it to lasting prominence. It is perhaps even more likely that originalism will be fashioned into just another tool for pragmatic manipulation by the Court and modern theorists who typically equate judging and legislating. This book explains the emergence and development of originalism and clarifies its presentation of what seem to be these basic options for American constitutionalism at the beginning of the twenty-first century.

CHAPTER 1

From Textual Originalism to Modern Judicial Power

Before the triumph of modern judicial power in the twentieth century, constitutional interpretation was understood as the ascertainment and application of the fixed, unchanging meaning of the written Constitution. Traditional interpreters recognized distinctions between law and politics and between legislation and adjudication. Their understanding of the judicial role required limits on interpretive discretion so that rights were protected and representative government at both the federal and state levels was maximized.

The traditional approach was regarded as axiomatic in a regime based on popular sovereignty, social contract theory, a written constitution, and the overarching constitutionalist goal of maintaining limited government under the rule of law. The intellectual and jurisprudential universe of traditional interpreters did not require elaborate theoretical defenses of their approach or its epistemological commitments. Interpretation as ascertainment and application of the meaning of the text was so much a part of legal consciousness that usually it was simply assumed rather than theorized. Adapting the received common law approach to statutes, traditional interpreters often described the object of interpretation as a search for "intent," and they usually sought it in the text of the Constitution and only rarely in extrinsic evidence such as convention debates or the *Federalist Papers*. This approach tended to collapse the firmer modern distinction between originalism and textualism. It also insisted that judges were limited by the separation of powers and federalism, thus obscuring another later distinction between originalist recurrence to extrinsic evidence and structuralist forms of argument.

The first half of this chapter surveys traditional, axiomatic "textual originalism" and shows that, in theory if not always in practice, it was regarded as the orthodox approach to constitutional interpretation until the early twentieth century. The second half of the chapter shows how this approach was marginalized by the modern intellectual "revolt against formalism." This major shift produced the "legal realist" equation of law and politics, the concept of a "living Constitution," and modern "balancing" tests. Together, these developments constituted a modern form of judicial power that eventually was elaborated by the Warren Court in the 1960s. At the outset it must be cautioned that traditional textual originalism and contemporary originalism should not be ahistorically equated, nor should we read modern realist conceptions of law and adjudication back onto the different intellectual self-conception of traditional-era jurisprudents. To understand how a new group of originalists in the second half of the twentieth century built on the traditional approach, we must first recognize its distinctiveness and then trace the fundamental modern departure from it.

Textual Originalism: From Blackstone to the *Lochner* Era

The Blackstonian Inheritance

The American political, legal, and intellectual heritage encouraged legal thinkers to understand the Constitution as a super-statute, an act of sovereign will whose preexisting intent could be ascertained by judges through normal legal methods. Therefore, while common law in nineteenth-century America was often instrumentalist and rapidly changing, public law was treated more formalistically even before the rise of the systematized and self-conscious formalism associated with classical legal thought in the *Lochner,* or economic substantive due process, era (treated below).[1]

The lawyerly Americans derived their method of constitutional interpretation most immediately from English jurist William Blackstone's *Commentaries* (1764–69). By Blackstone's time, parliamentary supremacy was no longer seriously questioned in English constitutionalism. He made this clear in a well-known observation about the interpretation of legislative acts: "to set the judicial power above that of the legislature" would be "subversive of all government." This reality defined the proper approach to statutory interpretation. The goal was to achieve the rule of law by ascertaining the legislative intent or will. Clear legislative intent, even in derogation of the common law, was understood to control the content or meaning of the law. Accordingly, numerous authorities agreed with another of Blackstone's famous enunciations: "the fairest and most rational method to interpret the will of the legislator, is by exploring his intentions at the time when the law was made, by signs the most natural and probable. And these signs are either the words, the context, the subject matter, the effects and consequence, or the spirit and reason of the law" or "the cause which moved the legislator to enact it."[2]

Blackstone derived canons of interpretation, well-known to the American founders, from the overall goal of ascertaining legislative intent. These canons oriented the task of constitutional interpretation until the rise of modern judicial power. The most important was the "plain meaning," or "literal" rule, in which the best indication of legislative intent was the words of the text, understood, as Blackstone said, "in their usual and most known signification . . . their general and popular use." A term of legal or professional art would be given its usual meaning as understood by those who regularly used it. In the comparatively rare case when the words of the law were too ambiguous to be used alone, the "mischief" rule was invoked. This rule authorized examination of the "evils" the law was designed to remedy (also referred to as its "purpose" or "object" or "end") or, in Blackstone's words, "the reason and spirit of it; or the cause which moved the legislature to enact it."[3] Accordingly, the context and subject matter of the statute could be used to discern the meaning of its words.

Blackstone also derived a rule to ensure consistency: departure from the words, even in their literal or unambiguous meaning, was permitted when they "bear either none, or a very absurd signification, if literally understood."[4] However, the absurdity issuing from literal application had to be a matter of logic, not merely a disfavored policy result. Absurdity could obtain if application of the plain or literal meaning yielded an internal *self-contradiction* in the law, meaning a conflict within its own provisions or between the law and a background principle of constitutional or higher law dimensions. Either kind of contradiction meant that the act was "impossible to be performed." Thus, an appeal to higher or fundamental law as a limit on legislative enactments existed in Blackstone's rule of consistency and his understanding of statutory interpretation. Of course, such appeals also issued from many other sources and were central to American constitutional thought at the founding, but Blackstone carefully highlighted how the political reality of parliamentary supremacy made parliament's clear intent the source of law, even if it was contrary to traditional common law practice or a judge's view of reasonableness.[5] After ratification of the Constitution secured its status as fundamental law, the Blackstonian approach helped define the limited parameters of early judicial interpretation.[6]

The Founding and the Marshall and Taney Courts

Interpretation of the American Constitution based on its original intent was a natural outgrowth of the Blackstonian inheritance and the principles of social contractarianism and popular sovereignty that informed the founding. American constitutional interpreters from the late eighteenth to the late nineteenth century regularly referred to the "intent" and "purpose" of the framers, the ratifiers, and the Constitution. Although Americans occasionally consulted extrinsic sources, the usual practice, following Blackstone and the English inheritance, sought the originally intended meaning by examination of the constitutional text. This traditional practice has aptly been described as "textual originalism"; in attempting to maintain the constitutional design, it usually collapsed "the contemporary distinction between textualism and originalism."[7] Of course, interpreters were not unanimous about the content or proper application of intent and frequently insisted that political opponents had assayed it incorrectly. However, the idea that interpretation was something other than a search for intent or that a judge could balance competing policy goals or "update" the living Constitution to his view of contemporary requirements was almost never heard before the late nineteenth century.[8]

In the *Federalist Papers*, Alexander Hamilton, James Madison, and John Jay, writing as "Publius," consistently employed Blackstone's rules, both explicitly and in the overall style of argument, to explain the political philosophy of the Constitution. In number 82, for example, Publius explained that state court decisions involving federal questions would be appealable to the Supreme Court: "The evident aim and plan of the convention is that all the causes of the specified classes [in Article III]" would be determined either originally or on appeal by the Supreme Court. To confine the Court's appellate jurisdiction to subordinate federal courts would be to subvert "the intent, contrary to every sound rule of interpretation." Moreover, in explaining the meaning of the Constitution, Publius frequently referred to the "plan of the convention," the "tenor of the instrument," and the "intent of the Constitution."[9] While Publius, like John Locke, conceded that language inevitably conveyed human thought imperfectly in the complex area of political principle, he also thought, again like Locke, that language could be reasonably precise.[10] Thus, in elucidating what all understood as a fixed, unchanging Constitution, Publius examined its text and structure and defended it in terms of its intent, purposes, and objects.

Perhaps most importantly, Publius's famous argument for judicial review in *Federalist* 78 likened the Constitution to a statute and argued that the Supreme Court would effectuate its purpose by using the standard legal interpretive techniques that aimed at ascertaining and applying original intent. This argument in turn depended upon popular sovereignty as the source of the Constitution's status as supreme law: "the constitution ought to be preferred to the statute, the intention of the people to the intention of their agents."[11] Moreover, Publius understood legal reasoning as different in kind from that of legislation. He insisted the Court would exercise only legal "judgement" in effectuating the will of the sovereign people as expressed in the "intention" of the Constitution. Legislative "will" was foreign to legal interpretation and the Court would instead be "bound down by [the] strict rules and precedents" of the legal craft.[12]

Congressional organization of the new government in the 1790s also reflected the standard textual originalist view. This was evident in the controversies over the presidential removal power, the creation of a national bank, and the Jay Treaty (1796).[13] Much in these debates concerned the practical application of a doctrine of implied power under the "necessary and proper" clause (Article I, section 8). Accordingly, debates in the 1790s reflected the tension between nationalists and advocates of a decentralized, state-centered union, a tension that had also been central to the ratification debate and continued in the first party system of Federalists and Jeffersonian Republicans. Yet for most of the nineteenth century, as the historian Morton Horwitz has observed, "debates over constitutional meaning took place entirely within Jefferson's and Chief Justice Marshall's framework of express versus implied powers and loose versus strict meaning of words. But if the debate between narrow and broad readings introduced a measure of flexibility into early constitutional interpretation, it was a flexibility firmly anchored in the premises of originalism."[14]

A detailed recounting of the 1790s is beyond the scope of the present work, but a brief consideration of congressional interpretation in this much-studied period confirms that it generally followed the prevailing rules of interpretation by seeking intent primarily in the text and only secondarily and rarely in evidence from the Philadelphia convention or state ratifying conventions.[15] Yet during the bank debate Madison attempted to establish the original meaning of the "necessary and proper" clause by invoking the Philadelphia convention and by quoting both state ratifying conventions and public defenders of the Constitution. Although Hamilton also occasionally referred to such extrinsic sources, in the bank debate he defended the more generally accepted idea that "intention is to be sought for in the instrument itself, according to the usual and established tools of construction."[16]

Recent scholars have emphasized the range of sources that Congressmen of the 1790s examined as evidence of originally intended constitutional meaning, such as the text, the debates of the Philadelphia convention, the *Federalist,* debates in state ratification conventions, and even the "sense," "spirit," or overall "purpose" of the document. Such studies have sometimes charged the founders with politically inspired inconsistency in order to undermine the recent originalists' claim that the original meaning of the Constitution exists and can be recovered.[17] To be sure, there was inconsistency in the kind of evidence averred in various debates, James Madison's being the best known. Politics surrounded interpretation, as it always had, but politically interested members of Congress still had to persuade their colleagues that their positions fell within the range of plausible interpretations of the document.[18] Moreover, none of the disputants fundamentally rejected the methods of their adversaries.[19] These facts underscore the more basic point that, despite disagreement about what the Constitution meant or required and the variety of sources invoked, few at the time thought interpretation was anything other than the ascertainment and application of original intent. The very features of these debates that modern scholars often regard as trimming or self-deception are better understood as evidence of the axiomatic, tacit, and untheorized nature of originalism in this period. Madison made this clear in a telling statement during the removal debate. In opposing anything diminishing the "principle" of executive responsibility that pervaded the "spirit" of Article II, he said it would be "contrary to [the Constitution's] spirit and intention, and unless it is saddled upon us expressly by the letter of that work, I shall oppose the admission of it into any act of the legislature."[20] Even when not pointing to a specific textual provision and speaking of "principle" and "spirit," Madison thought he was engaged in elucidating original intent. Interpreters debated the application and emphasis of original intent and sometimes the extent to which relatively rare appeals to extrinsic evidence were admissible. But interpretation was understood as effectuating the preexisting sovereign will of those who legitimated the words and structure of the Constitution that the framers wrote, as revealed by the text, historical evidence, reason, and common sense.[21] The rule of law ideal embodied in a written constitution of enumerated powers and deriving its legal force from the sovereign act of ratification further reinforced this established notion of interpretation.[22]

The scattered evidence of state court adjudications in the founding period also reflected the traditional view of law and legal interpretation that we have been charting, and it was further evident in Chief Justice John Marshall's jurisprudence.[23] Like other interpreters of the era, Marshall regularly used the tools of Blackstonian statutory interpretation and usually ascertained original intent by reading the text and only occasionally by consulting extrinsic sources (primarily the *Federalist*). Marshall used Blackstone's rules in light of the intent of the Constitution, not in a rote or lexicographic fashion. That is, he considered the overall structure, purpose, and political science of the Constitution when applying its discrete phrases as law. This approach blurred what have been later distinguished as originalist, structuralist, and textualist forms of argument. It also inevitably meant that Marshall's nationalist inclination shaped American constitutional law from the unformed condition in which he found it, which in turn generated criticism based on competing conceptions of original intent. But whatever the legitimate range of dispute about the originalist accuracy of some opinions, most scholars agree that Marshall did not understand himself as acting in a fundamentally creative fashion, let alone in a legislative or instrumentalist one.[24]

Further, most scholars now agree that in the famous case of *Marbury v. Madison* (1803), despite its charged political context, Marshall carried forward the established understanding of interpretation and the judicial function under a written constitution. Regarding his duty as explication of the Constitution by the "plain import of the words" in their "obvious meaning," Marshall held that the Judiciary Act of 1789 unconstitutionally enlarged the Court's power by authorizing it to issue writs of *mandamus*. Marshall rooted the power to disregard the statute in the nature of the American regime, among whose distinguishing features was a written constitution that had created three coequal branches of government. He thus echoed and paraphrased the argument in *Federalist* 78 about the popular sovereignty embodied in the written constitution as a fundamental limit on the legislature. Marshall added that the judicial oath and the supremacy clause not only empowered judges to disregard unconstitutional acts but also confined their interpretations of the document. Such close attention to the language, structure, and purpose of the Constitution tethered judicial interpretation to the rule of law by ensuring that judges always pointed to the source of their power in the document, which itself had not placed the *mandamus* power within the Court's original jurisdiction. In this way the purpose of the Constitution—the protection of liberty by limiting government, including judges—was part of the intent, subject matter, and context that interpreters were duty-bound to consider.[25]

In *Ogden v. Saunders* (1827) Marshall gave the clearest statement of his method, emphasizing that intent was to be gleaned primarily, although not exclusively, from the text of the Constitution. He restated the established Blackstonian idea that "the intention of the instrument must prevail; that this intention must be collected from its words; that its words are to be understood in that sense in which they are generally used by those for whom the instrument was intended; [and] that its provisions are neither to be restricted into insignificance, nor extended to objects not comprehended in them, nor contemplated by its framers."[26] This understanding of interpretation also was evident in *McCulloch v. Maryland* (1819). There Marshall exhaustively and brilliantly analyzed the "necessary and proper" clause in light of Congress's need for latitude in choosing the means of exercising its power. In Marshall's understanding of interpretation, powers delegated by the sovereign act of ratification were established in the constitutional text and created fixed categories for legitimate government action. Judicial interpretation in *McCulloch* was a matter of determining whether particular problems or policies fit within the categories of power established in the text. If so, they were susceptible to a legislative choice of means to effectuate legitimate legislative control over the subject matter of the category. Implied powers, such as creation of the national bank at issue in *McCulloch,* ultimately derived legitimacy from the constitutional text, structure, and design, and therefore from the intent of the Constitution. (Here again we see the blurring of originalist, textualist, and structuralist forms of argument.) It was no part of judicial interpretation to assess the wisdom or expedience of the legislative choice of means to execute a power that was within a category of legitimate legislative authority. Such capacity for legislative choice is what Marshall meant in writing that the Constitution could be "adapted to the various *crises* of human affairs."[27]

Other examples of Marshall's method could be multiplied, and while it may be debated whether he achieved the dictates of his textual originalism in every case, he always understood constitutional interpretation as the effectuation of intent, purpose, and design, as revealed primarily through textual analysis.[28] Indeed, *McCulloch* raised debate about Marshall's opinion, but in a pseudonymous defense of it he was blunt about his method: "The object of language is to communicate the intention of him who speaks, and the great duty of a judge who construes an instrument is to find the intention of its makers."[29] Additionally, while James Madison criticized Marshall's interpretation in *McCulloch* as "latitudinary," his complaint was that it seemed "to break down the landmarks intended by the specification of the Powers of Congress."[30]

The established textual originalist approach to Constitutional interpretation continued beyond the founding generation. The numerous commerce clause decisions of the Court under Chief Justice Roger B. Taney illustrated the same style of categorical reasoning about intent and design as under Marshall, even if they sometimes reached results he might have resisted. A good illustration is *Cooley v. Board of Wardens* (1852). The Court reasoned that the subject matter at issue, regulation of pilotage in local waterways, was more intrastate commerce than interstate, even though in the large port city of Philadelphia the challenged regulation touched foreign and interstate commerce. The Constitution intended federal regulation of interstate commerce, but the Court judged that the activity at issue in *Cooley* was not within this category. Rather, the nature of local pilotage demanded consideration of the tremendous diversity in local circumstances and was therefore not sufficiently national to be regulated as interstate commerce. Again, interpretation in this case was understood as the elaboration and maintenance of the categories and relationships contained in and intended by the Constitution.[31]

Taney further illustrated the traditional approach to interpretation, even as he failed its requirements, in the infamous *Dred Scott* decision (1857). He argued that the Constitution was not intended to apply to blacks (slave or free), nor did it intend congressional regulation of slavery in the territories, as in the Missouri Compromise (1820). Taney defended this view with a weak historical argument and also linked the orthodox originalist approach to the rule of law and the maintenance of constitutional limitations. Distinguishing political power from legal interpretation, Taney stated that "the duty of the Court is . . . to administer [the Constitution] as we find it, according to its true intent and meaning when it was adopted. . . . It must be construed now as it was understood at the time of its adoption." Justice Benjamin Curtis effectively rebutted Taney's historical argument, yet readily agreed that the rule of law depended upon the traditional approach to interpretation: "When a strict interpretation of the Constitution, according to the fixed rules which govern the interpretation of laws, is abandoned, and the theoretical opinions of individuals are allowed to control its meaning, we have no longer a Constitution; we are under the government of individual men."[32]

Legal Treatises and Late Nineteenth-Century Debates

Early national and antebellum legal commentators also adhered to the established textual originalist approach in announcing the orthodox method of statutory interpretation.[33] Antebellum constitutional treatises agreed that the Constitution could only mean what it was originally intended to mean, even as they reflected the politics of the period by debating the locus of sovereignty and the nature of the union, as had been done more famously by nationalists like Daniel Webster and states' rights advocates like Robert Hayne and John C. Calhoun.[34] This also was true of John Taylor of Caroline's *New Views of the Constitution* (1823), which argued the states rights position based on the newly published *Journal of the Federal Convention* (1819) and the notes of Robert Yates (1821), a delegate to the Philadelphia convention from New York.[35] William Rawle, a Northern commentator who uniquely recognized a theoretical right of secession, nonetheless held the orthodox textual originalist view of constitutional interpretation.[36]

Joseph Story's *Commentaries on the Constitution* (1833) defended the nationalist view of sovereignty and the union and also contained a long historical section that also drew from the *Journal of the Federal Convention* and Yates's notes. Story defended the liberal constructions of the Marshall court but wrote that the Constitution, like any other written law, should be met with "the first and fundamental rule in the interpretation of all instruments [which] is, to construe them according to the sense of the terms, and the intent of the parties." He then recapitulated Blackstone's rules of interpretation and held that interpretation based on intent was the best protection for limited government.[37] Abel P. Upshur directly and at length attacked Story's history of the Confederation and the creation of the Constitution but not the idea that the Constitution had a fixed meaning or that to interpret it was to ascertain and abide by its original intent. For Upshur, like John Taylor, the governing historical fact was that the union was a compact created by the states as sovereign entities and thus that the federal government itself was a creation of the compact. But the object of interpretation remained original intent.[38] Henry Baldwin, a Supreme Court justice and commentator who tried to steer a middle way between liberal and strict construction, likewise assumed that intent was the object of interpretation.[39]

Francis Lieber's influential *Legal and Political Hermeneutics* (1839), the first American treatise devoted solely to the topic of interpretation, defined it as finding "the sense [of the words] which their author intended to convey, and of enabling others to derive from them the same idea which the author intended to convey."[40] Lieber's German education and orientation toward an organic, nationalist conception of the state raise questions about the precise relationship of his subtle thought to American constitutionalism, but his conception of interpretation was compelling enough to win him the respect and admiration of James Kent and Joseph Story, notable expositors of the orthodox textual originalist view.[41]

As noted above, much of Story's treatise, like those of Taylor and Upshur, called on sources and facts extrinsic to the text of the Constitution. Such evidence was thought useful for understanding the true nature of the union created by the instrument. Nevertheless, Story restated the orthodox position on extrinsic evidence: intent was discerned primarily by a close reading of the text. Statements of individuals at the Philadelphia or the state ratifying conventions, or the *Federalist,* should be used only secondarily and with caution.[42] However, Chief Justice Marshall, for example, cited the *Federalist* in several cases and echoed its arguments in others, as the Taney Court occasionally did.[43]

The publication of James Madison's notes on the Philadelphia convention in 1840, like Yates's notes and the *Journal of the Federal Convention,* provided further extrinsic evidence of original intent. William Lloyd Garrison's wing of the antislavery movement was among the first to base an originalist argument on Madison's notes. In *The Constitution a Pro-Slavery Compact* (1844), Wendell Phillips collected extracts from the notes to prove that "these Debates show that our fathers intended to make" the Constitution proslavery.[44] Another notable use of such evidence was Justice John Catron's citation of Madison's notes in *Dred Scott* to elucidate his reading of the scope of congressional power to regulate the territories. In refuting Taney's historical argument about the citizenship status of blacks at the founding, Justice Curtis also agreed to conduct the debate in originalist terms.[45] Thus, in the nineteenth century extrinsic evidence was sometimes used to ascertain the originally intended meaning of the Constitution, although justices and commentators denied that it could dislodge a careful textual interpretation based on the long-established Blackstonian canons.

The traditional textual originalist approach, with occasional use of extrinsic evidence, continued during the drafting and early interpretation of the Reconstruction Amendments. As in earlier periods the approach remained more tacit and axiomatic than carefully theorized. Accordingly, it was again manifested not as a theory continuously in need of defense, but as an orthodoxy whose tenets periodically required affirmation when interpretive controversies arose. For example, in 1866 even Charles Sumner, a radical Republican who advocated a broad interpretation of the Fourteenth Amendment, clearly espoused the traditional view, while in 1872 the same point was made explicitly in a unanimous Senate Judiciary Committee Report, signed by many who had voted for the Reconstruction Amendments in prior congresses. Moreover, the committee, like most other interpreters of the era, also insisted that the rule of law required fidelity to original intent.[46]

The framers and ratifiers had hoped that the Fourteenth Amendment would both maintain the traditional design of federalism and increase federal protection for black civil rights. Over time tension between these purposes grew, but for contemporaries they were compatible, and the Supreme Court understood its responsibility as elaboration of doctrine faithful to these goals. Accordingly, the originalist orientation governed initial judicial interpretation of the Fourteenth Amendment.[47] This was evident in the *Slaughterhouse Cases* (1873), in which plaintiffs argued that a local ordinance creating a monopoly for cattle-slaughtering unconstitutionally deprived them of a property right in the pursuit of their trade. Justice Miller's majority opinion, echoing Blackstone, was based on the amendment's "purpose," "spirit," and the "evil [it was] designed to remedy." The "privileges or immunities" of national citizenship were decidedly limited and did not include freedom from regulation of slaughterhouses under the state's traditional police power. The amendment, said Miller, had not intended to give the national government power to superintend such areas of state regulation: "no such results were intended by the

Congress which proposed [the Reconstruction Amendments], nor by the legislatures of the States which ratified them."[48] Justice Stephen J. Field's dissent urged that the amendment's protection of private property should be used to void the regulation but also sought to effectuate what he thought "was intended by the Congress which framed it and the States which adopted it."[49]

The original intent of the Constitution was involved in another of the most important constitutional issues of the late nineteenth century, the use of paper money as a legal tender. The Supreme Court held in a series of cases that Congress had the power to make paper money a legal tender for public and private debts, including retrospective and prospective contracts, during the Civil War[50] and in peacetime.[51] Justices debated the original intent of the Philadelphia convention concerning the Article I, section 8 power of Congress to coin, borrow, and regulate the value of money and the Article I, section 10 denial of state power to "coin money; emit bills of credit; [and] make any thing but gold and silver coin a tender in payment of debts."[52] The central issue was whether excision from the draft Constitution of congressional power to "emit bills of credit" intended an entire prohibition or permitted implication of the power from some other provision. In addition to the dissenting justices, two of the era's leading constitutional scholars, George Ticknor Curtis and George Bancroft, made originalist arguments against paper money as a legal tender.[53]

As in the antebellum period, most treatise writers of the late nineteenth century continued to regard original intent as the object of interpretation. Nationalist commentators took it for granted that the Civil War had discredited the compact theory, and they defended the originally intended nature of the constitutional union as a national government.[54] Thomas M. Cooley's noted treatise reiterated the traditional originalist view, stating that "the object of construction, as applied to a written constitution, is *to give effect to the intent of the people in adopting it*. In the case of all written laws, it is the intent of the law giver that is to be enforced." Likewise, only this traditional approach could safeguard the rule of law.[55] Henry Campbell Black agreed and defined interpretation quite similarly.[56] Arthur W. Machen Jr. also defended a fixed Constitution interpreted according to its original intent and explicitly rejected the nascent notion of an "elastic" living Constitution that judges expediently altered to suit their views of current needs. As in the antebellum era, those who favored strict or broad interpretation might disagree on "the means to be employed in discovering the intent; but both agree—and this is the important point—that the object of all interpretation is the ascertainment thereof."[57]

The Originalist Idea in the *Lochner* Era

In the last decades of the nineteenth century the axiomatic originalist-cum-textualist approach was influenced by the trend in private law jurisprudence toward systematization and increasingly categorical, deductive, and formalist approaches to adjudication. The larger context of this development was the negotiation by courts of the conflicts derived from the contested role of government in the new industrial economy. A brief summary of these closely connected and well-known developments is necessary to understand how they built on the inherited form of originalist thinking and then were eventually displaced by modern judicial power.

Like their forebears, judges in the late nineteenth and early twentieth centuries sharply distinguished state from federal power, law from politics, and judicial from legislative reasoning. They continued to understand themselves as discovering and applying established law to the facts of a given dispute and to regard the legal categories they used as preexisting, derived either from the constitutional text or as immanently contained in extant decisions. But legal reasoning also began to get more rigid and scientistic in this period. Legal categories were more rigorously induced from decisions, an approach that was systematized in the case method of legal education pioneered by Christopher Langdell at Harvard. Additionally, as the formalist and systematizing trend advanced, legal categories often were treated as mutually exclusive and usually existing in dichotomous pairs, such as state/federal, direct/indirect, fact/law, or manufacturing/commerce. Judges decided which category covered the facts of a dispute and deduced a rule from that category to resolve the case, often rigorously following analogous instances of deduction in earlier precedents. This kind of jurisprudence marked the so-called *Lochner,* or economic substantive due process, era, which eventually gave way to the New Deal, and it has aptly been characterized as "legal formalism" or "classical legal thought."[58]

The Supreme Court was not immune from the influence of social Darwinism during this period, but this influence was laid over the older and more fundamental jurisprudential insistence that clear lines existed between legal categories and between departments and levels of government, which were established ultimately by the constitutional text. Only the federal government could regulate interstate commerce; traditional state police powers could be used only to regulate in the interest of health, safety, and morality, but not to defeat economic liberty; and legislation had to have a truly public purpose and treat neutrally all classes of citizens. The Court vindicated these notions in constitutional law by using early precedents, sometimes supplemented with judicial dicta on natural law, to create a formidable tool for overseeing legislatures that was usually applied via a "liberty of contract" derived from the due process clause of the Fourteenth Amendment. This economic substantive due process jurisprudence assessed the "reasonableness" or "arbitrariness" of the legislative regulation of property and contract rights. It is important to emphasize, however, that it did not do so with a modern "balancing" approach but rather by considering whether regulation existed within the established and originally intended categories.[59]

A detailed recounting of the *Lochner* era would be superfluous here, but we must recognize that textual originalism remained a confident and usually tacit concept in this period.[60] The idiom of "intent" occurred with some frequency, and recourse to historical investigation was still quite limited. Indeed, judges of the era did not understand themselves as engaged in a non-originalist or quasi-legislative project any more than had their antebellum counterparts. On the contrary, the premise and rationale for the *Lochner*-era goals of limiting power, ensuring its neutral use, and securing individual rights were understood as rooted in the founders' republicanism and their conception of the purpose and legitimacy of a written constitution. Judges thought they were guarding the integrity of the original constitutional design by maintaining the boundaries between the categories the popular sovereign had established in the text.[61] As one scholar has summarized, the maintenance of such boundaries reflected judges' conception that they were "elaborating general principles. Whereas the other actors exercised their own wills, [judges] obeyed the will of the people who had set up the whole system in the first place."[62] From this perspective it is understandable why the *Lochner* era contained little self-conscious originalist theorizing or historical investigation—judges were confident that they knew what the Constitution originally intended and that interpretation was properly an effort to apply that intent via the legal categories and relationships inscribed in the text.

The interweaving of the older textual originalism and the new formalism can best be illustrated by considering a few notable antiregulatory decisions of the era. In *Pollock v. Farmers' Loan and Trust Co.* (1895), the Court invalidated a federal income tax statute. Referring to the Article I, section 9 requirement that "direct" taxes be apportioned according to population, the Court stated that its responsibility was to decide whether the income tax belonged in the category of direct or indirect taxation as established by the text. The Court next announced that it would confirm the originally intended meaning of the constitutional text with an investigation of "the circumstances which surrounded the convention and controlled its action, and the views of those who framed and those who adopted the constitution." There followed an examination of the context and debates of the Philadelphia convention with respect to revenue and taxation, the *Federalist,* and the opinions of Madison and Hamilton regarding the carriage tax upheld as an indirect tax in *Hylton v. United States* (1796).[63] With this support the Court concluded the income tax was a direct tax within the originally intended meaning of the Constitution and was invalid because it had not been apportioned.

More methodologically typical, because the Court used no historical evidence extrinsic to the text, was *United States v. E.C. Knight Co.* (1895). This decision employed a textual originalist categorical distinction between Congress's power to regulate under the commerce clause and the impermissible regulation of the sugar trust's manufacturing that Congress had undertaken pursuant to the Sherman Antitrust Act (1890). Consistent with the distinction first stated in Marshall's opinion in *Gibbons v. Ogden* (1824), Chief Justice Melville W. Fuller's majority opinion stated that "Commerce succeeds to manufacture, and is not a part of it"; the Sherman Act could not therefore reach the sugar trust.[64] Likewise, in *Lochner v. New York* (1905) the Court invalidated a statute that restricted work in bakeries to ten hours a day or sixty hours a week as a violation of the liberty of contract protected by the Fourteenth Amendment. Justice Peckham's majority opinion posed the issue in terms of the rigorous and mutually exclusive categories of the police power and liberty of contract. Despite the state's argument that effects on the bakers' health was a question of degree that could be scientifically demonstrated and thus was for its legislature to decide, the Court maintained the categorical position that baking "in and of itself, is not an unhealthy [trade] to that degree," such that it would permit police power regulation.[65]

A final example is *Adkins v. Children's Hospital* (1923), in which the Court used the liberty of contract to invalidate a minimum wage for women and minors. The statute was not in the category of police power regulation because it was not limited to businesses affected with a public purpose or to inherently dangerous ones; neither was it an effort to prevent fraud in the payment of wages. It followed that the statute was in the other category, that of arbitrary infringements on the liberty of employers and employees to fix the terms of their contract. This made it "class legislation" designed to benefit one group (employees) at the expense of another (employers).[66] Such examples of the formalist, categorical approach could be multiplied.[67] However, by the 1930s the basis of such decisions in now more rigidly formalist textual originalism conflicted with modern intellectual trends and directly confronted the New Deal reform program. A new constitutional order and a distinctly modern form of judicial power were in the ascendance.

The Revolt against Formalism and the Rise of Modern Judicial Power

Modern judicial power was rooted in the "revolt against formalism." This extended intellectual revolution was a defining feature of the late nineteenth and early twentieth centuries.[68] In this period thinkers attacked and largely abandoned the established, categorical, and deductive ways of thinking about social life, including the nature of law, the Constitution, and adjudication. American legal and constitutional thought was penetrated by philosophic antifoundationalism, pragmatism, legal positivism, Darwinian evolution, and Progressive political demands for more regulatory and interventionist government. The ultimate result, after several decades of intellectual and constitutional struggle, was the marginalization of the untheorized form of textual originalism that had become intertwined with economic substantive due process and formalist adjudication. It was replaced by what has aptly been termed a "pragmatic instrumentalist" approach to law.[69] This new way advanced the regulatory-welfare regime of the New Deal, itself effectuated under the rubrics of a living Constitution, judicial self-restraint, and a doctrinal system based increasingly on the quasi-legislative weighing and balancing of competing social interests.

Oliver Wendell Holmes Jr. led the legal revolt against formalism and inspired "legal realism," which elaborated his thought into a fundamental attack on the old textual originalist and formalist order.[70] For Holmes adjudication was only superficially about legal reasoning. At bottom hard cases presented "a conflict between two social desires," and when not clearly resolved by legal rules, "judges are called upon to exercise the sovereign prerogative of choice."[71] Following Holmes, academics developed legal realism, especially at Yale, Columbia, and Johns Hopkins, and it flourished in the 1920s and 1930s.[72] Realism was more a critical mood reflective of the fundamental intellectual shift surrounding it than a systematic body of jurisprudence. As such, and despite their differences, realists were united in opposing the categorical, deductive, and formalist approach to adjudication typical of classical legal thought and the *Lochner*-era Supreme Court. The "core claim" of the realists was that in deciding cases judges responded primarily to the facts and reached a result based on what they thought would be fair or right—decisions were not motivated or constrained by legal reasons or the constitutional text.[73] The legal reasons upon which formalist judges purported to rely were too abstract, and therefore too indeterminate, to compel a particular outcome in a given case. Realists held, as Holmes had put it in his *Lochner* dissent, that "general propositions do not decide concrete cases."[74] Rather, flexibility and imprecision inhered in deduction from an abstract general principle, whose selection was itself discretionary, to application of a rule in a particular factual circumstance. This was especially true at points where intermediate minor premises were selected and inferences from them were drawn.[75] Furthermore, analogical reasoning, statutory interpretation, and facts themselves were often too indeterminate to resolve a case.[76]

If legal reasons were too indeterminate to explain decisions and judges responded to the facts, what explained their responses? Here the realists split, but generally in a way that reflected the era's fascination with the more behavioralist and empiricist aspects of the emerging social sciences, especially psychology and economics.[77] One group thought responses to facts were utterly unpredictable because they depended on the idiosyncratic, personality-driven "hunches" of particular judges.[78] A larger, more behavioralist and sociologically oriented group thought that judges had common traits, such as legal education, professional experience, and political ideology, that permitted prediction of their responses to certain kinds of fact situations. For this group empirical, social scientific investigation of judges' psychosocial profiles could be correlated with the outcome of cases of a particular fact-type, and this could establish a predictable pattern.[79]

Thus, realism was essentially a debunking, descriptive claim about how adjudication actually worked and then a set of competing explanations about how various nonlegal influences really determined judicial decisions. But its basic assertion that legal decisions were made for nonlegal, idiosyncratic or political reasons was a fundamental rupture from the textual originalist and formalist approaches.[80] The negative and descriptive realist view of adjudication had precious little to say to judges about how to decide cases, amounting to little more than "a constant invitation to the judge to do what he would, on the realist theory, do anyway."[81] As one realist put it, judges should only be clearer that they were deciding cases by doing the "economically or socially valuable thing."[82] Accordingly, scholars rightly mark legal realism as the watershed development in the history of American jurisprudence. By attacking the law/politics distinction it undermined nothing less than the traditional rationales for democracy, judicial review based on a written constitution, and the rule of law.[83] In so doing it established the theoretical agenda for generations of jurisprudents, judges, and democratic theorists. Realism set them the task of firming up the old foundations and rationales of the American legal-constitutional order or constructing new ones.[84]

The following chapters will show that originalism eventually reemerged in response to the modern form of judicial power rooted in realism and vigorously exercised by the Warren and early Burger Courts. At this point, however, we must recognize that irrespective of the problem realism set for later theorists, the realists themselves replaced classical legal thought not with a unified or wholly theorized jurisprudence but rather with a call for change or adaptation.

The formalist jurisprudence the realists opposed might not have had a necessary logical connection to the conservative, antiregulatory policies it generally produced,[85] but the realist critique was meant to impress upon judges the realities of modern, urban, industrial life and impel them to move the law toward the Progressive, interventionist regulatory program.[86] The idea of an evolving, adapting law integrated the broader instrumentalist, updating, and organic tendencies of pragmatist philosophy, Progressive politics, and Darwinist evolutionary theory.[87] Eventually this new thinking explicitly reconceptualized the Constitution as a malleable, living document. Advocates of the living Constitution viewed it as a summation of social and political practices at any given time; the document stated vague ideals that required constant updating, specification, and balancing by judges. Consequently, constitutional interpretation could not effectuate the chimera of original intent, but judges could balance political interests, weigh questions of necessity and expedience, and pragmatically adjust the Constitution to modern times.[88]

Accordingly, as legal realism and Progressive politics developed, the idea of a judicially adapted and updated living Constitution and the allied tendency to replace categorical, deductive reasoning with the balancing of interests became increasingly apparent. Balancing, in which judges decided cases by identifying, comparing, and assigning values to competing interests, has been aptly described as an outgrowth and response to legal realism. As such it became "a methodology for bringing pragmatic instrumentalism into constitutional doctrine."[89]

The tendency toward balancing and updating the living Constitution that became typical of modern judicial power was present amid the other elements of Holmes's thought.[90] Likewise, in deriding classical legal thought as "mechanical jurisprudence," Roscoe Pound argued that the "law in books" of the liberty of contract decisions needed to be updated to the new realities of the "law in action." The Court's insistence on the formal equality of the contracting parties blinded it to the fact that "actual industrial conditions" were "conditions of inequality."[91] The current gap between the outdated law and "social justice" existed because "our settled habits of juristic thought are to no small extent out of accord with current social, economic and philosophical thinking."[92] Moreover, Pound also advocated balancing, arguing that the task of the legal order, including constitutional law, was "to give effect to the greatest total of interests or to the interests that weigh most in our civilization."[93]

Benjamin Cardozo influentially advanced the trend toward pragmatic judicial balancing and updating of the Constitution by identifying common law reasoning with modern American pragmatism. In difficult cases, he argued, judges used assorted grounds of decision in an ultimately subjective, personal way. Because Holmes-influenced moderns were convinced that all legal issues were a "question of degree," Cardozo advised the "useful judge" to "balance all his ingredients, his philosophy, his logic, his analogies, his history, his customs, his sense of right, and all the rest" to decide a case according to his understanding of the "mores of the day" and the "furtherance of the common good."[94] Cardozo did not recognize any basic distinction between constitutional interpretation and his pragmatic understanding of the common law; he claimed that "the great generalities of the constitution have a content and significance that vary from age to age." On this view, "interpretation, thus enlarged, becomes more than the ascertainment of the meaning and intent of lawmakers whose collective will has been declared. It supplements the declaration, and fills the vacant spaces, by the same processes and methods that have built up the customary law."[95]

Progressive-era judicial treatments of the First and Fourth Amendments marked the first sustained judicial elaboration of the modern living Constitution and balancing approaches. Traditional interpretation of the First Amendment had assessed whether speech was rational argument designed to per-suade on issues of political concern and whether it had been restrained prior to publication. In the context of World War I, Holmes, Louis Brandeis, and civil libertarian scholars abandoned the original approach and the resulting pros-ecution of seditious libel. The first step in doing so was to abstract the language of the amendment to a higher level of generality than was contemplated by those who drafted it and then to argue that it embodied a general principle of free speech. This required, in turn, that judges specify the degree of "clear and present danger" that speech presented to the public and then balance it against other generalized nontextual principles, such as national security or public order. Zechariah Chafee, a noted commentator, vigorously defended the new approach. Justice Brandeis took a similarly broad view of the Fourth Amendment in *Olmstead v. U.S.* (1928), dissenting from the majority holding, which upheld government use of a telephone listening device. He insisted that the Constitution must have a "capacity of adaptation to a changing world."[96]

The Great Depression and New Deal advanced the Progressive tendency to-ward the living Constitution and balancing approaches but further marginal-ized formalist adjudication and the conception of interpretation as an attempt to ascertain and apply original intent. Here we need not retell every familiar detail of the New Deal victory, such as the formation of the dominant Demo-cratic political coalition, President Franklin Roosevelt's Court-packing plan (1937), and the subsequent judicial validation of the regulatory state under the commerce clause, the general welfare clause, and the taxing power.[97] The present analysis will focus on how the New Deal displaced the textual origi-nalist approach and advanced the reconceptualization of the Constitution as a judicially updated living document and illustrate how central components of formalist, categorical constitutional doctrine were replaced by judicial def-erence to legislative regulation and judicial balancing of interests.

To begin with, the Roosevelt administration's rhetoric voiced the modern view of the Constitution. Because it was "what the Justices say it is rather than what its framers or you might hope it is," the solution for the nation's ills was "Judges who will bring to the Courts a present-day sense of the Constitution." Inaccurately attributing the modern view to the past, Roosevelt called on the Court to "resume its high task of building anew on the Constitution 'a sys-tem of living law.'"[98] Likewise, Homer Cummings, attorney general from 1933 through 1939, said that "the American constitutional method is a process of adaptation and growth" and bemoaned justices who denied its "adaptability to modern conditions." Opponents of the New Deal made the mistake of "interpret[ing] the law and the Constitution as a check rather than as a guide to the flow of life."[99]

The Court exemplified the living Constitution idea perhaps most clearly in *Home Building and Loan Association v. Blaisdell* (1934).[100] It held that a Minnesota law permitting temporary delay of property foreclosures did not violate the contract clause of the Constitution. The statute was in essence a "stay" law of the type that had caused chaos in the confederation period and encouraged the drafting of the contract clause in 1787. Chief Justice Charles Hughes's majority opinion conceded this point, but he characterized the purpose of the contract clause abstractly enough to validate an activity it had been intended and always understood to forbid. Echoing Cardozo's treatise, Hughes wrote that the contract clause was "general" and afforded "a broad outline" in which "the process of construction is essential to fill in the details." Although the evils that gave rise to the clause were clear, they did not "suffice to fix its precise scope," which was done by judicial interpretation that assessed contemporary needs. The question for the modern Court "was no longer merely that of one party to a contract as against another, but of the use of reasonable means to safeguard the economic structure upon which the good of all depends."[101] Hughes concluded that the economic emergency of the Depression made the Minnesota law a reasonable means of achieving this generally stated end. Once the purpose of a constitutional provision was abstracted into generality, the judge took on the expanded, highly discretionary power of specifying and balancing. Hughes thus illustrated how modern judicial interpretation was becoming a process of declaring a rational balance between a vague standard and the interests involved in a particular case.

It is significant that Hughes quoted John Marshall in *McCulloch* to defend a judicial power to keep the Constitution "adapted to the various *crises* of human affairs" and Holmes that its words "have called into life a being the development of which could not have been foreseen completely by the most gifted of its begetters."[102] These authorities were called upon to establish the Court as adaptor of the Constitution in a decision that validated a law that clearly abrogated the intent of the founders. For the rest of the century interpreters and commentators, like Hughes, invoked these dicta to justify judicial adaptation of the living Constitution and judicial balancing of abstract values deemed fundamental. Indeed, this occurred immediately and was animated by support for the New Deal. Edward S. Corwin, the most important commentator of the period, approved Hughes's use of Marshall and actively supported judicial adaptation of the Constitution in the same way judges historically had adapted the common law.[103]

Modern judicial power took doctrinal form as the logic of the living Constitution was worked into the jurisprudence of the New Deal Court. This process was neither immediately complete nor doctrinally tidy, but the Court made it clear enough that it was "rejecting classical doctrine and validating its antithesis as the correct reading of the Constitution."[104] A central aspect of this shift was the substitution of consequentialist and deferential standards of review for the categorical distinctions that the old Court had understood as derived from the original Constitution and that had been used to void economic regulations. For example, in *Nebbia v. New York* (1934) the Court upheld a price regulation scheme as a valid exercise of police power under the due process clause, but in doing so it abandoned the inherited, categorical public/private distinction for a deferential "reasonableness" standard. No longer would a business have to be "affected with a public interest" in order to be regulated. Rather, the requirement of due process was satisfied so long as the law was not "unreasonable, arbitrary or capricious" and "the means [of regulation] shall have a real and substantial relation to the object sought to be obtained." Consequently, "the state is free to adopt whatever economic policy may reasonably be deemed to promote the public welfare."[105]

This new logic was elaborated in *West Coast Hotel v. Parrish* (1937). Justice Hughes's majority opinion upheld a state minimum wage law based partly on the public/private distinction but also suggested that the decision was not dependent on such an old bright-line distinction. Regulation could be upheld if it was "reasonable in relation to its subject and is adopted in the interests of the community." Moreover, Hughes indicated that the boundary of liberty of contract and permissible regulation could be affected by the circumstances of the case and the consequences of the decision. The opinion therefore took notice of "the economic conditions which have supervened, and in light of which the reasonableness of the exercise of the protective power of the State must be considered."[106] In *Wickard v. Filburn* (1942) Justice Robert Jackson's opinion for the Court announced the abandonment of any further attempt to limit regulation under the commerce clause.[107] Filburn had planted more than his allotment of wheat under the Agricultural Adjustment Act of 1938 but used the extra solely on his own farm. The Court upheld the act and stated that it would no longer measure categorical distinctions arguably related to the text and original intent of the commerce clause, such as whether an activity was commerce or manufacture, whether commerce was interstate or intrastate, or even whether it had some effect on interstate commerce. Jackson rejected "the mechanical application of [such] legal formulas [as] no longer feasible." Congress would decide what had a "substantial economic effect" on interstate commerce, and congressional estimation of what interests were involved in the economic effects of regulation was not a fit subject for judicial review.[108] Thus, the meaning of the commerce clause would expand or contract as Congress saw fit, and the Court would not interfere. As one historian has recently concluded of *Wickard*: "An interpretive revolution had taken place. The 'living Constitution' rubric had been internalized by the Court."[109]

In this way the New Deal Court adopted Progressive-era demands for judicial self-restraint and deference to the legislative balancing of social interests in matters of economic regulation. But the Court also indicated that it would take a more active role in the balancing process when noneconomic fundamental rights were asserted. This shift was announced somewhat obliquely in the now famous fourth footnote of *United States v. Carolene Products* (1938), although the preferred position of some rights and the balancing approach had been suggested in earlier First Amendment cases. The Court stated that economic regulations generally would be presumed constitutional, while laws affecting the protections of the Bill of Rights, the political process, or "discrete and insular minorities," would be subject to "more searching judicial inquiry." The Court suggested that challenged laws in these categories would place the burden of justification on the government. As one scholar has observed, the new "strict scrutiny" approach "was a call for judicial balancing—one that gave extra weight to the interests of ignored or underrepresented groups."[110] The new model came to be known as the "preferred freedoms" doctrine. The Court soon clarified that only property rights were presumptively regulable, while laws that employed "suspect classifications" and affected other rights would be balanced, with varying degrees of judicial scrutiny, against competing interests. The outcome would depend upon how fundamental the Court thought the rights were when balanced against other interests. The *Carolene Products* approach, which usually found its textual home in the equal protection clause of the Fourteenth Amendment, outlined the new orientation of activist judicial supervision and the vague balancing standards that typified modern judicial review for the rest of the century. Like the substantive due process jurisprudence it replaced, the "substantive equal protection" jurisprudence of *Carolene Products* provided judges with minimal textual or historical guidance.[111]

Another closely related doctrinal pillar of modern judicial power was erected in the New Deal period as the Court linked the ideas expressed in *Carolene Products* and the living Constitution to its own abstract definition of which "fundamental" rights required federal protection against the states. This was achieved through the due process clause of the Fourteenth Amendment and came to be known as "incorporation." In *Palko v. Connecticut* (1937) Justice Cardozo tied the judicial definition of fundamental rights to the incorporation doctrine. The decision reviewed a state criminal conviction on appeal under the due process clause. The Court had been struggling for some time to articulate the requirements of due process in its review of state criminal convictions and had been haltingly developing the idea of "fundamental" rights in this context and in the speech cases. However, in *Palko* the Court dispensed with its reserve and claimed the power to say what was or was not fundamental in the rest of the Bill of Rights. The First Amendment protection of speech was "fundamental" and therefore incorporated, but only aspects of the Second through Eighth Amendments that were deemed "of the very essence of a scheme of ordered liberty" and "so rooted in the traditions and conscience of our people as to be ranked as fundamental" would be applied to the states as well as the federal government. As one historian has noted, this process of "selective incorporation," as it came to be known, "lodged enormous power and discretion in the Court. Nothing in the Constitution provided guidance; rather, the justices had to modernize the Bill of Rights and decide which parts of it applied to the states, based on their own views (guided in some small degree by history and precedent) of what constituted a fundamental right." *Palko* thus "made it possible to expand constitutional safeguards without having to amend the document."[112]

During the following decades and with great controversy under the Warren and early Burger Courts, the modern form of judicial power elaborated from the "revolt against formalism" came to characterize Supreme Court decision-making. Judicial adaptation of the living Constitution frequently included the definition of a fundamental right, the highly discretionary balancing of it against other interests, and often the incorporation of it against the states on the model first sketched in *Carolene Products* and *Palko*. In this approach the text and original meaning of the Constitution receded into the jurisprudential background.

The Eclipse of Originalism

It is important to note, however, that an originalist and historical orientation was too fundamental to the American constitutional order to be wholly expunged, even as modern judicial power ascended. Recognition of the endurance of this fundamental orientation, albeit in a subdued form, helps explain how the originalist idea could later be revived.

For example, in 1905 Justice David Brewer expressed both the originalist idea and the link that it had developed with the formalist, categorical approach to adjudication by writing that "The Constitution is a written instrument. As such its meaning does not alter. . . . It embraces in its grasp all new conditions which are within the scope of the powers in the terms conferred. In other words, while the powers granted do not change, they apply from generation to generation to all things to which they are in their nature applicable."[113] Likewise, in one of the most important historical monographs of the early twentieth century, Charles Warren echoed this thinking.[114] As momentum for the New Deal built in the 1930s, Justice George Sutherland reiterated the traditional view with increasing urgency. In *Blaisdell* (1934) he argued that the majority had collapsed the distinction between constitutional interpretation and the interstitial legislation of common law adjudication. He wrote that "the whole aim of construction, as applied to provisions of the Constitution, is to discover the meaning, to ascertain and give effect to the intent, of its framers and the people who adopted it." History, argued Sutherland, demonstrated that the Minnesota law at issue was precisely the kind meant to be outlawed under the contract clause. He insisted that "A provision of the Constitution . . . does not mean one thing at one time and an entirely different thing at another time."[115] Sutherland reasserted this view one final time in *West Coast Hotel v. Parrish* (1937), a crucial confirmation of the New Deal victory: "To say . . . that the words of the Constitution mean today what they did not mean when written—that is, that they do not apply to a situation now to which they would have applied then—is to rob that instrument of the essential element which continues it in force as the people have made it."[116]

As Sutherland made clear, the textual originalist principle usually opposed modern jurisprudence in the Progressive and New Deal periods. However, originalism was not merely a pretext for conservative politics. Even as modern jurisprudence and the living Constitution took shape, Progressive legal commentators and historians attacked the old Court with arguments based on original intent and historical inquiry. For example, Louis Boudin insisted that the founders did not intend judicial review and thus that the Court had usurped power and become an unchecked tool of propertied interests. Charles Beard, an eminent Progressive historian, argued that *Marbury* and "judicial supremacy" *were* intended as part of a conspiracy among property holders at the Philadelphia convention. They feared democratic government and instituted a silent *coup* to protect their interests. Such antijudicial originalist arguments were a staple of scholarship before the New Deal.[117]

Inquiry into original intent also was central to reformers' destruction of the "conspiracy theory" of the Fourteenth Amendment. An important foundation of antiregulatory constitutionalism first propagated by Roscoe Conkling in *Santa Clara County v. Southern Pacific Railroad Company* (1886), the theory held that the covert original intent of the amendment was to protect corporations as legal persons from legislative regulation and taxation.[118] Most Progressive scholars regarded, and lamented, the conspiracy theory as the original intent of the amendment,[119] but Howard Jay Graham led an effort to formulate an original intent argument in response to it.[120] Graham assumed that "the evidence which is found in the congressional debates of 1866" would demonstrate what "the framers themselves conceived to be the meaning of the language they employed." He found no "direct contemporaneous evidence that the drafters of the Fourteenth Amendment devised its phraseology with corporations in mind" but rather that it was intended to embody the natural law tenets of antebellum abolitionism in order to protect "Negro freedom."[121]

The work of Boudin, Beard, Graham, and others showed the power of the originalist idea even in the period when it was being marginalized. Indeed, in a survey of the subject Jacobus tenBroek concluded that the Supreme Court had always "insisted, with almost uninterrupted regularity, that the end and object of constitutional construction is the discovery of the intention of those persons who formulated the instrument or of the people who adopted it."[122] TenBroek studied academic works and Supreme Court opinions to test what he took to be the widespread assumption that "the actual intention of the framers of the Constitution of the United States . . . may legitimately be discovered from sources other than the constitutional document itself."[123]

Still, tenBroek advanced the cause of modern jurisprudence by arguing that "the intent theory of constitutional construction falsely describes what the Court actually does."[124] The Court actually manipulated history or used it only to support a previously held political position, and tenBroek dismissed as fanciful the idea that history could or should direct constitutional interpretation.[125] Yet, despite tenBroek's modern view of the judicial process, even he could not fully reject the idea that the intent or purpose of the Constitution could be truthfully restated through historical investigation. After analyzing several Court opinions he concluded that "there are instances in which the holding of the Court has directly conflicted with the undeniable will of the Constitution makers" as determined on the basis of the Philadelphia and state ratifying conventions.[126] Thus, even as tenBroek dismissed the notion that history had directed or could direct interpretation, his study nevertheless demonstrated that this notion was the traditional one; that original intent could be independently verified irrespective of what the Court said about it; and that history demanded attention in controversial cases or periods of deep interpretive disagreement, as in the struggle for the New Deal.[127]

TenBroek was not alone in demonstrating the hold of originalist presuppositions even among those who attacked or dismissed them. New Dealers seemed to recognize that the modern abandonment of constitutional interpretation based on original intent, if trumpeted too loudly, would imperil the basis of the Court's own authority. In the crucial moment of the New Deal victory, the Court reneged on the logic of a living Constitution. It claimed to have restored judicial interpretation to the original intent of the Constitution that had been abandoned in the antiregulatory economic substantive due process era. For example, validation in *West Coast Hotel* of the legislative power to set wage rates was said to fulfill the intent of the Constitution because it was not expressly forbidden: "The Constitution does not speak of freedom to contract. It speaks of liberty . . . [but] the liberty safeguarded is liberty in social organization which requires the protection of law against the evils which menace the health, safety, morals and welfare of the people. . . . The *Adkins* case [voiding a minimum wage law] was a departure from the true application of the principles governing the regulation by the State of the relation of employer and employed."[128] This logic actually inverted the idea of a fixed constitution with enumerated and delegated powers, yet it claimed original intent for the modern project of judicial adaptation. Such a "failure of nerve" at the birth of the New Deal constitutional order further underscored that the idea of intent and the sanction of history were not easily dismissed from constitutional discourse, despite the jurisprudential sea change marked by modern judicial power.[129]

With the originalist idea submerged and marginalized, modern judicial power was constrained for a time by the jurisprudence of "legal process" and "self-restraint," as we shall see in the next chapter. In order to round out the current discussion it is helpful to show briefly how the Warren and early Burger Courts used modern judicial power in a manner that often overcame such limits and eventually helped induce reconsideration of the originalist idea.

Scholars frequently describe the Warren Court as a vigorous elaboration or the culmination of legal realism, the living Constitution, and the *Carolene Products* balancing approach.[130] Like the realists, the liberal core of the Court (Warren, Brennan, Douglas, Fortas, Goldberg, and later, Marshall) had no coherent jurisprudence "apart from the results reached."[131] Scholars sympathetic to the Court readily testify to the justices' essentially realist focus on reformist, "updating" results over legal reasons, and it is instructive to let such evaluations speak for themselves. Warren disdained "analytical reasoning" and "technical details," consistently recasting issues in "moral terms." For him "what counted in decision making was the conviction that a result was right."[132] Douglas, a leader of the realist movement at Yale, aimed "to do justice and to write moral ideals into the law" and "never pretended that he was anything but a results-oriented judge."[133] Fortas, also a realist in the 1930s, surprised a sympathetic biographer with his "cavalier attitude toward the rule of law" and his "crude instrumentalism."[134] Brennan, the liberals' best legal craftsman, had a "pragmatic conception of law" that allowed him to pursue "empathy, compassion, and justice." Marshall too had a "pragmatic jurisprudence" and regarded "law as social engineering."[135] As one noted historian has recently concluded, "Warren Court liberals shared a vision of law that the Legal Realists of the 1920s and 1930s had incorporated into New Deal legal consciousness." That vision was of the law "as a malleable instrument of social policy" and was often embodied in the idea of a living Constitution.[136]

Such modernist views of law and adjudication affected the results that were reached and the opinions that were written. The Court usually supported the modern liberal agenda of egalitarianism and social (but not economic) libertarianism and was thus aligned with the Great Society liberalism of the 1960s. Often enforcing national liberal values on outlying areas of the United States, particularly the South, the Court typically benefitted members of the Democratic New Deal coalition, such as blue-collar workers, the unemployed, government employees, African Americans, and liberal intellectuals.[137] Its decisions made the electoral system more egalitarian and the states' systems of criminal justice more solicitous of the accused; advanced racial integration, often ahead of the political process; liberalized the law of speech and obscenity; and restricted the role of religion in public life.[138] It also created the "right to privacy" and verged on declaring welfare a constitutional right.[139] To put it rather mildly, decisions in each of these areas were "deemed political and wrongheaded by a significant sector of [the nation's] politicians and electorate."[140]

Political dissatisfaction and jurisprudential criticism of the constitutional foundations of such decisions combined to prompt reconsideration of originalism, as later chapters will show in detail. Presently a few examples must suffice to indicate how the jurisprudential turn toward originalism initially developed. In *Brown v. Board of Education* (1954), the famous school desegregation case, litigants were ordered to investigate the original intent of the Fourteenth Amendment, but Warren's opinion for a unanimous Court deemed it "inconclusive." Despite having ordered the investigation, the Court refused to "turn the clock back to 1868 when the Amendment was adopted." Instead, it held that state-imposed school segregation "generat[ed] a feeling of inferiority" in black children, which violated the *contemporary* notions of equality it located in the equal protection clause of the Fourteenth Amendment.[141] Further articulating this living Constitution updating approach that drove many of the Court's equal protection decisions, Justice William O. Douglas wrote on another occasion that the clause was not "shackled to the political theory of a particular era."[142] Indeed, the Warren and Burger Courts accelerated the confused equal protection doctrine that was elaborated from *Carolene Products,* with its "discrete and insular minorities," "suspect classifications," and various "levels of scrutiny." Decisions in this area typically undertook an ad hoc balancing approach that many observers (including some dissenting justices) found incoherent, highly discretionary, quasi-legislative, and increasingly unrelated to the original intent of the Constitution.[143] In one example that typified the method, Brennan's majority opinion in *Shapiro v. Thompson* (1969) argued that the equal protection clause had created a "compelling interest" standard that outweighed a state's attempt to exclude nonresidents from welfare payments. Critics increasingly questioned the foundation of such equal protection balancing jurisprudence in the original Constitution.

Additionally, in reapportionment cases, First Amendment establishment clause cases, and others,[144] justices argued with each other about original intent and what influence it should have. Such conflicts heightened scholarly and jurisprudential concern about the relationship among original intent, judicial review, and the role of the Supreme Court—and unavoidably about the legitimacy of some of the Court's boldest reforms.[145] The Court further exacerbated concern about the source and legitimacy of its far-reaching decisions by basing the privacy right on the "penumbras" and "emanations" of provisions in the Bill of Rights and by revolutionizing state criminal arrest procedures with an opinion in *Miranda v. Arizona* (1966) that read like a legislative code.[146] Nor did the Burger Court curtail modern judicial power, as many had expected, but continued to use it for liberal reformist ends by ordering bussing as a remedy for segregated schools and by taking the first judicial step toward validating race-based affirmative action in employment.[147] In *Roe v. Wade* (1973) the Burger Court gave constitutional protection to abortion based on the right of privacy. In the same period the Court struck down state laws imposing the death penalty and validated race-based affirmative action in university admissions.[148]

Various types of academic "legal liberal" theorists soon stepped in to offer the justifications that many observers had deemed lacking in the Court's opinions, thus defending and seeking to elaborate modern judicial power in general and the work of the Warren and early Burger Courts in particular. Originalism emerged to combat modern judicial power and the legal liberal theorizing that defended it, at first by protesting that the historical Constitution did not mean what the Court now said it did, and thereafter with increasingly well-articulated theoretical arguments and historical investigations. Before continuing with this story, however, we must more precisely locate originalism in the flow of American constitutional history by understanding how the post-realist jurisprudence of "self-restraint" and "legal process" failed to constrain the Warren Court's exercise of modern judicial power. The next chapter takes up this task, and then we can investigate how originalism emerged to serve many of the same goals as the process-restraint approach.

CHAPTER 2

Modern Judicial Power and the Process-Restraint Tradition

The displacement of textual originalism and the formalism of classical legal thought by the rise of modern judicial power did not succeed in wholly effacing the originalist idea, even though it did recede. Originalism was not immediately reasserted because the radical potential inherent in modern jurisprudence was obscured by its initial link to the judicial "self-restraint" and "legal process" approach. Progressives had first deployed the restraint idea against the antiregulatory jurisprudence of economic substantive due process, but after the victory of modern judicial power during the New Deal, process thinkers attempted to constrain that power by further refining the restraintist approach. Although in the context of statutory interpretation process jurisprudence resuscitated the notion that law had a real, preexisting content that judges could know and apply, in the constitutional context it undertook no such project. Ultimately, the inability of process jurisprudence to prevent or reconcile itself to the Warren Court's reassertion of modern judicial power helped pave the way for reconsideration of the originalist idea.

The Tradition from Thayer and Holmes to *Brown*

Process jurisprudence originated at the Harvard Law School and was closely associated with the earlier Thayer-Holmes tradition of judicial self-restraint. The tender of self-restraint as a limitation on judges, like the process approach it shaped, tended to accept that interpretation was a fundamentally un-bounded practice. It therefore confirmed the arrival of modern judicial power while simultaneously obscuring it. These points were evident in a famous 1893 essay by James Bradley Thayer. Contrary to many scholars of the period who attacked economic substantive due process by attacking judicial review itself, Thayer clearly accepted its legitimacy. Like John Marshall in *McCulloch*, Thayer sought limits on judicial review by reasserting its basis in a written document that was founded on consent and that ordinarily permitted a broad scope for republican self-government. Accordingly, he insisted on a seemingly quite traditional distinction between legislation and adjudication, cautioning judges not to usurp power by replacing democratic value choices with their own. Nonetheless, he held that constitutional provisions were frequently am-biguous and therefore amenable to more than one reasonable interpretation. To maximize the scope of legislative regulation, judicial assessment of the "reasonableness" of legislation should operate with a presumption in its favor. If reasoned analysis could conclude that the Constitution permitted a legisla-tive enactment, then courts should uphold it, even if they thought a better interpretation of the Constitution would disallow it. If a "reasonable doubt" in favor of constitutionality existed, legislation must be sustained. The judicial function, on his view, was "merely that of fixing the outside border of reason-able legislative action."[1]

Although Thayer wanted to narrow the scope of judicial review and defend republican self-government, the "reasonableness" standard treated constitu-tional adjudication as unlimited by anything antecedent to the process itself, such as a constitution with a fixed, limited meaning. In this way Thayer was distinctly modern. His call for self-restraint assumed that "the ultimate arbi-ter of what is rational and permissible is indeed always the courts." This view exemplified the approach to the Constitution that was coming to characterize modern judicial power. Thayer understood the Constitution as "so much law" to be "interpreted and applied by the court."[2]

Nevertheless, when first articulated, the notion of judicial self-restraint was an attempt to constrain assertive judicial power. Holmes's understanding of law, as well as his moral skepticism, also led him to self-restraint. Holmes insisted on judicial deference to the legislature in the absence of an overtly unreasonable violation of the Constitution and advanced this position in several famous dissents.[3] As with Thayer, deference to other branches of government was an act of self-denial, not an imperative required by an interpretation based on the original intent of the Constitution or the limited legitimate power of the judiciary. In 1936, on the eve of the New Deal constitutional victory, Justice Harlan Stone strikingly articulated the basic idea: "The only check upon our own exercise of power is our own sense of self-restraint."[4] In the 1950s, Justice Felix Frankfurter elaborated this view. As has been well-documented by other scholars, some of Frankfurter's most noted opinions not only practiced restraint by using jurisdictional techniques to avoid the hearing of a case (a technique analyzed in more detail below) but also used the modern "balancing" approach with the usual result of restraint and deference to the legislature.[5]

Accordingly, modern balancing constituted an assumption and not a target of process jurisprudence, whose refinement of Thayer-Holmes self-restraint dominated legal education and constitutional thought in the 1950s.[6] It was known as the "process" school because it emphasized the basis of the rule of law in an adherence to forms, procedures, and reasoned judicial elaboration of legal principles generated from legitimate democratic processes. Although process jurisprudence has been the subject of scholarly inquiry, its significance for the emergence of originalism has not been adequately explored. Process jurisprudence and originalism were similarly concerned with constraining the growth in judicial discretion characteristic of modern legal thought and fostering judicial deference to legislative value choices.[7] Unlike the originalists to be analyzed in the chapters to come, process thinkers did not usually consult extrinsic evidence of legislative or original constitutional intent. However, to some extent they rehabilitated the concept of intent in statutory interpretation by insisting that statutes had a purpose, extant prior to adjudication, that could be discerned and should limit judicial application. Rigorous textual exegesis in the common law tradition could discern the purpose of a statute without making judges a law unto themselves. Likewise, process scholars argued that in the American system of representative government, political legitimacy and the rule of law normally required judicial deference to the legislative will and always required convincing legal reasoning in judicial opinions that overturned that will. The rule of law was endangered when the outcome of a case was seen to derive simply from the judicial desire for a particular result. Such themes would be carried forward in originalism. In the constitutional context, however, process jurisprudence typically relied on the Thayer-Holmes concept of judicial self-restraint instead of anything resembling originalism. Abstention from review in most cases, it was hoped, would realize the self-restraint goal of judicial deference to legislative majorities. Probing process jurisprudence and its context more deeply will explain how its content and its failure to prevent or incorporate the Warren Court's reassertion of modern judicial power helped create the space for the reassertion of original intent as the proper basis of constitutional interpretation.

Process jurisprudence must be understood in the context of the "consensus" thinking that developed in response to World War II and the birth of the Cold War. Consensus thought held that the American past and the current functioning of the American political system demonstrated profound agreement on the basic values of constitutional democracy and individual liberty. Most consensus academics abandoned the Marxist-inspired "conflict" explanations of Progressive political theory, historiography, and constitutional commentary. Consensus thinkers regarded political conflict in America as nonideological—essentially an intramural disagreement about means, consistently resolved within a deeper agreement on the institutional and procedural mechanisms of constitutionalism, representative government, and interest group pluralism. Within this intellectual environment many observers thought that the modern realist attack on legal formalism and on the idea of a fixed Constitution pushed in the same direction as the massive affronts to democracy and the rule of law evident in European fascism and Stalinist communism.[8]

Accordingly, process thinkers held that modern legal ideas threatened the rule of law by blurring the line between ad hoc substantive preferences and disciplined, constrained legal judgments. Process theory was conservative in the sense that it offered a rejoinder to the aspects of modern legal thought that questioned or undermined the rule of law at a time when totalitarianism threatened the American political and social system. However, process judges and scholars were New Deal liberals who embraced the skepticism, value relativism, and pragmatism of modern thought. They regarded the Constitution more as a symbol of shared but imprecise "values" than as a source of fundamental law properly interpreted according to its original intent. Traditional originalism smacked of the "absolutes" or "ideologies" that, they thought, implied the very authoritarianism they abhorred. Renewed judicial activism based on "absolutes," they cautioned, could undermine democracy and invite a constitutional crisis like that brought on by the old Court's economic substantive due process jurisprudence. In their "relativist democratic theory," as one historian has described it, process thinkers defended limited government and the rule of law by ensuring judicial deference to the legislatively enacted results of pluralistic political struggle.[9] The older way of protecting natural rights through formalist adjudication of the original intent of the Constitution was unavailable for this purpose: it was too closely associated with the previous era of assertive judicial power that process thinkers had rejected.

Because process jurisprudence located legal legitimacy in judicial deference to legislative commands and rigorously reasoned judicial opinions, *process* had two distinguishable but interrelated meanings.[10] In one sense it meant that each institution should decide the kinds of issues that its role in the American governmental process made it most fit it to decide. Courts should restrain themselves from encroaching on legislative determinations of what values would stand as law. Institutions naturally vary in their competence and responsiveness to public sentiment, and courts are far less democratic institutions than legislatures. Therefore, they should adhere to the jurisdictional and structural constraints that limited their own power, thereby promoting efficient but accountable government in the legislative branch. Thus, federalism, the separation of powers, and the jurisdictional questions they raised were central components of process thinking. The second meaning of *process* referred to the requirement that, in a democracy, judicial opinions—especially those of the Supreme Court—should be based on rigorous legal reasoning that would preclude judicial willfulness or assertiveness. In this second sense "process" came to be known as "reasoned elaboration," and to some extent it recovered the idea of interpretation as the effectuation of legislative purpose, if not historical original intent, from the oblivion to which the realist attack on formalism had consigned it. This style of interpretation and application of laws with a discernible purpose aimed to realize democratic decision-making by constraining judicial interpretation to ends and objects approved by the legislature. As the legal revolt against formalism ever more clearly suggested that law was politics, jurisdictional technique and the preservation of some distinction between adjudication and legislation replaced the traditional concern with constitutional interpretation based on original intent as the preferred method of constraining the Supreme Court.

As suggested by their debt to Thayer and Holmes, the judges and scholars who became the leaders of process jurisprudence in the 1950s had long been concerned with the first basic feature of the approach: how the Court, in relation to other branches and levels of government, could preserve limited republican government under the rule of law by restraining the exercise of its own power. This concern took the form of abiding attention to the intricacies of federal jurisdiction, as when Felix Frankfurter and James Landis evaluated the new discretionary *certiorari* power under the Judiciary Reform Act of 1925.[11] In 1934 Frankfurter and Henry Hart, both law professors who supported the New Deal, warned of the dangers posed by cavalier treatment of jurisdictional complexities. Constant vigilance "against undue suction [of the Supreme Court] into the avoidable polemic of politics" required "reaffirmation of old procedural safeguards and the assertion of new ones against subtle or daring attempts at procedural blockade-running."[12] Careful use of jurisdictional and procedural devices would allow the Court to regulate access to the ultimately political power of judicial review. Infrequent recourse to the Court would preserve the diversity of local self-government afforded by federalism. Such limits also would help preserve the rule of law by giving the Court time to produce persuasively reasoned judicial opinions. Furthermore, sparing use of judicial power would permit the Court to husband its reserve of prestige and authority for use in matters of high statesmanship.[13] This understanding of the relationship among jurisdiction, judicial review, the rule of law, and opinion-writing became central to the process defense of judicial self-restraint in the 1950s.

In particular, Hart, Frankfurter, and Landis advocated prudent and sometimes even strict use of complex jurisdictional doctrines that operated at the intersection of law, fact, and politics. Justice Louis D. Brandeis influentially summarized such doctrines in 1936, the most famous of which was the "political questions" doctrine. It excluded from court jurisdiction issues that in a constitutional republic were properly left to the legislative or executive branches. Two additional doctrines were insistence on a live "case or controversy" and a clear demonstration of "standing" to sue. These doctrines prevented the Court from prematurely undertaking constitutional interpretation or issuing advisory opinions. The doctrines of "ripeness," "mootness," and "justiciability," as well as clear demonstration of a "federal question," were similarly recommended. Such tools enabled the Court to serve as the gatekeeper to block those who sought the full and perhaps precipitous exercise of its power.[14] Frankfurter was instrumental, moreover, in advancing the academic study of "federal jurisdiction [as] an important part of the public law of the United States." In co-editing one of the first casebooks on federal jurisdiction, Frankfurter held as a guiding principle that "questions of jurisdiction were questions of power as between the United States and the several states." He consistently argued that the maintenance of federalism required limits on federal court jurisdiction and toleration of the conflict of laws at the state level, at least in some areas.[15]

Henry Hart and Herbert Wechsler's *The Federal Courts and the Federal System* (1953), an influential work that reflected Frankfurter's thought, also defended the process view of the properly constrained judicial role by appealing to the principles and policies underlying federalism and the separation of powers. Consideration of "'who should do what?'—that is, 'which institution within the legal process might be considered best equipped to deal with which problems?'"—was treated as central to modern jurisprudence. In the process approach, legal uncertainties were understood not as questions about the original meaning of the Constitution but as issues that could be settled by reference to appropriate conceptions of the various functional relations among institutions of government, as expressed primarily in jurisdictional concepts. Students were asked to consider the concept of a "case or controversy" and the related issues of advisory opinions, the "political questions" doctrine, feigned or mooted cases, and standing. Also considered were the scope of congressional control over federal courts jurisdiction, the establishment of a "federal question" in the removal of state court decisions to the federal system, and the proper exercise of "diversity jurisdiction."[16]

The Legal Process (1958), a casebook edited by Henry Hart and Albert Sacks, further illustrated the attempt to preserve republican government and the rule of law through legal techniques sensitive to federalism and the separation of powers.[17] A fundamental concept in the book was "institutional settlement." This referred to outcomes reached as a "result of duly established procedures" for making a certain kind of decision, which "ought to be accepted as binding upon the whole society unless and until they are duly changed." In the intellectual climate of "relativist democracy," in which substantive, absolute, or formalist claims about the nature of law, rights, or the concept of original intent were unavailable, Hart and Sacks explicitly linked the obligatory force of law to the regularity and integrity of the procedures by which legitimate institutions settled upon ultimately subjective choices. Once the principle of institutional settlement became effective, "we say that the law 'is' thus and so, and brush aside further discussion of what 'ought' to be. Yet the 'is' is not really an 'is' but a special kind of 'ought.'"[18] The law is compelling because of the legitimacy, integrity, and regularity of the procedures that produce it. Governmental power and judicial discretion could be limited through well-ordered institutional relationships that carve out a broad sphere of deference to the value choices produced by legitimate legal-institutional procedures. Although values ultimately might be subjective, people agree far more on procedures for arriving at a workable consensus on the values that should inform public policy. Judges could defend these procedures and defer to the results they produce without imposing their own ad hoc value judgments. Thus, process jurisprudence constrained judges in the era of modern judicial power by directing them to identify as law the result of a "morality of process."[19]

The process attempt to constrain modern judicial power clearly reflected the belief in proceduralism and rationality typical of the consensus intellectual and jurisprudential climate of the 1950s. Process thinkers, like consensus thinkers more generally, regarded American representative democracy as real and defensible. Maintenance of commonly accepted procedures for lawmaking allowed public goals to be articulated, discussed, and compromised in a rational, democratic process that was superior to European totalitarianism. Likewise, the consensus view of American society reinforced the process jurisprudence elaboration of the Thayer-Holmes tradition of judicial self-restraint. Although that tradition had emerged from the conflict-ridden Progressive view of American life in the early twentieth century, by midcentury it was consistent with the consensus view. Like the earlier creators of judicial self-restraint, process thinkers assumed that the legislative value choices to which judges normally deferred would represent the will of society as a whole. Whether or not this assumption was always valid, their republican and constitutionalist political theory did not permit judges to substitute their own definition of what was reasonable public policy. Thus, consistent with the older restraint tradition, Hart and Sacks wrote that a "statute ought always to be presumed to be the work of reasonable men pursuing reasonable purposes reasonably, unless the contrary is made unmistakably to appear."[20] So although process theory accepted the modern view that subjective values were the basis of law, it insisted that republican constitutionalism and the rule of law demanded deference to value choices made in the legislature.

As previously noted, the second basic element of process thinking was the idea that, in a regime under the rule of law, a judicial opinion should be a rigorously well-reasoned elaboration of statutory purpose. This was required to convince citizens that judgments conformed to preexisting standards or prin-

ciples and were not mere acts of will. In this way the process view of adjudication refrained from fully embracing the realist assertion of radical interpretive
indeterminacy and purely subjective political choice. Process scholars felt that
legal realists, in their zeal to highlight idiosyncrasy and indeterminacy in legal
reasoning, had underestimated the extent to which judges in fact responded
to the limitations imposed by the expectations of legal professionals and citizens of a reasoned judicial interpretation of a legislative enactment that was
thought to have a preexisting meaning or purpose. Henry Hart, for example,
saw process jurisprudence as a response to the Holmesian-realist assertion that
law was simply what judges said it was. He rejected the realist counsel that
judges "are not really thinking, they only think they are." Instead, he insisted
that the reasons officials give for their actions and decisions did matter and
should be taken seriously. To take the Holmesian-realist path was to abandon
the rule of law ideal and concede that "man's most elaborately contrived instrument [law] for the application of thought to human affairs we [would]
seem to have transformed into a gesture of futility."[21]

Consequently, Hart and other process thinkers argued that, within the
unique fact situation of a particular case, a judge could exercise discretion
that was constrained by values previously enunciated by a democratically responsive institution. The demand that adjudication not be ad hoc was not
understood to mean that judges could completely avoid making law as they
confronted a novel set of facts in a lawsuit, but it did require that such lawmaking ascertain, build upon, and conform to the legislature's purpose.[22] In
this sense, the "process of reasoning" defended by process theorists was the
recrudescence and rehabilitation of the traditional common law approach to
statutes, shorn of appeals to formally derived or "found" law by the power of
the realist critique. As Hart's teaching of the legal process course evolved at
Harvard, he clearly understood judging as the elaboration of principles and
application of policies that were ultimately traceable to the choices of more
democratically legitimate decision-makers. In his teaching notes he wrote that
statutory interpreters should "try in good faith to carry out what the legislature has decided" because it was "the chief policy-making agency of the government." Thus, first among the "reasons why judicial law-making should be
limited to the rational development of authoritative starting points" was that
"the power of judges otherwise [would be] subject to no adequate check."[23]

Since process jurisprudence staked so much of its defense of the rule of law
on a distinction between adjudication and legislation—between courts and

legislatures—its approach to statutory interpretation perforce resembled the traditional originalist view that "the intent of the lawgiver is the law." This was evident in an early essay by James Landis, who wrote that the "Anglo-American scheme of government" conceived of lawgivers who made law via the "formalism of passing statutes. It is from such a conception that one derives the rule of statutory interpretation emphasizing the intent of the passer of statutes."[24] Likewise, over time the writing of process thinkers rang with calls for "reasoned elaboration" in judicial opinions and "purposive interpretation" of statutes.[25] Reasoned elaboration of a purposive law premised that "every statute and every doctrine of unwritten law developed by the [judicial] decisional process has some kind of purpose or objective." Indeed, "every statute must be conclusively presumed to be a purposive act. The idea of a statute without an intelligible purpose is foreign to the idea of law and inadmissible."[26] Accordingly, the beginning point for the interpreter, as Hart wrote in his teaching notes for 1951, was to "determine the purpose of the statute and carry it out as best you can."[27] Frankfurter, too, articulated these concepts in a noted 1947 article: "Legislation has an aim," which "may fairly be said to be imbedded in the statute, even if a specific manifestation was not thought of."[28] The purpose of the statute could be understood through its text and context, the ancient canons of common law interpretation, and, for the Supreme Court, the background of federalism. These would guide and constrain the judge in elaborating the purpose of general laws to cover specific facts.

In defending the process approach Frankfurter readily conceded to the legal realists that the activity of interpretation was one of judgment and in no sense determined, yet he also insisted that "judges are not unfettered glossators" and warned that "the judicial process of dealing with words is not at all Alice in Wonderland's way of dealing with them."[29] Rather, the reasoned elaboration of a purposive statute fostered the impartiality and neutrality associated with the rule of law. It accomplished this by constraining the application of the law to fact situations sufficiently analogous to be comprehended under the purpose of the statute, as evinced by its words and structure. Hart and Sacks too held that the judge was "obliged to resolve the issue before him on the assumption that the answer will be the same in all like cases." When interpreting a statute the judge must "relate his decision in some reasoned fashion to the . . . statute out of which the question arises. He is not to think of himself as in the same position as a legislator taking part in the enactment of the statute in the first place."[30] This approach to interpretation served the larger goal of preserving the rule of law, which was buttressed primarily by constraining the discretion of the judge so that it was a "trained and responsible discretion" whose "permitted scope" was limited by the fundamental differences between adjudication and legislation.[31]

Process thinkers thus rehabilitated the traditional understanding of statutory interpretation as the effectuation of the will of the lawgiver, usually expressed in terms of "purpose" and sometimes "intent," and attended to the canons of statutory construction familiar to the common law. They maintained, as one put it in another important text, that "in the application of a statute the intent of the legislature seems important. The rules of construction are ways of finding out the intent."[32] Reasoned elaboration of a purposive statute, because it was consciously aimed at maintaining the rule of law, did not allow the "importation of any old purpose in to the words of the statute, but only 'a purpose which may reasonably be imputed to "those who uttered the words."'"[33] Process jurisprudence insisted that lawmaking authority resided in legislatures, which were "entitled to assume [that] language puts limits" on judges, whose job it was to effectuate the legislative purpose.[34]

Of course, process jurisprudence never claimed to eliminate discretion from interpretation—a problem as old as legal interpretation itself. Frankfurter recognized this point and denied that judicial inquiry into the subjective, individual motivations or expectations of legislators could resolve the difficulty in any determinative way. Yet he also approvingly cited John Marshall's dictum that "where the mind labors to discover the design of the legislature, it seizes everything from which aid can be derived," and he indicated his willingness to consider evidence extrinsic to the text of a statute.[35] Landis, too, had earlier defended recourse to legislative history for establishing the intent of the legislature: "Such material frequently affords a guide to the intent of the legislature conceived of in terms of purpose."[36]

Frankfurter clarified the methodological point about extrinsic evidence by distinguishing between the meaning or purpose of a statute on the one hand and the subjective intent or expectation of the legislator on the other. For process thinkers, interpretation aimed to ascertain the meaning (purpose) of a statute, accomplished primarily by examination of its words. Evidence of subjective legislative intent was admissible to the extent that it cohered with the meaning of the statutory words "as used in the common speech of men" or, if a term of legal art was in question, as a "familiar legal expression in [its] familiar legal sense."[37] So "the purpose which a court must effectuate is . . . that which [the legislature] did enact, however inaptly, because it may fairly be said to be *imbedded* in the statute." In a slightly different formulation, Frankfurter wrote that "legislative ideas which laws embody are both explicit and imma-nent. And so the bottom problem is: What is below the surface of the words and yet fairly a part of them?"[38]

In this approach the law could not be controlled by extrinsic evidence of the subjective, individuated intent, understanding, or expectation of the leg-islator if it was contrary to the meaning or purpose of the enactment as re-vealed through the judge's reasoned interpretation of its words in their over-all context. Hart also exercised common sense in cautioning that reliance on extrinsic evidence of legislative intent could mislead about the true purpose of a statute or unduly confine a court. While legislative history was part of the overall context of the statute, it was "useful mainly in answering only the more general questions of purpose."[39] Still, if "direct evidence is available and a specific intention can be established, that of course must control the more general purpose. But . . . rarely can the conclusion be justified that the two are at variance. The search for purpose and specific intention, accordingly, is complementary; and the same materials may have relevance for each."[40] Thus, the process approach, as one scholar has observed, generally subordinated specific intent to a more abstract general purpose, but it is nonetheless true, as another concluded, that its bedrock was the claim that the law was a set of general directive arrangements that could "'speak from one point in time to another'—that is, that there is some meaning which laws convey, and that interpreters of that meaning can get it right or wrong."[41] Frankfurter clearly recognized that the practice of judicial interpretation would be neither intel-ligible nor legitimate without the concept of legislative purpose. He further urged that judicial construction of statutory purpose should never usurp the "power which our democracy has lodged in its elected legislature." Yet he also lauded John Marshall's language of adaptation in *McCulloch* (1819) as "the single most important utterance in the literature of constitutional law" and consistently advocated "the evolution of social policy by way of judicial ap-plication of the Delphic provisions of the Constitution."[42]

In the statutory context the room for judicial adaptation fostered by the process approach may often have been unobjectionable. The legislature could remedy an erroneous interpretation with relative ease. But in the constitu-tional context, judicial adaptation of allegedly "Delphic" provisions raised fundamental issues about the rule of law and the legitimate role of the Court.[43]

In constitutional interpretation, as noted above, Frankfurter did not empha-size limiting judges with the concept of purposiveness, much less limiting them with extrinsic evidence of intent or purpose, as his process approach permitted in the statutory context. His thinking thus exemplified how in con-stitutional interpretation the judicial restraint goal of process jurisprudence was in tension with the modern judicial practice of adapting the supposedly vague "living Constitution." As we shall see in the next chapter, when it be-came clear that the New Deal settlement had institutionalized this approach to the Constitution, historical inquiry would once again become prominent in the debate about interpretation.

Brown's Challenge to Process-Restraint Jurisprudence

During the process jurisprudence attempt to constrain modern judicial power, the Supreme Court decided *Brown v. Board of Education* (1954) and thus presented theorists with a major challenge. *Brown* held that racially segre-gated public educational facilities were "inherently unequal."[44] The Court es-chewed reliance on either original intent or legalistic argumentation, citing instead contemporary psychological evidence that segregation lowered the self-esteem of black students. The Court held that the equal protection clause of the Fourteenth Amendment was violated because such evidence offended contemporary notions of equality.

As political liberals, process critics applauded the result reached in *Brown,* but they were gravely troubled that it signaled a renaissance in judicial activ-ism and therefore threatened the rule of law. Still, at the time of *Brown* process critics remained disinclined to present original intent or historical inquiry as possible limitations on the Court, and, as we shall see, Alexander M. Bickel supported the living Constitution approach to justify the decision. Rather than focusing on the historical issues, process-restraint thinkers typically crit-icized the quality of the Court's reasoning and warned that, as an institution, it was moving into a highly controversial arena that might undermine its own authority.

Herbert Wechsler, a process critic, offered such an assessment of *Brown* in one of the most famous and most-cited law review articles ever written.[45] He considered the opinion's "process of reasoning" and found it wanting. Despite approval of the result, Wechsler feared that a continuation of *Brown's* style of reasoning could make the Court a "naked power organ," which would simply read its policy preferences into law. He advocated interpreting the Constitution with "criteria that can be framed and tested as an exercise of reason and not merely as an act of willfulness or will." Elaborating the process view of the problem, he argued that the application of such criteria to analogous fact situations ensured the impartiality that law required to command obedience from a free people. He wrote that "the main constituent of the judicial process is that it must be genuinely principled, resting with respect to every step that is involved in reaching judgment on analysis and reasons quite transcending the immediate result that is achieved. [Courts must] decide on grounds of adequate neutrality and generality, tested not only by the instant application but by others that the principles imply."[46]

Poorly reasoned opinions such as *Brown* were essentially ad hoc assertions of power. Although made in the name of the Constitution, they threatened limited constitutional government and the very freedoms protected by judicial review. Simply put, shoddy reasoning damaged the authority the Court needed to vindicate the Constitution.[47] In *Brown* the Court had not shown clearly how "separate but equal" was "inherently unequal." It had simply announced that the doctrine had no place in public education because the separation was said, on the basis of social scientific authority, to provoke a feeling of inferiority in black children. Wechsler did suggest a defensible principle upon which the Court seemed to have silently based its decision: that blacks' freedom to associate trumped whites' freedom not to. Yet he insisted that the Court utterly failed to reason its way to this position, and its opinion bore little connection to this posited premise.[48]

It should be emphasized that Wechsler was actually defending judicial review by drawing attention to the proper limits of it in the process conception, thereby reflecting the lessons learned from judicial activism prior to the New Deal. More immediately, Wechsler was responding to a lecture given by Judge Learned Hand of the Second Circuit Court, a noted self-restraint judge, the previous year. Wechsler thought Hand would too tightly circumscribe judicial power and that Hand's approach bordered on an unprincipled abdication of constitutional duty.

Hand had argued that judicial review and judicial supremacy were not required by the Constitution but were in fact merely an expeditious means of securing the practical operation of the constitutional system. Accordingly, he concluded that broad interpretations of the Fifth and Fourteenth Amendments could not be sanctioned by a general power of judicial review because the power itself was legitimate only as a mere practical contrivance. So the Court was increasingly acting as a "third legislative chamber" in its recent opinions, like *Brown*, which relied on the Fourteenth Amendment.[49] He could not understand *Brown* as anything other than a *"coup de main."*[50]

In response Wechsler defended the legitimacy of judicial review by inferences from the text and structure of the Constitution but cautioned that it could remain vital only if it conformed to the dictates of process jurisprudence. Because he believed judicial review was "anchored" in the text, Wechsler rejected what he regarded as Hand's lawless claim that it could be undertaken, as a jurisdictional matter, "depending on 'how importunately' [the Court] considers the occasion to demand an answer." Rather, the assumption or denial of jurisdiction had to be as defensible, constitutional, and lawlike as a sound Court opinion. Wechsler further emphasized that the ultimate recourse in jurisdictional matters was to the congressional power to regulate the appellate jurisdiction of the Court under Article III, section 2.[51] Thus, true to the process approach and the lesson it took from the excesses of the pre–New Deal Court, Wechsler defended judicial review by highlighting both its legitimacy and its limitations. Only in this way could the Court retain even the opportunity to satisfy moral sentiments of the kind ham-handedly vindicated in *Brown*. Indeed, Wechsler maintained this attitude throughout his life, continually wondering at those who thought that "the credibility, authority, and power of the federal judiciary is an asset that can be extended to the moon without any loss anywhere."[52]

Even though part of Wechsler's motivation was to defend judicial review from critics like Hand who he thought would irresponsibly eviscerate it, he was attacked for daring to criticize the liberal triumph of *Brown*. Wechsler was usually understood as having appealed to an objective consensus on the requirements of interpretation, which many felt legal realism had long since vanquished. Wechsler assumed, said his critics, that all reasonable people could agree upon principles of adequate "neutrality and generality."[53] Further, Wechsler also had conceded that the modern judge inevitably would have to balance competing principles and admitted that some estimation of the results could be undertaken.[54] Moreover, said the critics, principles would eventually come into conflict, so the judge would be forced to look to his own preferences or to the results of a particular decision (which amounted to the same thing) in order to resolve a case.[55] Here indeed was the reassertion of the legal realist critique of interpretation. Wechsler's critics insisted that he had not fundamentally constrained the judge by merely intoning the need for reasoned elaboration of principles—these remained a mere obfuscation of inevitably political judging.[56] To the extent that Wechsler sought to constrain the court with a method of reasoning that did not seem capable of determining how to prefer one contending value to another, he had failed to constrain judicial discretion or prevent judicial activism.[57]

It was not true, however, that Wechsler claimed the mantle of objectivity. Insistence on a coherently reasoned judicial opinion was the heart of Wechsler's process-based criticism. The call for "neutrality" in legal reasoning referred to the establishment of a "basis for decision that [a person] would be willing to follow in other situations to which it applies." In effect this was a call for sound common law analogic reasoning in which an interpreter would give reasons for interpretive choices at every step in the interpretive process.[58] A principled decision was not necessarily a correct or morally salutary one. Likewise, a thoroughly reasoned, principled decision could be based on a misinterpretation of the Constitution.[59]

The subtleties and caution of the process approach were lost on reformers who wanted the Court actively to advance social change on the model of *Brown* and the emerging civil rights movement. Judicial decisions should be assessed by how well they comported with the current understanding of good politics and not by "issuing blanket condemnations" based on an "abstract model" of legitimate policymaking.[60] It was nearly self-evident to some critics that there had never been any line between law and politics or between legislation and adjudication. Judges should squarely confess their individual values and issue opinions according to the requirements of the "democratic ideal" and the goals of the welfare state.[61] Law professors Addison Mueller and Murray Schwartz similarly made the familiar points about interpretive indeterminacy, then argued that Wechsler's criteria were met only when the Court ceased judicial review in a particular area of law. Such de facto deference to the legislature, they insisted, would imperil individual freedom when the Court should be vindicating it. Individual freedoms "must be interpreted and applied by a select few" and "our Supreme Court are those who have been chosen under our system of government."[62] While dismissing process jurisprudence as wedded to a discredited notion of judicial "objectivity," liberal reformist critics seemed to think that obedience to the Court's view of justice would follow unproblematically upon its announcement.

Paradoxically, critics also condemned Wechsler's "pure reason" because it might not reliably produce objectively good, substantive justice in concrete circumstances such as *Brown*.[63] The irrelevance of process jurisprudence to these goals of liberal reform was increasingly urged.[64] Wechsler's approach, which emphasized reason, a distinction between adjudication and legislation, and the limits of legitimate judicial power, would not necessarily realize the reformers' seemingly objective conception of "justice" or "progress."[65] Additionally, the difficulty process jurisprudence had with *Brown* was indicated in the omission of the case from the 1958 edition of Hart and Sacks's *The Legal Process*. As one scholar has noted, the omission was significant because it revealed a fundamental problem: "If a court is able to produce laudable results without elaborating its reasons for those results, why treat the requirement of soundness [in legal reasoning] seriously?"[66]

Bickel and the Limits of Process-Restraint Jurisprudence

Alexander M. Bickel, one of the most important process thinkers, recognized the depth of *Brown*'s challenge to his school of thought. One way of legitimating the decision was to reconceptualize the original intent of the Fourteenth Amendment toward the living Constitution idea. In 1955 Bickel published a version of the memorandum he had written as Frankfurter's clerk during the *Brown* litigation.[67] It argued that the 39th Congress, which passed the Amendment, intentionally used capacious language. Although the historical facts showed that the 39th Congress assumed segregation would continue in nearly all social interactions, including schools, this could be overcome if the phrase "equal protection" were understood at a sufficiently abstract level and the Court could specify or update its substantive content.[68]

Bickel recognized that the concept of intent involved here raised fundamental issues about legitimacy and the rule of law. Indeed, the ultimate issue was the legitimate source of law. "Original intent" or "understanding" (Bickel used the terms interchangeably) "may raise a fundamental question concerning the Court's function in construing the Constitution." This was true because "the original understanding forms the starting link in the chain of continuity which is the source of the Court's authority, and it is not unnatural that appeals to it should recur as consistently as they do."[69] Bickel concluded that if the Fourteenth Amendment "were a statute, a court might very well hold, on the basis of what has been said so far, that it was foreclosed from applying it to segregation in public schools." But the Constitution was not a statute, and Bickel was not deterred. Following Hughes's transformation of John Marshall's defense of legislative prerogatives in *McCulloch* (1819), Bickel said that the framers of the Amendment were aware "that it was a *constitution* they were writing, which led to a choice of language capable of growth." He concluded that "the record of history, properly understood, left the way open to, in fact invited, a decision based on the moral and material state of the nation in 1954, not 1866."[70] Bickel thus showed that history could be transcended or translated into the present once the Court was assumed to be the arbiter of the nation's "moral and material state" via a living Constitution.

A key part of his argument for "open-ended" language was that the radical Republicans held the balance of power in the 39th Congress. Radicals were able to strike a deal with moderates, suggested Bickel, so that the party could "go to the country [in the Congressional elections of 1866] with language which they could, where necessary, defend against damaging alarms raised by the opposition, but which at the same time was sufficiently elastic to permit reasonable future advances." A year later Bickel clarified what the capacity for growth of constitutional language meant in practice. In the field of race relations, he wrote, "we have been paralyzed in two of the institutions of government. . . . It remained for . . . the Supreme Court, to quicken the conscience of the nation." Bickel thus sanctioned an appeal to the moral sense of the Court as a justification for making the Constitution mean what it had not meant to those who wrote and ratified it, elevating his, or the Court's, estimation of the requirements of contemporary morality over the limits of history.[71]

Bickel soon undertook a more elaborate attempt to reconcile *Brown,* if not the rest of the Warren Court's decisions, to process theory's concern for the rule of law and judicial deference to legislatures. Like Herbert Wechsler, Bickel's overall goal was to preserve the power of judicial review by conserving the Court's prestige and authority for deployment in a case like *Brown.* While Wechsler wanted the reassertion of judicial power to be measured by the "process of reasoning" standard of the legal process tradition, Bickel's more complex theoretical justification first took up the older process approach to jurisdictional and procedural issues, then built on his initial living Constitution justification of *Brown.* The goal of his attempted reconciliation was to "allow leeway to expediency without abandoning principle" and thus "make possible a principled government."[72]

Bickel expanded upon Brandeis's dictum that "the most important thing [the Court does] is not doing" and polished the process techniques for "staying the Court's hand" so that judicial review could command obedience in cases of grave national significance.[73] These methods, outlined as we have seen in Frankfurter's early work at Harvard, were gleaned from Thayer, Holmes, and Brandeis. Bickel famously dubbed them the "passive virtues."[74] The concepts of "standing," "case or controversy," "ripeness," "justiciability," and the doctrine of "political questions" could be used by the Court to reject the hearing of a case. These were complicated doctrines whose prudential exercise was intimately tied to the facts and political environment in each case, but as the "vivid metaphors of jurisdiction," Bickel urged that they be used so that the Court could preserve its authority. Sometimes avoiding a case and refusing to enter the maelstrom of politics was required for the long-term authority of the institution. This conservation of prestige and power permitted the Court to resolve rare controversies of truly great moment by having the parties accede to its enunciation of a basic constitutional principle.[75]

An important example was Bickel's approval of Frankfurter's dismissal for the Court of *Poe v. Ullman* (1961) because it was not "ripe." The Connecticut law challenged in this case forbade the use of contraceptives. Reformers wanted it repealed to pave the way for birth control clinics but had repeatedly failed to sway the state legislature. Bickel recognized that there was an extant controversy, but not the kind that the Court should try to resolve: its function was "not necessarily to resolve issues on which the political processes are in deadlock." The Court should not relieve Connecticut of the "burden of self government."[76] Bickel similarly approved the dismissal of *Naim v. Naim* (1956), a challenge to a state antimiscegenation statute, even though it flouted the principle of *Brown*. It would not have been "wise" to void this statute at a moment when many howled that integration would lead to the "mongrelization of the race."[77] The prestige the Court required for obedience to the principle of *Brown* was simply too precarious to be used for such rapid change.

Bickel's "passive virtues," like Wechsler's "neutral principles," aimed to preserve judicial review by preventing its precipitous exercise. The looming threat of renewed judicial willfulness required that any theory of judicial review must set limits on it. This was necessary because judicial review was ineluctably "countermajoritarian" and therefore a "deviant institution" in the American democratic system. But where were the limits on it to be found? It is perhaps unsurprising that, given Bickel's general approach, he explicitly denied that history was of much use for this purpose.[78] He argued that the "intentions of the framers," Hamilton's argument in *Federalist* 78, and Marshall's in *Marbury v. Madison* (1803) did not delineate clear limits for judicial review, although he conceded that historical inquiry demonstrated that the practice was intended to some ill-defined extent. Likewise, he criticized Justice Hugo Black's historical inquiries as searches for a nonexistent certainty, one which in fact obscured the process of judgment. Bickel thought Black was simplemindedly asking the past to resolve questions it could not have foreseen. Yet Bickel simultaneously averred that the framers meant to bind posterity by providing "quite specifically for certain forms of government that must necessarily be known to all, [and] they prescribed a very general allocation of competencies among several institutions." Indeed, he recognized that "this itself is a judgment based on the sort of materials in which Justice Black seeks his answers." Nonetheless, Bickel claimed that history also demonstrated that the framers had "no specific intent" regarding the scope of judicial power and the modalities of its exercise. Instead, they left it "open-ended." Bickel also lauded the logic of a living Constitution in which a "useable past" was available for rhetorical and aspirational (but not historically specific) support of adjustment to new circumstances.[79]

Thus liberated from the nonexistent limitations of the past, Bickel argued that "judicial review is a present instrument of government . . . . Ultimately we must justify it as a choice in our own time." The justification lay, as in his initial approbation of *Brown,* in what Bickel's judge assessed to be a value that was both fundamental and capable of vindication in the extant political environment. At this point in his career Bickel felt that the Supreme Court could be the "pronouncer and guardian" of "enduring values" because "judges have, or should have the leisure, training, and insulation to follow the ways of the scholar in pursuing the ends of government. This is crucial in sorting out the enduring values of a society." Judicial review in this scheme functioned as an "educational institution" and the justices as "teachers in a vital national seminar."[80] Bickel therefore found it necessary, like Frankfurter, to move beyond James Bradley Thayer's reasonableness rule. In modern times judicial invalidation of only clearly unreasonable laws would allow the legislature too much power to offend individual "rights" or shared national "values." Bickel counseled that "Thayer's rule of the clear mistake should, therefore, be expanded to read as follows: What is rational, and rests on an unquestioned, shared choice of values, is constitutional."[81] Like Frankfurter, Bickel was confident that judges could conduct this project without becoming continually activist or behaving like an ongoing constitutional convention.

Thus, *Brown* presented an issue Bickel regarded as fundamental, and he seemed to have found a way to legitimate it. Although the profound principle vindicated in the case had to be inferred from the opaque opinion and the Court's later *per curiam* desegregation orders, it was "clear that the principle in question is that racial segregation constitutes, *per se,* a denial of equality to the minority group against whom it is directed." The Court properly had exercised its authority to vindicate its own formulation of a principle fundamental to the national character. Such "activism of high principle," as Alfred H. Kelly termed Bickel's jurisprudence, allowed the Court to choose when and how to vindicate its own definition of constitutional fundamentals.[82]

Critics generally responded to Bickel as they had to Wechsler: Bickel's counsel of prudence in the use of judicial power did not offer a reliable limitation on judicial discretion, nor did it seem reliably to produce the results admired by the Warren Court's defenders. One piercing criticism was that Bickel's "passive virtues" were tantamount to "100% insistence on principle, 20% of the time." Bickel's approach "would endorse conjecture about the complexities of political reactions as a primary ingredient of Court deliberations." Thus, the prudence Bickel saw as inherent in the passive virtues also could be characterized as unmoored discretion.[83] Another observer keenly declared that where "Wechsler had tried to confine the Court's discretion within boundaries sufficiently narrow to obviate the justices becoming the Platonic Guardians feared by [Learned] Hand," Bickel had postulated "Guardians who are Platonic not only in their exercise of power, but also in their wisdom."[84] Bickel's judges required more Platonic wisdom because he had given them more discretion.

Bickel clearly had a moral desire to approve and defend *Brown* while also preserving the limited judicial role process theory required. In light of *Brown* he had concluded that moral sensibility or good social policy could be a legal-constitutional trump in the "proper" circumstances. But in this way Bickel's response to *Brown* laid bare the difficulties besetting the process tradition. In the consensus intellectual environment of the early Cold War, process thinkers had successfully theorized a route between the Scylla of modern jurisprudence and the Charybdis of a willful Court. This was required because at the deepest level they were convinced by the philosophical skepticism of modern legal thought—allowing one's sense of justice to trump the legal process or reasoned elaboration too closely resembled the simple political will, disguised as natural law, that the old Court had used to subvert reform legislation before the New Deal. But guiding the Court by neutral principles, precedent, and jurisdictional prudence could solve this problem. Constitutional adjudication would come to resemble the slow, careful interstitial legislation of the common law, the modern balancing of interests, and the occasional updating of the living Constitution. Although at the outset the process school had routinely warned against "running the blockade" of jurisdiction, procedure, and legal reasoning, it now allowed the occasional exception of high principle à la *Brown*. Thus, in 1962 Bickel's attempted theoretical reconciliation was marked by a far more discretionary role for the Court than was suggested by his jurisprudential roots: "One can imagine Holmes, Hand, and even Frankfurter blinking."[85] Bickel's effort brilliantly but poignantly illustrated the struggle of the process tradition, after conceding so much of the modern claim about the nature of law, to guarantee both judicial self-restraint and politically salutary results.

As the 1960s wore on Bickel himself intensified his criticisms of the Warren Court and became more dissatisfied with process jurisprudence. In his 1969 Oliver Wendell Holmes Jr. lectures at Harvard Law School, Bickel rethought his earlier attempt to reconcile the process tradition to the Court's reassertion of modern judicial power. He now questioned the propriety and efficacy of a Court that made its own determinations of political prudence or the requirements of national values.[86] He doubted that Felix Frankfurter, and by implication process jurisprudence, had reconciled judicial review to democracy or could have prevented the judicial activism of the 1960s. This was clear in Bickel's analysis of Frankfurter's explanation of how he "balanced" constitutional principles and defined the content of the due process clause. Bickel considered Frankfurter's statement that "striking the balance implies the exercise of judgment . . . founded on something much deeper and more justifiable than personal preference." For Frankfurter this judgment rested on "fundamental presuppositions rooted in history to which widespread acceptance may be fairly attributed."[87] But now Bickel concluded that Frankfurter "never successfully identified sources from which this judgment was to be drawn that would securely limit as well as nourish it, he never achieved a rigorous general accord between judicial supremacy and democratic theory, . . . he was thus unable to ensure that the teaching of a duty of judgment would be received as subordinate to the teaching of abstention."[88] With all values held to be individual and subjective, and original meaning too dismissed, process jurisprudence lacked a source of legal judgment capable of limiting judges.[89] This suggested that the jurisprudential field might now be more open to ideas about what such a source could be.

Before originalism stepped in to offer a solution, it was clear to Bickel which thread of Frankfurter's teaching the Warren Court had taken up: "The teaching of the duty of judgment, although more an undertone than the dominant note in Frankfurter's work seen as a whole, was destined to have the more willing reception."[90] Bickel was increasingly troubled by the Warren Court's demonstrated preference for its own judgment because he retained the central process assumption that judicial review was inevitably in tension with the imperatives of pluralistic, democratic decision-making in a constitutional republic. Consequently, he had come "to doubt in many instances the Court's capacity to develop 'durable principles'" and rejected the new reforming faith that "judicial supremacy can work and is tolerable in broad areas of social policy." As one scholar of Bickel's thought observed, such "rank apostasy" from the "liberal creed" marked the distance he had traveled from his earlier theory.[91]

Process criticism was thus becoming more urgent even as it failed to constrain modern judicial power or stem the flow of decisions that process critics regarded as poorly reasoned. Still, this vigilance derived from the properly constitutionalist goals of limiting government power and ensuring the rule of law. Process critics genuinely feared that the recent reassertion of modern judicial power undermined the constitutional order. Nevertheless, their jurisprudence had from its beginnings accepted the realist critique of formalist adjudication. Like their realist predecessors, process critics assumed that at their core the superficially legal processes of constitutional interpretation and adjudication were determined by individual political choices, themselves essentially relative and subjective, and not by objective legal sources or reasons. This view fundamentally constrained their attempt to rein in modern judicial power and helped make way for the more formalist, rule-oriented, and historical originalist response.

Indeed, although by 1969 Bickel openly reproached the Warren Court, he retained the modern idea that judges could only be warned of the delicacy of their essentially political power. Identification of law with politics and politics with subjective will yielded Bickel's insistence that judicial vindication of "fundamental values" be prudent, cautious, and supportive of an emergent consensus. Overly active judicial pursuit of controversial political goals could undermine the Court's authority and erode the public support required for obedience to its decisions. As one historian has noted, "Perhaps it was because [Bickel] believed one could only 'caution' judges that he came to caution them so forcefully."[92] Philip Kurland, another important process critic, was equally convinced of the fundamental modern claim. He wrote that "at least since Holmes's day we have recognized judicial lawmaking as a conscious project of creation [and] not discovery." He too urged judicial caution in setting aside the will of the majority, which should be done only when the prudence of the judge (or commentator) counseled that it was "essential to [the Court's] functions as guardians of interests that would otherwise be unrepresented in the government of the country."[93]

Based on this view of interpretation and the Court's proper role in the constitutional system, use of historical evidence of original intent as a way of limiting judicial power held little attraction for process thinkers. Kurland and Bickel recognized that historical meaning was at issue, but neither emphasized history in the late 1960s, even as they amplified their criticisms.[94] Their increasingly urgent calls for judicial self-restraint were still based on the premise that the Constitution was what courts said it was—it did not have a historically demonstrable meaning that could limit judges. Thus, in the late 1960s the process attempt to restrain the Warren Court simultaneously sharpened and foundered on its own limitations. The Court's reassertion of modern judicial power simply bypassed the careful process attempts to limit it. The Court continued to issue controversial decisions, like *Brown*, which an increasing number of observers criticized as inadequately supported by the original intent of the Constitution. As we shall see in the next chapter, just at the point when process jurisprudence fell most into disarray, and despite its ahistorical thrust, decisions raising historical issues helped return consideration of original intent to a prominent place in the intensifying discussion about the legitimacy and limits of modern judicial power.

CHAPTER 3

The Return of Originalist Analysis in the Warren Court Era

In the 1960s the Warren Court rapidly repudiated several established constitutional doctrines and plunged into social reform primarily on the basis of the Reconstruction-era Amendments. It did so in ways that invited attention to history, often by inquiring into original intent or by disregarding its relevance in constitutional decision-making. Increasingly the response was protest that the original Constitution did not mean what the Court now said it did and that the Court's new reformist direction paid too little attention to original intent as a source of legitimating authority. To be sure, some reformist judges and supportive commentators tried to enlist history to defend the established modern notion of a judicially updated "living Constitution." But as Charles A. Miller noted in a perceptive study, there was a gap between the limited legal-constitutional reformism of the Reconstruction Amendments and the demands placed on them in the 1960s. Judges and commentators engaged in "attempts to reconstruct the reconstructionists [that] foundered each time on the facts of social and constitutional history."[1]

The widening of the gap in historical justification made history a more pressing concern at the very time when process jurisprudence was under strain. Some commentators and some Supreme Court justices began to pay more attention to history, sometimes appealing to original intent to insist that the universe of meaning available to judges was limited.[2] Further, they argued that federalism and the separation of powers, central to both the historically verifiable original intent of the Constitution and the process-restraint tradition, were undermined by the reassertion of modern judicial power. Most of these judges and commentators, such as Hugo Black, Robert G. McCloskey, Charles Fairman, and Alfred H. Kelly, did not make history the consistent core of their jurisprudence, nor should they be understood as originalists in today's terms. However, it is necessary to recall their criticism of the Court because by charging it with ignoring or misunderstanding history, they raised the issues that later made possible a more theoretically self-conscious originalist jurisprudence. This chapter first will backtrack slightly to show that the importance of historical issues in the modern era initially re-emerged in the 1940's debates about "incorporation" and the establishment clause of the First Amendment. In the Warren Court era, history became a major component of the controversy surrounding *Brown v. Board of Education* (1954); the "state action" requirement under the Reconstruction Amendments; voting and legislative apportionment; the religion clauses of the First Amendment; and the renaissance of the Ninth Amendment in *Griswold v. Connecticut* (1965).

Debates on Incorporation and the Establishment Clause

Incorporation was somewhat casual and relatively uncontroversial until *Adamson v. California* (1947). This case clearly presented a fundamental disagreement between Justices Felix Frankfurter and Hugo Black about the original intent of the Fourteenth Amendment and the relevance of the concept itself for constitutional interpretation.[3] Both men wanted to set limits on judicial power in the incorporation context, but only Black did so with a historical argument.[4]

The issue in *Adamson* was whether a state law that permitted a prosecutor to comment on the failure of a criminal defendant to testify in his own defense violated the Fifth Amendment protection against self-incrimination. Justice Reed's majority opinion upheld the statute based on the *Palko* approach (see chapter 1) and reaffirmed an earlier holding that the privilege was not a "fundamental" part of Fourteenth Amendment due process and therefore was not incorporated. Black's dissent argued for incorporation of the first eight

Amendments by analyzing evidence from the 39th Congress and insisting that the framers had not intended to allow judges the discretionary power to discern fundamental rights. Frankfurter's separate concurrence denied that history supported full incorporation and championed the *Palko* formula of ad hoc "selective incorporation" of judicially defined fundamental rights.

On the jurisprudential level, Frankfurter argued that even if an influential framer clearly intended incorporation, his remarks in Congress were "not to be deemed part of the amendment. What was submitted for ratification was his proposal, not his speech." Incorporation was not intended because, during and after ratification, the states clearly had not understood their criminal justice systems now to be subject to the Fifth Amendment requirement for a grand jury indictment or the Seventh Amendment requirement for a jury trial in cases involving a claim over twenty dollars. Thus, judicial review of state court proceedings under the due process clause should follow the *Palko* formula and determine what rights were "of the very essence of a scheme of ordered liberty." Standards for this effort were not "authoritatively formulated anywhere as though they were prescriptions in a pharmacopoeia" but required "judgment." Frankfurter believed that this approach did not leave judges "wholly at large" to effectuate the "idiosyncrasies of a merely personal judgment" because their views would derive from and represent the community of which they were a part.[5] He had articulated this typically modern approach before *Adamson* and had consistently held that judges must discern fundamental values and "balance" them against other interests. As in *Adamson*, Frankfurter usually eschewed extrinsic evidence of original intent as a constraint on this process, typically preferring discretionary jurisprudential techniques for abstaining from judicial review and deferring to the legislature.[6]

Black's *Adamson* dissent relied on the legislative history of the Fourteenth Amendment as a way of combating Frankfurter's approach. In an appendix, Black quoted extensively from framers in the 39th Congress and the later Reconstruction period, but he paid little attention to the ratification debates. He argued that the framers originally intended the Amendment to abrogate *Barron v. Baltimore* (1833) and to apply the first eight Amendments to the states. Close adherence to text and legislative intent, argued Black, would constrain what he termed Frankfurter's dangerous "natural law" approach, which erroneously held that the "Court is endowed by the Constitution with boundless power . . . periodically to expand and contract constitutional standards to conform to the Court's conception of what at a particular time constitutes 'civilized decency' and 'fundamental liberty and justice.'" Although this illegitimate power had recently been used to prevent state violation of the Bill of Rights, there was no guarantee that it would remain so limited. Black thus undertook the search for original intent to guide and constrain modern judicial interpretive discretion, though he was imprecise about whether incorporation had been intended and accomplished by the "provisions of the Amendment's first section, separately, and as a whole" or through the privileges or immunities clause, which constituted the focus of most of his historical evidence.[7]

Black's dissent provoked a lengthy scholarly debate about the original intent of the Fourteenth Amendment. An important response to Black came from Charles Fairman, a former student and correspondent of Frankfurter's and a law professor at Stanford University. Fairman studied the legislative history of the Amendment and inquired "what the country understood to be the import of Section 1 of the proposed Amendment" through analysis of state-level political speeches, newspapers, and records of ratifying legislatures. Like Frankfurter, Fairman rejected incorporation in part because he found no evidence that people at the time thought state criminal justice systems would be subjected to the requirements of the Bill of Rights. Moreover, Fairman found no clear agreement among the framers or understanding among the ratifiers that "privileges or immunities" was intended to include the entire Bill of Rights. The overriding goal was to provide former slaves with equality before the law through some federal oversight of state action, but the record was "overwhelmingly against" Black's view that this was intended or understood to have been accomplished by full incorporation. Fairman ended by seemingly endorsing the process of selective incorporation the Court had initiated under the due process clause.[8]

The incorporation debate also attracted William Winslow Crosskey, a colorful and controversial figure, because it was related to his own unorthodox scholarship. Crosskey defended Black's view of the privileges or immunities clause and responded directly to Fairman. Crosskey's role in the incorporation debate is best understood in light of his unique attempt, since the early 1940s, to formulate a massive historical argument against established constitutional opinion. Its main thesis was that the framers of the Constitution had intended Congress, under the general welfare and commerce clauses, to possess plenary power for realizing the abstract goals of the Preamble. As a corollary he claimed that the Supreme Court was intended to be the final authority on all matters of state and federal law but had no power to overturn an act of Congress unless it directly breached the Court's own Article III powers. From this perspective Crosskey argued that the Bill of Rights was originally intended to apply to the states and that *Barron,* in which Chief Justice John Marshall held the opposite, was incorrectly and illegitimately decided. Though the Court was only slowly realizing it in practice, the originally intended limits on the states were being restored by the incorporation of the Bill of Rights through the Fourteenth Amendment.[9]

Crosskey's study was a major event in constitutional scholarship, and although a few initial reviews were favorable, the tide rapidly turned against him.[10] Fairman wrote an unfavorable review of Crosskey's treatment of the Bill of Rights, attacked Crosskey's claim that *Barron* was wrongly decided, and briefly reiterated his own argument against incorporation. Crosskey responded with a lengthy defense of incorporation and another attack on *Barron,* to which Fairman offered a brief rejoinder.[11]

The Fairman-Crosskey debate, like the Black-Frankfurter debate from which it grew, showed that consideration of historical evidence of original intent remained an important component of arguments about proper constitutional interpretation and the role of the Court. But it also demonstrated the generally untheorized nature of the debate. This was evident, for example, in the differing and uncontested practices concerning when extrinsic evidence or the text (or both) should be used to establish the original intent of the Constitution. Crosskey's inconsistency demonstrates the point: His monograph's argument for plenary Congressional power and limited judicial review had strained the Constitutional text and rejected use of both Madison's notes and the *Federalist.* But in his debate with Fairman he used legislative history, as had Justice Black, to corroborate what he understood as the plain meaning of the Fourteenth Amendment's privileges or immunities clause. Thus, in contrast to the argument in his book, in the incorporation debate Crosskey held that the meaning he found plainly embodied in the text of the Fourteenth Amendment could not be trumped, even if its legislative history or the understanding of the ratifiers had not also corroborated incorporation (which he thought they did). On the other hand, Fairman insisted that the absence of an understanding for incorporation among the ratifiers was crucial because they provided the Amendment with its power as law, and he was skeptical that the legislative history supported incorporation.[12] Still, despite their substantive disagreements and methodological inconsistency, both Fairman and Crosskey were engaged in reconstructing the original intent of the Constitution and assumed that the

Supreme Court should be bound by it.[13] The incorporation debate thus reflected the persistence of the traditional constitutionalist concern that Supreme Court interpretation be based on the original intent of the Constitution.

Another debate in the immediate aftermath of the New Deal further illustrated the persistence of originalist presuppositions. In *Everson v. Board of Education* (1947) and *McCollum v. Board of Education* (1948), the Court took up the interpretation of the establishment clause of the First Amendment.[14] In *Everson* Justice Black studied the founding era and concluded that the clause effected a "wall of separation" between church and state, invoking a metaphor first used by Thomas Jefferson in a private letter in 1802. But Black's majority opinion held that the state's interest in education permitted the bussing of parochial school students at public expense and that this action was not a breach of the "wall."[15] In *McCollum* the Court voided a statute allowing time in the school day for voluntary religious instruction ("released time") and held that the incorporation doctrine made this interpretation of the establishment clause binding on the states.[16] Justice Reed's dissent noted the same history examined in *Everson* but said of the "wall" metaphor that "a rule of law should not be drawn from a figure of speech." He could find no justification in history for "barr[ing] every friendly gesture between church and state."[17]

Reed went further and suggested that the original intent of the establishment clause might in fact be much narrower. It "may have been intended by Congress" only to have prohibited a legally preferred, state-financed church while allowing nonpreferential aid or accommodation of religion. In 1949 this position, which became known as the "nonpreferentialist" interpretation of the establishment clause, was defended in a historical argument by Edward S. Corwin, an eminent liberal constitutional scholar better known for his defense of the living Constitution. The "unhistorical conception of what is meant by 'an establishment of religion'" and the Court's hitching of the wall metaphor to the incorporation doctrine (in *McCollum*) yielded a decision that in Corwin's opinion was as mistaken as *Dred Scott*. In short, the Court had contravened original intent, illegitimately displaced local governance of a local issue, and made itself into a "national school board."[18] An expanded historical investigation by J. M. O'Neill (who had consulted on the state's brief in *McCollum*) reached the same nonpreferentialist conclusion and noted the same threat to the rule of law. Like Corwin, O'Neill recognized the centrality of inquiry into the "purpose or intent" of the First Amendment—particularly since the Court had rested its holding in *McCollum* on historical authority. He accepted as a matter of course that the "meaning of an ambiguous phrase in the Constitution [was determined by] what that phrase must have meant to the men who wrote it, adopted it, and ratified it." Constitutional government depended upon this enterprise: "If the 'purpose' of any passage in the Constitution becomes whatever a majority of the Supreme Court think it *ought to be,* the days of constitutional government are over."[19]

The debate on the establishment clause, like the one on incorporation, showed that even in the post–New Deal era of modern judicial power, constitutional argument gravitated to the originalist idiom when fundamental issues were at stake. This occurred again as the Warren Court extended judicial power in ways that stimulated basic questions about original intent, the legitimate scope of judicial review, and the rule of law.

Brown: A Spur for Historical Inquiry

Historical inquiry into original intent, initiated by the Court itself, was a conspicuous feature of the most famous decision of the twentieth century, *Brown v. Board of Education* (1954). Litigants were ordered to investigate whether "the Congress which submitted and the state legislatures and conventions [*sic*] which ratified the Fourteenth Amendment contemplated or did not contemplate, understood or did not understand, that it would abolish segregation in public schools."[20] The Court also asked if it was "the understanding of the Framers of the Amendment" that Congress had such power under section 5 of the Amendment. The Court thus identified the categories of historical actors whose "contemplation or understanding" had been traditionally understood as relevant to the determination of constitutional meaning: ratifiers and Congressmen who voted for the measure, referred to collectively as "framers." If historical investigation did not "dispose of the issue," the litigants were ordered to discuss whether the Amendment might "of its own force" have created rights the Court itself could construe and then vindicate through the exercise of its equity powers.[21]

The Court's order produced several historical studies. Thurgood Marshall, who represented appellants through the National Association for the Advancement of Colored People (NAACP), enlisted several scholars, including Alfred H. Kelly, Howard Jay Graham, C. Vann Woodward, and John Hope Franklin. The historical brief written for the NAACP was based mostly on the work of Graham and Jacobus tenBroek and advanced the "Negro Freedom" interpretation of the original intent of the Fourteenth Amendment. This interpretation held that the 39th Congress intended to incorporate the natural rights concepts of the antebellum abolitionist movement into the first section of the Amendment, most particularly its equal protection clause. By this reading, the intent of the Amendment was quite broad: abolition of racial discrimination in all of its forms.[22] Although these scholars were confident that original intent required school desegregation, Graham was also willing to appeal to a judicially updated living Constitution.[23]

Justice Earl Warren's opinion for a unanimous Court deemed the original intent "inconclusive" on the question of segregated schools. Although the Court had ordered the historical investigation, the *Brown* opinion said it could not "turn the clock back to 1868 when the Amendment was adopted." Instead, it held that state-imposed school segregation generated "a feeling of inferiority" in black children, which violated contemporary notions of equality it located in the equal protection clause of the Fourteenth Amendment.[24] The Court's request for reargument on historical grounds and dismissal of the resulting evidence advanced debate about the original intent of the Amendment and its relationship to judicial review and the role of the Supreme Court.

Despite, or because of, *Brown*'s appeal to contemporary, Court-defined notions of equality, several scholars involved in the litigation publicly offered the historical rationale the Court had deemed "inconclusive." A major part of their argument was that the framers of the Fourteenth Amendment intended the Court to update the Constitution to contemporary needs. That is, a judicially updated living Constitution was the original intent.

As we saw in the last chapter, this was how Alexander M. Bickel had first attempted to reconcile *Brown* and process-restraint jurisprudence. Kelly also used historical evidence to defend a broad reading of the Amendment and an "updating" role for the Court.[25] He built on the Graham and tenBroek argument about antebellum abolitionist theory and also echoed Bickel's contention that radical Republicans, who subscribed to the broad abolitionist notion of equality, held the balance of power in the 39th Congress. They had used vague, abstract language to allow an open-ended interpretation. Kelly concluded that as a part of the "living and dynamic constitutional system" the "meaning of [the Amendment] consequently was ultimately to reflect through the medium of the judicial process the evolution of democratic aspiration."[26]

Yet upon reflection Kelly thought he had helped blur the line between legislation and adjudication, observing that in *Brown* "the Court was 'legislating,' for sweeping aside state decisions and decisions based on mere law and precedent, it vested [*sic*] its opinion on broad considerations of national welfare." He was troubled that during the litigation he had "ceased to function as a historian" and instead "took up the practice of law without a license" by "using facts, emphasizing facts, bearing down on facts, sliding off facts, quietly ignoring facts, and above all interpreting facts" in a way favorable to a broad reading of the Amendment.[27] Kelly justified this to himself and his profession by observing that opposing counsel was doing the same thing and that the Court would hear each side, but also by the result of the case. Misgivings about manipulating history for the purposes of advocacy did not undermine his pride that "we [historians] had something to do with the victory." Indeed, he thought that in ordering the historical investigation the Court was seeking possible cover for a result it meant to reach, with or without the sanction of the historical record.[28]

Recent evidence suggests this possibility may have been truer than Kelly realized. It appears that Justice Frankfurter courted impropriety by helping shape the Department of Justice *amicus* brief so that the limitations of original intent would not jeopardize a holding for desegregation. The brief buttressed the contention that the history of the Amendment, if understood at a sufficiently abstract level, permitted the Court to order desegregation. Combined with the NAACP brief and the Bickel memorandum, the government brief helped cloud the issue of intent so that the Court could plausibly dismiss the history as "inconclusive."[29]

Although Frankfurter was willing to use history in this instrumental manner, he disparaged the notion that historical inquiry into the Fourteenth Amendment could justify desegregation. In internal Court deliberations on segregation cases just prior to *Brown* he explicitly rejected Hugo Black's invocation of the "basic purpose" of the Amendment as a ground for desegregation, asking, "How does Black know the purpose" of the Amendment? Frankfurter argued that such cases "should be decided aside from any doctrinaire [views] or intentions as we construe them of the 14th Amend[ment]. No one knows what was intended."[30]

Additional scholarly defenses of *Brown* similarly diminished the relevance of original intent and ultimately applauded the Court's updating of a living, evolving, and informal constitution with its own measure of reason, morality, and "fundamental values." Simply put, the "nature" of the Constitution was to be "ordained by the people," it belonged "to the living, and not to the dead."

Even Charles Fairman made a similar argument, despite having earlier presented an originalist rebuttal to Hugo Black's argument for full incorporation of the Bill of Rights.[31] In such analyses, disgust with racial segregation facilitated disregard of the traditional view of the limited original intent of the Fourteenth Amendment or generalization of that intent to a high degree of abstraction.

The corollary of this development was that the concept of original intent was sometimes equated with conservative politics or segregation. Sober conservatives argued that the written Constitution as a limit on government was in peril if the Court substituted its estimation of contemporary needs for original intent. This view was apparent in the neglected work of L. Brent Bozell,[32] a lawyer and intimate of the circle that coalesced around William F. Buckley and *National Review,* and Charles S. Hyneman, a political scientist.[33] Bozell and Hyneman thought *Brown's* explicit dismissal of original intent as the basis of constitutional interpretation, plus its prospective desegregation decree and the Court's language of judicial supremacy in *Cooper v. Aaron* (1958), all combined to present a potentially ominous departure from limited government and the normal consensus-building and give-and-take of democratic politics.[34]

Similarly, although there is room to doubt the Virginia Commission on Constitutional Government's disavowal of any position on segregation, it condemned *Brown* as an affront to constitutional government and insisted that original intent was the only legitimate basis of interpretation.[35] Likewise, a South Carolina resolution condemning *Brown* and foreshadowing "massive resistance" in the South to integration further associated originalism with segregation. It stated that "the action of the Court ignored the principle that the meaning of the Constitution and its Amendments does not change. It is a written instrument. That which the Fourteenth Amendment meant when adopted it means now."[36] The segregationist former Justice James F. Byrnes expressed a similar view.[37] The John Birch Society's well-known "Impeach Earl Warren" publicity campaign similarly tainted originalist criticism of the Warren Court with racism and undermined its claim to be a defense of the rule of law.

Overcoming the State Action Problem

Brown showed that historical inquiry and the idea that interpretation should be based on original intent were fundamental to the American constitutional order and could not be easily set aside, even for the sake of better race relations. The persistence of originalist thinking also was evident in other areas of constitutional law revised by the Warren Court. For example, litigation derived from sit-ins at segregated restaurants prompted substantial originalist inquiry. This litigation forced the Court and scholars to wrestle with the disputed legal concept of "state action," which must be explained briefly to illuminate how originalist inquiry developed in this area.

Since the *Civil Rights Cases* (1883) it was generally agreed that the Fourteenth Amendment was originally intended only to prohibit discriminatory state action, not discriminatory acts by private citizens. This in turn protected a sphere of choice in private activity and association often seen as a crucial limit on government power. In the twentieth century, interaction of the state action doctrine with issues of race drew the Court into hard decisions that produced laudable results but also seemed capable of undermining the neutrality required for the rule of law. For example, the Court voided a private housing covenant among whites that prohibited the conveyance of property to blacks in the important precedent of *Shelley v. Kraemer* (1948), thus encountering the complexities of state action that returned in the sit-in cases of the 1960s. In *Shelley* the Court held that enforcement of the contract in federal court would have constituted state action and therefore was prohibited. Herbert Weschler observed in his famous "Neutral Principles" article that the opinion in *Shelley* did not explain why a court that merely gave effect to a private contract should be seen as an agent of discrimination rather than simply an enforcer of property rights. Nor had the Court indicated what fact situations might prompt extension of this practice and thus give it the sanction of a neutral principle that could be stated independent of the particular case.[38]

With these questions unresolved, the sit-in cases arrived at the Court. In *Bell v. Maryland* (1964) several blacks were charged with criminal trespass for holding a sit-in at a segregated restaurant. A majority of the Court refrained from deciding on either the state action issue or the merits of the case, but the concurring and dissenting opinions addressed them.[39]

Justice Arthur Goldberg's concurrence, joined by Justices William Douglas and Warren, circumvented the state action requirement by arguing that the Fourteenth Amendment was originally intended to ensure equal protection in public accommodations, such as the restaurant in question. He insisted that the Court was required to read the Constitution "to effectuate the intent and purposes of the Framers." He then argued that this purpose and intent, along with the "contemporary understanding of the general public," was that public accommodations would be subject to the equal protection standard, quoting from the debates in the 39th Congress and contemporary court interpreta-tions to make his case. Goldberg concluded by pleading in the alternative: if the historical evidence was not dispositive, the logic of a Court-updated living Constitution demanded that the equal protection clause be interpreted with enough generality to cover the situation in *Bell*.[40]

Justice Black dissented in part on historical grounds, attacking Goldberg's assertion that the Fourteenth Amendment was originally intended to bar dis-crimination in privately owned establishments.[41] He argued that Goldberg's evidence from the Reconstruction period was scant, sometimes contradictory, and frequently taken out of context. For example, Black showed that state-ments quoted by Goldberg referred to debates on proposed civil rights legisla-tion, not the Fourteenth Amendment, upon which *Bell* was contested. Finally, Black rejected the idea that the logic of a living Constitution could justify the process of judicial amendment the majority had undertaken.[42]

Scholarly assessment of *Bell* recognized the inevitable historical component in arguments about state action. Alexander M. Bickel briefly observed that to "anyone who has read the debates of the Reconstruction Congress" Goldberg offered a "dubious proposition." Alluding to the incorporation debate, Bickel noted that Black, "himself the notable author of some dubious readings of Four-teenth Amendment history on other issues," rejected Goldberg's effort in the case. Alfred Avins, a conservative law professor who responded to the Court's treatment of history throughout the 1960s, collected a series of quotations from the 39th Congress and court decisions that supported the state action requirement. Additionally, he argued that the legislative history of the Civil Rights Act of 1875, passed pursuant to the Fourteenth Amendment and ulti-mately voided in the *Civil Rights Cases,* showed that contemporary constitu-tional opinion had been that the Amendment contained the requirement.[43]

Alfred H. Kelly described Goldberg's opinion as "law office history" that was fabricated in an attempt to overcome the state action precedent of the *Civil Rights Cases.* Kelly judged that the evidence from the 39th Congress did not support the conclusion that the framers intended to outlaw anything be-yond discriminatory state legislation. Charles A. Miller agreed in his study of the Supreme Court and the uses of history. He observed that in several places Goldberg relied upon general statements not germane to public accommoda-tions or offered his own inferences as if the historical record contained them.[44] Monrad G. Paulsen also found Goldberg's historical argument "unimpressive." In large measure this was because it did not demonstrate that the "general public" understood the Fourteenth Amendment to compel equality in public accommodations. Paulsen also reiterated Black's point that Goldberg had quoted Congressional debates on proposed statutes but none on the Amendment itself. He added that Bickel's 1955 study, unrebutted by Goldberg, demonstrated convincingly that the 39th Congress had not intended to abolish segregation in public accommodations.[45]

Four years after *Bell* the Court constructed an original intent argument to overcome the state action problem, again illustrating its willingness to reform the law and its desire to do so with the apparent sanction of history. In *Jones v. Mayer* (1968) the Court obviated the Civil Rights Act of 1968, which was to become effective in January 1969, by enacting a general ban on religious and racial discrimination in the sale and rental of housing. *Jones* held that the Thirteenth Amendment empowered Congress to ban private discriminatory action, such as housing policy, and that Congress had intended to accomplish this in the Civil Rights Act of 1866, which was passed pursuant to the Amendment and which contained no state action requirement. Justice Potter Stewart's majority opinion relied heavily on debates in the 39th Congress to break with precedents holding that the Act was intended to affect only state action. He concluded that housing discrimination was a "badge or incident" of slavery within the meaning of the Thirteenth Amendment and thus that the 1866 Act also did not require state action to outlaw housing discrimination.[46]

Justice John Harlan dissented in *Jones*, joined by Justice Byron White. While he felt that the case should not have been heard because Congress had just legislated on the very topic of housing discrimination, he also argued that imputation of this concern to the 39th Congress was historically dubious. Harlan analyzed Stewart's citation of debates in the 39th Congress and found that they were irrelevant to the issue of state action, taken out of context, or could easily be read as evidence that Congress intended the Act to embody the state action requirement. Likewise, Stewart had quoted opponents of the Act who described its power as sweeping, but supporters responded by disavowing such broad constructions of it.[47]

The scholarly response to the original intent theory in *Jones* was similar to that of *Bell*. Gerhard Casper opined that the Court's history was of the "law office" variety. He criticized Stewart and Harlan for portraying the historical record as more straightforward and unambiguous then it actually was, although he concluded that Harlan had the far more defensible argument. Casper did discern scattered evidence that the Act was meant to reach some private discriminatory activities but none that it was intended to confer on blacks a right to buy from an unwilling seller, as Stewart had argued.[48]

The state action issue in *Bell* and *Jones* showed that the reassertion of modern judicial power by the Warren Court was focusing attention on the relationship between judicial review, original intent, and the rule of law. The two most important legal process critics of the 1960s, Philip Kurland and Alexander M. Bickel, noted the exposure of the "law office history" in *Jones*. While both men remained dissatisfied with the Court primarily because of its dubious legal reasoning, as befitted the emphasis of the process tradition, each also found that contrived history was no more satisfying than poor legal logic.[49] Likewise, Monrad Paulsen observed that while Justice Goldberg's turn to history in *Bell* "fail[ed] of proof," the decision provided an occasion to consider how the state action requirement was related to the rule of law. If the state could be charged with the discrimination of those who appealed in its courts for vindication of property rights, as occurred in *Shelley* (and as Douglas urged in *Bell*), the reach of government into aspects of private life and association was virtually unlimited. Such a development was anathema to the American tradition of limited government under the rule of law. The problem for all who sympathized with the civil rights movement was "the nature of law itself—its demands for some degree of universality and generality." If resolution of something like the state action issue could not be tied to the constitutional text, then constitutional law might become "nothing more than the political and social values of nine learned men."[50] Although he did not emphasize the point, Paulsen's analysis of Goldberg's failed historical argument clearly implied that it posed the same threat to the rule of law.

There was far too much at stake for defenders of the Warren Court to concede that their critics were correct about the original intent of the Civil Rights Act of 1866 or the Reconstruction Amendments. Accordingly, Robert L. Kohl delved far more deeply into debates in the 39th Congress than had Justice Stewart to argue that the act did not require state action. Kohl insisted that the government could use the act to punish any private activity synonymous with the present-day notion of "prejudice" that prevented blacks from acquiring property. He concluded that "by using the legislative history properly, the Court could have extended the Act still further" than it did in *Jones*.[51] This assessment, combined with an increased emphasis on the Thirteenth Amendment, which indisputably lacked any concept of state action, was characteristic of the originalist arguments of scholars who sought increased judicial authority for dealing with racial prejudice. In another example, civil rights lawyer Arthur Kinoy argued that the Thirteenth Amendment had not conferred mere ordinary civil rights but rather had created a special right of national citizenship that implied significant further government action. The right could be directly enforced by the federal government to excise what it defined as the relics of slavery.[52]

Reapportionment: A New Task for the Equal Protection Clause

Another major constitutional development of the 1960s that encouraged originalist inquiry was the Court's move into legislative reapportionment. In the twentieth century state legislatures had not consistently changed their representational schemes to account for increased urbanization. Many states did reapportion their legislatures in the 1950s, but they frequently emulated the Congressional model and maintained equal representation by district in one house in order to account for rural or agricultural interests. This left legislative representation unequal when measured solely by population. In a series of decisions the Court required state legislatures to organize both their houses, and their method of Congressional apportionment, as nearly as possible on the principle of "one person, one vote." A brief recapitulation of the holdings in the major cases will show how they increased concern about original intent, judicial review, and the rule of law.

In *Baker v. Carr* (1962) the Court held that the "political questions" doctrine did not bar it from ordering reapportionment of the Tennessee legislature based on the equal protection clause of the Fourteenth Amendment. The state had not done so since 1901.[53] Justice William Brennan declined to say what a remedy under the equal protection clause might be and remanded the case to the district court to fashion relief. A year later Justice Douglas articulated the "one person, one vote" standard in *Gray v. Sanders* (1963), which overturned a state apportionment scheme.[54] In *Wesberry v. Sanders* (1964) the Court overturned Georgia's method of apportioning representatives to Congress. Justice Black's opinion linked "one person, one vote" to the Article I, section 2 command that congressional representatives be chosen "by the people of the several states."[55] In *Reynolds v. Sims* (1964) the majority opinion of Chief Justice Warren returned to the equal protection clause to require that both houses of the Alabama legislature be apportioned by population, disallowing one house modeled on the

United States Senate. Warren claimed that the provision in the Northwest Ordinance of 1787 for solely population-based apportionment in the territories
proved that the "Founding Fathers clearly had no intention of establishing a
pattern or model for the apportionment of seats in state legislatures when the
system of representation in the Federal Congress was adopted."[56] If this were
not bold enough, in *Lucas v. Forty-Fourth General Assembly of Colorado* (1964),
Warren's majority opinion used the equal protection clause to strike down as
insufficiently majoritarian a state apportionment plan that recently had been
approved as a constitutional amendment in a statewide referendum.[57]

The reapportionment decisions fostered dissenting opinions, academic criticism, and congressional hearings in which original intent, the scope of judicial power, and the rule of law were central concerns. Frankfurter's dissent in
Baker veritably shouted that there was not a more eminently political question
than legislative apportionment—the separation of powers meant that a court
of law had no business in the issue. He and Harlan would have dismissed *Baker*
for failure to state a claim on which relief could be granted. Frankfurter skewered the Court for a "massive repudiation of the experience of our whole past
in asserting a destructively novel judicial power" and correctly predicted that
by taking on the issue the judiciary headed into the "mathematical quagmire"
of measuring the equity of state apportionments. The equal protection claim
the Court held to be justiciable was "in effect, a Guarantee Clause claim masquerading under a different label," and the Court was being asked to take on
the task it had refused since *Luther v. Borden* (1849). Neither the guarantee clause
nor the equal protection clause provided a standard by which the Court could
settle a dispute over the makeup of a legislature, and Frankfurter saw Brennan's
refusal to fashion a remedy in the case as a "sorry confession of judicial incom-
petence in place of a frank acknowledgment that there is not under our Constitution a judicial remedy for every political mischief." Frankfurter then restated the traditional separation of powers argument and concluded that the
entire issue should have remained with the legislature and not the Court.[58]

Some scholars also saw *Baker* as a dangerous judicial foray into politics. In
an article acerbically titled "Politics in Search of Law," Phil C. Baker feared
that the Court was acting like a legislature by enforcing its values instead of
remaining content to behave like a court and interpret the law. Although reformers exalted the Court's move into reapportionment as a "great example
of the rule of law in our society," Baker observed that "law makes demands on
courts as well as legislatures," and one of them was "a more satisfying explana-

tion of the authority and principles by which courts decree reapportionment." Unless and until this was done, *Baker* would "serve better as an example of the role of fiat in the exercise of judicial power" than of the rule of law.[59]

By focusing on the rule of law, judicial restraint, institutional competence, and judicially administrable standards, this kind of criticism and Frankfurter's *Baker* dissent bridged the older, process-restraint approach and the more self-conscious examination of original intent that Justice Harlan's dissents undertook in examining the equal protection clause of the Fourteenth Amendment (*Reynolds*) and Article I, section 2 of the Constitution (*Wesberry*). Additionally, both Harlan dissents argued that by manipulating or ignoring original intent the majority transgressed the separation of powers and usurped the power of constitutional amendment.[60] Invalidation of detailed apportionment schemes, said Harlan, began the dangerous process of "extracting from the very general language of the Fourteenth Amendment a system of delusive exactness." To ratchet down the level of abstraction at which the Court understood the equal protection clause, Harlan cited specifics from the 39th Congress. He analyzed the text of the amendment in light of these debates ("the understanding of those who proposed and ratified it"), the "political practices of the States" at the time of ratification, and the common public understanding and judicial interpretation until *Baker* "made an abrupt break with the past in 1962." He concluded that the amendment was "never intended to inhibit" a state's choice of methods for apportioning its legislature. Moreover, Harlan lambasted the Court's appeals to the logic of a court-updated living Constitution. To intone "constitutional 'development' [was meaningless] when both the language and meaning of the controlling provisions of the Constitution are wholly ignored." Harlan thought the Court's error grew from the reforming zeal of the era and attributed the holding to the "current mistaken view of the Constitution" that held that "every major social ill in this country can find its cure in some constitutional 'principle' and that this Court should 'take the lead' in promoting reform when other branches of government fail to act."[61] In *Wesberry* Harlan supplemented textual exegesis with analysis of the Philadelphia convention of 1787, the ratification debates, and the *Federalist* to demonstrate that Black's reliance on Article I, section 2 confused the founders' debate about apportionment of representatives *between* states with the issue in *Wesberry*, which was apportionment of representatives *within* states.[62]

Although the Court's majorities in the reapportionment decisions had no doubt that they were advancing progress, academic critics also faulted the historical dimensions of the decisions. Charles A. Miller observed that Harlan "pulveriz[ed]" Black's majority opinion in *Wesberry*. Alfred H. Kelly opined that Black had "mangled" the past and committed a "historical felony." L. Brent Bozell parsed the historical evidence and offered a detailed refutation of Black, concluding that if the Court could fabricate the law of the land in derogation of original intent, as in *Wesberry*, while Congress failed to constrict its jurisdiction or amend the Constitution, than "we are in the grips of a judicial despotism."[63]

The Court's treatment of the equal protection clause attracted probably the most heated scholarly debate about original intent and the level of generality at which the contemporary Court legitimately could restate it. Kelly found "amusing" Justice Warren's invocation of the Northwest Ordinance to help justify "one person, one vote" under the clause, but more importantly he noted that Harlan's evidence from the 39th Congress on the meaning of "equal protection" concerned the framers' understanding of its effect on voting, not apportionment. William Van Alstyne expanded on this point, arguing that the decreased representation mandated in section 2 of the Fourteenth Amendment was not intended by the 39th Congress as the exclusive remedy for a state's denial of suffrage. Rather, the "original understanding" was that the equal protection clause of section 1 was sufficient authority. Thus it was available to compel reapportionment, as the Warren Court had done. Van Alstyne linked this originalist argument to Bickel's argument that the language of section 1, including "equal protection," was intended to be open-ended—and therefore that the Court had broad latitude in its application.[64] This approach was common: other commentators documented their reasons for disagreement with Harlan's originalist argument and then appealed to the salutary results produced by a Court-updated living Constitution.[65] A blunter liberal response was that history simply did not matter. Conceding that the equal protection clause was "not originally intended to deal with [legislative representation]," one need only invoke Bickel's "open-ended" language, argue that "one person, one vote" was at the heart of democratic politics, and then welcome the Court as "the first authoritative faculty of political theory in the world's history."[66]

Other critics defended Harlan and rejected the idea that the Court legitimately could ignore the original intent of the equal protection clause while using it to bring about major changes in American political life. Alfred Avins, who represented states in two cases challenging the Voting Rights Act of 1965, insisted that disregard of the original meaning of equal protection and sub-

stitution of the Court's own measure of the "reasonableness" of state legislation endangered limited government and the rule of law. He further agreed
with Harlan that the Court was usurping the sovereign power of the people
to amend the Constitution under Article V.[67] Avins scoured the legislative debates of the entire Reconstruction era and concluded that the equal protection
clause was intended only to guarantee limited, absolute equality to former
slaves in their civil rights to life, liberty, and property.[68] It was not intended to
apply to political rights like voting, so "the Supreme Court's slogan, 'one person, one vote,' which it alleges it has derived from the Equal Protection Clause
is simply a figment of the Court's imagination."[69] As a result the Court was
unmoored to the written constitution and consequently "today, in this area,
we have all cases and no constitution."[70] Professor Robert G. Dixon agreed
that Justice Harlan's historical and textual arguments were "overpowering"
and unrebutted by the majority opinions. However, he observed that to make
a historical argument to a Court that had decided *Brown* "on broad principles
of developing Constitutionalism was like trying to get Bertrand Russell to take
Holy Communion."[71]

This was an accurate description of the Warren Court majority, and the
complaint persisted that judicial opinions contrary to original intent threatened the rule of law. This view was strong enough in Congress to provoke
hearings on constitutional amendments to revise the results of the reapportionment decisions or else to use the Article III, section 2 "exceptions" clause
to withdraw future reapportionment cases from federal court jurisdiction. The
debate on the latter proposal, offered by Representative William Tuck (D-VA),
presumed the relevance of the original intent of constitutional language and
the structures of federalism and the separation of powers.[72] Both supporters
and opponents of the bill constantly defended their positions with historical
examples and quotations about what was intended or required by those who
wrote the Constitution and the Fourteenth Amendment.[73] The historical elements of this debate were not especially scholarly or nuanced, but congressmen found it impossible to argue about the constitutional legitimacy of the
Tuck proposal without appealing to original intent.

Representatives also engaged the concept of intent when considering their
power over congressional districting. They often spoke in terms of intent when
they struggled to accommodate the Court's holding that the Constitution required "one person, one vote" to their belief that their own constitutional

authority permitted deviation from this formula. Recognizing that the Court had diminished their constitutional power, they approached the problem by considering what "the framers of the Constitution intended—as the Supreme Court [has said] they intended." Despite consistent recurrence to the idiom of original intent, this congressional attempt to respond to the Court failed largely because most representatives agreed that the Constitution was what the Court said it was.[74] Such unreflective acceptance of judicial supremacy hampered most critics from arguing that the Court's interpretation did not square with what the Constitution meant to those who wrote and ratified it.

School Prayer: The Return of the Establishment Clause Debate

The school prayer decisions of the early 1960s further fueled the debate about original intent. In *Engel v. Vitale* (1962) the Court held that recitation of a nonsectarian prayer in a public school violated the establishment clause of the First Amendment. In *Abington v. Schempp* (1963) the Court struck down a law requiring daily Bible readings in a public school.[75] Reaction was swift and intense, encompassing the general public, academia, and Congress. In the course of this reaction many people investigated the original intent of the First Amendment. Partisans on both sides frequently assumed, as a matter of course, that original intent should control the contemporary meaning of disputed constitutional provisions. Moreover, historical arguments were used not only to attack or justify the legitimacy of the decisions but also were part of the continuing and more fundamental debate about whether a Court-updated evolving Constitution could be reconciled to the rule of law.

Before *Engel* and *Schempp* the Supreme Court used the "wall of separation" metaphor to uphold most statutes attacked under the establishment clause.[76] But in these decisions the Court used it to strike down state laws. In *Schempp* the Court formulated a test for reconciling the free exercise and establishment clauses of the First Amendment. The test asked whether the primary purpose and effect of a challenged statute was to advance or inhibit religion. If it was either than the statute was invalid: "To withstand the strictures of the Establishment Clause there must be a secular legislative purpose and a primary effect that neither advances nor inhibits religion." Simultaneously, the Court explicitly rejected the contention that the establishment clause merely required nonpreferential official treatment of different religions or sects.[77] The *Schempp* test would make government "neutral" in the face of religion, thus creating a "wall of separation." Of course, both *Engel* and *Schempp* also depended upon the incorporation doctrine to invalidate the state laws at issue.[78]

A scholarly summary of the issues in this debate concluded that "tank cars of ink [were] spilt" in arguing about the "intent" of the "Framers" of the First Amendment.[79] For example, Leo Pfeffer, an attorney for the challengers in *Engel*, considered the "intent" of the First Amendment in a noted monograph. He concluded that historical evidence showed "unmistakably that in the minds of the fathers of our Constitution" government could have no interaction with religion. He concluded that they "intended to impose on future generations" an "obligation to preserve" and "adhere strictly to the principle" of separation.[80] After studying the historical record and tracing the constitutional cases, another scholar concluded that "Jefferson and Madison understood the language in much the same sense as did Justice Black" in his strict separationist *Engel* opinion.[81]

Advocates of some government support for religion also thought that history should limit judicial interpretation and that the historical record supported their position. One meticulously researched study began with the assumption that there "should be no doubt of the propriety of turning to the lessons of history in interpreting the United States Constitution," which required "recourse to the intent of the Founding Fathers who sat in the First Congress that proposed the Amendment, as well as to the intent of the citizens of the states that ratified it." Research in historical sources convinced the authors that the "intention" of the First Amendment was not strict separation of church and state but rather that government could nonpreferentially aid or accommodate religion when it served the public interest.[82]

Robert G. McCloskey, a noted commentator, recognized that the controversy over the religion clauses inevitably involved original intent. Neither original intent nor sound legal reasoning could be excised from the calculus of legitimacy if obedience to the Court were to continue. If the "historical-technical" base of a decision was weak, then the overall justification for the decision was diminished. The Court's reliance on its own ethical goals and its prestige as an institution simply were not enough over the long term.[83] Moreover, the incorporation of the establishment clause of the First Amendment did not seem to McCloskey to be "in [the] mind" of the "Framers of the Fourteenth Amendment."[84] Turning to the eighteenth century, he argued that "neither the constitutional text nor historical intent [gave] a positive mandate

to the Court to outlaw non-discriminatory and non-compulsive state aid to religion, and even those who fervently endorse the broad disestablishment idea
would be better off to admit this forthwith." The only other way to reconcile
the results of the school prayer decisions with original intent was to increase
the level of generality at which that intent was understood, as Bickel and
Kelly had in defense of *Brown*. This was the route taken in Justice Brennan's
Schempp concurrence, which argued that "a too literal quest for the advice of
the Founding Fathers" was "futile and misdirected." Rather, the Court should
ascertain whether present practices "threaten those consequences which the
Framers deeply feared," in effect the "interdependence between religion and
state which the First Amendment was designed to prevent."[85] McCloskey further noted that concern with the level of generality at which to apply constitutional provisions was central to constitutional interpretation. Yet this was
precisely where the line between law and politics was most unclear. "Once we
accept this [Brennan's] not unreasonable conception of the inquiry, however,
we are free to roam widely among our own prepossessions in deciding what
does or does not threaten those consequences."[86]

Other scholars concluded that in the school prayer decisions the Court
was undermining the rule of law by straying too far from the original intent
of the First Amendment. Charles E. Rice presented the standard historical evidence for a nonpreferentialist interpretation and excoriated the Court for
"enthron[ing] the abstraction" in its religion clause jurisprudence. The Court
had "deconsecrat[ed]" American public life in derogation of history, tradition,
and the political science of the Constitution. Rice recommended a constitutional amendment "not to change the Constitution, but to restore it, to repair
the breach opened by the federal judiciary."[87]

Rice was not alone in favoring a constitutional amendment, and original intent was part of the debate in 1964 when both houses of Congress considered
amendments to overturn the school prayer decisions.[88] Representative Frank
Becker (R-NY) proposed the most far-reaching of these measures. It would
have permitted voluntary prayer and Bible reading in public institutions, including schools, and allowed invocation of God in public documents, ceremo-
nies, and proceedings. Similar to the hearings on reapportionment, those on
school prayer amendments contained debate conducted in terms of the original intent of the Constitution, especially the First Amendment. Proponents
insisted that constitutional meaning depended on original intent and that
the rule of law was endangered if the Court departed from it.[89] For example,

Representative Louis Wyman (R-NH) insisted that the Becker amendment would clarify but not undermine the protections of the First Amendment. It "would be a slight modification of [it] as interpreted by this Court, which is what has caused all the difficulty anyway. Nothing in the First Amendment has caused it. Only what this Court has said about it."[90] Some members considered intent as they addressed the difficult problem of the proper level of generality at which to apply constitutional language. Representative Roland V. Libonati (D-IL) insisted that the Becker amendment would eviscerate the "specificities" of the "concept and intent" of the First Amendment on the issue of church and state. It was a "whittling away" of the "original intent of [the First Amendment]." Wyman replied: "It is not . . . a question of specificity; it is a question of whether or not such generality is to be given to the First Amendment as to mean that you can't even have the Lord's Prayer on a voluntary basis in the public schools." He insisted that "the Founding Fathers never intended to prohibit that sort of thing."[91] Although they disagreed on what original intent required in the circumstances, these congressmen adhered to the traditional idea that it was fundamental to the meaning of constitutional language and that the Court should be bound by it.

Law professors steeped in modern legal thought were more skeptical. Yet they could not avoid engaging the assumption of many in Congress that original intent should resolve the controversy. For example, Harvard professor Paul Freund was asked how history should inform the debate. He said that "to try to derive our answers from what we think Jefferson would have said, given our conditions, seems to me really putting our words in his mouth." He then added "we have got to make up our own minds on the philosophy of the Amendment."[92] The rub was that the very controversy prompting the hearings demonstrated that people disagreed on the "philosophy" of the Amendment while insisting that history could be adduced to show that the Court had gotten it wrong or at least that it was never intended to have the final word on church-state relations.

The Supreme Court's interpretation of the First Amendment in *Engel* and *Schempp* survived the amendment challenge. Opponents of the Becker amendment warned of dire consequences, arguing that it could be read to permit precisely the kind of "establishment of religion" or "religious test" all agreed that the extant Constitution already forbade.[93] Over two hundred law professors supported this view by signing a letter to the Committee on the Judiciary urging rejection of the proposed "experiment" because it would "impair by amendment" the Bill of Rights to satisfy short-term political goals. The professors said the Becker amendment encouraged lawlessness, even though its sponsors thought that it was a remedy for the Court's own lawlessness. The letter suggested that it was incorrect to think an amendment could have *restored* the original intent of the First Amendment from the Court's misinterpretation of it. Instead, it successfully equated the Becker amendment with "an alteration of the Bill of Rights" and helped produce enough "alarm" to defeat it.[94] As the professors saw it, fidelity to the rule of law required the protection of "rights" and defeat of the proposal, while substantial opinion in Congress and the public held that the rule of law required an amendment to retrieve the true, originally intended meaning of the Constitution from judicial misinterpretation. Plainly, the rule of law and its relation to the text, intent, and history of the Constitution were becoming increasingly contested.

The Right of Privacy: Somersaults with History

Griswold v. Connecticut (1965) also focused attention on issues of original intent and judicial power. Justice Douglas's majority opinion held that a Connecticut law against the use of contraceptives violated a new constitutional right of privacy he derived from the "penumbras" and "emanations" of the Bill of Rights.[95] In a concurring opinion Justice Goldberg relied on the Ninth Amendment's protection of unenumerated rights "retained by the people," which Douglas mentioned only in passing. Like Frankfurter and Cardozo before him, Goldberg held that the Court could move beyond the text of the Constitution and protect new rights by drawing on "'the traditions and conscience of our people' to determine whether a principle is 'so rooted [there] to be ranked as fundamental.'"[96] Claiming to reject the discredited Fourteenth Amendment economic substantive due process approach of the pre–New Deal era, Goldberg nonetheless wrote that judicial announcement of new rights was consistent with the text and original intent of the Ninth Amendment.[97]

Justices Black and Stewart dissented. Black, obviously piqued, charged the Court with usurpation of the legislative and amending powers in derogation of the text, intent, and political theory of the Constitution. "Penumbras," "emanations," and the Ninth Amendment were no more convincing or stable bases for judicial power than was the old economic substantive due process approach. Quoting extensively from *The Records of the Federal Convention,* Black concurred with Stewart's conclusion that reliance upon the Ninth Amendment "turn[ed] somersaults with history." Black wrote that "the idea that a federal court could ever use the Ninth Amendment to annul a law passed by the elected representatives of the people of the state of Connecticut would have caused James Madison no little wonder." Far from creating a judicial power to create new rights, the amendment simply stipulated that the federal government could not regulate rights left unenumerated merely because they were unenumerated. If the Court used it to void a state law based on its own creation of an unenumerated fundamental right, it had amended the Constitution and usurped legislative power from those who passed the law.[98]

Before *Griswold* the Supreme Court had recognized the Ninth Amendment only a few times, but Goldberg's opinion in the case cited recent broad, activist readings of its intent.[99] Most importantly, Norman Redlich had specifically advocated use of the Ninth Amendment to overturn the challenged Connecticut law. If the Court were to continue the modern liberal project of expanding federal rights against the states, and particularly if it were to overturn the Connecticut law, it needed a tool other than the discredited notion of substantive due process. When combined with the Tenth Amendment and the expanded federal power of incorporation under the Fourteenth Amendment, the Ninth Amendment supported judicial articulation of nontextual rights that were analogous to those in the text of the Bill of Rights. Redlich conceded the subjectivity inherent in moving beyond the text but was undeterred because American constitutional history and theory projected "through the ages the image of a free and open society."[100] Goldberg clearly followed Redlich's advice when he tried to locate the desired judicial power in the authority of original intent while actually updating the living Constitution.

Griswold provoked numerous articles analyzing the history of the Ninth Amendment and pondering the implications for American constitutionalism if the Goldberg version were elaborated.[101] Several echoed the historical arguments of Goldberg or Black.[102] In his analysis in "Clio and the Court," Alfred H. Kelly found the Goldberg opinion to be "a curious mixture of law-office history and vaulting legal logic." It surely would have been convenient, argued Kelly, if Goldberg could have called upon positive evidence for his historical interpretation, but it did not exist. Kelly felt that some ambiguities in Madison's statements could be read to support a limited version of the Goldberg thesis, but the record lacked any positive corroborative evidence.[103] Although the founders were steeped in the natural rights tradition, this did not permit the Court to pull "new natural rights from the air to allow for an indefinite expansion." Echoing Justice Black's dissent, Kelly concluded that under a "thin veil of constitutional history" Goldberg and others in the majority had attempted a return "to an open-ended concept of substantive due process after *Lochner.*"[104] Black himself also likened the Court's announcement of the privacy right in *Griswold* to the jurisprudence of the *Lochner* Court. He condemned the Court for ignoring the constraints of text and history and for resurrecting the self-bestowed power to overrule legislation according to its own view of justice. He marked the distance between his own generation of New Dealers and the Warren Court majority by rejecting those who "look to the judiciary to make all the major policy decisions of our society under the guise of determining constitutionality." Referring to the New Deal crisis, Black wrote, "I have known a different court from the one today. What has occurred may occur again."[105]

At the end of the 1960s there was a growing sense that the Court was straining the limits of its legitimacy and straining the relevant historical facts in doing so. Leonard W. Levy, a noted commentator of the period, observed the "notorious fact" that the Warren Court "flunked history."[106] Decisions consistently based on contested historical claims prompted scholars and dissenting justices to undertake their own evaluations of the evidence, although most reformers were unperturbed with the gap in historical justification and did not bother to seek it out. Chief Justice Warren's oft-repeated query during oral argument—"Is it fair?"—consistently produced results they approved. Yet it is not entirely accurate to say that "no one cared" that the Court flunked.[107] Those who thought the reassertion of modern judicial power threatened the rule of law did care, and they protested the Court's treatment of history with their own investigation of the facts. Even some reformers, as we have seen, occasionally tried to find a plausible basis for Warren Court decisions in the historical record. Thus, justices and scholars of the period unsystematically but more frequently invoked the "intent" and "understanding" of the framers and ratifiers of the Constitution and its amendments or what words "originally meant" to them and the general public at the time of their enactment into law. Historical debate increased, even though it produced neither sustained reflection on historical method nor agreement on the role history should play in constitutional interpretation. Indeed, theoretical considerations of relevance, what counted as proof of a given contention, or the legitimacy of different kinds of history remained largely submerged jurisprudential issues. Nevertheless, the return of historical analysis highlighted the difficulty of reconciling modern judicial power to the traditional understanding of the constitutional rule of law and also indicated the direction originalist jurisprudence would take once it became clear that the process-restraint tradition could no longer restrain the Court. Process thinkers, as we saw in the last chapter, declined any sustained theoretical pursuit of the originalist idea as a response to the reassertion of modern judicial power. Unable to restrain the Court on its own terms, the troubled process tradition left the way open for others who were more concerned about the role of history in Supreme Court decision-making. This situation made originalism an attractive option at the end of the 1960s, when both party politics and constitutional theory had reached a crossroads.

CHAPTER 4

At the Crossroads

The Originalist Idea in Post–Warren Court Politics
and Jurisprudence

Constitutional thought was at a crossroads by the late 1960s. The Warren
Court had attracted widespread attention to the role of original intent in
constitutional interpretation, but midcentury inheritors of the legal process–
judicial self-restraint approach did not return to this traditional idea to check
the Court. Instead, the established forms of process criticism gave way to new
varieties of jurisprudence. A new generation of liberal theorists, usually unconcerned with original intent as a limit, embarked on ever more complex
justifications for the continued reformist use of modern judicial power. However, at the same time the American political party system had reached its
own crossroads: the New Deal coalition, dominant since the 1930s, began to
fragment in the 1960s. The coalition had sustained the liberal constitutional
order and the Warren Court's updating of the "living Constitution," but by
the end of Earl Warren's tenure as chief justice it was giving way to a conservative, grassroots political movement. Waning support for liberal politics and
Supreme Court decisions plus rejection of original intent by both the new defenders of judicial power and its older process-restraint critics combined to encourage reassertion of the originalist proposition as a way to limit the Court.

At first haltingly and then with increasing theoretical self-consciousness, politicians, scholars, and some justices began to argue that the original meaning of the Constitution should be accorded more normative weight in Supreme Court adjudication. By the mid–1970s recurrence to original constitutional meaning was a notable feature of work critical of recent liberal reformist uses of modern judicial power.

The Parties and the Court

In the late 1960s America was divided over the Vietnam War, urban riots, the black power and feminist movements, and the beginning of an economic downturn.[1] These dislocations encouraged complex political shifts that began with the fragmentation of the New Deal Democratic coalition of unionized labor, urban Catholic ethnics, Jews, public sector employees, liberal intellectuals, white Southerners, and northern blacks. This coalition had dominated the party system since the presidential election of 1936, but the political issues of the 1960s alienated several of its member groups from one another. The end of the decade marked the end of liberal dominance of American politics as a new conservative coalition emerged.[2]

The conservative coalition consisted of socially traditionalist lower and middle income northern ethnics, southern whites and midwesterners, Catholics, evangelical Protestants, plus corporate elites and everyday citizens who were dissatisfied with the tax and regulatory policies of the welfare state. Although Barry Goldwater lost the presidential election of 1964 by a wide margin, his nomination and campaign clearly demonstrated the coalescence of a reinvigorated conservative response to modern liberalism, a trend confirmed by the election of Richard Nixon in 1968 and 1972. After the interlude of Watergate and the Ford and Carter presidencies, the new conservative coalition that began to take shape in the late 1960s elected Ronald Reagan president in 1980.[3]

In the 1960s the Supreme Court had advanced liberal goals and garnered the admiration even of student radicals.[4] However, the breakdown of the New Deal coalition and the emergence of the new conservatism made the Court the focus of renewed attention and controversy, as it had been in earlier periods of transition in the party system.[5] At this crossroads, the political shift, advanced in some measure by the results of the Court's own decisions, helped create an environment conducive to conservative, majoritarian, and eventually originalist criticism. This was evident when Richard Nixon made the Court an issue in the presidential campaign of 1968. He attacked recent decisions that had increased procedural protections for accused criminals, insisting that an activist Court had undermined law and order at a time when it was greatly threatened. Such criticism was part of Nixon's appeal to a "silent majority" of Americans who opposed the alleged usurpations of radicals and liberal elites. As a remedy Nixon vowed to nominate to the Court only "strict constructionists" who would "interpret the Constitution strictly and fairly." He reiterated this point at the Republican national convention in Miami, stating that it was "the job of the courts to interpret the law, not to make the law."[6] Such rhetoric concretely expressed the deeper political changes that were underway. It showed that conservative politics was moving toward populism and majoritarianism and linked this move to a call for a return to constitutional orthodoxy, thus directly challenging decades of liberal dominance of American politics and the Supreme Court.

There is further evidence that the politics of the period contested the proper direction of constitutional law when, in 1968, Chief Justice Earl Warren tried to control who would nominate his successor. Fearing a Nixon victory, he offered his resignation to President Johnson. This plan was widely perceived at the time as a political ploy to safeguard the Court's controversial liberal decisions, but it failed when the Senate rejected Justice Abe Fortas, the man Johnson nominated.[7]

Warren retired in 1969 and Nixon nominated Warren E. Burger to replace him. Soon thereafter the Court gained three more of Nixon's choices: Harry A. Blackmun, Lewis F. Powell, and William H. Rehnquist. While Rehnquist repeatedly stated in his nomination hearings that judicial interpretation should be based on the original intent of the framers of the Constitution, his view never came close to dominating the Burger Court.[8] Indeed, the early Burger Court still contained the liberal voices of Brennan, Marshall, and Douglas, while Blackmun, Powell, and later John Paul Stevens similarly showed no interest in reviving the kind of formalist jurisprudential constraints central to Rehnquist's originalism. Rather, Burger Court decisions typically reflected pragmatic, shifting alliances among the justices and often pivoted on and were expressed in the modern ad hoc balancing approach favored by Justice Powell.[9]

Consequently, in the short term Nixon's appointees altered neither the Court's direction nor the growing political resistance to it. In addition to the criminal procedure decisions that so exercised "law and order" conservatives like Nixon, Congress contemplated resistance to Court-mandated reapportionment until the death in 1969 of Senate minority leader Everett Dirksen (R-IL), the champion of that cause. Dissatisfaction with the school prayer decisions also continued, and the issue remained alive in grassroots resistance to the Court.[10] Additionally, the Court sparked new controversy in *Shapiro v. Thompson* (1969). Citing no "particular constitutional provision" as the source of a right to interstate travel, it overturned a durational residency requirement for welfare benefits, and states were required to provide for all comers.[11] In 1971 the Court ordered bussing as a remedy for segregated schools and took the first judicial step toward validating race-based affirmative action in employment.[12] In *Roe v. Wade* (1973), the most controversial decision of the period, the Court gave constitutional protection to abortion based on the right of privacy that in *Griswold v. Connecticut* (1965) had been created from the "penumbras" and "emanations" of the Bill of Rights and the Ninth Amendment. In the same period the Court struck down state laws imposing the death penalty and validated race-based affirmative action in university admissions.[13] These decisions offended the moral and political sensibilities of many Americans, so they had the unintended effect of helping establish the new direction of political change by hastening the fragmentation of the New Deal coalition and drawing some of its elements into the ascendant conservative political movement. Conservatives and Republicans increasingly attacked the Court as an undemocratic institution that thwarted legislative majorities and adopted liberal policies that had bad social consequences, such as forced school bussing, the release of criminals, legalized abortion, and the promotion of welfare programs and culture.[14]

Scholarly assessment of the Supreme Court in this period also reflected the idea that the constitutional system, like the party system, was at a crossroads. Scholars increasingly observed that the Court frequently was acting as a more powerful and discretionary institution than had been originally intended. Widespread recognition that the Burger Court's exercise of modern judicial power was fundamentally consistent with that of its predecessor underscored this view. Four Republican appointees had made little difference. As one critic noted, "In 1969 something was supposed to happen, and didn't." The Burger Court's bussing, abortion, and death penalty decisions made it clear that there had been no "counterrevolution" against the liberal activism of the Warren Court.[15]

More technically, scholars saw in the Burger Court no abandonment of the discretionary equal protection balancing jurisprudence that had been central to so many of the Warren Court's decisions. Indeed, commentators who took the long view of constitutional history argued that modern equal protection jurisprudence mirrored the ad hoc, essentially legislative discretion and activism of the Court's economic substantive due process decisions before the New Deal. The "counterrevolution that wasn't" suggested that the New Deal constitutional settlement and the Warren Court had made modern judicial power an institutionalized servant of liberal political goals. An increasing number of observers now thought that the Court had accepted that its decisions did not derive from the Constitution but rather reflected the justices' political and essentially legislative "estimates of where the factual data point and their own vision of what the good life in the good state would be."[16] Likewise, scholars began more pointedly to distinguish the discretionary and prescriptive practice of modern judicial review from its traditionally more limited scope. Donald Horowitz's noted study articulated well this aspect of the period's scholarship. He wrote that the modern Court's willingness to reform such things as schools, prisons, hospitals, and executive agency policies, accomplished in part by hurdling jurisdictional barriers and then prescribing and overseeing detailed remedies, distinguished it "sharply from the traditional exercise of the judicial function."[17]

Constitutional Theory

The crossroads of the political system, in which the Court was a factor, was mirrored by developments in constitutional theory that brought it to a crossroads as well. As we saw in chapter 2, process-restraint scholars had led scholarly criticism of the Supreme Court in the 1960s. Although after World War II they had expended substantial effort to safeguard the rule of law by domesticating the radical implications of legal realism, in a very short time the Warren Court had undermined their achievement. Moreover, at the end of the decade process-restraint attempts to limit the Court did not call for a return to original intent, even though the salience of historical evaluation was on the rise, as we saw in chapter 3.

Eschewing the turn to history, process theory continued to offer prudence, proceduralism, jurisdictional technique, and rigorous legal reasoning. But the new generation of liberals who defended the Warren Court regarded these tools as obstructions to the achievement of good results.[18] *Brown*, the "simple justice" of much of the civil rights movement, and the Warren Court in general convinced many liberal legal academics to abandon the moderating and braking tendencies of the process-restraint tradition.[19] Many liberals now viewed the process-restraint approach as outdated, internally contradictory, and unresponsive to the contemporary demands of justice and fundamental rights. For example, in a noted article that served as a key marker of this crossroads in liberal constitutional theory, federal judge J. Skelly Wright condemned the process failure to welcome the active use of modern judicial power that now supported liberal goals. Rejecting the process premise that pluralistic political struggle, and not the justice of judicial decisions, provided public policy with the surest basis of legitimacy, Wright suggested that "the ultimate test of the Justices' work . . . must be goodness." He noted that the Warren Court had inspired the maturing generation to view judicial review in this way. Like Wright, they welcomed a Court that would eschew the "judicial obstructionism" of the process tradition and instead defend the liberal view of goodness.[20] This new generation of students and academics saw the law as a "romance" and the Warren Court as a "judicial Camelot" that could realize justice. To them the constitutional crisis of the 1930s that so affected process thought did not present any continuing intellectual or practical difficulties, and in the 1960s few of them stepped in to provide a theoretical justification for the more daring if constitutionally and historically dubious of the Court's achievements.[21]

This sanguine and untheoretical mood was shaken by *Roe v. Wade* (1973), the abortion decision. It helped spur new theoretical justificatory endeavors because it had achieved a major liberal reform with an opinion that seemed barely concerned with the Constitution and that almost no one found convincing.[22] In a caustic and widely noted criticism, John Hart Ely pointed out that the Constitution "simply says nothing, clear or fuzzy, about abortion." More to the point, Ely noted that constitutional commentators had to take some of the blame for the damage done to judicial authority because they had failed to discipline the Court. They should have been insisting that if the basis of a decision "lacks connection with any value the Constitution marks as special, it is not a constitutional principle and the Court has no business imposing it."[23] Similarly, a seminal article by Thomas Grey highlighted the need for new theory but wanted it oriented to a goal that was the opposite of Ely's. Courts *should* apply values not articulated in the constitutional text, and this view had tacitly guided "constitutional doctrine developed by courts over the last generation." But "the trouble [was] that this view has been too tacit.

It has not been clearly stated and articulately defended, as basic constitutional doctrine should be."[24] Thus, in the wake of the Warren Court and *Roe* "legal liberal" academics offered numerous theories for rationalizing, defending, and elaborating the use of modern judicial power for liberal reformist ends.[25]

To trace all the manifestations of "legal liberal" theory would take us too far from the story of originalism, but it is worth briefly observing that, like Bickel and the process approach generally, legal liberals either regarded history as no limit on judicial power or as the basis for an even more expansive judicial role.[26] For example, Ronald Dworkin claimed that in the Constitution "'vague' standards were chosen deliberately, by the men who drafted and adopted them, in place of more specific and limited rules." Judges should protect fundamental values or principles by giving specific content to the assertedly vague "concept" the framers had in mind—judges need not be bound by the merely time-specific "conceptions." Dworkin's "concept-conception" formulation was crucial to his desired "fusion of constitutional law and moral theory."[27] Dworkin's work defended a major legal liberal theme, that the Court had a special competence and responsibility to effectuate justice as understood by contemporary moral and political philosophies, often by vindicating unenumerated rights, or even more abstractly, fundamental constitutional "values."[28] On the other hand, Ely rejected Dworkin and the fundamental rights/ values approach as too discretionary and too closely bound to contestable theories of justice. He argued that judicial review was legitimate only if the Court was limited to ensuring equal access to the process of political representation and decision-making. This innovative move illustrated that while the process tradition had been transformed, it was not wholly eliminated. Still, Ely's theory was no more historically grounded than Dworkin's or earlier process theory was. Ely also claimed that constitutional language was sufficiently "openended" to justify elaborating the logic of footnote four of *Carolene Products* (1938; see chapter 1) into a rationale for most of the liberal reform decisions of the 1960s and 1970s, many of which earlier process critics had protested.[29]

Between Dworkin and Ely were many other complex and competing theories that developed throughout the 1970s and 1980s. Moreover, at the doctrinal level liberal commentators almost uniformly defended and elaborated the discretionary balancing tests that came to typify most areas of constitutional law in the aftermath of the legal realist attack on formalism.[30] On the whole, though, the direction legal liberalism took at the crossroads was to encourage the Court to discern and protect its own definition (that is, the theorist's preferred definition) of norms, values, or rights not clearly part of the Constitution as originally understood. The Court should get on with realizing the modern liberal program, whether through judicially created visions of "goodness" or "moral courage,"[31] judicially determined moral "conceptions" of constitutional "concepts,"[32] or judicially determined levels of participation in the political process.[33] Legal liberals "essentially . . . were serving up boiled-over Bickel" in that they elaborated the general approach of Bickel's justification for *Brown* with theories designed to expand the occasions on which the Court could trump legislative judgments with an "updated" version of the Constitution.[34] But as one theorist observed, the explosion in justifications for the liberal reformist use of modern judicial power was "plainly designed to protect the legacy of the Warren Court,"[35] and they usually offered what another observer frankly called "advocacy scholarship—amicus briefs ultimately designed to persuade the Court to adopt our various notions of the public good."[36] The embrace and elaboration of modern judicial power that defined legal liberalism at the jurisprudential crossroads of the late 1960s and early 1970s was an important shift in the history of American constitutional theory. Although a restrained, cautious role for the Court had been a central component of liberal jurisprudence for over half a century, a new generation favored an active, reforming Court as the best way to achieve liberal goals.

The Originalist Idea

In contrast to the new direction of liberal legal theory, concern with original intent became a salient characteristic of the partisan, scholarly, and jurisprudential criticism of judicial power that also was present at the political and jurisprudential crossroads of the period. As shown by the initial history-based criticisms of the Warren Court analyzed in chapter 3, reliance on the Constitution as a historically demonstrable and legally enforceable fundamental ordering had remained a basic if submerged premise of American politics and jurisprudence. It had persisted in the midst of the rise of modern judicial power in the early twentieth century and the later legal liberal use and defense of that power. Accordingly, the traditional originalist conception of the Constitution was available and now was increasingly attractive to those politicians, judges, and theorists who sought a basis for legitimacy, order, and limits in response to the deep political and jurisprudential changes surrounding them.

The trend toward originalist thinking was becoming more noticeable even when it did not immediately result in carefully theorized arguments. This was evident when the Separation of Powers Subcommittee of the Senate Judiciary Committee met in June 1968 to consider using the "exceptions" clause (Article III, section 2) to constrain federal jurisdiction over state criminal convictions. The proposal would have prohibited federal courts from overruling "any trial court of any State in any criminal prosecution admitting in evidence as voluntarily made an admission or confession of an accused if such ruling has been affirmed or otherwise upheld by the highest court of the State."[37] The proposal was a response to the Court's recent sweeping assertion of power in the field, and the hearings showed that dissatisfaction with the Court was heightening.[38] As one would expect, the established process–self-restraint criticism intensified, but the hearings also contained a tendency toward originalist thought and rhetoric, albeit still in inchoate form. For example, Senator Sam J. Ervin Jr. (D-NC), the chairman of the subcommittee, stated at the outset that in the opinion of many the Court was acting beyond "its Constitutional mandate, and has assumed a position of judicial superiority out of keeping with its historically accepted role." Senator Everett Dirksen (R-IL) more directly linked this opinion to the idea of intent, stating that "it was not the intention of the Framers of the Constitution that the Supreme Court should be a policy-making body."[39] While it is possible to dismiss such statements as unsophisticated partisan incantations of the Constitution as a national symbol or "civil religion," it is important to recognize their substance, that the Constitution stood for limits on government and that the Court should be constrained by returning to some notion of original intent.

Scholars at the hearings also were concerned about the "quantity of things [the Court] takes on and the loss of public support that builds up" as well as the seeming equation in *Cooper v. Aaron* (1958) of its own constitutional opinions with the rule of law, which tended to blur the distinction between "legitimate constitutional disagreement with the Court's position and law-breaking."[40] The historian Alfred H. Kelly thought that the Court had always been part of politics as well as law but that in recent times it seemed to have begun acting in a fundamentally new and more powerful way. In school desegregation, the ensuing movement toward compelled integration more generally, and legislative reapportionment, the Court "gets into the process of minutely administering the details of the situation in terms of the structure of local government or State government. This seems to me to be quite new." Alexander M. Bickel agreed that such new endeavors engaged the Court too deeply in everyday politics: "The deeper you get into administration the more unmoored you become from any kind of . . . connection back to your initial constitutional principle, the more you become involved in myriad policy choices that are simple, political or judgmatical [*sic*] kinds of choices."[41]

Bickel's concern for a mooring to the Constitution suggested why the turn to history characteristic of later originalists also was limned in the hearings. Even though historical argument about original intent was not central to the critical stance of most scholars who were present, concern over limiting judicial power haltingly pushed some of them, and other attendees, to grapple with the originalist idea. Kelly noted that the gap in historical justification for many Warren Court decisions meant that it had "falsifi[ed] history in order to produce continuity where there is not any."[42] Philip Kurland, who had clerked for Felix Frankfurter and was chief consultant to the Subcommittee on the Separation of Powers, even as he emphasized standard process criticisms, stated that "the essential problem of the Court at the moment is its lack of recognition of its obligations to history." Senator Ervin argued that "the Constitution should not be interpreted as to give the same words one meaning at one time and another meaning at another time" because "if the judge is at liberty to change the meaning of the Constitution [than] we are not ruled by the Constitution."[43]

Originalist thinking also informed consideration of whether Congress had authority to check the Court through the exceptions clause or section 5 of the Fourteenth Amendment. The Court itself seemingly endorsed the latter option by upholding congressional interpretation of the equal protection clause in a Voting Rights Act case, *Katzenbach v. Morgan* (1966). But use of section 5 or the exceptions clause would have constituted a direct confrontation between coordinate branches of government based on disagreement over the meaning of the Constitution. Given such high stakes, scholars at the hearings in 1968 were no more agreed that original intent provided a firm basis for such a momentous step than during other recent attempts at curbing federal appellate jurisdiction.[44]

The congressional decision not to use the exceptions clause or section 5 meant that any response to the reassertion of judicial power would occur within the parameters of professional criticism of the Court and within the Court's own adjudications. Additionally, the hearings had shown once again that controversial Warren Court decisions raised not only political resistance but also scholarly concern about their historical basis and legal justification.

Two widely noted studies of the period further reflected this concern and con-tributed to the enlivening discussion of the place of history in Supreme Court decision-making.

The historian Alfred H. Kelly's noted "Clio" essay, which he referenced in the hearings, pointedly condemned the Court's use of history in many of the cases analyzed in the last chapter. He described them with such phrases as "historical felony," "amateurish historical solecism," and "mangled history." Kelly forthrightly insisted that history had a real existence that should limit judicial decision making: historical truth did not stem from its utility to a Court bent on "a constitutional equalitarian revolution," nor should it be written merely "to serve the interests of libertarian idealism." Kelly feared that the Court's historical fiction was moving it toward the disastrous level of activ-ism associated with *Dred Scott* and *Lochner*. He thus illustrated the traditional and now growing tendency in American constitutionalism to hold Supreme Court interpretation to the measure of original intent and thus to treat it as the ultimate justification of adjudicatory outcomes. Yet his own activities in *Brown* had illustrated the wrenching choices that arose when political liber-alism confronted its erstwhile enemy, judicial activism. Kelly had worked as-siduously on the NAACP brief, which he conceded had "manipulated history in the best tradition of American advocacy, carefully marshaling every scrap of evidence in favor of the desired interpretation and just as carefully doctoring all evidence to the contrary." Nonetheless, ten years after *Brown*, Kelly demon-strated a loyalty to historical accuracy that seemed to diminish his confidence in the project he had helped inaugurate.[45]

The traditional importance of history in the justification of Supreme Court opinions was addressed at more length by Charles A. Miller, a political sci-entist. His landmark study of the Court and the uses of history noted that the idea of binding law in America was intimately tied to the principles of a historically discernible event—the founding of the republic. No amount of law review encouragement could stop the Court from invoking the ultimate source of its own authority in the Constitution, which stood as the result of the founding. Neither would popular sovereignty, an integral principle of the American regime, ever permit the Court wholly to ignore the intent of the founders or the will of contemporary legislative majorities. Although Miller failed to see any philosophical reason why the Court ought to be bound by the historic meaning of legal-constitutional terms in a particular case, he ac-knowledged that abuse or ignorance of history would weaken its authority.[46]

In several case studies Miller found that the Court most frequently provoked criticism with what he termed "ongoing history." This was in essence the logic of a living Constitution. It took the form of an appeal to the Court's own notion of "what this country has become" and helped to dismiss the original, narrower meaning of the terms it was interpreting. Miller thought some such practice must occur if the law was to adjust to changing circumstances. Yet he insisted that the stability and obligatory force of law were diminished if the Court undertook such development with bad history or in spite of contrary historical facts. The Court inevitably spoke with "special public authority"—with the force of law—in its capacity as the highest legal institution in the land. Hence "when declaring the meaning of the past . . . where it matters most to society, it matters most that the story be a true one."[47] Indeed, liberal reformers themselves occasionally recognized the force of this point. Jacobus tenBroek, who also was involved in the *Brown* litigation, subsequently chided the Court for dismissing the liberal-reformist original intent theory of the Fourteenth Amendment. He declared it "little short of remarkable that the Chief Justice [in the *Brown* opinion] should have cut himself off from these historical origins and purposes."[48]

Though not originalists in today's sense, such respected scholars clearly had reencountered the force of history as a legitimating concept in constitutional decision-making. Significant judicial statements of the same type also became more noticeable. Dissenting opinions by Justices John Marshall Harlan and William H. Rehnquist illustrated the renewed focus on the text, history, and structure of the Constitution that characterized the emerging historical rejoinder to the judicially updated living Constitution. Moreover, these justices said directly that the Court was exceeding its proper role in the constitutional system by abandoning the original intent of constitutional provisions. Justice Harlan maintained that the Court's reapportionment decisions were historically unjustified arrogations of power, as he had done in earlier dissents in this area. Transformation of "a political slogan" ("one person, one vote") into a "constitutional absolute" exhibited a distrust of the legislative process that was "completely alien to established notions of judicial review." In 1970 the Court upheld amendments to the Voting Rights Act of 1965, but Harlan condemned it for disregarding the original intent of the Fourteenth Amendment so that it could monopolize the process of constitutional change. Although he agreed that the Court inevitably would apply some general constitutional principles to unforeseen circumstances, he warned that "when the Court disregards the express intent and understanding of the framers, it has invaded the realm of the political process to which the amending power was committed, and it has violated the constitutional structure." Harlan was further concerned that the Court's relaxation of standing requirements would "go far toward the final transformation of this Court into the Council of Revision which, despite Madison's support, was rejected by the Constitutional Convention."[49]

Rehnquist rejected the Court's decisions on the death penalty and abortion as unwise assertions of judicial power that had little historical basis. Echoing the *Federalist Papers,* he called the Court's overturning of a state death sentence "not an act of judgment, but rather an act of will" and warned that judicial overreaching under the guise of protecting rights "may result in sacrifice of the equally important right of the people to govern themselves."[50] In the abortion cases Rehnquist argued that the majority's trimester regulatory scheme "partakes more of judicial legislation than it does of a determination of the intent of the drafters of the Fourteenth Amendment."[51] In *Trimble v. Gordon* (1977) Rehnquist's dissent aimed directly at the Court's equal protection jurisprudence.[52] The majority held that the equal protection clause was violated by a state statute that allowed illegitimate children to inherit by intestate succession only from their mothers and not their fathers. Such a regulatory scheme, wrote Rehnquist, was surely not "mindless and patently irrational," and the fact of the matter was that the Court had no legitimate basis for overturning the law. The majority had simply substituted its own judgment of good public policy "without any antecedent constitutional mandate." Rehnquist underscored a fundamental originalist point: of course making distinctions was inherent to legislation, but they had "little or nothing to do with the Equal Protection Clause of the Fourteenth Amendment, unless they employ means of sorting people which the draftsmen of the Amendment sought to prohibit."[53]

As dissenting members of the Court sounded originalist arguments, there were scattered initial indications that legal liberals too might attempt to link their jurisprudence and the recently expanded role of the Court to the text and history of the Constitution. Judge J. Skelly Wright, for example, argued that attention to the constitutional text would return constitutional theory to the issue of "values," which had been obscured by the recent process focus on the restraining subtleties of jurisdiction, legal reasoning, and relative institutional competence. Wright suggested that because process critics such as Bickel had betrayed their willingness, albeit rarely, to have the Court make basic value choices, the debate about judicial review now should proceed in terms of "the true meaning and scope of particular constitutional protections." Likewise, Charles Black, a "judicial activist proudly self-confessed," recognized that basic questions about the legitimacy of judicial review required closer attention to the constitutional text and structure. Black argued that the structures, relationships, and procedures outlined in the text of the Constitution could serve as a basis for liberal jurisprudence. Further, in a review of Black's book Vincent Blasi warned that most activists had recently contented themselves "with flat assertions when it comes time to dismiss the significance of the framers' original understanding." Black's approach seemed to indicate dissatisfaction with the liberal judicial method and signaled "a belief that fidelity to some conception of the framers' intentions is a *necessary* component of decisional legitimacy." Blasi encouraged his fellow liberals to investigate original intent as a rebuttal to those who would use the method to limit judicial power.[54]

Nevertheless, renewed attention to constitutional history, text, and structure was advanced primarily by those seeking to limit the recent liberal reassertion of judicial power. For example, Hans A. Linde counseled that decisions should be based on a "most serious inquiry into historic constitutional imperatives" rather than a "diagnosis of and prescription for contemporary social problems." Likewise, treating the text too generally improperly regarded constitutional provisions as "more or less suitable pegs on which judicial policy choices are hung." Such an approach glossed over the fact that the text and its legal rules derived from decisions "made by particular men at particular moments in history" and therefore that constitutional interpretation ineluctably attributed "the asserted principle [of decision] to the political act of adopting that text, in the sense that without that political act, the principle would lack its constitutional basis."[55]

Linde recognized that the current need to reconsider legitimacy in light of original intent derived from the dependence of most commentators on the intellectual assumptions of legal realism. The realist equation of law with what courts announced improperly treated constitutional law "as a consequence of judicial review, rather than vice versa." Such realist functionalism was better understood as a critical description than as a prescription of what judges should do or why citizens should listen to them. Thus, in a move that served as another crucial marker of the changes that were underway in constitutional theory, Linde criticized process thinkers such as Alexander M. Bickel and Philip Kurland for their attachment to, if not self-conscious defense of, the modern, legal realist view of law. The jurisprudence of Kurland and Bickel, though critical of the Warren Court's reassertion of modern judicial power, no more rejected the legal realist equation of constitutional law and judicial opinions than had J. Skelly Wright. All three assumed that the Constitution had no more or less meaning than what the Court gave it. Therefore, they either attempted to limit the Court's concededly illimitable power for use as their prudence dictated, or else they justified active use of that power by approval of the results it achieved. Such a "Court-centered constitutional jurisprudence" put too much discretion in the hands of judges by treating constitutional adjudication as if it were the interstitial legislation of common law judging rather than the "application of prior political law making." Linde concluded that the vitality of judicial review depended upon belief in its legitimacy, which the Court could best ensure by treating exposition of the Constitution as a "most serious inquiry into historic constitutional imperatives."[56]

Thomas Grey's noted article (mentioned above) observed the renewed attention being accorded to constitutional text, structure, history, and the intent of draftsmen as defenses of the limited judicial role most recently identified with Justice Hugo Black.[57] In addition to Linde, Grey cited as exemplars of the new trend John Hart Ely, Richard A. Epstein, Ralph K. Winter, and Robert H. Bork.[58] Of this group Bork became the leading originalist and his thought will be treated as a whole in chapter 7. Grey dubbed the ascendant method of these scholars "interpretive," meaning that it viewed the Constitution as something that could be interpreted according to its original intent. Grey did not use the term "originalism" but instead distinguished "interpretivism" from "noninterpretivism." This nomenclature guided the debate until the early 1980s, when the terminology of "originalism" versus "nonoriginalism" began to predominate. While Grey favored noninterpretivism, which looked beyond the original intent of the Constitution to natural law or the judge's estimation of contemporary values as a basis for decision, he cautioned against ignoring interpretivism. It had deep roots in the history and practice of constitutional law, and its defense of the prerogatives of legislative majorities reflected fundamental American principles of political legitimacy. Indeed, Grey noted that it was harder to justify "noninterpretive" judicial review, that is, the judicial vindication of values or rights not expressed as positive law in the written Constitution.[59] He completed his sketch of the opposed camps in constitutional jurisprudence by observing that what has come to be known as legal liberalism was in his terms "noninterpretive" and by suggesting that protection of nontextual rights through the judicial updating of a living Constitution might be justified by the natural law tradition in American constitutionalism. On the other hand, Grey concluded that the emerging body of "interpretive" jurisprudence provided little purchase for nontextual rights, so, as noted above, he urged theorists to establish the "legitimate pedigree of noninterpretive judicial review."[60] Grey was one of the first analysts to see that the battle lines of constitutional jurisprudence were being redrawn by the growing insistence that original intent should constrain interpretation.

An important article by Justice Rehnquist quickly echoed Grey's analysis. Rehnquist attacked the noninterpretive, legal liberal view of constitutional interpretation and defended majoritarianism, the separation of powers, and a limited judiciary. He did so primarily by rejecting the metaphor of a living Constitution that frequently served as the shorthand expression of legal liberalism. Although the metaphor was rhetorically appealing, it had become a way of exhorting the judiciary to substitute "some other set of values for those which may be derived from the language and intent of the framers."[61]

Rehnquist also illustrated how the emerging body of originalist thought was based on a positivist understanding of law. He located the obligatory force of the Constitution in its status as popularly enacted fundamental law by reiterating the standard interpretation of Marshall's opinion in *Marbury v. Madison* (1803). This emphasized that the Constitution was law because of its basis in "the people [as] the ultimate source of authority." The problem with the idea of a living Constitution from this perspective was that it encouraged judges to decide cases based on their own views of justice, thereby ignoring "totally the nature of political value judgments in a democratic society." In constitutional adjudication properly understood, the values and rights enshrined in the text were obligatory and constraining "neither because of any intrinsic worth nor because of any unique origins in someone's idea of natural justice but instead simply because they have been incorporated in a constitution by the people." Therefore, "it is the fact of their enactment that gives them whatever moral claim they have upon us as a society."[62]

Finally, Rehnquist made it clear that judicial adaptation of the Constitution according to values not found in its text or history was a rejection of the separation of powers and a usurpation of legislative prerogatives. Accordingly, he emphasized the majoritarianism of the originalist position by concluding that the legislature was the proper institution for adapting the law to social change. The notion of a judicially updated living Constitution, on the other hand, was often "a formula for an end run around popular government."[63]

American politics and constitutional thought were brought to a crossroads at the end of the 1960s in part by the fact of modern judicial power and the legal liberal defense of it and more generally by the fragmentation of the New Deal order and the rise of the new conservatism. Debate about the legitimate basis, extent, and function of judicial review was at perhaps its most intense level since the constitutional crisis of the 1930s. At this crossroads constitutional theory went in new directions as the new generation of legal liberals defended modern judicial power and called for its further elaboration. But those judges and scholars who criticized legal liberalism did so by according renewed attention to the original intent of legal-constitutional terms, along with historically based arguments about the proper role of courts in the American system of government. Like the process-restraint tradition that preceded and influenced them, commentators and judges who appealed to original intent were concerned that the legal liberal exercise of modern judicial power threatened the separation of powers, republican government, and the rule of law. Thus, originalism began to fill the gap created when liberals abandoned the process-restraint approach; by the mid–1970s it was an identifiable and cogent position in American constitutional thought. It next found expression in the work of Raoul Berger, one of its most famous exponents.

CHAPTER 5

Raoul Berger and the Restoration of Originalism

Over the course of his career Raoul Berger produced a massive body of writing on a variety of topics in law and legal history.[1] Born in Russia in 1901, Berger was a concert violinist until he abandoned that career for the law, serving as a government attorney and then maintaining a private practice in Washington, D.C., until 1961. From 1962 to 1965 he taught law at the University of California at Berkeley, and from 1971 until his retirement in 1976 he was the Charles Warren Senior Fellow in American Legal History at Harvard University.[2]

Berger consistently regarded originalist constitutional interpretation as a continuation of the founders' dedication to the rule of law and to the limitation of all official power. Accordingly, he viewed the Constitution in the traditional way—as fundamental law. Interpretation of this legal text, like any other, was the ascertainment and application of the intent of its creators through the long-established methods and conventions of the common law. Its meaning did not change in response to social developments or through ignorance or misinterpretation. Berger's historical scholarship was meant to show that original intent (or "intention," or "meaning," or "understanding"—he drew no distinctions among these terms) was usually recoverable and therefore available as a limit on those who spoke in the name of the Constitution.

Considered in the history of twentieth-century American jurisprudence, Berger's originalism elaborated the legal positivist majoritarianism of the Progressive and process-restraint approaches. As a legal positivist, Berger always insisted on the test of empirical evidence in the written record as the only legitimate source of constitutional law. He saw natural rights and natural law as imprecise, infinitely manipulable notions that the pre–New Deal Court had used merely to force its policy preferences on unwilling majorities.[3] Additionally, Berger reasoned in a formalist style: the unchanging original intent, once identified, established a premise for reasoning that was deductive and categorical. The old Court also employed a formalist style of legal reasoning, but Berger eschewed any connection to its jurisprudence.

This positivist and formalist stance led Berger to conclude that the Warren and Burger Courts, like the Court prior to the New Deal, overcame constitutional limitations with their own convictions about natural rights or true morality. The glaring difference between the eras was that the new judicial power supported liberal political goals. Berger always identified himself as a Democrat, but he rejected the legal liberal insistence on immediate, Court-led change that had displaced the process-restraint approach at the crossroads of the 1960s. Instead, he defended originalism, as he had for decades, as a neglected but still fundamental interpretive method. Moreover, although Berger's originalism was marked by far more historical research than was process-restraint jurisprudence, like its advocates he defended the legitimacy and limits of judicial review in a system he regarded as ultimately consent-based and majoritarian.

Berger's Originalism before the 1970s

A productive and influential scholar long before originalism achieved prominence, Berger became interested in legal history and originalism during the New Deal era, as his first published writings show.[4] Indeed, it was in the constitutional crisis of the 1930s that Berger's suspicion of judicial power was formed, as illustrated in an article from 1942, when the Supreme Court was issuing decisions usually in accord with his political sympathies. First, Berger warned of the awesome potential in judicial "adaptation" of the Constitution. Then he used historical evidence to argue that a decision whose result he favored was rooted more in the justices' political inclinations than in the original intent of the Constitution. Finally, he asked: "Can the liberals, after steadily criticizing the tendency of the pre-'reconstructed' court to read laissez-faire into the Constitution, afford to sanctify by their own example an interpretive approach which for a generation was employed to block social legislation and may once again be turned against themselves?"[5] The lesson Berger learned from the crisis of the 1930s, one that he never forgot, was that assertive judicial power almost invariably disregarded original intent and threatened limited constitutional government.

Yet his originalism was never simply antijudicial. In 1969, a time when judicial review was under severe attack from opponents of the Warren Court, Berger turned to history to defend the practice. His first book, *Congress v. The Supreme Court,* argued that judicial review was originally intended by the framers of the Constitution but that plenary congressional power to withdraw federal jurisdiction under the Article III, section 2 "exceptions" clause was not.[6] Such usage threatened not only to destroy the originally intended practice of judicial review but also the separation of powers and the rule of law itself. Berger addressed the issue by first arguing that judicial review, although not explicit in the text of the Constitution, was intended by the framers and knowingly validated by the ratification conventions for which records existed. Approaching the historical evidence with the assumption that law was a public act, Berger eschewed the subjective, private intent of particular historical actors as evidence of the original meaning of the Constitution. He built his case for the original intent of judicial review on what advocates of the Constitution said in public when defending and voting for its provisions.[7] After concluding that judicial review could only be legitimated by reference to public historical sources extrinsic to the text, Berger argued that the scope of congressional regulation was limited by the same kind of evidence. Thus, the exceptions clause was intended only to permit congressional regulation of federal appellate jurisdiction over questions of fact.[8] The clause was not intended to grant Congress the greater power of negating judicial interpretations of the Constitution via the withdrawal of jurisdiction.[9]

These historical conclusions had implications for the burgeoning Warren Court–era debate about the legitimate scope of judicial power. For his part, Berger thought his evidence supported the position of Henry Hart, a noted process-restraint scholar. According to Hart's influential theory, the exceptions clause could not legitimately be used to "destroy the essential role of the Supreme Court in the constitutional plan," understood as the protection from legislative majorities of life, liberty, and property through due process of law. Berger agreed with Hart that a plenary power to regulate jurisdiction, which the text of the exceptions clause alone seemed to allow, would in fact defeat judicial review as a check against unconstitutional legislation.[10] It is important to note that Hart too seemed to have understood Berger's work as an important historical buttress to the position Hart had argued in theoretical terms, thus illustrating how Berger's originalist method was initially closely linked to the process approach. Indeed, unsolicited by Berger, Hart praised Berger's book manuscript and urged the Harvard University Press to consider publishing it; upon its acceptance Berger dedicated the book to Hart. Berger was greatly impressed and motivated by Hart's theory but thought it was not sufficiently grounded in history. He observed to a correspondent that Hart's theory was an axiom "and like Euclidean axioms, it merely represent[ed] an assumption. My task was to undergird that premise from the Constitutional history."[11]

In supporting Hart's view, Berger also supported a version of judicial supremacy consistent with the process-restraint approach, in which the Court kept the other branches within constitutional limits as the Court interpreted those limits, but Berger rejected emerging legal liberal defenses of the "living Constitution."[12] He attacked the idea that the meaning of the Constitution was created by interpretation or that specific salutary results of judicial review could justify expanding its scope. This position stemmed from his insistence that the founders understood the Constitution as a "fundamental law" that derived its obligatory force from the sovereignty of the people. This foundation of the constitutional rule of law established a crucial distinction between judicial interpretation and partisan politics that should always circumscribe the role of the Court. Accordingly, Berger rejected the notion of Alexander M. Bickel and others, later developed by legal liberals, that the Court could be an "educator of public opinion" or "national conscience" capable of "leading" in the resolution of social problems. Rather, judicial review was intended to be a countermajoritarian force that ultimately was legitimated by the popular sovereignty embodied in the Constitution.[13] The historical evidence from the founding period, said Berger, much better supported James Bradley Thayer's "rule of the clear mistake." This rule, which held that courts should uphold legislation unless its violation of the Constitution was "not open to a rational question," had undergirded the majoritarianism and judicial deference of liberal jurisprudence from the late nineteenth century until the middle of the twentieth. But Berger sensed that the tide was turning in the 1960s, now that liberals were abandoning or reworking Thayer to defend a broader conception of judicial power. He sketched the direction his originalist scholarship eventually would take by concluding that "the most generous interpretation of the Constitutional text must still rely on history to buttress the legitimacy of judicial review, [so] it would be arbitrary to invoke history for the establishment of the power and to repudiate it when the scope of the power comes into question."[14]

Berger's study was further evidence that historical inquiry into the original intent of the Constitution was becoming more prominent at the jurisprudential crossroads of the late 1960s. Further, although history would become central to originalist criticism of judicial power, Berger showed that the search for original intent was not inherently opposed to courts. Indeed, his next two books investigated the original intent of impeachment and the historical basis for claims of an "executive privilege" to withhold information from Congress.[15]

This scholarship played a significant role in the Watergate affair. Berger analyzed the English historical roots of impeachment and executive privilege and how the framers of the Constitution had understood them. He argued that the framers intended impeachment for offenses of a political nature, such as "abuse of power" or "subversion of the Constitution" but did not require indictment for a common law crime in order to impeach. In the context of Watergate this suggested that President Nixon need not be accused of ordinary crimes to be impeached. Berger also argued that impeachment was intended by the framers as an exception to the principle of the separation of powers. Impeachment ensured that the president could not flout the Constitution, notwithstanding a claim of executive privilege to withhold information from congressional investigation, as the Nixon White House had asserted during Watergate. Berger found no firm historical basis for executive privilege that could overcome the overwhelming evidence that Congress was intended to have authority to investigate fully any possible malfeasance by the executive or judicial branches.

Far from setting out to provide a scholarly foundation for attacks on Nixon, Berger had begun and nearly completed this aspect of his scholarly inquiry before Watergate became a national preoccupation. But at the time most analysts, including Berger, agreed that his work undercut Nixon's legal and constitutional positions. This put Berger in the national spotlight and made him a hero to Nixon's political opponents. Members and staff of the House Judiciary

Committee consulted Berger's *Impeachment,* and an article that had preceded the book was reprinted in the committee's background materials. Berger's attack on Nixon's reliance on executive privilege was featured on the front page of the *New York Times,* and Berger was profiled in the *Atlantic Monthly.* Additionally, he spoke before the Organization of American Historians about his originalist methodology and argued that the Supreme Court was mistaken to recognize executive privilege in *United States v. Nixon* (1974).[16]

Berger's examination of impeachment and executive privilege evinced his abiding concern with limited constitutional government, the rule of law, and accountability for all officeholders under the Constitution. Consequently, he rejected as historically insupportable defenses of executive privilege that appealed to "modern" requirements of government or to an "inherent" executive power. Such appeals to abstractions were themselves inherently illimitable.[17] The original, limited meaning of the Constitution did not change because a practice or interpretation was based on a highly generalized treatment of its language or principles.

Despite the prevailing trend in legal thought toward subjectivity, informality, and a judicially updated living Constitution as the best way to achieve liberal goals, Berger's originalist scholarship and traditional interpretive method did advance liberal goals in the context of the debate over the exceptions clause and Watergate. Berger did not undertake an extensive defense of the originalist method in the mid–1970s, nor did those who welcomed the contemporary implications of his findings suggest that he should have. Instead Berger usually simply put forward the established Anglo-American ideas that the intent of the lawgiver is the law, that historical evidence could help reveal that intent, and that absent contrary evidence, traditional common law terms in the Constitution were intended by the framers to retain their traditional meaning.[18]

It bears repeating that Berger's originalism favored no particular governmental institution and was not inherently antijudicial, as his stance during Watergate further illustrated. Berger was convinced by his earlier research into the origins of judicial review that the framers intended the Court to defend the constitutional boundaries between branches of the federal government and between the federal and state governments. ("Coordinate" or "departmental" review, obviously a challenge to judicial power, was historically insupportable.) Conflicts between Congress and the executive or a judge, as in the case of a claim of executive privilege, were reviewable by the Supreme Court. The

Court legitimately could settle not only rival claims to obtain or withhold information but also could review the Senate trial of an impeached judge or president. Thus, at the same time that Berger attacked Nixon for using executive privilege to elude Congress, his view of original intent compelled him to argue that Nixon could appeal to the Supreme Court if he thought his constitutional rights or the powers of his office had been invaded.[19] Berger did not regard judicial supremacy in interbranch or federal-state conflicts as presenting the danger of unlimited judicial power because the fixed and defined meaning of the Constitution was ordinarily recoverable through historical investigation. The Court could resolve such conflicts, but in the process it could not exceed the original, limited meaning of the Constitution without undermining its own legitimacy.

Thus, well before he was identified with originalist opposition to legal liberalism—and while his originalism supported liberal goals—Berger was insisting that legitimate interpretation properly applied original intent but did not extend beyond it. Although the Constitution could be misinterpreted, interpreters could never make it mean what it did not already mean. Berger argued that "there is no surer way to defeat the Founders' intention to create a government of enumerated, 'limited' powers than to interpret the common law terms they employed to fashion the 'limits' in a freewheeling fashion." Likewise, he believed, as Thomas Jefferson did, that the Constitution should be administered "according to the safe and honest meaning contemplated by the plain understanding of the people at the time of its adoption—a meaning to be found in the explanations of those who advocated . . . it." He further noted that James Madison had similarly clung "to the sense in which the Constitution was accepted and ratified by the nation," adding that "if that be not the guide in expounding it, there can be no security for a consistent and stable government, more than for a faithful exercise of its powers." Adherence to the limited meaning of the words in the Constitution was the best way to preserve the rule of law and constrain the Court within the limits of federalism and the separation of powers.[20]

Government by Judiciary

As the Watergate affair illustrated, Berger's work intersected at key moments with fundamental issues in American politics. His own reliance on historical argument was long-standing, but it contributed to the trend toward originalism that occurred at the historical and jurisprudential crossroads of the late 1960s and early 1970s. As we saw in the last chapter, the overall political climate in this period was becoming more conservative, and the Supreme Court was often the focus of intense controversy, especially since changes in personnel and the official end of the Warren Court did not curtail controversial opinions that often compelled liberal policy results. Berger was acutely aware of growing popular resistance to the Court's decisions on abortion, school prayer, bussing, affirmative action, pornography, and the death penalty. Political mobilization in reaction to such decisions was clear evidence that a sizeable portion of the polity rejected the Court's new legal liberal role. This background of growing conservative dissatisfaction with the Court contributed to the impact of Berger's most famous book, *Government by Judiciary: The Transformation of the Fourteenth Amendment* (1977) and linked it to the larger political developments of the period.

Government by Judiciary carried forward the originalist method of Berger's earlier works, but this time it was the Supreme Court that was found wanting. The book argued that the Court had subverted the Constitution by invading the prerogatives of legislatures both state and federal. Berger attacked modern judicial power, most often wielded through interpretation of the Fourteenth Amendment, with a historical argument that the amendment originally had a far more limited meaning than what the Court attributed to it in such cases as *Brown* and the reapportionment decisions of the 1960s.[21] Berger also provocatively claimed that in these decisions and others the Court had usurped the sovereign power of amendment under the guise of constitutional interpretation.

In order to explain the original meaning of the Fourteenth Amendment, Berger analyzed the legal and constitutional situation that confronted the 39th Congress, which drafted it in the spring of 1866. After the Civil War and despite the abolition of slavery by the ratification of the Thirteenth Amendment in December 1865, southern state governments enacted restrictive "black codes." These laws created strict apprenticeship requirements, instituted harsh punishments for vagrancy, and restricted access to courts, thus relegating the newly emancipated slaves to an inferior form of citizenship that in the opinion of many was tantamount to bondage. The 39th Congress passed the Civil Rights Act of 1866 to redress the black codes. The act provided the freed people with basic civil rights to own, inherit, lease, or sell property; make and enforce contracts; sue, be parties of cases, and give evidence in court; and generally to receive the full and equal benefit of all laws that secured and protected persons and property. However, many Republican members of Congress doubted that the Thirteenth Amendment in fact supplied adequate constitutional authority for the act, so the Fourteenth Amendment was thought necessary to provide the requisite authority for accomplishing its goals. The Fourteenth Amendment was drafted and debated in the 39th Congress by the same men who had passed the Civil Rights Act of 1866.

Basing his reasoning on a minute dissection of the debates in the 39th Congress, Berger argued that the Fourteenth Amendment was intended by its drafters and supporters to constitutionalize only the basic rights contained in the act. This was the extent of the amendment's meaning, despite section 1's general terminology of "due process," "equal protection," and "privileges or immunities." These words were not intended to expand the meaning of the amendment or confer rights beyond those enumerated in the act. Rather, the substance of the "privileges or immunities" contained in the new category of national citizenship was those rights specified in the act. Blacks were entitled to "equal protection" from any laws that denied or deprived them of their rights, which could be vindicated by the traditional procedural guarantees of "due process" in a court of law. Through the amendment the federal government ensured that states could not racially discriminate in the legal deprivation of life, liberty, or property.[22]

This assessment of the original intent of the Fourteenth Amendment was based on the same historical approach, interpretive method, and attention to constitutional structure employed in Berger's earlier scholarship. As in his earlier work, he understood "original intention" as "shorthand for the meaning attached by the framers to the words they employed in the Constitution and its amendments." Understanding the Constitution as it was understood by its creators could be accomplished by a close reading of the records they left, supplemented by the centuries-old canons of statutory construction, by which, he argued, the framers of the original Constitution and the Fourteenth Amendment thought themselves bound.[23]

Berger's analysis of the historical evidence frequently attended to the canons of construction, which were in themselves uncontroversial.[24] For example, he held that formal public statements by proponents of the amendment were the best indication of how it was understood at the time. The statements of opponents or the private, subjective, undisclosed sentiments of proponents were of little or no weight.[25] Additionally, he argued that exclusion of suffrage from the scope of the amendment also meant that it provided no authority for courts to enter the area of apportionment, on the traditional canon that "the greater includes the less." In another example, he hewed to the canon that laws *in pari materia*—that is, dealing with the same subject matter, like the Civil Rights Act of 1866 and the Fourteenth Amendment—must be construed consistently, as if they were one law. In the drafting of the act, and in its final text, the general terms "privileges or immunities" were constantly specified by reference to equal protection for the enumerated rights of life, liberty, and property. It also was an established canon, known to the framers, that general words followed by a specific enumeration constrained the terms to the enumeration. Thus "privileges or immunities" were *in pari materia* and equally limited in the amendment and in the act, which were drafted in the same Congress by the same men. Berger found confirmation for this interpretation in congressional support for segregated schools in the District of Columbia, which occurred contemporaneously with the drafting of the Civil Rights Act of 1866 and the Fourteenth Amendment. This indicated that neither enactment was thought capable of invalidating the practice.[26]

Berger also frequently linked appeals to canons of construction with the persistent attachment of the 39th Congress to the structural constraints of federalism and the separation of powers. These fundamentals of constitutional design were for Berger a binding part of original intent, as his earlier scholarship also had made clear. Like fidelity to the original intent of textual provisions, federalism and the separation of powers safeguarded the rule of law and limited government. The Supreme Court could only police the boundaries of the separation of powers and federalism; it could not legitimately invade these structural restraints by "interpreting" constitutional provisions to mean what they were never intended to mean. The logical outcome of this view was Berger's insistence that rather than subvert the constitutional structure with erroneous interpretations, change in the fundamental law should occur through the process of amendment created by the provisions of Article V of the Constitution.[27]

This originalist tack directly challenged liberal orthodoxy, which held that the amendment was intended to incorporate the natural rights theories of antebellum abolitionists, thereby empowering the Court to fashion an openended living Constitution from its terms.[28] A major component of Berger's rebuttal of the neo-abolitionist, open-ended theory was that the radical Republicans, who were most attracted to this thinking and the fundamental alteration of federalism it entailed, did not in fact control the 39th Congress.

Instead, it was controlled by a moderate-conservative coalition that persisted in racial prejudice and an attachment to federalism. These loyalties thwarted the sweeping radical goals. Radicals repeatedly lost votes on proposed amendment language that moderates and conservatives thought too destructive of the traditional state regulatory power over such local concerns as schools and suffrage. Moreover, Berger argued, the language used in the amendment was not understood by its authors to be prospectively capable of "living" or "growing" to accomplish such goals. For them it retained its traditional meaning and thus merely constitutionalized the 1866 Civil Rights Act.[29]

Berger's historical argument also revisited the earlier debate over whether the amendment had been originally intended to "incorporate" the Bill of Rights and make it applicable to the states. If, as Berger insisted, the 39th Congress was not controlled by abolitionist advocates of more centralized federal power, than the amendment was not intended fundamentally to alter the federal-state balance by incorporating the Bill of Rights. He concluded that incorporation was not intended, despite the Warren Court's application of nearly all of the Bill of Rights to the states.[30]

After laying out his historical case in the first part of *Government by Judiciary*, in the second part Berger pointedly underscored how his historical conclusions challenged the notion of an evolving fundamental law. He insisted that treatment of the Fourteenth Amendment on the model of *Palko v. Connecticut* (1937)[31] and *U.S. v. Carolene Products* (1938),[32] as if it were an open-ended invitation for ad hoc judicial adaptation, went beyond its original intent. Such treatment usurped the sovereign power of amendment and displaced both Congress and state legislatures from their primary responsibility of adapting the law to social change. Attribution of the living Constitution idea to the Fourteenth Amendment depended not only on misreading or ignoring its original intent but also on the famous "living Constitution" dicta of John Marshall, Oliver Wendell Holmes Jr., and Felix Frankfurter themselves. Berger noted that reformers frequently invoked Marshall's dictum in *McCulloch v. Maryland* (1819) that the Constitution must "be adapted to the various *crises* of human affairs" or Holmes's in *Missouri v. Holland* (1920) that "the case before us must be considered in the light of our whole experience." Reformers often had combined these and similar dicta with the allegedly vague terms of the amendment to justify decisions beyond its original intent. As a remedy, Berger carefully contextualized these dicta with the limited holdings of the cases in which they occurred. Additionally, he noted with relish Marshall's contemporary pseudonymous rejection of claims that his dictum was a grab for more judicial power under the guise of interpretation. Marshall explicitly denied that the defense of implied powers in *McCulloch*, of which the dictum was a part, could support any extension of judicial power beyond the limits of the Constitution.[33] Berger concluded that none of the other seemingly expansive dicta frequently quoted by advocates of a living Constitution was ever understood in its own time as a basis for judicial updating of the fundamental law.[34]

As in 1969, Berger's originalism still reflected the influence of process-restraint jurisprudence, but this time in a more critical way. He still shared the process-restraint dedication to proceduralism and judicial deference, but he thought that its emphasis on prudence and jurisdictional technique could not adequately constrain judicial discretion because of its insufficient roots in the facts of history. For example, Berger told one correspondent that he found "all the talk about 'neutral principles,' pro and con, a morass."[35] To another correspondent he wrote that "Wechsler's 'neutral principles' distracted attention from the much more crucial issue: may the Court revise the Fourteenth Amendment in contradiction of the framer's design?"[36] Berger emphasized that "given clearly expressed 'intention,'" the Court's misinterpretation of the Fourteenth Amendment posed "the issue of power to revise the Constitution, a far more solid issue than 'craftsmanship,' 'netural [*sic*] principles[,]' etc."[37] Likewise, Berger criticized Felix Frankfurter for retaining the "adaptive" logic of the living Constitution insofar as Frankfurter's approach to the Fourteenth Amendment's due process clause imputed to it a historically inaccurate and discretion-inducing vagueness. This allowed Frankfurter and later legal liberals to rationalize the "updating" of the "fundamental values" of the Constitution to their own sense of contemporary needs, which in turn assumed that judges had a special competence for discerning and articulating national commitments and aspirations—or, indeed, even for serving as the nation's conscience.[38]

Once the liberals of the 1960s and 1970s exploited the discretion that, according to Berger, had remained latent in the failure of process-restraint jurisprudence to account sufficiently for history, they recreated the same problems that had led to the constitutional crisis prior to the New Deal. Berger saw little difference between the assertive, discretionary natural right jurisprudence of the pre–New Deal Court and Warren Court–style legal liberalism. Both frequently ignored or perverted the original intention of the constitutional provisions they purported to interpret, substituting instead a view of justice or good public policy that many in the polity rejected. In Berger's view, then, the watershed development in American constitutionalism after Word War II was the legal liberal abandonment of the traditional process-restraint suspicion of judicial power. Approving the results achieved by the Warren Court, liberals now defended and promoted a highly discretionary jurisprudence and judicial adaptation of the Constitution.[39] Berger lamented that this shift seemingly blinded liberals to the threat their new approach presented to constitutional government as understood and defended by his own earlier generation of liberals as well as by the founders of the republic. Thus, on one hand Berger's originalism carried forward the majoritarian, deferential, and rule of law aims of process-restraint jurisprudence. On the other hand, he combated legal liberalism by pursuing these ends through historical investigation and the traditional concept of original intent, which were not central components of the process-restraint approach and which were usually ignored by legal liberals.

The originalist approach emboldened Berger to criticize the most far-reaching decisions of the Warren Court: the desegregation and reapportionment decisions directly contradicted the original intent of the equal protection clause of the Fourteenth Amendment. He concluded that the 39th Congress, dominated by racial prejudice and not abolitionist sentiment, had explicitly denied that the amendment gave the federal government, let alone the judiciary, any power over segregation or apportionment in the states.[40] Referring to the ratification of the Amendment, Berger regretted that what "the sovereign people were prepared to do in 1868" was "tragically limited."[41] Clearly, Berger put primary value on the constitutionalist principle that alteration of fundamental principles required the formally expressed consent of the governed. Despite professed sympathy with the liberal results of these and other Warren Court decisions, Berger insisted that such personal political sentiments could never properly be the measure of constitutional legitimacy. Good results justified neither the Court's importation of new meaning into the terms of the amendment nor the attendant overstepping of the separation of powers and federalism. To approve such action when it satisfied one's political predilections would sanction the notion that the political end justified the judicial means, thus marking an end to the rule of law and constitutional government.

Berger and His Critics

Berger's insistence on original intent as the basis of constitutional interpretation had an explosive effect on constitutional debate in the late 1970s and 1980s. *Government by Judiciary* was reviewed widely in both the academic and popular press, and a noted constitutional historian recently opined that possibly only Charles Beard's *An Economic Interpretation of the Constitution* (1913) provoked as much controversy. At the time a law professor critical of Berger observed that the book "stimulated an explosion of academic interest in the framers' intent and its significance for constitutional adjudication." Responding to Berger became "somewhat of a cottage industry in constitutional scholarship."[42]

Some reviewers derided Berger's scholarship. It was said to be "simplistic and myopic" and "persistently distorted to support his thesis." Moreover, Berger's claim that the Constitution had a fixed and limited meaning would condemn Americans to "be governed by the dead hand of the past."[43] In rejecting Berger, many reviewers agreed with Arthur S. Miller that judges should put "contemporary meaning" into the "delphic words of the 14th Amendment." The proper function of the Supreme Court, argued Robert Cover, was to interpret such words "in light of its own best judgment about the proper meaning of the principle [in the text]." The intent of the framers regarding the words they wrote or the role of the Court was irrelevant because "it is for us, not the framers, to decide whether [the] end of liberty is best served by entrusting to judges a major role in defining our governing political ideas."[44]

However, Berger convinced other observers, including some legal liberals, that the Fourteenth Amendment was not originally intended to affect state control of segregation or suffrage.[45] Other reviewers rejected Berger's historical conclusions and argued that the Fourteenth Amendment was intended to have a broader or vaguer meaning than Berger had allowed or that it was intended to incorporate the Bill of Rights.[46]

Berger's insistence on the relevance of the concept of original intent in constitutional adjudication was especially criticized, particularly by updated forms of the legal realist charge of inevitable indeterminacy, and thus political choice, in the activity of interpretation.[47] For example, Ronald Dworkin criticized Berger for insensitivity to the possible complications in attempting to generalize about the shared intent of a multimember body such as the 39th Congress or in reconciling its intent to that of the ratifiers. Further, it would be difficult at best to identify the level of abstraction at which the authors of a constitutional text intended their words to be understood. Thus, appeals to intent as a way to constrain judicial power were too indeterminate to prevent personal or political choice from settling the outcome of interpretation.

Dworkin concluded that "there is no stubborn fact of the matter—no 'real' intention fixed in history independent of our opinions about proper legal or constitutional practice—against which the conceptions we construct can be tested for accuracy." Interpretive choices could be justified only by a political theory that took on the full burden of reconciling representative democracy, claims of principle or right, and judicial power.[48]

Reviewers also recognized that Berger's attack on the "open-ended" living Constitution was a fundamental challenge to the recent activism of the Court and supportive liberal commentators.[49] Even when reviewers conceded Berger's historical conclusions, nearly all wanted the Court to continue the broader, more powerful role it had played since *Brown*. The achievements of the Warren Court should be protected and extended by using the Fourteenth Amendment—or other allegedly "open-ended" constitutional provisions—to articulate new rights and update the Constitution.[50]

Berger answered nearly all of his critics. He wrote point-by-point responses to the criticisms of his historical argument, often reiterating, amplifying, and occasionally supplementing the historical evidence presented in the book.[51] These responses sometimes charged critics with a failure to come to grips with the facts in their zeal to defend legal liberalism. The debate continued well into the 1980s, sometimes becoming repetitive or duplicative. Still, the drive to attack or refute Berger, plus his tenacity in responding to his critics, was a major reason originalism became a central topic of debate in American constitutional theory.

Berger's rejection of the living Constitution idea made it clear that his originalism was much more than a plea for historical accuracy. In the debate with his critics he tirelessly recapitulated how this erroneous view of an intentionally vague or "open-ended" Fourteenth Amendment was offered by Alexander M. Bickel to Frankfurter in the *Brown* litigation. Whatever complexities the record of the 39th Congress might contain, Berger insisted that it was unmistakably clear that segregation and the regulation of suffrage were not within the scope of the amendment and that no one thought they eventually would become so according to any notion of a living Constitution. While historical evidence could be "inconclusive and murky," this was not the case with this aspect of the Fourteenth Amendment.[52] Similarly, Berger consistently emphasized the error in thinking that judicial updating of the Constitution could be justified by John Marshall's dictum in *McCulloch*, referring to it as the legal liberal "Rock of Ages [that served as] a refuge from the rigors of analysis."[53]

Constitutional provisions had a fixed meaning and were not like common law principles that could be elaborated or adapted by interstitial judicial legislation or the living Constitution approach.[54] Berger's historical argument thus clarified the fundamental issues at stake between originalism and legal liberalism. As one observer noted, the legal liberal answer to Berger's basic question—can the Court contradict clearly expressed intent?—"has been a somewhat tentative, seldom straightforward, and mysteriously convoluted 'yes.'"[55]

As Berger's rejoinders indicated, in the debate surrounding the book he relentlessly focused on constitutional fundamentals. Another way he did so was by continually invoking, as he had in *Government by Judiciary,* the limits meant to be imposed by the originally intended structure of the separation of powers. As in the process-restraint approach, this limitation would maximize the space for legislative politics and preserve the rule of law by maintaining distinctions between constitutional law and constitutional amendment and between constitutional law and ordinary political preference. Accordingly, Berger also regularly defended legislative formation of public policy and the reservation of basic constitutional change for the Article V amendment process. He thus offered originalism as the bulwark of the majoritarian, legislative power that the process approach also had defended against the tendency of legal liberalism to undermine legislative power and the rule of law.[56] In this way the debate over Berger's book showed how originalism related the complex and seemingly arcane topic of legal and constitutional interpretation to the fundamental political issue of how to allocate and limit official power within a system of constitutional government.

Because such fundamentals ultimately were at stake, the debate sharpened Berger's defense of the nature of originalist interpretation. Intent was the critical concept because, Berger argued, the framers of the original Constitution and the Fourteenth Amendment regarded the Constitution as a special kind of statute or contract. Once popular ratification had legitimated the original text or an amendment, the drafters and ratifiers thought it would be interpreted according to their intent. Thus the original Constitution and the Fourteenth Amendment were "written against a background of interpretive presuppositions that assured the Framers their design would be effectuated." Consequently, it was Berger's insistence that effectuation of intent was the proper goal of interpretation that caused him to undertake detailed investigation of legislative history as a supplement to traditional textual analysis. Ascertaining intent was always the goal of his historical research: "The draftsmen's 'intention' is the genus, and the use of legislative history to illuminate it is the species." A provision in the Constitution whose intent was unclear or contested could be illuminated by evidence of intent extrinsic to the text, if it was available. As noted above, Berger also ascertained the intent of the lawgiver by using the traditional canons of statutory interpretation known to each group of framers. Although Berger used them to buttress the evidence of intent contained in the text and legislative history, he readily conceded that canons could never displace the clearly expressed intent of the framers as revealed in evidence extrinsic to the text.[57] He similarly insisted that general terms in the text could not overcome clear extrinsic evidence that the framers intended the terms to have limited meaning, as was the case when they explicitly denied that the Fourteenth Amendment would affect state control of segregation or suffrage.

From the perspective of originalist interpretation, then, legal liberals undermined the rule of law by encouraging judges to raise words in the text to such a level of generality that they went beyond the intent of the framers. Such abstraction defeated the interpretive goal of discovering intent and undermined the limitations on judicial power necessary for constitutional government. Although Berger agreed with his critics that interpretation inevitably involved discretion in the application of words to unforeseen circumstances, "the necessity of choosing does not empower the Court to *displace the choices of the framers*." If extrinsic evidence of these choices was clear, it controlled constitutional meaning, notwithstanding general terms in the text or precedents that ignored or distorted such evidence.[58]

The debate also made it clearer that Berger did not hold, as some critics charged, that the private, subjective intent or state of mind of a particular legislator or ratifier could determine the original intent of a constitutional provision. Rather, original intent came from the traditional meaning of common law terms, unless explicitly modified, and the meaning attributed to other terms by those who drafted, voted for, and publicly advocated them. As we have seen, *Government by Judiciary* concentrated on the legislative history of the drafting of the Fourteenth Amendment, and Berger understood ratification as the acceptance of the meaning of the text as articulated by those who publicly formulated and advocated it. He demanded presentation of any evidence that showed that the ratifiers understood its meaning differently. Moreover, Berger noted that those who attempted to complicate out of existence the idea of intent by pitting framers against ratifiers also invariably viewed the Court as the guardian of the national conscience or principles or the up-dater of a living Constitution containing amorphous "fundamental values." This seemed to Berger simply to beg the basic question of whether there were limits on judicial interpretation and, if so, what they were, if not the mean-ing of constitutional provisions as understood by those who wrote and rati-fied them.[59] Later interpreters who substituted new meanings of the text for its original meaning would put an end to constitutional limitations and the rule of law. Although "the meaning of words may change over the years, it does not follow that we may saddle the framers with our meanings." Berger said that his critics "would permit judges to give [the words of the Constitution] a different meaning as they list." Words whose meaning changed through interpretation could no longer serve the limiting purpose of a written Constitution.[60]

In the ongoing debate Berger also emphasized the fundamental point that only interpretation based on original intent could relate judicial decisions to the ultimate source of their legal legitimacy in the sovereign act of ratification. In this context he understood the rule of law as the public announcement of legal principles and standards, and thus their limitation, prior to enforcement by government officials. Ratification conferred the status of law on the pro-posed Constitution, and officeholders who enforced it derived their powers from the text that was ratified. Indeed, ratification of a Constitution designed to limit government had legitimated a text of finite meaning, not one that was open-ended, hopelessly vague, or infinitely manipulable. Accordingly, Berger held that an interpretation was legitimate only if it was tied to, indeed had emerged from, a provision's original intent and likewise had been fitted into the limitations imposed by the overall form and structure of the Constitution. Original intent, if recoverable, fostered the rule of law by serving as a previ-ously announced legal limit on judicial interpretive discretion.[61]

During the debate Berger, who was seventy-six years old in 1977, pointed out with relish that the dismissal of original intent and the aggressive liberal defense of judicial power was part of a generational shift in academia. He con-demned this "turnabout of the libertarians" as he had in the book, rejecting both the confident assertion of judicial power for liberal ends and the weak reed of judicial self-restraint it had overcome. Thus, although Berger echoed the positivist proceduralism of process-restraint thought and defended the Constitution as a "framework within which each generation can strive for a peaceable solution of clashing aims," he also lamented that judicial self-restraint found few liberal supporters when judicial power achieved liberal goals.[62] Likewise, Berger ruefully observed that liberal praise of his earlier originalist scholarship on impeachment and executive privilege had now turned to scorn. His prior studies "invoked the selfsame intention of the framers to determine the meaning of the terms they employed," and "liberals were ready enough to embrace that approach to topple Richard Nixon, but [they] condemn it bitterly when it is used to test the Warren Court's espousal of causes dear to their hearts."[63] Berger, a liberal of an older generation, had more in common with the goals of the process-restraint tradition than he did with the new generation of liberals, who were quite eager to reject that tradition once they found that it obstructed their goals.

Berger's Legacy: The Attraction and Influence of Originalism

The majoritarian, restraintist thrust of *Government by Judiciary* closely aligned originalism with the steadily growing conservative criticism of Warren and early Burger Court decisions. In 1980 the new conservative political coalition elected Ronald Reagan as president, and Republicans won control of the Senate for the first time in decades. In this atmosphere, Berger's originalism appealed to conservative critics of legal liberalism, some of whom served in or were sympathetic to the Reagan administration. In June 1982, for example, Berger spoke at a conference on judicial reform sponsored by the Free Congress Research and Education Foundation, a conservative public policy organization with close ties to the Republican Party and the Reagan administration. Berger introduced Judge Robert Bork of the United States Court of Appeals for the District of Columbia Circuit. Bork was a prominent originalist eventually nominated by Reagan to the Supreme Court in 1987. Berger praised the seminal contribution to originalism Bork had made in a 1971 law review article, which Berger cited in his book and frequently thereafter in the debate with his critics.[64] Observing Bork's conclusion that the text and original intent of the Fourteenth Amendment did not support the Court's reapportionment decisions, Berger noted that Bork's article had encouraged his own research. Additionally, Berger suggested that Bork would make a fine Supreme Court justice because he had shown himself able to "lay bare the identification of personal predilections with constitutional requirements" that was a defining characteristic of legal liberal attacks on originalism.[65]

The Center for Judicial Studies, a conservative organization that began producing the legal periodical *Benchmark* in the fall of 1983, was another group that heralded Berger as one of its guiding lights. *Benchmark* vigorously advocated originalism and regularly contained articles and reviews by members of the Reagan Justice Department and conservative scholars. In 1987 *Benchmark* ran an issue in tribute to Berger. In the midst of the originalism debate, one contributor concluded that "in many ways Raoul Berger stands behind this great and robust public debate about our most fundamental principles."[66]

Even though he was a former New Deal lawyer and had remained a Democrat, Berger welcomed such acknowledgment. Political differences with conservative Republicans did not undermine Berger's advocacy of originalism as a defense of American constitutionalism and its wide latitude for popular government. Indeed, as the originalism debate gained strength Berger reconsidered his earlier conclusion about the power of Congress to constrain judicial power under its Article III, section 2 authority to create "exceptions" to the appellate jurisdiction of the Supreme Court. The language of the exceptions clause was unqualified, yet Berger's earlier scholarship had emphasized the founders' fear of legislative power and concluded that the clause was intended only to prevent revision of local jury findings of fact, not to authorize plenary congressional control over the Court's jurisdiction.[67] However, by the early 1980s Berger had reconsidered the evidence. He now highlighted the threat modern judicial power posed to popular government. He concluded that the clear intent of the exceptions clause to insulate jury findings of fact was "unaccompanied by overtones of exclusivity," in contrast, for example, to the clear rejection of suffrage and desegregation from the coverage of the Fourteenth Amendment. This meant that "the 'exceptions-regulations' clause may be regarded as part of the machinery available for correction of judicial encroachment on the paramount legislative domain." Likewise, he defended the power of Congress under section 5 of the Fourteenth Amendment to enforce its terms. Replying to the perennial argument that regulation under the exceptions clause or section 5 would eviscerate the Court's ability to vindicate constitutional rights, Berger thought that the Court, urged on for decades by reformers, had created new rights out of whole cloth and used them to trump the policy choices of elected legislatures. Therefore, defenders of such illegitimate judicial power should not be allowed to help the Court continue its errors by appealing to a misinterpretation of the exceptions clause or a renunciation of section 5. He concluded: "liberals should be the last to abandon the rule of law because the desires of Demos are antipathetic to their own."[68]

Berger took his own advice. His originalist defense of popular government and the rule of law occurred while proposals to curtail the Court's jurisdiction over school prayer, among other issues, were pending in the first years of the Reagan administration and the new Republican-controlled Senate. He noted that his views on the substance of such proposals were "diametrically opposed to those of the Jesse Helms *coterie*" but that personal political sentiments could not undermine the constitutionality of using the exceptions clause.[69]

To abide by the original meaning of the Constitution as he understood it, wherever it might lead, was typical of Raoul Berger. More than any other single scholar Berger highlighted the issues that separated originalism from legal liberalism and brought them to a wide audience. *Government by Judiciary* attained a level of renown and influence achieved by only a handful of books in the history of American constitutional scholarship. It clarified the basic contours of originalism by seeking to constrain the interpretive discretion and institutional role of the Supreme Court through inquiry into the historical meaning of constitutional terms, defense of federalism and the separation of powers, and a reassertion of the traditional concept of interpretation as the ascertainment and application of original intent.

While few later originalists understood themselves as systematically elaborating Berger's understanding of the doctrine, he made originalism impossible to ignore. One noted historian has suggested that Berger "almost single-handedly revised the terms of debate in constitutional law" and that his book "was promptly accepted as the bible of original intent jurisprudence."[70] Some originalists associated with *Benchmark* credited Berger with having influenced them.[71] Others not so associated did likewise. Richard Kay, who advanced originalism in the 1980s and 1990s, wrote that in "forcing us to face" the issue of adherence to original intent as "vital to a government where power is delegated and limited by a constitution," Berger had "made his most important contribution."[72] Reflecting on a recent law journal symposium, Kay told Berger "how profoundly your work has changed the assumptions and questions of modern constitutional law scholarship. In a sense, almost everything being written, explicitly or implicitly, is a response to *Government by Judiciary*. You have brought us back to the basic—and therefore the most troublesome questions. The whole field is better off for it."[73] Larry A. Alexander, who also defended originalist interpretation in the 1990s, wrote in the same symposium that "credit must go to Raoul Berger, a true gadfly of constitutional theory" for forcing "all serious constitutional theorists to deal with questions regarding proper principles of constitutional interpretation and the proper role of the courts, questions that many theorists, basking in the warm glow of Warren Court decisions on individual rights, felt content to ignore."[74] Alexander too personally thanked Berger for performing "an immense service by forcing all 'liberal' constitutional theorists either to abandon the pretense of interpretation, to develop a theory of interpretation, or to improve upon your historical research."[75] Even when critical of aspects of Berger's later work, originalists such as Michael McConnell observed that Berger had long stood "for the honorable tradition that a scholar must put aside his own social and economic predilections and look only to original sources in seeking the meaning" of the Constitution.[76] Further, as noted above, responding to Berger had become a cottage industry in the 1980s. Michael Perry, for example, insisted that "a debt of gratitude" was due to Berger because his book challenged "those who approve the Court's policymaking function to elaborate a theory in defense of that function."[77] Other major legal liberals such as Ely and Dworkin also recognized Berger as an important exponent of a position each rejected.[78]

Although originalism would become a more refined and contested doctrine after Berger, his efforts ensured that it would not be quickly dismissed. Despite his Democratic politics and his careful distinction between political aspiration and constitutionality, Berger's book encouraged the further interaction of originalist criticism and conservative politics. Appearing in the midst of growing academic and popular criticism of legal liberalism, the book unambiguously presented originalism as a challenge to the continued realization of liberal goals through judicial creation of new rights and expansion of an allegedly amorphous, judicially updated living Constitution. *Government by Judiciary* was often seen as a major contribution to the general conservative trend that elected Ronald Reagan, and in the 1980s it encouraged his administration to offer originalism as a counter to legal liberalism.

CHAPTER 6

Originalism in the Era of Ronald Reagan

Ronald Reagan was reelected as president of the United States in 1984, and his landslide victory confirmed that the conservative political ascendancy that began at the crossroads of the 1960s had displaced the New Deal coalition and the disunited forces of modern American liberalism.[1] As we have seen, originalism had emerged at the coinciding crossroads in constitutional thought, gaining further attention in the 1970s through the galvanizing work of Raoul Berger. In the 1980s originalism steadily became a more systematic and readily identifiable set of jurisprudential ideas. While those who would identify themselves as originalists were few in number compared with their opponents, the debate in academic constitutional theory revolved around originalist claims about constitutional interpretation and the role of the Court in the constitutional system.

Additionally, originalism was politically and rhetorically attractive to the Reagan administration. Many administration officials, as well as supporters in the electorate and Congress, regarded several Supreme Court decisions as politically distasteful, constitutionally mistaken affronts to limited, representative government. In this environment originalist criticism of legal liberalism portended policy consequences beyond the legal-academic debate.

In the 1980s critics sometimes dismissed originalism as nothing more than a partisan ploy to advance the immediate policy goals of the conservative coalition and the Reagan administration. Originalism was not, however, merely a call for conservative results in constitutional adjudication. As we have seen in previous chapters, in one form or another its appeals to the principles and rhetoric of limited government and consent-based politics, as well as its traditional understanding of the nature of constitutional interpretation, had long been characteristic features of American constitutionalism. The centrality of these ideas to the American constitutional project helps explain why both scholars and political partisans advanced originalism with such noticeable effect in the welcoming conservative political climate of the 1980s.

The Terminological and Theoretical Context of the 1980s

Clarification of the sometimes cumbersome terminology of the 1980s academic debate is required to appreciate how much the advance of originalism raised fundamental constitutional issues. We saw in the previous chapter that Raoul Berger's seminal *Government by Judiciary* (1977), like some judicial opinions and scholarship well before it, had argued in terms of "original intent" and "original understanding." However, from the mid–1970s until the mid–1980s academics usually debated judicial review in terms of "interpretivism" versus "noninterpretivism," following a noted article by Professor Thomas Grey.[2] After John Hart Ely employed this nomenclature in his widely read work, Berger's reassertion of the traditional idea that interpretation was properly the ascertainment and application of original intent informed by extrinsic historical evidence meant that in the idiom of the day he was an "interpretivist."[3] Berger accepted this terminology in his law review essays of the late 1970s and 1980s. Nonetheless, as the criticism of modern judicial power intensified in the wake of Berger's work, the nomenclature of the debate took another turn. In a noted article, Paul Brest, who had earlier attacked Berger, applied modern hermeneutic analysis to what he called "originalism." Brest described "originalism" as the "familiar approach to constitutional adjudication that accords binding authority to the text of the Constitution or the intentions of its adopters."[4] After Brest's essay, "interpretivism," "originalism," and "original intent" frequently were used interchangeably, although a few commentators then and since have attempted fine and occasionally pedantic conceptual distinctions among these and related terms.

The term "original intent" became even more popular after the widely publicized and debated speeches Attorney General Edwin Meese III delivered in 1985 and 1986 (analyzed below). "Original intent" or "originalism" then gradually supplanted "interpretivism" as the name for arguments opposed to modern judicial power. In the early 1980s these various terms made up a common critical vocabulary. Theorists who sought to justify and extend modern judicial power were often cast as "noninterpretivists" or "nonoriginalists," whom Brest aptly described as "purposely depart[ing] from the text and original understanding."[5] Additionally, the older appellation of "judicial activist" endured as a general description of judicial assertiveness or as a condemnation of judicial decisions overturning policy decisions that arguably should have remained with another level or branch of government. However, the newer nomenclature indicated that the debate about judicial review was getting more fundamental and moving beyond older concerns about "strict" versus "loose" construction or "active" versus "restrained" review. "Originalism" raised the far more basic issue of whether the Court could or should be constrained by the text and history of the Constitution or if it was free to disregard them.

Amid the shifts in nomenclature, originalist scholarship in the 1980s typically argued that the liberal reformist use of modern judicial power threatened the rule of law and the formulation of public policy in legislatures. The development of originalism can be best understood by briefly recalling the general contours of liberal arguments in this period. As observed in chapter four, "legal liberal" theory emerged in the wake of the Warren Court and *Roe v. Wade* (1973). Legal liberal academics offered theories to rationalize, defend, and advance recent reformist decisions, and they usually did so by treating constitutional language as inherently vague or at a high level of generality. While some scholars of the period noted that a dominant theme of legal liberal scholarship was to get courts to advance the liberal view of moral principles and justice, by the late 1970s and early 1980s it was becoming clearer that there was disagreement about how best to direct modern judicial power to liberal goals.[6]

As in the 1970s, the primary division was still between process and rights theories.[7] As exemplified by John Hart Ely, process theories aimed to keep open and smoothly functioning the pluralistic political process, while rights theories, as exemplified by Laurence Tribe and Ronald Dworkin, rejected the moral skepticism they associated with process approaches and argued instead that judges should discern and vindicate "fundamental" rights or values beyond those formalized in the text of the Constitution. Variations on these general approaches, as well as other versions of legal liberalism, could be adduced. But most observers agreed that "all represent[ed] a common enterprise, [creation of a] basis for the expansive review power of the federal courts."[8] As the 1980s wore on, legal liberals became more catholic (or desperate), turning more directly to various contemporary political theories (especially John Rawls) and, as the shadow of the originalist ascendance advanced, eventually to their own versions of history to justify continued "activism by a liberal court."[9]

Additionally, at the rhetorical level the generalized treatment of constitutional language characteristic of legal liberalism was often defended in the metaphor of a "living Constitution." Although in the early twentieth century this metaphor had been arrayed against judicial obstruction of legislative initiatives, legal liberals since the 1960s typically used it to advocate judicial "updating" of the Constitution to their understanding of contemporary needs or fundamental values. For example, Justice William J. Brennan Jr. offered a widely noted defense of the living Constitution in the midst of the originalism debate of the 1980s. He described the document as a "sublime oration on the dignity of man" and understood the Supreme Court as the primary vehicle for updating the law to the evolving standards of this "sparkling vision." The judge's role was to "seek out the community's interpretation of the Constitutional text." He also emphasized his own desire to "embody a community striving for human dignity for all" in areas such as the death penalty and the "new property" of government entitlements.[10]

Originalists also confronted critics influenced by modern hermeneutics, which by the 1980s was migrating from literary criticism to the law schools. Hermeneutic critics said that the concepts of intent and historical investigation were too indeterminate to constrain judicial interpretation and insisted that originalist interpreters inevitably make an "arbitrary choice among levels of abstraction" when applying constitutional language to unforeseen circumstances. They further claimed that originalism prevented legal adjustment to new circumstances because it would limit constitutional interpretation to specific issues contemplated at the time of the Constitution's creation or amendment. (This criticism undermined the claim that historical inquiry was too subjective or indeterminate to reveal what the framers intended, but the critics rarely attempted to reconcile these positions.) Another favorite hermeneutic criticism was the use of extrinsic historical evidence from the founding era to argue that the drafters and ratifiers of the Constitution did not intend future judges to consult such evidence; still another was to argue that the original intent of a multimember body such as the Philadelphia or state ratifying conventions was too complex to be recovered. It was then usually argued that the founders thought judges would settle the meaning of the Constitution through common law–style adjudication, in which recurrence to extrinsic evidence of intent was rare, or by some version of the "special judicial competency" to discern and protect "fundamental values" and/or the living Constitution.[11] Eventually a sizeable body of criticism informed by hermeneutics urged that law should be reconceived as a "process" or communal "conversation," which could dispense with the foundational notions of political and legal authority typical of a traditional theory such as originalism.[12] More radical hermeneutic critics sometimes went so far as to claim that their ideas proved that constitutionalism and the rule of law were impossible. The intricacies and conundrums of the sometimes anti-legal hermeneutic movement need not detain us, but its co-evolution with the legal liberal notion that judicial review should advance liberal definitions of justice and the good society suggested why originalism might be attractive to those interested in limiting judicial power.[13]

Developing the Originalist Idea

Originalists and even some legal liberals observed that the very nomenclature of the debate in the 1980s suggested that liberals had left the Constitution behind. "Noninterpretivism" undeniably connoted that its practitioners were in fact doing something other than interpreting the Constitution. Michael Perry, a noninterpretivist who argued that the Court should lead society to a fuller realization of correct moral principles, clearly recognized this point.[14] Likewise, a commentator who earlier was sympathetic to the Warren Court opined that noninterpretivism signaled "a frank resolve to detach judicial review from the Constitution itself." Gary McDowell, a political scientist who became associate director of the Office of Public Affairs in the Justice Department in June 1985 and helped formulate Meese's speeches on originalism, observed that in the earlier debate between "strict" and "loose" construction "the question was how to read the Constitution; in the new [debate on inter-pretivism versus noninterpretivism] the question is whether to read the Constitution."[15]

This terminological point helped originalists raise the stark question of whether legal liberals actually thought the Constitution established limits on legal-political actors. If it did not, than a noninterpretive "interpretation" could enact a judge's own values or versions of morality in the name of the Constitution. Constitutional interpretation and ordinary political preference were essentially indistinguishable, even though obedience to the Court's decisions had always depended in some sense on the proposition that what it did was based on preexisting law and not on the politics of the moment—that is, that there was a difference between what was contained in the Constitution and what was not. Robert H. Bork, who taught at the Yale Law School in the early 1980s, continually used this "inside/outside" method of criticism to query whether liberals regarded the Constitution as legally binding. He approvingly quoted Ely's description of interpretivism as the "insistence that the work of the political branches is to be invalidated [by a court] only in accord with an inference whose starting point, whose underlying premise, is fairly discoverable in the Constitution." Bork then emphasized the mistake of his opponents (including Ely) by stating that "the judge who looks outside the Constitution always looks inside himself and nowhere else." Other critics similarly understood noninterpretivism as "a methodology that permits the judiciary to decide the difficult moral issues of our time under the rubric of constitutional law." In Bork's pithy formulation, judges who looked to themselves or to the various mutually conflicting recommendations of the "value-choosing" theorists of "moral abstraction" would be effectuating their own political predilections or moral theories. Thus, "not surprisingly, the politics of the professors becomes the command of the Constitution."[16]

Bork further developed the inside/outside point by attacking Frank Michelman, a prominent legal liberal who advocated a "fundamental" right to welfare as a way to increase participation in the political process. Bork insisted that such a right could not be fairly inferred from the text, history, structure, or function of the Constitution, but rather was derived from a moral philosophy outside of it. Echoing the title of Raoul Berger's seminal work, Bork said that legal liberals who went beyond the Constitution in hopes of judicial realization of their moral philosophy would "convert our government from one by representative assembly to one by judiciary."[17]

Bork further noted that the Michelman fundamental rights argument for welfare also called on Ely's claim that judicial review should reinforce representation in the political process. Although many commentators regarded Ely's theory as more moderate than fundamental rights theories, Bork took the opportunity to argue that Ely's process-oriented theory was no more of a limit on judges. He observed that Ely accepted a basic premise of legal liberalism by positing that constitutional provisions such as the Ninth Amendment and the equal protection and privileges or immunities clauses of the Fourteenth were vague and "open-ended" and then insisting that such provisions should be used only to effectuate values actually located in the Constitution (primarily those ensuring equal representation in the political process). But Bork held that if provisions such as the Ninth Amendment were as vague as Ely claimed, then judges should not use them to void legislative enactments. The Ninth Amendment did not in fact provide that "the Supreme Court shall, from time to time, find and enforce such additional rights as may be determined by moral philosophy, or by consideration of the dominant ideas of republican government." All Ely seemed to have accomplished was the substitution of the vague value of "participation in the political process" for the equally illimitable values advocated by legal liberals like Michelman.[18]

As suggested by Bork's criticism of allegedly "open-ended" language, in the 1980s originalists bolstered the claim that legal liberal jurisprudence was not bound by the Constitution by more frequently attacking the modern practice of treating constitutional language at high levels of generality. One of the best examples of this criticism in the early 1980s was the work of the political scientist Christopher Wolfe. He argued that since the Warren Court era liberal supporters of modern judicial power (and judges they praised) characteristically considered constitutional language at ever higher levels of generality. To do so they often obfuscated or ignored the original intent of legal-constitutional terms or else restated them at a level of generality that was then specified in an ad hoc manner to resolve a particular case. Once the historically limited original meaning of legal-constitutional language was abandoned or abstracted, the Court was invited to mold to "contemporary needs" various formulae that usually were designed to effectuate the imperatives of a favored fundamental values approach.[19]

In seeking to combat the legal liberal preference for a high level of generality, originalists insisted that there was a difference between abiding by the limits of the Constitution and the discredited idea of "mechanical" in-

140 of Originalism in American Law and Politics

terpretation. Bork argued that a "judge must not state [constitutional values and principles] with so much generality that he transforms" them. Rather, a judge should choose "no level of generality higher than that which interpretation of the words, structure, and history of the Constitution fairly support." Bork recognized that this method could not determine results in every case: like any interpretive methodology it could be manipulated by a disingenuous judge. He thus conceded that judgment in the application of general terms to concrete, unforeseen circumstances was inevitable; the Constitution did not provide the interpreter with "a conclusion but with a major premise."[20] Despite inevitable indeterminacy, the originalist interpretive methodology was more legitimate than competing alternatives because "at the very least judges will confine themselves to the principles the Framers put into the Constitution." Bork provided an example by remarking on the valid inclusion of electronic media in the protection of the First Amendment and interstate trucking within the coverage of the commerce clause, though neither was foreseen at the time the Constitution became law. On the other hand, he condemned Justice William O. Douglas's derivation of a right to privacy from the "penumbras" and "emanations" of the Bill of Rights in *Griswold v. Connecticut* (1965). Bork said, "The level of abstraction chosen makes application of a generalized right of privacy unpredictable." Without constitutional text or history to define the right, privacy became an unconstrained source of judicial power.[21]

As we have seen, originalists attempted to counter the drift into abstraction by defending the traditional idea that, as in other areas of law, interpretation of the Constitution was accomplished primarily by a close reading of the text. Its terms were not to be treated in an overly general way or divorced from their context, and traditional canons of interpretation were guides to effectuation of the intent of the lawgiver as well as constraints on the discretion of the interpreter. Originalists further held that abstract readings could be defeated by consulting sources extrinsic to the text to elucidate not only the meaning of particular clauses in it but also the constraints that federalism and the separation of powers originally imposed on interpreters.[22] Indeed, the originalist view was that a historically informed appreciation of the political theory embodied in federalism and the separation of powers was as much a part of original intent as a particular clause in the text.[23] Historical knowledge of both the text and the political theory realized in the Constitutional structure could illuminate how particular provisions were understood at the time of their enactment. This knowledge could limit, but not necessarily determine, the level of generality at which contemporary judges derived, restated, and applied constitutional language.[24]

As this analysis suggests, originalists rejected the modern hermeneutic notion that meaning was created as much by the interpreter of a text as its creator. If the judiciary was to be limited by the Constitution as law, wrote Bork, "one of the things this means is that the words constrain judgment." Henry Monaghan agreed that a legitimate interpretation could encompass subjects beyond the specific contemplation of the drafters and ratifiers, yet within their general purpose. But interpreters could not legitimately "mold [the text] to the views of contemporary society, irrespective of the sorts of evils that concerned the Framers." He recognized that originalist interpretation depended upon "the coherence and intelligibility of a line much favored by lawyers but frequently criticized: the distinction between meaning and application." Rejecting the idea that to interpret something is to give it meaning, Raoul Berger stated that "'Give' denotes the grant of something to one who obtains something he did not have before, whereas 'to interpret' is to ascertain, not to add." Bork similarly noted that proper interpretation translated "the framer's or the legislator's morality into a rule to govern unforeseen circumstances." This task did not permit the judge to apply his personal view of morality or the public good.[25] Originalists were thus confident that the traditional activity of interpretation as the ascertainment and application of intent was not only possible but also necessary for a constitutional government responsible to the consent of the governed. Although originalists readily conceded that inevitable lacunae and ambiguity in the historical record would always necessitate judgment, they insisted that historical evidence supported the conclusion that the adopters of the Constitution never understood the judiciary to possess the power, through adjudication, to revise or update its recoverable meaning.

Originalism and Established Features of the Constitutional Order

In the 1980s originalists were developing more sophisticated defenses of their position, but they still confronted established features of the constitutional order that supported legal liberalism. One of these was the entrenched sense that the Court's role was to serve as the ultimate guardian and protector of fundamental values or rights, a position that, as we have seen, many legal liberal theorists elaborated from the early work of Alexander M. Bickel.[26]

In response, originalists contended that the Court and the new generation of liberal commentators had revealed the potential for abuse at the core of this modern understanding of the Court's role. Such criticism convinced even William Van Alstyne, a noted commentator previously more sympathetic to legal liberalism, that any such "special role" or "duty-at-large" could not be reconciled to the constitutionally limited function of the Court. Further, originalist critics typically agreed that "Bickel skewed his theory in favor of those who would come after him who would be more inclined to confuse 'fundamental values' with policy choices that were the result of their personal predilections."[27] One insightful originalist critic, William Gangi, painstakingly schematized and summarized his view of the complex, interrelated arguments "noninterpretivists" used to justify fundamental values jurisprudence: "The past is dead—the Constitution is living. When a vacuum exists in pursuing societal ideals the Supreme Court is best suited to obtain results. In the context of a cumbersome amendment process the Court has the responsibility of securing individual rights. This new Court role has been accepted by the American people and is irreversible. The time has come explicitly to recognize [the Court's new legislative role]."[28] These propositions aptly summarized the originalist view that legal liberals wanted judges to move beyond the traditional limits on the judicial function, especially via the vindication of rights or values they had empowered themselves to announce.

As Gangi's analysis suggested, originalists also had to confront the popular metaphor of a living Constitution that often was invoked to defend the preferred legal liberal role for the Court. William Rehnquist had earlier attacked it and offered instead a legal positivist defense of majoritarianism, the separation of powers, and a limited judiciary. Like Rehnquist, originalists in the 1980s noted that although the metaphor was rhetorically appealing, it had become a way of imploring the judiciary to substitute "some other set of values for those which may be derived from the language and intent of the framers."[29] The metaphor now should be recognized for what it was: a tool that gave the Court too much power over the process of constitutional change.[30] The fundamental issue obscured by the friendly metaphor should not be ignored in a regime dedicated to limited government and the republican principle of consent.

Another established feature of the constitutional order that originalists had to address was the relationship of their theory to *Brown v. Board of Education* (1954), the famous school desegregation decision, and to the issue of *stare de-*

cisis, that is, a court's consideration of whether to follow a precedent, more generally. Legal liberals often noted that Raoul Berger had argued that the equal protection clause of the Fourteenth Amendment was not intended by its framers or ratifiers to prohibit segregation and could not support *Brown,* a position he never relinquished. Bork, on the other hand, had suggested in 1971 that *Brown* could be justified by reasoning that the equal protection clause protected a "core idea of black equality against racial discrimination" that the Court must neutrally apply.[31] Earl Maltz built on Bork's view in the 1980s, arguing that historical experience with segregation by the time of *Brown,* even if it (arguably) was not intended to be prohibited by the clause, had shown that separate facilities were never equal and that attempts to change this fact had invariably met with resistance. Therefore the *Brown* opinion "could have established a virtually irrebuttable presumption that all such segregation was maintained for the purpose of denying blacks equal opportunity. Such a presumption would justify an interpretivist Court's decision in favor of the *Brown* plaintiffs." Maltz admitted that the more generalized restatement of the clause need not require such a presumption—an interpretivist judge could hew to a narrower reading that was arguably supported by the evidence—but his point was that "one can claim to be a consistent interpretivist and at the same time support the *Brown* decision."[32]

Berger had never called for a rollback of *Brown* and its progeny but rather had admonished that in the area of segregation, for example, the Court should "go and sin no more" instead of returning to original intent. But *stare decisis* also raised questions for originalism. As Maltz described the challenge for originalist jurisprudence, the problem was to describe "criteria that determine which illegitimate decisions should be overruled and which should be left inviolate. No plausible theory for drawing such a distinction has yet emerged."[33] The issue of *stare decisis* consistently circulated around the debate, and originalists sometimes noted the strong liberal defense of precedents minted since the Warren Court era. Some scholars did contemplate the problems presented by reconsideration of precedents that seemingly were well established, although suspect by originalist tenets. At this point, however, no consensus emerged among originalists about how to handle this important constitutional and jurisprudential issue.[34]

Thus, in the 1980s originalists faced established features of the constitutional order that presented problems for their theory, as seen in the idea of a living Constitution and the identification of the Court with the protection of rights, as well as *Brown* and *stare decisis*. However, originalists did successfully pit other fundamental features of American constitutionalism against legal liberalism. One scholar observed that a major limitation of legal liberalism was that its frequent appeals to hermeneutics persisted "in finding noninterpretivism in the slightest showing of 'indeterminacy' without addressing the political arguments for interpretivism." The liberal attempt to center the debate on the inevitable discretion in legal exegesis—a very old issue—was a "sideshow" that avoided the fundamental issues of what limited interpretation and what was the proper role of the Court in the American constitutional system.[35] Indeed, as we have seen in previous chapters, Anglo-American legal interpretation and the practice of judicial review had long recognized that interpreters had discretion while also consistently holding that the rule of law required judges to interpret the Constitution according to its original intent. The liberal captivation with hermeneutics in the 1980s could not displace the originalist claim that judges should be limited by the original meaning of the documentary Constitution. This basic presumption of American constitutionalism was grounded in the reality of the document's creation and amendment as amply documented events that had actually occurred—no amount of law review hermeneutics could change these facts. Moreover, the text at the center of American constitutionalism, generated by recognizable historical events, embodied the principle that government, including the Supreme Court, must be limited.[36]

The staying power of these real and rhetorically powerful features of the American constitutional order profited originalists and undercut the legal liberal goal of a vague, amorphous but judicially updated living Constitution. The originalist attempt to ascertain and apply the intent and design of the Constitution in order to limit government and defend legislative policymaking was far easier to defend than liberal theories that began with hermeneutic deconstruction and/or ended in a living Constitution updated to judges' conceptions of fundamental values. As one inquiry into the condition of legal liberalism in the 1980s observed, its advocates were "in the precarious position of taking *public* stands against the interpretative legitimacy of the constitutional text and the framers' intent—this while *publicly* deprecating the need to abide by the legislative will of democratic majorities."[37]

Originalists pointed out that legal liberals faced another difficulty derived from their claim that, on the one hand, original intent was irreducibly subjective and offered no strong constraints on judges while insisting on the other hand that fundamental values were real and that the Court's announcement of them should be obeyed. Because the presumptions of American constitutionalism compelled legal liberals to argue that the values they advanced were in some sense derived from the Constitution, they had either to flout this premise directly or treat original intent at a level of abstraction that was so high as to be easily dismissed as meaningless.[38] This created a problem of legitimacy that put them at a disadvantage. Originalists observed that "if intent is irrelevant and the text ambiguous, courts are left with no constitutional source that defines the limits of their authority."[39] Moreover, originalists pointed out that if their opponents were correct about the irreducible indeterminacy, subjectivity, and ultimate willfulness of constitutional interpretation, citizens were left with little reason to obey a Supreme Court whose decisions they found disagreeable. Further, if judges did indeed have a special competence to discern and effectuate unenumerated fundamental rights or values, as many legal liberal theories claimed, it was unclear why a legislature or, for that matter, a written Constitution, was needed at all.[40]

Thus, by centering the early 1980's debate about judicial power on the limits of legitimate constitutional interpretation and the role of the Court in relation to legislatures, originalism drew attention to the most basic questions about the nature of constitutional government in America. In this way originalism addressed the same issues that had driven the process-restraint response to legal realism, as evidenced in its majoritarian thrust and its less precise appeals to the allied ideas of consent and democratic legitimacy.[41] This continuity was not usually at the forefront of originalist arguments, but in retrospect it is clearly discernible. Whereas legal liberals, elaborating the Warren Court model, sought judicial remedies for perceived injustices through highly generalized versions of constitutional rights or values, originalists held that the Constitution prescribed legitimate processes for consent-based, representative self-government—which did not always guarantee a particular view of justice. Henry Monaghan suggested that the Constitution guaranteed "only representative democracy, not perfect government." Bork similarly stated that the Constitution merely provided "a mechanism for a morality of process. It follows that real institutions can never be as pure as abstract philosophers demand, and the philosophers' abstractions must always teach a lesson in derogation of our institutions."[42]

The clear implication of the originalist argument—which in the 1980s was usually offered as a statement of fact—was that constitutional law had displaced the more representative and democratically responsive legislative process as the primary site for the formulation of public policy. Moreover, it had become a tool for advancing the modern liberal view of justice in spite of the more conservative political sentiments of most voters. Consequently, the majoritarian thrust of originalist criticisms of judicial power aligned the doctrine with the conservative political coalition that, by 1984, had twice elected Ronald Reagan president.

Originalism in the Constitutional Politics of the 1980s

The interaction of originalist academic criticism and the politics of the Reagan administration, especially in the Justice Department under Attorney General Edwin Meese III, was a significant feature of American constitutional history in the 1980s.[43] The Reagan administration found in originalism an academic expression of popular dissatisfaction with liberal Supreme Court decisions. The administration and Republicans in Congress quickly showed that, like originalists, they took a dim view of legal liberalism. Reagan's Justice Department announced that its litigation would not rely on courts to attain short-term political goals. Instead the department said it would attempt to pare back judicial power in favor of Congress and state legislatures. The creation of fundamental rights and the continued erosion of jurisdictional thresholds for access to the Court would not be pursued.[44] Additionally, judicial nominees would be screened to ensure that they adhered to a properly limited view of the judicial function, and throughout the 1980s the Reagan administration carefully examined the judicial philosophy of each candidate for the federal bench.[45]

Some Republicans in Congress even went so far as to propose constitutional amendments to allow school prayer or to prohibit abortion and mandatory school bussing. There were also bills that would have used Article III, section 2 of the Constitution to authorize congressional "exceptions" to federal court jurisdiction or equitable remedial powers. Some of these proposals would have withdrawn Supreme Court jurisdiction to hear cases relating to school prayer or would have prevented federal courts from using bussing as a remedy in school desegregation cases. One of the most comprehensive proposals was a Judicial Reform Bill introduced by Senator John East (R-NC), which would have repealed the incorporation doctrine—long condemned on originalist grounds—and the federal exclusionary rule, among others. Additionally,

Senator Jesse Helms (R-NC) sponsored the Human Life Bill under the "enforce-ment" power of section 5 of the Fourteenth Amendment. The Bill would have defined life to begin at conception and would have restricted federal courts from denying life without due process of law, thus forcing the Court into a head-on confrontation with Congress over the issue of abortion.[46]

These proposals showed that resistance to the legal liberal use of modern judicial power was broader than originalist academic criticism. However, as in prior attempts, the fundamental separation of powers issues involved in using Article III, section 2 or section 5 of the Fourteenth Amendment prevented any consensus on the constitutional legitimacy or prudence of such action. One originalist observed that "every time the idea [of limiting the Court] comes up, tour busses full of law professors from Harvard and Yale Law Schools come down to tell Congress that the idea is unconstitutional—or, if not unconstitu-tional, at least contrary to the 'spirit' of the Constitution." Yet Senator Barry Goldwater (R-AZ) condemned use of the exceptions clause, while Raoul Berger insisted that, as originally understood, it conveyed a broad power to check the Court by regulating its jurisdiction.[47] Robert Bork opposed the Human Life Bill on the grounds that it would undermine a Supreme Court interpretation by mere statute. Bork also held, with many liberal scholars, that curtailment of federal jurisdiction through the exceptions clause could thrust numerous is-sues into state courts, possibly resulting in an unwieldy or even chaotic legal system. Likewise, the Justice Department under Attorney General William French Smith cited historical evidence from the founding era and the politi-cal theory of the Constitution to reject congressional curtailment of federal jurisdiction under the exceptions clause. The Department also echoed Bork's narrow view of the enforcement power—it did not permit Congress, by stat-ute, to trump the Court with its own view of what the Fourteenth Amendment allowed or required.[48]

None of the judicial reform proposals of the early 1980s became law. Al-though they unmistakably illustrated that the new conservative political cli-mate had fostered challenges to judicial power, failure to enact any of them yet again maintained the primacy of jurisprudential argument and judicial review as the venues in which constitutional change would occur. This resolution contributed to the further elaboration of originalism as the best way to contest legal liberalism and continued the interaction between originalist ideas and the Reagan Administration.

An important early site of such interaction was the Federalist Society, a group of conservative and libertarian law students and scholars founded in 1982 to combat what they regarded as the liberal domination of the legal academy.[49] The group held annual conferences, whose proceedings were reprinted in the *Harvard Journal of Law and Public Policy* and in which originalist attacks on legal liberalism were a prominent theme.[50] Charles Cooper, assistant attorney general for the Office of Legal Counsel, later recalled that the Federalist Society "was to the Reagan Administration a philosophical supporter and intellectual resource. . . . [It] supplied not only [intellectual] product and venues but personnel to an eager consumer." Indeed, a recent study has concluded that "membership quickly became a prerequisite for law students seeking clerkships with many Reagan judicial appointees as well as for employment in the upper ranks of the Justice Department and White House."[51]

The interaction of originalist ideas and the Reagan administration also occurred at the Center for Judicial Studies, an organization headed by James McClellan, a political scientist and lawyer who had been chief counsel to the Separation of Powers Subcommittee of the Senate Judiciary Committee during its consideration of some of the recent judicial reform proposals. The Center published *Benchmark*, a legal periodical dedicated to originalism that began in the autumn of 1983. McClellan and Gary McDowell, a political scientist who was associated with *Benchmark* and helped write Meese's speeches over the next few years, immediately rejected the recent spate of failed single-issue amendments. They viewed such maneuvers as ill-conceived, politically unfeasible, and capable of diminishing the necessary distinction between the Constitution and ordinary law. As originalists their view was that the problem lay not in the original Constitution; it did not need to be amended. Rather, the problem was the Supreme Court's recent ignorance or, at best, misinterpretation of the document's original intent. Moreover, McClellan explicitly rejected judicial supremacy, that is, the view that Court interpretations were the final authority on the meaning of the Constitution for other branches and government officials. He wrote that "amendments to our fundamental law to correct misinterpretations by the Supreme Court . . . tend to wink at judicial supremacy, and color the Court's usurpations with the tint of legitimacy." Like Berger, McClellan and McDowell advocated vigorous use of the exceptions clause and the enforcement power, provisions already in the Constitution, to constrain modern judicial power.[52]

McClellan thought that acceptance of judicial supremacy explained why some originalist critics, a majority in Congress, and the Justice Department failed to use the originally intended congressional power available in the exceptions clause or the enforcement power. On these grounds he also criticized Rex Lee, Reagan's first solicitor general. McClellan condemned as a half-measure Lee's *amicus* brief in support of local regulations of abortion in *City of Akron v. Akron Center for Reproductive Health* (1983). Lee's brief advocated judicial deference to the superior democratic legitimacy of legislative processes in this controversial area and warned of dangers to the separation of powers and self-government if the Court continued closely to censor legislative action. McClellan described this effort as a "slavish submission to prior rulings" that failed to attack the Court's reliance on the illegitimately derived privacy right undergirding legalized abortion. Nor was McClellan satisfied with Lee's performance in *Lynch v. Donnelly* (1984), in which Lee's *amicus* brief supported the inclusion of a Nativity scene in a municipally funded Christmas display as a constitutional accommodation of religion that did not violate the Court's First Amendment precedents. Following the recent *Marsh v. Chambers* (1983) decision, Lee argued that the Court should uphold the challenged practice in *Lynch* because accommodation of religion in public life was recognized in history and custom as well as in the purpose, understanding, and practice of the founders and subsequent generations under the First Amendment. McClellan lamented that Lee did not more strongly challenge the Court's "confused and inconsistent" precedents under the establishment and free exercise clauses or the doctrine of incorporation, by which the Court had long held that the Fourteenth Amendment applied the First Amendment (and subsequently nearly all of the Bill of Rights) to the states. McClellan remained dissatisfied even though the majority opinion in *Lynch* invoked extrinsic historical evidence and the "intent of the framers," as the Court had in *Marsh*, to uphold the Nativity scene as a constitutional accommodation of religion. Although the outcome of the case was laudable, prior erroneous interpretations of the First and Fourteenth Amendments "emerged unscathed to haunt future generations." In McClellan's view, Lee's arguments made it impossible "to know where the intent of the Framers ends and that of the Court begins, [which] establishes the Court as a permanent constitutional convention. . . . In short, Rex Lee is a judicial supremacist."[53]

Another notable First Amendment case further involved originalists at the Center for Judicial Studies in attacking modern judicial power. McClellan and Charles Rice, a law professor at Notre Dame, contributor to *Benchmark*, and originalist opponent of the school prayer decisions since the 1960s, became heavily involved in the litigation of *Wallace v. Jaffree* (1985). The case was an establishment clause challenge to an Alabama law that permitted a moment of silence at the beginning of the day in public schools for "meditation or voluntary prayer." Federal District Court Judge W. Brevard Hand upheld the law in an opinion resting primarily on originalist grounds. Hand held that the incorporation doctrine was illegitimate because it violated the original intent of both the founders and those who adopted the Fourteenth Amendment. He argued that the founders intended the establishment clause merely to prohibit imposition by the federal government of a particular sect; in his view it was intended to permit nondiscriminatory government encouragement of religion and left church-state interaction to state regulation. A footnote in Hand's opinion acknowledged McClellan's contribution, and the Center also filed an *amicus* brief in the Eleventh Circuit, which later overturned Hand.[54]

The Center for Judicial Studies submitted another *amicus* brief to the Supreme Court in *Jaffree,* reiterating the argument that incorporation was not intended by the drafters or understood to have been adopted by the ratifiers of the Fourteenth Amendment. It relied heavily on anti-incorporation evidence from the amendment's legislative history, ratification, and contemporary judicial interpretations, which previously had been recounted in the scholarship of Charles Fairman, Stanley Morrison, and Raoul Berger. Further, the brief emphasized the importance of the proposed Blaine amendment (first offered in Congress in 1875), which would have made the establishment clause a limit on the states and therefore tended to establish that this had not already been accomplished by the Fourteenth Amendment. Finally, the brief argued that, even if incorporation were conceded, the regime of nearly absolute church-state separation in the Court's establishment clause precedents conflicted with the far more limited manner in which historical actors had originally understood the clause.[55]

Justice John Paul Stevens's majority opinion in *Wallace v. Jaffree* held that the moment of silence law was an establishment of religion. He reaffirmed the incorporation doctrine and stated that it was far too firmly embedded in constitutional law to be abandoned. However, the originalist arguments did make an impression on the Court. Justice Byron White dissented briefly and called for a basic reconsideration of the Court's precedents in light of Justice Rehnquist's lengthy historical dissent. Rehnquist did not challenge the incorporation doctrine but insisted that the metaphor of a "wall of separation" between church and state that had guided the Court's religion clause jurisprudence since the 1940s was historically inaccurate as a description of the original intent of the founders. He wrote that the "greatest injury of the 'wall' notion is its mischievous diversion of judges from the actual intentions of the Bill of Rights." Accordingly, the Court's doctrinal tests and resulting precedents in the religion clause cases were "in no way based on either the language or intent of the drafters." Rather, like the Hand opinion and the *amicus* brief of the Center for Judicial Studies, Rehnquist urged that "the true meaning of the Establishment Clause can only be seen in its history. As the drafters of our Bill of Rights the Framers inscribed the principles that control today. Any deviation from their intentions frustrates the permanence of that charter and will only lead to the type of unprincipled decision making that has plagued our Establishment Clause cases since [the 1940s]." Rehnquist's reading of the history convinced him that the establishment clause was intended merely to prohibit a national church or "governmental preference of one religious sect over another" but did not require "neutrality on the part of government between religion and irreligion."[56]

Originalist argument in the First Amendment cases established the context for the Reagan administration's challenge to *Roe v. Wade* (1973), one of the most hallowed recent accomplishments of legal liberalism. In July 1985 Charles Fried, Reagan's second solicitor general, submitted an *amicus* brief asking the Court to overturn *Roe*. Fried argued that *Roe*'s intricate strictures had "no moorings in the text of our Constitution[,] in familiar constitutional doctrine," or in "the historical facts" Justice Harry Blackmun had attempted to adduce in support of the holding. Fried added that *Roe* had grave difficulty satisfying appeals to the two major sources of the Court's legitimacy, the "framers' intention as revealed by history, or, failing sufficient help from history, by the interpretive tradition of the legal community." Fried therefore cautioned that "the further afield interpretation travels from its point of departure in the text, the greater the danger that constitutional adjudication will be like a picnic to which the framers bring the words and the judges the meaning."[57]

Roe was not overturned, but the very attempt, as well as the Fried brief, evinced a palpable shift in the constitutional atmosphere, as had the originalist arguments in the briefs and opinions in some of the recent First Amendment cases. A full analysis of Burger Court decisions during Reagan's presidency cannot be undertaken here, but some developments in other areas also suggested that the Court was according more attention not only to history, but also to the constitutional text and structure, and more generally to the limits of judicial power.[58] Of course the Court did not simply "follow the election returns," but if "legal liberalism" remained an accurate description of many decisions in the 1970s, the same could not be said of the 1980s.[59]

The separation of powers, a feature of the American constitutional system that originalists had been attempting to reinvigorate for some time, was another area in which the more formalist jurisprudential ideas associated with their approach were gaining traction. For example, in *Valley Forge Christian College v. Americans United* (1982), a group of taxpayers made an establishment clause challenge to the federal practice of transferring surplus property to church-related schools, but the Court reinvigorated the doctrine of standing as a key component of the separation of powers. The doctrine had been a critical component of the judicial restraint orientation of process jurisprudence until the Warren Court severely undercut it in *Flast v. Cohen* (1968). In *Valley Forge* Justice Rehnquist held that taxpayers had not demonstrated the potential for a concrete injury and therefore had no standing to invoke the Court's jurisdiction. Rehnquist trenchantly insisted that "federal courts were simply not constituted as ombudsmen of the general welfare." Also in the separation of powers area was *INS v. Chada* (1983). This decision overturned the legislative veto, which had become a major means of controlling the legislative power Congress delegated to the federal bureaucracy, even though such vetoes were not presented to the president for approval. In *Chada* the Court invalidated Congress's overruling of an executive agency decision via the veto. In a close analysis of the constitutional text, the Court held that the veto violated the separation of powers because it did not meet the requirement of Article I, Section 7 that all legislation be presented to the president for his signature.[60]

The opinions in these cases demonstrated concern with the separation of powers as an originally intended feature of the Constitution, even though they relied on textual and structural reasoning instead of the extrinsic historical evidence often invoked in recent originalist arguments. Additionally, although it was not entirely clear that *Chada* vindicated the originalist defense of the separation of powers so much as the modern Court's view of itself as the final arbiter of the Constitution, in early 1987 originalists in the Justice Department noted it, along with Rehnquist's dissent in *Jaffree* and Burger's opinion in *Marsh,* as praiseworthy recent examples of "interpretivism."[61] Bruce Fein, a conservative constitutional commentator earlier employed in the Reagan administration, concluded that such recent Court decisions might fore-cast a return to properly limited judicial power. He observed in *Benchmark* that the 1983–84 term of the Court marked a "decisive swing towards principles of judicial restraint . . . [and] deferen[ce] to the policies forged by representative institutions."[62]

Decisions in other areas that had attracted originalist criticism also seemed to evince a similar tendency. In *Firefighters v. Stotts* (1984) the Court overruled a lower court injunction, issued under Title VII of the Civil Rights Act of 1964, that had allowed an employer to make layoffs on the basis of race without first having established that retained individuals actually were the victims of discrimination. *Stotts* thus suggested an end to the Court's emphasis on nu-merical quotas in affirmative action. The Reagan administration had urged this position in lower federal courts and also submitted an *amicus* brief in July 1985 in *Wygant v. Jackson* (1986), a seniority case that argued that quota-based affirmative action violated the "colorblind" original intent of the equal pro-tection clause of the Fourteenth Amendment.[63] In *United States v. Leon* (1984) the Court recognized a "good faith" exception to the exclusionary rule, declar-ing that evidence collected under a search warrant reasonably thought valid but later proven faulty did not violate the rule and therefore was admissible at trial. It is notable that the liberal Justices Thurgood Marshall and Brennan, along with Blackmun, dissented in these cases. Still, the Court's affirmative action decisions were limited to the seniority context, and in subsequent de-cisions it demonstrated a majority in favor of affirmative action in most other contexts. Likewise, as a commentator in *Benchmark* observed, at least in the area of criminal procedure, the expansive legal liberal jurisprudential method that had created the exclusionary rule in the 1960s remained unaffected.[64]

The Attorney General Advocates Originalism

Notwithstanding the clear shift in the constitutional atmosphere evident in the early 1980s and the attraction of originalist and structuralist arguments for some justices, originalism did not roll back modern judicial power or the legal liberal precedents of the Warren and early Burger Courts. The Court, sup-ported by legal academics, retained the discretion inherent in the typically modern balancing of abstract, ahistorical concepts with its own view of con-temporary interests.[65] Relatively few academic commentators identified themselves as originalists, the incorporation doctrine and the right of privacy were as secure as ever, and there certainly was no originalist majority on the Supreme Court. This situation contributed to a conviction among conservative activists that the intellectual structure of modern constitutional jurisprudence had to be confronted in a more direct and public manner.[66] Accordingly, in 1985 and 1986 members of the administration, led by Attorney General Edwin Meese III, undertook a public campaign to present originalism as an alternative to modern judicial power and liberal reform through the courts.

Meese was advised by scholars associated with *Benchmark* and other conservative organizations. In a series of speeches beginning in July 1985 he forcefully articulated the established originalist appeals to majoritarianism and the need to limit judicial discretion. Reflecting on the recently completed term of the Court, Meese lamented the expansion of the commerce clause at the expense of the Tenth Amendment in *Garcia v. San Antonio Metropolitan Transit Authority* (1985) but lauded the criminal procedure decisions and Rehnquist's originalist rejection of the "wall of separation" metaphor in *Jaffree.* He went further than Rehnquist, suggesting that the incorporation doctrine was "intellectually shaky." In an equally fundamental way Meese criticized the discretionary interpretive method of modern judicial review, saying that the Court was "unpredictable" and had a "jurisprudence of idiosyncrasy" that yielded "more policy choices than articulations of constitutional principle." Seeking a more "coherent jurisprudential stance," Meese emphasized that the Reagan administration would continue to "resurrect the original meaning of constitutional provisions and statutes as the only reliable guide for judgment." He termed this a "jurisprudence of original intention" and later added that "original intent" could be found in "the text of the Constitution as illuminated by those who drafted, proposed, and ratified it."[67] Moreover, in these and subsequent speeches he frequently quoted Madison, Jefferson, and Joseph Story to the effect that limited government depended on constraining the meaning of legal and constitutional language.

Meese elaborated and reiterated other originalist themes, rejecting the legal liberal view that "judges [had] a special rationality to discover and apply hidden values." Likewise, he disapproved of the focus in numerous modern cases on the "determination of moral values or a [reformist] political and social program." Instead, he hewed to the originalist insistence that the Constitution was a "limitation on judicial power as well as executive and legislative." Originalism called on a "deeply rooted commitment to the idea of democracy," which was offended if "courts were allow[ed] to govern simply by what [they view] at the time as fair and decent." Modern judicial approaches not clearly anchored in the Constitution endangered the "rule of law" because they invited judgment based on "personal whim" rather than fixed and previously known principles.[68]

In place of the uncertainties of modern jurisprudence, Meese emphasized the majoritarian, process-oriented thrust of originalism, which was necessary because the Constitution contained "very little in the way of specific political solutions." Originalism aimed to depoliticize constitutional adjudication by defending the legitimate "process" for dealing with most new issues—that of majoritarian politics, which, according to the design of the Constitution, "was responsible for adapting and vivifying its principles in each generation." Indeed, Meese tellingly demonstrated the connection between the goals of originalism and the majoritarianism of post–World War II process-restraint jurisprudence by quoting Frankfurter's dissent in *Baker v. Carr* (1962): "There is not under our Constitution a judicial remedy for every political mischief, for every undesirable exercise of legislative power. The Framers carefully and with deliberate forethought refused to enthrone the judiciary."[69]

Just as Meese quoted Frankfurter to defend majoritarianism, he also invoked Hugo Black's originalist dissent in *Griswold v. Connecticut* (1965) to condemn the judicial creation of the right to privacy. This demonstrated the characteristic originalist attraction to Frankfurterian, process-based judicial deference to legislatures and Black's rigorous textualism and reliance on extrinsic evidence of original intent. Tying the implication of this synthesis to present circumstances, Meese amplified solicitor general Charles Fried's contemporaneous brief calling for the abandonment of *Roe*. Meese echoed Black's logic in *Griswold*, and unlike Fried he explicitly condemned the manner in which Justice Douglas had created the right to privacy in that case. He added, as Black said of *Griswold*, that in *Roe* the Court had illegitimately usurped state regulation of an area not conveyed by the Constitution to the federal government.[70]

After making it clear that *Roe* was an originalist target, Meese stepped back, arguing that originalism nonetheless could accommodate two of the major constitutional changes of the twentieth century. He said that the vast expansion of federal regulatory power under the commerce clause decisions of the New Deal era properly restored policymaking primacy to Congress. Likewise,

Meese said that *Brown* corrected the judicial error of *Plessy v. Ferguson* (1896) by restoring the proper "colorblind" original intent of the Fourteenth Amendment.[71] Although these historical claims could be disputed, this presentation made it more difficult simply to equate originalism with economic substantive due process or racial segregation.

In another important speech in October 1986, Meese targeted judicial supremacy. He forthrightly insisted on a "necessary distinction between the Constitution and constitutional law," which meant that Supreme Court opinions did "not establish a supreme law of the land that is binding on all persons and parts of government henceforth and forevermore." Adverting to the refusal of Presidents Jackson, Lincoln, and Roosevelt to consider themselves bound by judicial interpretations they thought incorrect, Meese challenged the common acceptance of judicial supremacy by raising the long dormant idea of coordinate or departmental review, in which each branch of government has a duty to interpret the Constitution in the performance of its official duties. He criticized the Court's dictum (but not the holding) in *Cooper v. Aaron* (1958), which stood as the clearest statement of modern judicial supremacy. *Cooper* compelled desegregation of a public school in Little Rock, Arkansas, and stated that judicial opinions were the "supreme law of the land." Following the suggestion of others before him, Meese regarded this as an elision of any distinction between judicial interpretation and the Constitution itself. He condemned this way of thinking about judicial review because it truncated criticism of the Court and improperly aggrandized its power, therefore threatening limited government and the rule of law.[72]

Meese's speeches were national news and aroused a host of commentary in both the popular press and scholarly journals.[73] Justice Stevens responded to Meese, as did Justice Brennan in his defense of the living Constitution (analyzed above), which in turn prompted a strong originalist critique by William Bradford Reynolds, the assistant attorney general for civil rights. While conceding the relevance of the "original intent of the Framers" and the necessity of trying "to read their words in the context of the beliefs that were widely held in the Eighteenth Century," Stevens noted the difficulty of this task and the importance of settled practice under the Constitution as a guide to its meaning. He also rejected Meese's criticism of the incorporation doctrine on the grounds that the Fourteenth Amendment profoundly altered the federal system—itself a claim about original intent.[74]

Meese, Reynolds, Stevens, and Brennan thus articulated positions that by the mid–1980s represented the deeply opposed understandings of constitutional interpretation and the role of the Court developed by originalists and legal liberals. Likewise, their exchanges, especially in the context of the administration's stance in recent controversial litigation, constituted the most direct constitutional debate between the executive branch and the Court since the New Deal. Meese, along with his colleagues and defenders, clearly understood originalism as a way to limit the reach of constitutional adjudication and as a defense of the rule of law. To them originalism could limit government by defending majoritarian decision-making from untrammeled judicial interpretive discretion and the creation of new, nontextual constitutional rights. They hoped that originalism would restore the resolution of contentious public issues, as well as more of the process of constitutional change, to legislatures or the amendment process.[75] However, Brennan and several legal liberals charged originalists with subverting the rule of law and taking the novel step of politicizing constitutional adjudication.[76] This was primarily because Meese criticized the notion of judicial supremacy articulated in *Cooper,* which had occurred in the context of race and thus could be portrayed as a threat to a core accomplishment of legal liberalism.

However, other opponents of originalism realized that Meese had indeed raised basic issues about judicial review and the constitutional system that resisted blithe dismissal or inflammatory misrepresentation. Mark Tushnet, for example, pointed out that Meese reopened the fundamental issue of how to maintain the distinction between law and politics in the practice of judicial review. Meese, said Tushnet, had "struck a chord" because he directed attention to "our fear that judges, like other government officials, can do us serious harm. The dilemma is that Justice Brennan's confident liberalism, though it recognizes that government and judges can do good, fails to express our concern that they do evil as well." Sanford Levinson found it ironic "that those associated with the left are so quick to denounce Meese's speech, for that denunciation further legitimizes government by legally trained elites, speaking an ever more esoteric language. [This revealed] a profound fear of the public in whose name the left pretends to speak."[77]

Meese and the responses he engendered put before a wider audience the fundamental constitutional issues raised in the academic debate about originalism. This made the phrase "original intent" more common in academic and political discourse, although to some extent it had always been part of the American constitutional lexicon. Critics seized on the recently publicized term *intent* to dismiss originalism as simpleminded and unworkable, frequently pointing out the difficulty of discerning the aggregated individual intentions of legislators or members of a ratifying convention. These critiques often yielded a confident dismissal of the originalist idea as "judicial autopsies on the framers' minds" or "a position [that] would keep the Constitution in a powdered wig and knee breeches."[78] To some extent the term *intent* invited the familiar assumption that originalism required knowledge of the subjective, in-dividuated mental state of those who wrote and ratified the Constitution and its amendments or the canard that originalists despised change.

Originalists responded tactically by de-emphasizing the term *intent,* though of course not the jurisprudential approach associated with it. Clarifying the position they had taken in the law review literature, originalists reiterated that their method did not depend on evidence of the subjective intent of a particu-lar drafter or ratifier, although such evidence could shed light on the publicly understood meaning of constitutional terms that had been formally ratified and made legally binding. Despite the profusion and overlap in terms, origi-nalists did attempt to avoid the closed-minded rigidity liberals associated with "intent" by suggesting that the terms "original understanding" or "original meaning" better described their position.[79] As the debate over originalism con-tinued, scholars often used interchangeably the terms "original intent," "origi-nal understanding," and "originalism" to refer to what, by the mid–1980s, was a readily identifiable set of responses to modern judicial power.[80]

Whatever appellation they chose, originalists generally agreed that extrin-sic evidence of the public positions of the drafters and ratifiers could be con-sulted to illuminate the meaning of language in the text and that the limits imposed on judges by the constitutional structures of federalism and the sepa-ration of powers should be observed. As Meese stated, "Where the language of the Constitution is specific, it must be obeyed. Where there is a demonstrable consensus among the framers and ratifiers as to a principle stated or implied by the Constitution, is should be followed. Where there is ambiguity as to the precise meaning or reach of a constitutional provision, it should be interpreted and applied in a manner so as to at least not contradict the text of the Consti-tution itself."[81]

Meese thus underscored that the basic goal of originalism was to constrain judicial power and encourage adherence to the written Constitution as law, re-gardless of tangential concerns about nomenclature or the long-recognized inevitability of judgment in the face of ambiguity. Any legitimate theory of the judicial function in a constitutional republic must recognize that the power of judges should be limited by the meaning of the text they claim to be interpreting. Originalists continued to insist that despite the challenges of their own approach and lacunae in the historical record, they at least were attempting to recognize limits on the Court—non-originalist theories, on the other hand, demanded obedience to the Court while encouraging it to take on even more power and discretion.

Originalism was widely discussed by constitutional theorists and the broader public in the 1980s, and it was clear that the interaction of originalist academic criticism and a renewed conservative politics had altered American constitutional debate.[82] As we have seen, it also was beginning to influence some arguments put to the Supreme Court and even a few of the opinions the justices wrote. Legal liberals increasingly were compelled to grapple with originalism, and for all of their attempts to dismiss it, they could not.

The changed legal-political climate was strikingly underscored in *Bowers v. Hardwick* (1986), one of the most publicized decisions of the decade. Justice White's majority opinion refused to include sodomy in the right to privacy, thus letting stand a Georgia statute. White, who dissented vigorously in *Roe* when the Court included abortion in the right, wrote that "the Court is most vulnerable and comes nearest to illegitimacy when it deals with judge-made constitutional law having little or no cognizable roots in the language or design of the Constitution." He placed the Court's current situation in the context of the constitutional crisis of the 1930s and stated that if the institution continually redefined "the category of rights deemed to be fundamental," it could again take "to itself further authority to govern the country without express constitutional authority."[83] Like most of the other decisions in the 1980s in which the Court declined to advance legal liberalism, *Bowers* was based on textual and structural arguments rather than extrinsic historical evidence. But while not cast directly in more readily identifiable originalist terms, the ruling in *Bowers* too was concerned with maintaining limits on the judiciary and marked the outer limit of both the judicially created right to privacy and legal liberalism. The decision thereby reflected the changed constitutional climate that originalism had helped create. Moreover, *Bowers* also served notice to legal liberals and interest groups about the likely trend of decisions if President Reagan were to make successive appointments to the Supreme Court. In late 1986 William Rehnquist was elevated to chief justice, and Antonin Scalia was confirmed as an associate justice. Both men had defended originalism. Another Reagan appointment would likely secure a center-right majority. So the stage was set for a major battle, which duly began in July 1987, soon after President Reagan nominated Robert H. Bork, the most prominent of original-ists, to replace Justice Lewis Powell.

CHAPTER 7

Robert Bork and the Trial of Originalism

President Ronald Reagan's nomination of Robert H. Bork to the U.S. Supreme Court in June 1987 produced a political battle that gripped the nation for most of the summer. The nomination was a crucial public test of originalism as an approach to constitutional interpretation and as a component of the conservative political renaissance. In the heat of the battle it sometimes appeared as if originalism was nothing more than Reagan-era conservatism or that Bork's defense of it was made for the moment. In fact, Bork had been defending the traditional legal ideas associated with originalism since the crossroads of American constitutional theory and politics that defined the late 1960s. Bork was perceived to be such a threat to legal liberalism that the jurisprudential issues involved in his confrontation with it were largely obscured and distorted in the nomination hearings. After losing the Senate vote on his nomination, Bork sought to present a clearer and more positive picture of originalism than was possible in the summer of 1987.

From Antitrust to Originalism

Bork first made his academic reputation in the field of antitrust law as part of the law and economics movement at the University of Chicago, a movement that was itself an important component of twentieth-century legal thought.[1] While there is no simple equivalence between the statutory context of Bork's quasi-originalist antitrust scholarship and his later constitutional originalism, they were motivated by similar concerns. The work culminating in his book *The Antitrust Paradox* (1978) was focused on economics, but to a lesser extent it was about the separation of powers, the rule of law, and legislative history as evidence of original intent.[2] Consulting the legislative history of the Sherman Antitrust Act (1890), Bork argued that it originally intended courts to use evolving economic knowledge to safeguard consumer welfare by ensuring competitive markets. Influenced by neoclassical economics at Chicago, Bork argued that the concept of consumer welfare required economy-wide efficiency in the allocation of resources. To this end, the pursuit of efficiency by a firm ("business efficiency") might decrease the number of firms in a given market to a few, while in terms of the entire economy this state of affairs could contribute to efficient resource allocation. On this basis Bork criticized existing antitrust law as reliant on inaccurate economics, inconsistent with the original intent of the Sherman Act, and protective of inefficient firms that charged high prices. Bork did not offer originalist analysis as the key to interpreting the Sherman Act; the historical argument was subservient to the economic one. He merely held that the notion of consumer welfare was at least consistent with the evidence of original meaning that he referenced. Bork's position gradually influenced courts and enforcement agencies to allow industries more flexibility in mergers and acquisitions and to allow firms more flexibility in the management of distribution agreements. Bork was cited in Supreme Court and lower court opinions, with leading judges and academics accepting that consumer welfare was the original intent of the Sherman Act, although not necessarily agreeing that it included business efficiency as Bork and the Chicago School understood it.[3] Although Bork's consumer welfare interpretation of the Sherman Act remains disputed, it helped redefine the field by offering a legal standard that, in contrast to the system it confronted, was stable, administrable, and more consistent with the constitutional separation of powers.[4]

After attempting to limit and legitimate antitrust, Bork turned his attention to the issues generated by the political and constitutional crossroads of the late 1960s. He had watched as the process-restraint approach defended by Alexander M. Bickel, his Yale faculty colleague and close personal friend, failed to forestall or constrain legal liberalism. At this crossroads Bickel argued more urgently that the Supreme Court was endangering its legitimacy by attempting to resolve issues better left to other venues. More fundamentally, Bickel thought that the liberal contractarian basis of American constitutionalism might be incapable of generating the required limits on the law and the Court. He therefore ceased further technical refinement of the process-restraint approach and turned to Burkean conservatism.[5] At the same crossroads Bork similarly diagnosed the challenges facing the Court and legal theory, and this period sheds some new light on how and why Bork began to develop originalism as a solution to the problems highlighted but inadequately resolved by process jurisprudence.

One of Bork's important early efforts was "We Suddenly Feel That Law Is Vulnerable," an article that has recently gone little noticed, even though Bickel described it in 1972 as "much discussed" when recommending Bork to Attorney General Richard G. Kleindienst for a seat on the Court of Appeals for the Second Circuit.[6] In it Bork warned that law was "claiming an omnicompetence it cannot sustain."[7] Law was now more pervasive and politicized—but simultaneously less respected and therefore less effective. Bork analyzed this development in numerous aspects of American life, but he reserved his greatest criticism for the Warren Court. It had been undermining "the most fundamental theory of representative democracy" by encouraging "litigation as a shortcut to the achievement of desired political and social ends" and dispensing with the "time-consuming, expensive, and messy process of persuading voters or legislators." The Court compounded this error by too often issuing unpersuasive opinions on controversial issues (even though Bork agreed with "many" of the results it reached). Although "the Warren Court majority pleaded that it was merely applying the Constitution, that pretense fooled fewer and fewer people."[8] In sum, the Court was undermining the rule of law when it was already under enough strain from other quarters. If this development went too far, "disrespect for the Supreme Court may easily become disdain for what the Court symbolizes, the ideal of government by law rather than by whim, prejudice, or raw power."[9]

Because overreliance on law and adjudication endangered not only their legitimacy but also government by consent and social stability, Bork consciously set out to provide a new theory for limiting the Court in the post–legal realist, post–Warren Court era. During the 1968–69 academic year he was on sabbatical and corresponded with Bickel regarding their "Proposal for an Institute of Legal Theory."[10] Although it never materialized, the memorandum they circulated to potential university sponsors revealed the general solution to the problems each had identified. "Law has not evolved a theory and a discipline of its own. . . . Without [normative models of judicial behavior] criticism tends to become ad hoc, subjective, and essentially trivial. The creation of such models would be one of our basic tasks."[11]

Bork elaborated this view and suggested a solution (analyzed below) in his "first venture in print into the rarefied atmosphere of the higher criticism of constitutional law."[12] He solicited Bickel's advice, wishing to avoid merely unconstructive naysaying. Bickel commented on Bork's first draft, cautioning him that he might not have succeeded and suggesting that Bork state his theory more tentatively and conclude by writing "that beyond judicial restraint, the problem with judicial review is to work out acceptable sources of constitutional law, that this is not only an unsolved but neglected problem, and that we ought to get on with it."[13] Bork's published essay concluded that after the Warren Court's experiment in elaborating legal realism, theorists should now "move on to new formulations of the Court's powers and responsibilities."[14] Three years later Bork described the task more starkly, writing that "a persistently disturbing aspect of constitutional law is its lack of theory."[15] Consequently, "law must become more self-conscious if it is to meet the challenges that are being put to it." Lawyers should "begin to create the body of theory that their profession so desperately requires."[16]

Bork's first theoretical venture was not originalism, but his initial experiment with ways to limit and legitimate judicial review reflected the same concerns evident in his earlier antitrust scholarship and his later originalism. He began by recognizing that the jurisprudential problems sharpened by the Warren Court, and the concomitant need for theory, were rooted in the legal realist attack on the formalism associated with the traditional sources of constitutional law in text, history, and precedent. Although these sources could "sometimes dictate results," more often they were "equivocal oracles."[17] However, Bork insisted that the appropriate "place of the judiciary in a democratic society" forbade judges who confronted this problem of indeterminacy from simply voting their preferences into law, as some realists had recommended and as Bork thought the Warren Court had done too often.[18]

While noting the attempted theoretical resolution associated with Bickel, and thus the process-restraint tradition, Bork devoted more attention to a second theoretical alternative, which he called "legitimate activism."[19] It was based on the American tradition of natural rights and had the potential to stand as an objective standard for thwarting the will of the majority. Although it seems strange in retrospect, *Griswold v. Connecticut* (1965) inspired this initial theory.[20] Despite Justice Douglas's derivation of the right to privacy in a "shallow, murky, and rhetorical" majority opinion, Bork was impressed by its general approach, by the concept of privacy, and even by the use of the Ninth Amendment in Justice Arthur Goldberg's concurrence. Based on the analogical reasoning familiar to the common law, judges could "construct new principles that explain existing constitutional rights and extrapolate from them to define new natural rights."[21] Here Bork was advocating neither the moral philosophizing which came to typify much of legal liberalism nor a more limited but still direct judicial engagement with the natural rights doctrine of the founding. Rather, he was attempting to give judges an essentially legal positivist starting point in the text of the Constitution from which they could adjudicate in a more formalist style than had the Warren Court. Starting from the first eight amendments as examples of a general set of natural rights, "the judge need not ask whether these provisions are wise or universally valid, whether they rest on religion, morality, or principles of some ultimate philosophy." They were "the givens of the system he is commissioned to operate. He is thus enabled to take as his starting point values that are exterior to himself."[22] Bork hoped that from this point the traditional process-style norms of legal reasoning would discipline the judicial derivation of new rights and that, as in the process tradition, judges would defer to legislative decision-making when dubious of their own authority. Such a theory could meet "the public expectation that the Supreme Court derives its results objectively from the Constitution through some standard process of legal reasoning" and thus it could meet the process-restraint tradition's plea for "'neutral principles' of constitutional law."[23]

Not long after exploring the theoretical potential of *Griswold*, Bork explicitly abandoned the effort as doomed to failure.[24] He offered instead "Neutral Principles and Some First Amendment Problems," a seminal statement of originalism that would become one of the most famous and most cited law review articles ever written.[25] In attempting to clear the way for originalism, Bork now skewered *Griswold* as illustrative of the Warren Court's too frequent dismissal of legislative judgment. In generating a right of privacy from the "penumbras" and "emanations" of the Bill of Rights, Douglas had reasoned loosely, strained the text, and ignored history in order to perform a "miracle of transubstantiation." This method was so undisciplined that "we are left with no idea of the sweep of the right of privacy and hence no notion of the cases to which it may or may not be applied in the future." Like others before and after him, Bork concluded that in *Griswold* the Court had revived the pre–New Deal substantive due process era by commanding, "without guidance from the Constitution, which liberties or gratifications may be infringed by minorities and which may not."[26]

Now Bork not only rejected the *Griswold* route, he also more directly criticized the process-restraint tradition, which he thought had failed to constrain the Court and exhausted itself in the attempt. Observing Bickel's recent conclusion that Frankfurter had never found a "rigorous general accord between judicial supremacy and democratic theory,"[27] Bork judged that heretofore commentators in Bickel's tradition had "had no better luck than the Justice."[28] Of course, Bork also rejected the other emerging theoretical alternative, some form of legal liberalism, because it obscured this fundamental question: "How free is the Court to choose values that will override the values chosen by elected representatives?"[29] A new theory might provide an answer.

Bork introduced the new theory of originalism with a point that was fundamental but recently had been too often overlooked: in the American constitutional system the Court's legitimacy depended upon judicial opinions able to persuade citizens of their basis in the Constitution.[30] Legal liberalism was illegitimate because it encouraged the Court to pursue its own political agenda, while Bickel's process-restraint tradition had not "carried the idea of neutrality far enough."[31] The latter had focused on legal reasoning without adequately considering the legitimate sources of constitutional law, and it was with this point that Bork distinguished the originalist idea. Observing Wechsler's criticism of *Brown* as a result-driven opinion lacking an adequately neutral principle, Bork insisted that the idea of "neutrality" had to be extended beyond the "process of reasoning." The time had come to return more systematically to the original meaning of the Constitution as the source of law and the object of interpretation. "If judges are to avoid imposing their own values on the rest of us," he wrote, "they must be neutral as well in the *definition* and the *derivation* of principles," adding that "the judge's power to govern does not become more legitimate if he is constrained to apply his principle to all cases but is free to make up his own principles." Instead, adjudication should be based on "the text and the history, and their fair implications." With these words Bork concisely stated the core originalist proposition. Immediately he juxtaposed it with a legal liberal Court that "construct[ed] new rights" or itself chose "'fundamental values.'" Bork also emphasized the positivism of the originalist approach by arguing that "where constitutional materials do not clearly specify the value to be preferred, there is no principled way to prefer any claimed human value to any other."[32] Finally, Bork made it clear that originalism aimed to contain judicial discretion better than alternative theories by encouraging a more formalist method of adjudication than had been seen since the advent of legal realism. Thus, he "insist[ed] at the outset that constitutional law, viewed as the set of rules a judge may properly derive from the document and its history, is not an expression of our political sympathies or of our judgments about what expedience and prudence require."[33]

Like Raoul Berger, Bork aimed originalism at the heart of legal liberalism by arguing that the equal protection clause of the Fourteenth Amendment had frequently been expanded beyond its original meaning. It was originally intended to apply only to situations involving race, and thereby "to enforce a core idea of black equality against governmental discrimination." However, Bork was careful to attempt an originalist justification for *Brown*: even if the framers and ratifiers of the Fourteenth Amendment intended both legal equality and racial segregation, once it was clear that equality could not be achieved with segregation, the text of the equal protection clause trumped any nontextual assumption that it could. In this way vindication of the original intent to establish legal equality, which was written into the text, required abandoning segregation, which was not. Even though the framers thought segregation would be unaffected, it had not been written into the text, thus *Brown* should stand.[34] Nevertheless, Bork continued, the general words of the Amendment "surely . . . would not permit us to escape the framers' intent if it were clear. If the legislative history revealed a consensus about segregation in schooling and all the other relations in life, I do not see how the Court could escape the choices revealed and substitute its own, even though the words are general and conditions have changed." Moreover, he argued that when the Court moved beyond race it had "no principled way of saying which non-racial inequalities are impermissible. What is done, therefore, is to appeal to simplistic notions of 'fairness' or to what it regards as 'fundamental' interests."[35] Emphasizing the majoritarian thrust of his originalism, Bork insisted that "courts must accept any value choice the legislature makes unless it clearly runs contrary to a choice made in the framing of the Constitution."[36]

Bork offered originalism because the process-restraint tradition had not forestalled legal liberalism, but at the same time he was defending the process concern with democratic legitimacy, proceduralism, and neutrality in legal reasoning.[37] But Bork's originalism was more overtly positivist and formalist than the process-restraint tradition, because he thought this approach could better limit the discretion and imprecision of legal liberalism and thereby yield a wider scope for legislative decision-making. As suggested by the strong historical, textualist, and majoritarian elements in Bork's thought, his originalism also retained the skepticism typical of the older process approach. In this way Bork embodied a historic transformation in the intellectual underpinnings of the opposed camps in American constitutional theory. He rejected legal liberalism as the judicial injection of views, whether morally relativist or realist, that came from outside the Constitution—just as Progressives and legal realists had similarly rejected the old Court's injection of a nontextual right to liberty of contract into the Constitution. When post–Warren Court liberals encouraged judicial vindication of "rights" or "values" not in the text of the Constitution as originally understood, Bork revived legal positivism and formalism, not the American natural rights idiom or any other form of moral realism that might generate a more limited form of judicial review.[38] Indeed, Bork attempted to close the judicial door on moral discourse once and for all, insisting that "where the Constitution does not embody the moral or ethical choice, the judge has no basis other than his own values upon which to set aside the community judgment embodied in the statute [under review]. That, by definition, is an inadequate basis for judicial supremacy."[39]

Raising the Public Profile of Originalism

Bork's pathbreaking article outlined the core components of the originalism he defended before, during, and after his nomination to the Supreme Court. In the last chapter we saw how he carried forward its arguments in the academic debates of the 1980s. He did so primarily by criticizing legal liberal theorists for raising the terms of the Constitution to levels of generality that obscured any distinction between what it did or did not contain, which permitted them to advance their preferred moral or political theories under the guise of constitutional interpretation. At the same time that Bork attacked legal liberal academics in this way, he also attempted to bring his understanding of originalism to wider attention in high-profile speeches. These efforts also more explicitly and confrontationally opposed originalism to the egalitarianism and moral relativism Bork saw in legal liberalism.[40]

Wider publicity of the intellectual struggle in constitutional law was required because its complexity and abstraction made it remote from the general public and most policymakers, despite its very real consequences for political life.[41] Reiterating his earlier diagnosis to his wider audience, Bork argued that this situation had occurred because "the law possesses very little theory about itself." This made it "vulnerable to the winds of intellectual or moral fashion." The permeability resulting from the law's lack of theoretical self-consciousness subjected it to the egalitarianism and moral relativism typical of modern American culture. Legal liberal theorists brought these tendencies into constitutional law by substituting "abstractions of moral philosophy" for the original Constitution, thus encouraging judges to set aside legislation embodying the "common sense of the community"—its own moral and aesthetic judgments.[42]

Originalism could serve the moral traditionalism found more often in statutes than in Supreme Court decisions because it provided a way for law to resist "influences that should properly remain outside." So Bork again declared, "Now we need theory." Originalism, understood as "the proposition that the framers' intentions with respect to freedoms are the sole legitimate premise from which constitutional analysis may proceed," could defeat "the theorists of moral abstraction." Originalism could accomplish this because it clearly distinguished what was actually in the Constitution as a source of law from theories or values not found there. While legal liberal judges would, without basis in the Constitution, redraw the line between individual and community in a far more relativist, permissive, and egalitarian fashion, originalists recognized that "in a constitutional democracy the moral content of the law must be given by the morality of the framer or legislator, never by the morality of the judge."[43]

Bork put theory into practice once he joined the District of Columbia Circuit Court of Appeals in 1982. For example, in a dissent in *Barnes v. Kline* (1985) he argued that a grant of standing to members of Congress to sue the executive branch would undermine the separation of powers and accrue a general supervisory role to the judiciary that it was never intended to have. He supported this argument by examining the records of the Philadelphia con-

vention of 1787, as well as Supreme Court precedents and the likely consequences of such a grant of standing.[44] In *Dronenberg v. Zech* (1984) Bork wrote
for a unanimous three-judge panel and refused to extend the right of privacy
to prevent the honorable discharge of a naval petty officer for consensual homosexual conduct. He wrote that Supreme Court opinions in the privacy field
provided "no explanatory principle that informs a lower court how to reason
about what is and what is not encompassed by the right." Accordingly, deference to legislative policymaking was a part of the proper relationship between
the branches in the area of unenumerated rights: "If the revolution in sexual
mores that the appellant proclaims is in fact ever to arrive, we think it must
arrive through the moral choices of the people and their elected representatives, not through the ukase of this court." Underscoring the majoritarian
point, he concluded: "When the Constitution does not speak to the contrary,
the choices of those put in authority by the electoral process, or those who are
accountable to such persons, come before us not as suspect because majoritarian but as conclusively valid for that very reason."[45]

Context and Strategy in the Bork Nomination

When President Reagan nominated Bork to the Supreme Court in 1987,
it was clear that the originalist theorist was also a reliable originalist publi-
cist and judge. The issues at stake in his possible elevation were the familiar
ones that had developed over recent decades in academic debate and constitutional politics, as well as in Bork's own thought. They were present in the
Senate hearings on Bork's nomination, but more often they were obscured by
a highly partisan and sometimes sensational atmosphere.

This controversy was somewhat surprising, given that Bork had been confirmed unanimously for his Circuit Court judgeship. Moreover, in September
1986 the Senate unanimously confirmed Antonin Scalia, a well-known conservative, as an associate justice of the Supreme Court. But the political context of the Scalia nomination insulated it from any of the fierce resistance that
confronted Bork in 1987. The most significant difference was that Republicans
controlled the Senate in 1986 but not in 1987. Additionally, before the Scalia
nomination, liberal senators and interest groups had staunchly opposed William H. Rehnquist, whom President Reagan also had nominated in June 1986
to be chief justice. Rehnquist was also confirmed in September 1986, but when
it came to Scalia liberals did not mount another attack. Scalia was helped by

the fact that he was a member of an ethnic group never before represented on the Court and that he was nominated by a very popular president whose nominee for chief justice had just been roughly treated. Further, the elevation of Rehnquist and the confirmation of Scalia did not alter the overall balance of the Court. Both men filled seats previously held by justices commonly identified as judicial conservatives.[46]

In 1987 the political context was different. Democrats controlled the Senate, and the recent retiree, Justice Lewis Powell, was a moderate and frequent "swing" voter whose departure left the Court evenly divided on such controversial issues as abortion, affirmative action, and school prayer. Bork's confirmation augured a solid right-of-center majority, so anyone nominated in this circumstance would have received more than the usual scrutiny from supporters of modern judicial power. Liberals also were well-prepared. They had undertaken a sustained and organized resistance to President Reagan's judicial nominees since the early 1980s, which was evident in the attacks on Rehnquist and some lower court nominees. Liberal interest groups in particular anticipated that Bork would be nominated for the next Court vacancy.[47] Likewise, in the 1980s the Senate slowly moved toward heightened scrutiny of judicial nominees as it became clear that the Reagan administration was making a concerted effort to nominate conservative and restraintist judges.[48] Reagan himself raised the stakes of his next Supreme Court nomination, who turned out to be Bork, by telling voters in several southern Senate races of the importance of confirmation of his judicial nominees.[49] Finally, in the summer and fall of 1987 the Reagan administration was increasingly distracted from judicial issues by the Iran-Contra affair, hostilities in the Persian Gulf, and arms negotiations with the Soviet Union. Reagan's personal popularity decreased and the administration was unable to devote the attention to the Bork nomination that otherwise it might have.

From the standpoint of originalist jurisprudence Bork was the best possible nominee. Possessing impeccable professional credentials, he had long argued the originalist proposition and criticized legal liberalism. Yet in the less tangible realms of image and political instinct, he had weaknesses as well as strengths. Bork's primary weaknesses as a nominee were a seemingly uncompromising quality of mind and inadequate adaptation to the political and prudential demands of the hearings themselves. His liberal opponents successfully portrayed him as an "extremist" and insisted that his originalism was "outside the mainstream" of American constitutionalism. Pursuing what they termed a "Southern strategy," Bork's opponents also claimed that he would reopen the divisive civil rights battles of the 1960s. Bork and his advisers in the Reagan administration did not respond promptly or adequately to this inflammatory and galvanizing portrayal. The administration was slow to counter early liberal political maneuvering in the battle for public opinion that occurred between the announcement of the nomination on July 1 and the opening of the Senate hearings on September 15. The Democratic Senate leadership used this time to coordinate with liberal organizations and to build political resistance to the nomination.[50]

The context of the nomination affected how originalism and Bork were portrayed in the hearings. Liberal Democrats depicted Bork as a grave danger to the American constitutional order. Senator Joseph Biden (D-DE), chairman of the Senate Judiciary Committee, and Senator Edward Kennedy (D-MA) led the opposition and helped coordinate the anti-Bork public relations campaign. Kennedy made it clear that liberals viewed Bork as a pariah. On the day the nomination was announced he set the low tone that characterized many of the ensuing attacks, saying that in "Robert Bork's America . . . women would be forced into back-alley abortions, blacks would sit at segregated lunch counters, [and] rogue police could break down citizens' doors in midnight raids."[51]

Liberal lobbying groups produced media briefing materials and advertisements that also sensationalized and misrepresented Bork's record. For example, Ralph Nader's Public Citizen Litigation Group produced a misleading statistical analysis of Bork's record on the Circuit Court to claim that his votes could be predicted by the identity of litigants.[52] The American Civil Liberties Union warned its members that Bork was "far more dangerous than previously believed." Confirmation not only risked "wrecking [the] entire Bill of Rights," it also "threaten[ed] our system of government." An advertisement by the National Abortion Rights Action League warned that Bork threatened abortion and "almost every major gain women have made since [they] won the right to vote."[53]

Liberal strategy had to account for the fact that in the twentieth century the Senate usually deferred to the president's judicial nominees, often confirming them even when opposing parties controlled the legislative and executive branches. Senators usually avoided publicly basing confirmation decisions on politics or ideology because of the political risks entailed by such a clear stance. Until the Bork nomination, the general pattern of deference and confirmation failed only when the nominee was portrayed successfully as incompetent or unethical. In the Bork nomination liberals combined arguments against senatorial deference with the portrayal of Bork as a dangerous extremist.[54] In an ironic example, Senator Biden argued at length on the floor of the Senate that the framers of the Constitution originally intended the Senate to have broad latitude in considering the philosophy of judicial nominees. Therefore, the tradition of deference evaded the responsibilities of the Senate under the Constitution as originally understood.[55] It was easier for Senators to abandon the custom of deference if it was contrary to original intent, while at the same time Bork's originalist philosophy itself was labeled as "extreme," radically "outside the mainstream" of constitutional development, and his temperament insufficiently "judicial."

The White House believed that capturing centrist votes in the Democrat-controlled Senate was the only hope of confirmation, so its strategy was to present Bork as a well-qualified, lawyerly moderate and to rely on the twentieth-century pattern of Senate deference to qualified judicial nominees. The administration emphasized Bork's intellect and professional achievements and presented him as a worthy moderate successor to Powell. The White House pursued this strategy in a briefing book on Bork's record submitted to the Senate on July 31. Attempting to counteract the demonization of Bork by downplaying his scholarly originalist criticisms of legal liberalism, the document highlighted his record as solicitor general, in which he successfully argued several important civil rights cases before the Supreme Court. The briefing book also noted that none of Bork's majority opinions for the Circuit Court had been overturned by the Supreme Court, that his judicial record on the First Amendment often protected free speech for liberal causes, and that his criticism of the right of privacy as the basis for abortion was well within the mainstream of legal opinion. Refusing to present Bork as a nominee who would do battle with legal liberalism, the White House briefing book even stated that his confirmation "would not change the balance of the Supreme Court."[56]

Conservatives questioned the White House strategy and usually advocated a more forthright defense of Bork as an originalist whose philosophy would change the balance of the Court. Some Justice Department officials derisively referred to the White House briefing book as the "Bork as a Liberal Book." Assistant Attorney General John Bolton asked in frustration, "If he wouldn't change the balance of the Court, why the hell are we nominating him?"[57] The administration's presentation of Bork seemed to invite charges of deception. Joseph Grano, a constitutional scholar, condemned the Biden media briefing book but also wrote that his own defense of Bork did "*not* attempt to portray Judge Bork as another Justice Powell." Many other Republicans thought the moderate strategy undermined the nomination. Richard Viguerie, a noted conservative political strategist, observed, "It was a disaster the way they repackaged Bork. It's hard to get people to go out and fight, bleed, and die for Lewis Powell." Bolton's Justice Department tried to seize the momentum just before the hearings by issuing a lengthy rebuttal to the liberal attacks. The rebuttal emphasized Bork's conservative and originalist credentials, but it came too late to have much effect.[58]

The White House strategy made sense in so far as Bork's intellectual and professional qualifications were indisputable, and the efforts to question his ethics were labored and unsuccessful.[59] Moreover, during Strom Thurmond's (R-SC) chairmanship of the Judiciary Committee in the 1980s, Republican control of the Senate and the norm of deference led to rapid confirmation of nearly all Reagan nominees. Additionally, in 1982 when Bork was nominated to the District of Columbia Circuit Court, the American Bar Association (ABA) unanimously gave him its highest ranking. By 1987, however, circumstances had changed somewhat: Bork received a positive evaluation from the organization, but the liberal members of the ABA who evaluated Bork found him "not qualified" to be a Supreme Court justice. They alleged that he lacked "judicial temperament," which they somewhat tendentiously defined as "compassion, open mindedness, his sensitivity to the rights of women and minority persons or groups," and cautiously noted his "comparatively extreme views respecting Constitutional principles or their application." The ABA votes against Bork and the implication of extremism attracted much attention and undercut the White House's confirmation strategy, notwithstanding that the overall evaluation was positive.[60]

The ABA dissenters and the anti-Bork public relations campaign came to the aid of politically astute centrist senators who desired neither to reject Bork on overtly political grounds nor to offend the constituencies who opposed him. The putatively apolitical but lukewarm ABA endorsement, combined with the sensational attacks on Bork and an alleged "confirmation conversion" to non-originalist views, permitted senators to reject him on grounds that at least superficially were congruent with the institutional norm of deference. Centrist southern Democrats, elected largely with black votes, could avoid offending a constituency that overwhelmingly rejected Bork. Likewise, centrist Republicans did not have to reject a Republican nominee on overtly political grounds.[61] In this way the sensationalism and distortion surrounding the nomination provided political cover for negative votes.

Thus, the White House underestimated the resistance Bork's nomination would provoke from liberals. In extenuation the ferocity and inaccuracy of the attacks were unprecedented, but the White House response was still inadequate. It was slow to counter the charges of reactionary extremism that began with Kennedy's diatribe and continued throughout the hearings. Presentation of Bork as a Powell-like moderate only hardened liberal opposition and alienated some conservatives. More importantly, the White House strategy ceded the terms of the debate to Bork's opponents, permanently placing the nomination on the defensive. Bork's opponents successfully framed the debate in terms of the "mainstream" of American constitutionalism and Bork's alleged "extremism." During the entire nomination process Bork and his supporters were forced to argue that as an originalist he was not in fact bent on destroying the constitutional system or individual rights. Likewise, in the hearings Bork did explicitly downplay some of his earlier criticisms of legal liberalism, and this was taken as a disavowal of the views that had gotten him nominated, proof that he had undergone a "confirmation conversion" to attain a seat on the Court.[62]

Originalism in the Nomination Hearings

The several contextual and strategic factors described above complicated the Bork nomination and to a considerable extent undercut Bork's defense of originalism. To understand the significance of the nomination for originalism, we must turn to the complex interaction of Bork's views with the charged political setting of the hearings. Bork offered originalism as a democratic constitutional philosophy and method of interpretation that would constrain countermajoritarian judicial power. Insisting on a distinction between law and politics as central to this vision, he described originalism as a defense of limited government, the rule of law, and legislative majorities.[63]

Bork's testimony made it clear that he held as an axiom of the American system of government that the text of the Constitution as originally understood was the source and limit of constitutional law. Despite legal liberals' decades-old and often overt rejection of this traditional position, he found it strange that it could be seriously challenged, let alone that some opponents would attack originalism as a cover for conservative judicial activism. Expressing this view while parrying the persistent canard that originalism required some sort of historical mind reading, he declared, "When I say original intent, what I mean is really original understanding, because law is a public act, and it is really what was understood generally at the time the Constitution was framed, not the subjective intentions of James Madison." It was all but self-evident to Bork that this was a proper approach to constitutional law. Further, he insisted that historical inquiry about the actual events of the American founding could provide "a pretty firm starting point" for judges because it could show "what the public understanding of the time was of what the evil was [the framers and ratifiers] wished to avert, what the freedom was they wished to protect." With this as a "major premise," the task of the judge was the traditional one of "supply[ing] the minor premise" and thus protecting, in changed contemporary circumstances, the "value" or "freedom" inscribed in the text.[64]

Bork again emphasized that originalism best clarified that the principles and rights, even the "values," contained in the Constitution were distinct from those it did not contain. Referring to one of his recent judicial opinions, he observed that "it is the task of the judge in this generation to discern how the framers' values, defined in the context of the world they knew, apply to the world we know. The world changes in which unchanging values find their application."[65] This was different than jurisprudence that asked judges to protect or advance values that had no recognizable basis in the text or history of the Constitution. Bork insisted that disengagement from the bounds of the Constitution placed judges in the abstract, contested realm of moral philosophy, encouraging them to invalidate democratically formulated policies based on values not in the Constitution and frequently not shared by most of the polity.[66]

This familiar originalist critique of liberal jurisprudence had utmost practical political significance in the context of Bork's nomination to the Court. Jurisprudence and politics intertwined as the hearings explored the possible constitutional law and policy results of confirming Bork. Judicial rights-creation and the jurisprudence of the equal protection clause of the Fourteenth Amendment were two areas in which liberals felt Bork's originalism would be unacceptable. These issues, as well as Bork's earlier scholarly criticism of particular decisions, provided his opponents with ample opportunity to portray him as an "extremist" who was outside the "mainstream."

As an example of judicial creation of nontextual rights that blurred the line between law and politics and displaced legislative adaptation of the law to change, Bork again criticized the privacy right created in *Griswold v. Connecticut* (1965).[67] He rejected the high level of abstraction and consequent indeterminacy of the right, again insisting that this uncertainty meant that judges' own political predilections likely would determine the outcome in privacy cases, thereby removing from legislatures the capacity to create public policy.[68] The privacy right announced in *Griswold* was the basis for *Roe v. Wade* (1973), but Bork's opponents usually avoided appearing to protect the controversial abortion license. They often subsumed their support for it under "privacy," a concept more vague and popular, albeit constitutionally suspect. Moreover, they claimed that Bork's originalist criticism of *Griswold* was a reactionary attempt not only to rekindle the long-settled issue of contraception but also to challenge individual natural rights.[69] Chairman Biden led this attack, charging Bork with failure to appreciate "that we are just born with certain rights as a child of God having nothing to do with whether or not the State or the Constitution acknowledges I have those rights."[70] As Biden illustrated, the majoritarian implication of Bork's originalist criticism of judicial rights-creation, and the privacy right in particular, made him vulnerable to charges that he was unconcerned with the American natural rights tradition or "simple justice."

Moreover, in responding to Biden's challenge Bork did not condemn what many conservatives regarded as the social evils that resulted from the judicial "rights revolution," such as abortion, affirmative action, forced school bussing, and hamstrung criminal law enforcement. Terry Eastland, a conservative in the Justice Department, believed Biden's defense of rights was vulnerable and lamented Bork's failure to present a better originalist rejoinder.[71] Thus, while Bork went out of his way to avoid comments that might offend liberals, he satisfied neither liberals nor conservatives on the topic of rights and the proper role of the judiciary in defending or creating them.

Bork's opponents found another opportunity to label him as an extremist based on his originalist criticism of the complex edifice of modern equal protection doctrine. This doctrine, of course, rested on the *Carolene Products* rationale of judicially defined "discrete and insular minorities" and "suspect classifications." Race was the quintessential suspect classification, but it had given rise to others more novel. Statutes involving distinctions based on judicially created suspect classifications triggered a presumption of unconstitutionality and received "strict judicial scrutiny," being upheld only if they met some judicially determined "compelling" state interest. Statutes reviewed under this test were almost never approved. Other statutory classifications had only to

rest on a "rational basis" and be reasonably related to a legitimate state interest; these were usually schemes for economic regulation that were nearly always upheld. Beginning in the 1970s the Court developed a third, middle level
of judicial scrutiny in equal protection cases. The new middle category was
created originally for gender classifications, which received "intermediate" or
"heightened" scrutiny. A gender classification was required to be substantially
related to an important governmental interest and was rarely upheld.[72]

Bork viewed this system as unsupported by the text or original intent of
the Fourteenth Amendment, a position he had long held and recently reiterated. The original intent of the equal protection clause concerned race: if
this category was abandoned it was difficult to find any principled way to include or exclude other classifications from the coverage of the clause.[73] As the
Court nevertheless proceeded in the attempt, the equal protection doctrine
had become increasingly incoherent, discretionary, and insufficiently deferential to legislative judgments. Like others before him, Bork insisted that the
Court's complicated legal tests forced it into essentially political judgments
about which groups were "discrete and insular minorities" and therefore entitled to different levels of judicial scrutiny and protection. Additionally, he
argued that the strict scrutiny and rationality tests were actually more conclu-
sory than evaluative, while decisions based on "intermediate scrutiny" were
unpredictable.[74]

Likely in response to the political demands of the hearings, Bork attempted,
somewhat extemporaneously, to fashion an alternative to the three-tier approach.[75] He said that the language of "any person" in the text of the equal
protection clause should be read to include women and other individuals,
even though the framers and ratifiers had not understood this to be the case.
He argued further that gender was sufficiently like race for most purposes to
be included within the now broader original intent of the clause. Like race,
gender was immutable and irrelevant to almost all regulable activities, so legislative classifications based upon it were almost always invidious.[76]

By analogizing gender to race Bork expanded the coverage of the clause
beyond what was originally intended by its framers and ratifiers. However,
his desire to constrain judicial power endured in the argument that the clause
should be applied to individuals, not groups, and should be applied with
a single standard, not three. Bork built on an opinion by Justice John Paul
Stevens that rejected the tiered approach and advocated a test determining
whether an "impartial lawmaker could logically believe that the classification

would serve a legitimate public purpose that transcends the harm to the members of the disadvantaged class." Stevens believed that the results produced by this test would not vary substantially from the nearly automatic invalidation and validation, respectively, of racial and economic classifications under the three-tier model, while those based on alienage, gender, or illegitimacy were "sometimes relevant and sometimes irrelevant to a valid public purpose." Stevens's test of rationality could account for this fact and would obviate the cumbersome and artificial tier method.[77]

Bork agreed that Stevens's general approach comported better with the constitutional language of "any person" than did the three-tier system. As he stated in the hearings, all he "meant was some distinctions are reasonable as to gender." Bork's approach, while not strictly originalist, would have constrained judicial discretion and required more deference to legislative judgments than the tiered balancing approach, although it would have reached nearly all of the same results as recent decisions that had overruled statutes containing invidious, empirically ungrounded gender classifications. Bork termed his proposal a "reasonableness" standard to distinguish it from the "rationality" test under the three-tier model.[78]

Even though Bork had clearly abandoned a strict originalist position in the area of equal protection, his opponents again characterized him as a dangerous extremist. They charged that he was bent on destroying the rights of women, oblivious to abundant evidence that belied the claim.[79] Senator Kennedy, for example, again conveyed the disgust and disdain opponents accorded Bork, lecturing him in his typically hyperbolic style: "Women are first-class citizens, Mr. Bork, and your views would take us back to the days when women were second-class citizens and the Supreme Court winked at discrimination and denied equal rights for women." Other Senators, encouraged by Bork's academic opponents, argued that his "reasonableness" standard would allow unequal treatment of women because it was too deferential to legislatures.[80] Bork's attempt to increase judicial deference to legislatures counted for little against the charge that he was intent on subordinating women.[81]

The notion that the Court was the ultimate defender of constitutional rights, and perhaps their creator, also helped Bork's opponents sensationalize his criticism of the reasoning in other equal protection decisions. They portrayed Bork as an extremist by emphasizing that he had been on the wrong side of what they offered as simple political choices between good and bad results. This characterized the reaction not only to Bork's criticism of the derivation of the right of privacy in *Griswold* but also his analysis of *Skinner v. Oklahoma* (1942), in which the Court overturned a statute requiring the sterilization of recidivist robbers but not embezzlers. Bork had pointed to the decision as evidence that the Court lacked a guiding principle to apply the equal protection clause beyond the originally intended context of race.[82] Senators and activists suggested that Bork supported police raids into marital bedrooms or the sterilization of criminals, despite his emphatic protests that "to say that the reasoning of any case seems not adequate is not to say you want to overrule it, and it is certainly not to say you want to bring back the underlying statute."[83]

Bork's criticism of the reasoning in decisions involving racial discrimination provided his opponents another opportunity to portray him as a radical by again obfuscating the basic distinction between criticism of legal-constitutional reasoning and the substantive outcome of a case. For example, Bork criticized the public accommodations provision of the 1964 Civil Rights Act; the Court's handling of the state action problem in the outlawing of racially restrictive private housing covenants; its use of the equal protection clause to overturn a poll tax that was not alleged to be administered in a racially discriminatory fashion; and its reading of an equal protection component into the due process clause of the Fifth Amendment to desegregate the District of Columbia schools. He had further criticized the Court's validation of Congress's use of section 5 of the Fourteenth Amendment to invalidate a literacy test for voting in New York, and the "one person, one vote" rule announced in the reapportionment case of *Reynolds v. Sims* (1964). Like numerous other critics over the decades, Bork said that in these decisions the Court had not adequately reasoned its way to the result or had not sufficiently explained how the rulings were consonant with the original intent of the Constitution. He and his supporters endlessly reiterated in the hearings that such criticisms echoed many other scholars, along with dissenting justices in several of the cases, and that he did not necessarily disagree with the results in the cases.[84]

Nevertheless, Bork's opponents stated that the substantive results in most of these cases helped racial minorities or the poor, thereby associating Bork's originalism and criticism of legal reasoning with racism or insensitivity to poverty. This was especially effective in advancing what Bork's opponents termed their "Southern strategy," an appeal to the fear of southern voters and Senators that Bork would reopen the divisive civil rights battles of the 1960s. As one observer of the nomination noted, "while fearing Bork would turn back the clock, the anti-Bork coalition actually *did* turn back the clock. . . . It forced the debate into the domain of issues long settled, raising the specter of birth control police, poll taxes, and literacy tests."[85] Bork's legal arguments could not overcome the sensationalized focus on results by most of his opponents.

Another complex legal topic that, in the charged political context of the hearings, provoked concern about immediate results was the relationship between originalism and *stare decisis*, that is, the judicial determination of whether to follow a precedent. As an originalist Bork held the traditional view that the ultimate source of constitutional law was the Constitution, not the Court's interpretation of it that might be appealed to as a precedent. This position rested on the distinction between the American system of written constitutionalism and the common law method of case-by-case judging. The distinction was real, but in American jurisprudence it was also a source of tension and debate. Bork's originalist critique of liberal precedents ensured that *stare decisis* would be an issue in the hearings. He testified repeatedly that criticism of the reasoning of a decision, or the observation that a decision exceeded the original intent of the Constitution, did not mean he would attempt to overrule such precedents.[86] For example, although as a professor Bork had criticized the *Brandenburg* (1969) position that advocacy of law violation was protected under the First Amendment unless there was a threat of imminent violence, he testified that "as a judge, I accept it, and that is all there is to that."[87]

However, Bork also said that the concept of original intent should be included in the judicial assessment of whether a precedent should be followed or overruled, in addition to consideration of a decision's legal reasoning, the expectations and institutions that had grown up around it, and the need for stability in the law.[88] Moreover, Bork stated that the privacy jurisprudence stemming from *Griswold*, including *Roe*, was an unsettled area and was not immune from reevaluation in the way that other nonoriginalist precedents might be.[89] In this context Bork's assurances about his respect for *stare decisis* did not satisfy his opponents that originalism would safeguard the logic of the judicially updated "living Constitution."[90]

The hearings also revealed at a deeper level how the issue of *stare decisis* remained a jurisprudential challenge for originalism.[91] Originalists like Bork were committed to the view that the legitimacy of constitutional law depended on judges who interpreted the Constitution according to its original intent. However, the question of how to treat an established precedent that contravened the original intent of the constitutional text, of which there were many, did not seem resolvable by recourse to original intent. According to Philip Bobbitt, Bork's explanation of the factors to be considered in a challenge to *stare decisis,* including original intent, were essentially prudential. That is to say, determining whether to follow a precedent by considering its age, the institutions that have grown up around it, or the need for legal stability, is to undertake a prudential evaluation not based on how well the precedent reflects the original intent of the Constitution. Bobbitt has written that "if a realistic assessment of practical political affairs—including even the public perception of the court's politicization—leads one to conclude that, whatever the historical inquiry reveals, the state of the case law will remain undisturbed, then, as a matter of argument, it is as if the historical inquiry were never made."[92]

Bork did not convincingly reconcile his proffered loyalty to liberal precedents he had earlier criticized with his equally strong insistence that original intent should guide and constrain interpretation.[93] If prudence ultimately determined Bork's approach to precedent, perhaps it was because it still bore the stamp of the process tradition, especially as articulated by his friend Alexander M. Bickel.[94] Or perhaps it was because considerations of *stare decisis* might inevitably be prudential regardless of the larger jurisprudential system in which they occur. In any event, Bork's difficulty in reconciling originalism with liberal precedents encouraged many observers and participants in the hearings simply to dismiss originalism, despite its deep roots in the American constitutional order, as mere conservative disagreement with liberal politics.

Bork's acquiescence to the nonoriginalist expansion of the First Amendment in the *Brandenburg* precedent also contributed to charges of a "confirmation conversion." Bork's stance on *Brandenburg* also further disappointed conservatives who had hoped that he would attack more directly a nonoriginalist decision that many held responsible for coarsening the culture. Ray Randolph, a friend and advisor, said that in the *Brandenburg* discussion Bork should have confronted Senator Arlen Specter (R-PA), a Jew, by asking: "Senator, we are talking about men with guns and knives under their gowns calling for the extermination of Jews and blacks. Is that really the kind of speech we want to protect in our society? Do you honestly believe that if a community forbids such speech, the First Amendment has been violated?" Noting that Bork nowhere made such a point, conservative stalwart Bruce Fein observed critically: "The basic message sent by the hearings so far is that the courts are about where they should be, that no great changes are needed. Bork is bending his views to improve his confirmation chances and it's a shame."[95]

The sensationalized and confrontational tenor of the hearings and the defensive caution it induced in Bork not only made it difficult for him to present a positive view of originalism, it also limited the thoroughness of the jurisprudential evaluation that did occur. A further example was the discussion of *Brown v. Board of Education* (1954). Bork had long recognized the necessity of reconciling originalism with this heroic liberal precedent, and in the hearings he reiterated his earlier position.[96] Bork's "acceptance" of *Brown* was not seriously in doubt, and in the political context of the hearings his explicit endorsement of this sacrosanct liberal decision was required.[97] Consequently, Bork's attempted reconciliation of originalism and *Brown* received little attention.

However, *Brown* highlighted jurisprudential challenges for originalism: how could an originalist accommodate liberal precedents or increase the level of generality at which to restate constitutional language (as Bork did for *Brown*) yet also remain moored to the original intent of the constitutional text in a substantive way? Indeed, Bork's originalist defense of *Brown* was subjected to searching criticism by noted legal liberal academic Ronald Dworkin.[98] Putting aside the tension between originalism and nonoriginalist precedents, Dworkin argued that Bork's willingness to increase the level of generality at which equal protection was applied in *Brown* did not prohibit, in fact it required, even more generalized applications—such as equal protection for the right of consensual homosexual activity. Dworkin insisted that once the original intent of equal protection and segregation was abandoned, there was no way based on original intent to choose a level of generality at which to apply the equal protection clause. Bork's exclusion of homosexuality merely expressed his political preferences, so the argument ran, not the requirements of originalism.[99] Without citing Dworkin, Senator Specter observed that this kind of critique could undermine originalism. Bork did not concede, however, that *Brown* was irreconcilable to the theory, and the conversation quickly moved on. On the national political stage of the confirmation hearings, senators were hardly likely to engage the complex jurisprudential problems of originalism fully, much less condemn it for failing to guarantee a right to homosexual activity. Nevertheless, Dworkin's critique, like the problem of *stare decisis,* suggested that originalism had not resolved some of the important jurisprudential issues it raised. But the difficulties of originalism as a developing body of jurisprudence contributed less to Bork's defeat than did the bitterly partisan attacks and distortions which dominated the hearings.

Defeat and the Continued Defense of Originalism

The Bork nomination was a battle of apparently upstart originalism against established legal liberalism. While frequently obscured, the legal-constitutional issues were the traditional ones at the root of a system based on a written Constitution, issues that originalists had reasserted against legal liberalism over the previous two decades. Bork's supporters in the hearings, like Bork himself, clearly regarded originalism as a return to traditional constitutional ideas. Bork's originalism, they said, aimed to constrain the vast new realm of modern judicial power and to defend democratic decision-making and the rule of law.[100] This was also the view articulated in the Minority Report of the Senate Judiciary Committee and by Bork's defenders in the Senate floor debate.[101]

But on October 23, 1987, Bork was defeated in the Senate and legal liberalism seemed to have weathered the originalist storm. Bork's opponents were unpersuaded that originalism was a worthy constitutional public philosophy that went deeper than simple dissatisfaction with the results of legal liberalism or that it could safeguard or create new rights under a judicially updated living Constitution. A more immediate lesson was that a Democrat-controlled Senate could be relied upon to protect legal liberalism.[102] Most senators were content to claim that "the Supreme Court is the basic guarantor of our liberty" and to praise it as "the guardian of individual liberties" whose reading of the Constitution must "save us" from the power of government.[103] The Senate was keen to retain its insulation from divisive political issues such as abortion and affirmative action, which originalism would turn back to Congress or state legislatures. Instead of tackling such issues, the Senate demonstrated its willingness to allow the Supreme Court to create and protect "fundamental rights" as it saw fit.[104]

In this sense Bork's defeat could be described as a "failed constitutional moment."[105] It confirmed the modern legal liberal, rights-creating role the Warren and Burger Courts had elaborated from *Carolene Products* and the general notion of a living Constitution. Originalism had challenged this role and its interpretive method; as a replacement for Justice Powell's swing vote Bork likely would have helped reduce this kind of judicial power. Had he been confirmed, Bork's fifth vote probably would have redirected constitutional change more than at any time since the Warren Court. Accordingly, his defeat marked the failure of originalism to change fundamentally the direction of constitutional development from its dominant course in the preceding thirty years, let alone its course since the New Deal. Further, it underscored that the conservative political renaissance was not in fact a classic "realignment" resulting in sustained Republican dominance but was more likely part of a new era of "dealignment," if not party decay.

However, Bork's defeat was not the final repudiation of originalism that some liberals trumpeted. The outcome also was determined by the concrete political context of the nomination, the strategies employed by both sides, and Bork's own difficulties in selling himself to the Senate. In the most basic sense, Bork was a controversial Republican who confronted a Democratic Senate—by simple arithmetic he did not have the votes to win. Moreover, the White House did not adequately defend Bork as either a solid constitutionalist or from the distorting charges of "extremism." For example, Judiciary Committee member Howell Heflin (D-AL), a conservative Democrat and defender of judicial restraint, explained his negative vote by stating that Bork's "proclivity for extremism in spite of confirmation protestations" led him to rely on the proposition "when in doubt, don't."[106]

Additionally, Bork was sometimes his own worst enemy. For example, Randall Rader, an aide to Senator Orrin Hatch (R-UT), advised Bork to "get a tear in your eye and wipe it away and say: 'I would dearly love to defend the constitutional rights of women and blacks'. . . . Leave the room ringing a bit." Bork responded: "Randy, I'm a lawyer, not a politician." Not thinking like a politician, at least during the hearings, resulted in a costly and widely noted response to a query about why he wanted to be on the Court. Instead of reassuring his audience along the lines suggested by Rader, Bork responded that it would be an "intellectual feast." This contributed to the perception that he was disengaged from the concerns of everyday citizens.[107] Further illustrating the disconnect between Bork and his audience, Terry Eastland defined the neologism "to bork" that emerged from the hearings: "What does it mean to be borked? Simply this: Your opponents attack you on a matter involving law and criticize you in terms of policy outcomes. You defend yourself by discussing the issue in legal jargon." Eastland recognized that Bork's opponents gained politically by ignoring the fundamental distinction between the result of a case and its legal rationale, but Bork did not adequately compensate by adapting his testimony to the political realities of the confirmation process.[108] The presence of such explanations for Bork's defeat meant that it was not a clear-cut or final judgment on originalism.

While the decades-old emergence and development of originalism did not culminate in a Supreme Court seat for its most noted exemplar, the very fact of Bork's nomination and the lengths to which his opponents went to defeat him showed that originalism had changed the climate of American constitutional law a great deal since the 1960s. The jurisprudence of original intention had to be addressed, and sometimes distorted, in order to defeat Bork. Although some liberals understandably hailed Bork's defeat as the end of originalism and the final victory of the living Constitution, such claims were belied not only by the complex reasons for the defeat but also by the further elaboration and influence of originalism in the 1990s.

Bork himself capitalized on his public recognition to advance originalism after the hearings, especially with his best-selling book *The Tempting of America* (1990). This book reassembled and elaborated Bork's scattered earlier work into the most cogent and accessible defense of originalism then available. Part of Bork's goal was again to clarify for a wide audience the issues of democratic legitimacy involved in the originalism debate, so he starkly described the core issue: "Either the Constitution and statutes are law, which means that their principles are known and control judges, or they are malleable texts that judges may rewrite to see that particular groups or political causes win." If the Constitution was law, by the originalist definition of the concept it had meaning that limited judges: "What does it mean to say that a judge is bound by law? It means that he is bound by the only thing that can be called law, the principles of the text, whether Constitution or statute, as generally understood at the enactment."[109] In America the authority of law was derived from popular sovereignty and consent, the principles of political legitimacy and obligation at the heart of the constitutional regime. The law made authoritative by these principles had a real existence, which confronted judges as a rule independent of their own desires. Moreover, maintenance of the limits in the constitutional design required originalism—"no other method of constitutional adjudication can confine courts to a defined sphere of authority. . . . [It was] thus a necessary inference from the structure of government apparent on the face of the Constitution."[110] Like Raoul Berger, Bork presented these arguments in a straightforward, lawyerly fashion rather than in a philosophical one, and he frequently emphasized that originalism was the "orthodox" approach to the American Constitution.

Tempting also made a few notable clarifications in defense of originalism (most of which, to be fair, were present in Bork's earlier work). The first was to say more distinctly than previously that originalists sought to interpret the "public understanding" of a legal text at the time of its enactment, not the "subjective intentions" of particular framers or ratifiers.[111] Bork also further clarified that the level of generality of a principle in the text could not be wholly separated from its original meaning; to determine that level was not an arbitrary and essentially political choice, as some critics had argued. In fact "to find the meaning of a text" was "a process which includes finding its degree of generality, which is part of its meaning."[112] The text, structure, and history of the Constitution carried its meaning, but if the level of its generality or breadth remained unclear after consultation of these sources, than the judge had no law to apply and should defer to legislative judgment. Here Bork was suggesting that the level of generality was empirically part of the meaning of the text, not something established by a separate theoretical inquiry any more than by a political choice. Finally, Bork also explained that because lawyers had no generally accepted theory about precedent, he did in fact regard it as a prudential issue, though this need not undermine originalism. Overruling long-settled non-originalist holdings would be destabilizing, imprudent, and unacceptable. But non-originalist precedents in currently contested areas of social policy, such as the right of privacy, should not be extended because the legitimacy of such new decisions would be undermined by their basis in relatively recent misinterpretations of the Constitution.[113]

We need not revisit *Tempting*'s reiteration of Bork's earlier responses to standard legal liberal claims that original meaning was unknowable, or that the living Constitution should be updated by abstracting its terms and infusing judicial-theoretical conceptions of politics or morality. But Bork now added that, by originalist standards, it was no more legitimate to read into the Constitution conservative interpretations of tradition or libertarian resuscitations of economic substantive due process. This move underscored just how deeply Bork regarded originalism and its traditional form of legal reasoning as "rooted in a concern for legitimate process rather than preferred results," a concern further reflected in the separation of powers.[114] In this way Bork showed that his originalism carried forward the concerns characteristic of postwar process-restraint jurisprudence—defense of the separation of powers, deference to legislatures, and neutrality in legal reasoning—at the same time that his originalism attempted to remedy the inadequate attention of process jurisprudence to the original Constitution as the fundamental source of law.

At another level Bork's jurisprudence still sounded the same skepticism and legal positivism, as noted above, that was typical of midcentury process-restraint arguments.[115] Nevertheless, a major theme of his writing after 1987 was that the recent abandonment of the original Constitution, whether for the abstractions of legal liberal theorists or the non-originalist decisions of the Supreme Court, usually advanced the relativist, radically individualist, and egalitarian values of a cultural elite. The more conservative values held by most of the political community were typically cast aside. Indeed, Bork has recently argued that the judiciary, headed by the Supreme Court, is the "enforcement arm" of the values of this elite and that this phenomenon is now noticeable in other countries.[116] From this perspective adherence to the Constitution's original meaning would constrain judges from drifting into theoretical abstraction and from moving beyond their jurisdiction. Courts would then be limited to the relatively small number of subjects in the Constitution, and legislative value choices upheld by a restrained court usually would be more conservative than those resulting from judicial review. Originalism, as Bork understood it, would defend the more conservative opinions generally held by the majority of the political community and would avoid unresolvable, abstract theoretical debates about natural rights or the features of the truly just society.[117]

Nonetheless, Bork doubted that jurisprudential argument alone could bring the Court back within the limits of the original Constitution and with it American politics to a more democratic and conservative balance between individual autonomy and community norms. He suggested a more drastic political-institutional solution: a constitutional amendment permitting a majority vote in each house of Congress to overturn a state or federal court decision. Bork was realistic about the slim likelihood of this proposal being accepted but thought it was necessary to "inject into the popular discussion the question of a democratic check upon a branch of government which is currently uncheckable."[118]

While Bork suggested that such an amendment might be the only way to check the Court and conserve traditional values, he never wavered from insisting that the rule of law required conservatives to abide by the original meaning of the Constitution instead of replicating the modern liberal error of reading their own political and moral preferences into it. In a recent example, he regarded as "absurd" the argument that the due process clause of the Fifth or Fourteenth Amendments allowed courts to find abortion unconstitutional because it arbitrarily deprived an unborn person of life. The original meaning of the clause simply had nothing to do with abortion, which besides was private and not state action. Cultural conservatives should not pretend that "a Constitution that is plainly silent on the matter does the job for us." Rather than further deformation of the Constitution, the solution was "moral education" of the majority, and conservatives ought to "fight the culture war where it belongs, in the arena of moral discourse and democratic politics."[119] As this example and Bork's earlier work show—and as he also has explicitly stated—he understood himself as a legal positivist but not a moral skeptic. He emphasized that "there is no apparent reason why the vitality of political conservatism depends upon abandoning a jurisprudence of legal positivism," which was merely a recognition that "in our system of government, it is not judges but the people and their elected representatives who are to make major policy decisions."[120]

Thus, Bork agreed with conservatives that politics was unavoidably about questions that should be informed by moral realist philosophy and religion. However, his jurisprudence, like the process tradition it built upon, sought to protect the originally intended processes and institutional relationships designed to root law in the community's norms and values—from whatever ontologically contestable source they might ultimately spring. As we shall see in the next chapter, the positivist and restraintist form of originalism associated with Bork formed the beginning point for the many other theorists who engaged the doctrine in the 1990s.

CHAPTER 8

Originalism in the 1990s

The Transformation of Academic Theory and the Limitations of Practice

Much of academic constitutional theory in the 1990s was devoted to elaborating, refining, coopting, or attacking originalism. In the process, originalism became a more subtle, complex, and fragmented doctrine. While academics were immersed in a debate largely driven by the ongoing and increasingly diversified influence of originalism, Supreme Court decision-making was affected, but not nearly as much. This chapter traces these changes and concludes with some reflections about what the emergence, development, and limited practical effect of originalism tells us about its place in twentieth-century American constitutional history.

It is worth emphasizing that the endurance of originalism in the 1990s derived in part from the same fundamental reasons that had helped it resurface decades earlier. The originalist understanding of the Constitution as law rooted in popular sovereignty persisted as a favored and powerful organizing concept. Like Robert Bork and Raoul Berger before them, but with more theoretical rigor and less polemic, originalists such as Richard Kay recently have emphasized that limited government under the rule of law necessitates rules with a content that is fixed prior to application. This proposition depended on the sovereign act of ratification, which had made politically authoritative and legally compelling rules with discernible content. Interpretation was the application of these rules. Any approach to judicial review that did not account for the Constitution only undermined its own claim to authority. Articulating this enduring core of originalism, Kay wrote, "What commands obedience is not a mere set of words, but the expression of an intentional historical-political act. Any attempt to apply the Constitution's terms in a sense not intended by the human beings participating in that historical-political act, therefore, fails to invoke the only phenomenon that marks the Constitution off as worthy of obedience."[1] Political scientist Keith E. Whittington's defense of originalism likewise argued that only interpretation based on original intent could limit the power of judges, justify judicial review, and safeguard the structures, forms, and procedures of the constitutionalist project. Further, only interpretation of the original intent of the Constitution legitimated by the sovereign people made possible respect for the potential sovereignty they might exercise in the present or future.[2] Other scholars who would not necessarily identify themselves as originalists recognized the force of the originalist appeal to such traditional Anglo-American concepts of law and the judicial function.[3]

Another closely related and equally fundamental reason that originalism persisted was that the various alternatives often seemed to deny the law/politics distinction that originalists had so insistently resurrected. Originalists made this point against commentators who rejected the distinction as impossible yet advocated a Supreme Court that adjusted the Constitution to contemporary needs in a pragmatic, case-by-case fashion or urged it to realize a particular moral philosophy or to create new rights as it saw fit.[4] Such normative arguments contributed to the persistence of originalism precisely because they provoked consideration of whether, in the American constitutional system, they could be reconciled to limited, consent-based government and the rule of law. The general originalist response was that only the originalist method could both justify judicial review and permit some distinction between written law and political aspiration.[5]

Elaborating and Refining Originalism

As we have seen in earlier chapters, the fundamental issues just described were central to the legal positivist, restraintist, and lawyerly version of originalism made prominent primarily by Berger and Bork. In the 1990s this version generated three general categories of response that we will trace in the following sections of this chapter. First, scholars defended, elaborated, and re-fined originalism. This included assessing whether originalism was necessarily restraintist and majoritarian and whether the Berger/Bork form of originalism left any room for moral realism or rather depended on moral skepticism. Origi-nalists also offered a more thorough response to hermeneutic criticism than they had offered in the 1980s. Second, liberal theorists increasingly attempted to make originalism, and historical analysis in general, more amenable to their goals. Third, as the jurisprudential debate increasingly turned on the content and relevance of original meaning, a steady stream of new and detailed his-torical research was produced not only by originalists but also by those who contested their findings.

To be sure, the positivist, restraintist, and lawyerly understanding of origi-nalism remained prominent in the writing of Berger, Bork, and Lino Graglia.[6] As before, such work aimed to puncture the abstraction and moral theorizing typical of much legal liberalism, but it did not elaborate originalism with argu-ments drawn from political philosophy, nor did it move beyond axiomatically regarding interpretation as aimed at determining original meaning. Other originalists, while also insisting that judicial review should be limited by the original meaning of the Constitution, argued that the best form of the doc-trine could not be simply equated with judicial restraint. For example, Keith E. Whittington, like Bork, emphasized popular sovereignty as the source of the Constitution's authority and insisted that originalism must defend some version of formalism in adjudication, but he argued that the doctrine should move beyond what he regarded as Bork's morally skeptical defense of restraint and majoritarianism. Whittington's conception of originalism allowed that upholding the original meaning of the Constitution might sometimes require active judicial review.[7] Another originalist, Earl M. Maltz, also rejected the equation of originalism with judicial restraint or majoritarianism.[8]

Straussian moral realist defenders of the natural rights/natural law read-ing of American constitutionalism also attacked the positivist majoritarian-ism associated with lawyerly originalism. They rejected its alleged Hobbesian moral skepticism and opposition to moral reasoning by judges. In their view legal positivist originalism too readily conceded modern secular liberalism's truncated understanding of human nature, the Constitution, and the legal-philosophical inheritance of the West. With this attack Straussians tried to move originalism toward the "higher law" tradition that informed not only the American founding but the entire Western legal tradition. American constitutionalism made no sense apart from the framers' philosophy of natural rights and the higher law of nature, and the political science and institutional design of the American constitutional order in fact depended upon the philosophical and legal presumptions of these traditions. Therefore they were integral to the true and guiding original intent of the Constitution. In some articulations this argument justified more active use of judicial power than the originalism associated with Bork or Berger.[9]

At the same time, however, other important moral realists such as Russell Hittinger and Robert P. George were too critical of the judicial penchant for moral philosophy to dismiss legal positivist originalism *tout court*. Rather, they attempted to reconcile a Borkian originalist approach with a Thomistic understanding of how legitimate authority for legal and moral decision-making was allocated in the American constitutional system. As George put it, calling on the Thomistic notion of *determinationes,* the ultimately moral purpose of law did not automatically give judges authority to vindicate their own conception of the natural law. Their role was determined not in the order of nature but rather by the practical choices made when the founders of a particular regime attempted to implement or approximate the natural law in the positive law. In the American case, George agreed with Bork that legitimate political authority had established that the natural law was best served by confining the judicial office to the legal application of moral decisions taken by more democratically responsible institutions. Thus, "Judge Bork's idea of a body of law that is properly and fully (or almost fully) analyzable in technical terms is fully compatible with classical understandings of natural law theory."[10] This nascent *rapprochement* between originalism and moral realism, like the insistence by Whittington and others that the Court should actively enforce the original meaning of the Constitution, meant that originalism could no longer be associated exclusively with moral skepticism or automatic judicial deference to legislative majorities.[11]

In addition to deeper consideration of the relationship among legal positivism, moral realism, and judicial activism, the originalists of the 1990s offered a more rigorous response to the persistent hermeneutic arguments about interpretive indeterminacy, the nature of the constitutional text, and related charges of historical indeterminacy. We must digress briefly to outline these arguments so we can better appreciate the now deeper originalist response.

As in the early 1980s, the hermeneutic tendency was to claim that if the constitutional text was vague or abstract, if all legal and historical interpretation was subjective and indeterminate, then there could be no distinction between originalism and non-originalism.[12] Ronald Dworkin continued to insist that the supposedly inherently abstract (if not wholly indeterminate) terms of the constitutional text necessitated moral reasoning by judges. On his view everyone could be understood as interpreting original intent: "The important question for constitutional theory is not whether the intention of those who made the Constitution should count, but rather what should count as that intention."[13] Recently Dworkin has entered the originalism debate even more directly by building on his earlier concept/conception distinction, now offering one between "semantic" and "expectation" originalism. He has distinguished "what some officials intended to say in enacting the language they used"—semantic—from "what they intended—or expected or hoped—would be the consequences of their saying it"—expectation.[14] Since, as a matter of "semantic" originalism, the authors of the rights-granting clauses of the Constitution wrote an abstract text that invited moral reasoning by judges, Dworkin's "moral reading" of the Constitution insisted "that the Constitution means what the framers intended to say."[15] This kind of claim permitted defenders of modern judicial power to make the rhetorically attractive assertion that "we are all originalists now," while continuing to advocate judicial moral reasoning based on highly abstract versions of the Constitution.[16]

In another apparently good faith effort to take originalism seriously, the noted constitutional historian Jack N. Rakove offered only another version of the indeterminacy thesis. The founding should be understood as an era of legal-political experimentation whose ingredients had no stable meaning that could bind the judges of today, so originalism failed as constitutional jurisprudence.[17] Rakove accordingly rejected a "strong" form of originalism while still holding that historical knowledge was possible.[18]

Originalists responded to such claims on several fronts. Most importantly, they used developments in the philosophy of language and literary criticism to offer more refined theoretical defenses of intent-based interpretation than they had in the 1980s. Additionally, originalists argued more robustly that to be workable their method need not attain the impossible goal of determinacy. They also undertook deeper consideration of what counted as evidence of original intent and benefitted from the related efforts of others.

Literary scholars and philosophers of language had for some time been attacking modern claims that readers or auditors could be understood to interpret texts or utterances by restating something other than an author's or speaker's intent.[19] Such work elaborated the insight of the later Ludwig Wittgenstein that speech was essentially communicative, arguing that an utterance or a text is a "speech act" undertaken to communicate the intention of the utterer or author. Absent the concept of intent there is no communication. For communication to be successful it is impossible to conceive of interpretation as anything other than the reader's or auditor's attempt to comprehend the intention of the author or speaker.

By the 1990s originalists developed these arguments and applied them to the constitutional context more frequently and effectively than they had in the more lawyerly debates of the 1980s.[20] Because the upshot of the philosophical claim was that there was no "language meaning independent of some human intention, real or postulated," interpretation was essentially an empirical act of recovery, not a creative or theoretical enterprise.[21] As another scholar put it, "Discovering what an author intended to say is simply identical to determining successfully what the author in fact said, which is to say that in matters of textual interpretation, textual meaning and authorial intention are the same thing."[22] Several scholars (like the one just quoted) who likely would eschew the conservatism commonly associated with originalism still agreed that the meaning of a text could only be what its author intended to communicate.[23]

The philosophically stronger reconnection of interpretation to the intent contained in the text also meant that the generality or abstraction of a particular clause could no longer simply be asserted or theorized—its level or breadth also was properly understood as a matter of empirical historical investigation. As Whittington put it in responding to Dworkin's famous and historically unsubstantiated claim that general constitutional terms were intended to refer to moral realities best articulated by judges, "That their language can be linked to broad moral principles through a purely semantic analysis, however, tells us little about the proper interpretation of the text. In order to discover the intended reference, we must investigate the historical intentions of the relevant actors, not apply an abstract semantic theory."[24]

The improved defense of the dependence of textual meaning on intent also clarified the separability of questions about the meaning of the text from those about its authority. The question of whether a political community wished to be bound by a text as an authority could not be settled by its original meaning but ultimately only in terms of that community's norms of legal-political obligation.[25] As we have seen throughout this study, originalists typically justified the authority of the constitutional text by arguments rooted in popular sovereignty and the text's status as law. Other scholars argued that with the passage of time authoritative norms may shift and the Constitution may no longer deserve adherence or that it may have to be "innovatively" interpreted to cohere with current understandings of justice that could make it authoritative.[26] While the distinction between the meaning of a text and its authority had often been collapsed by earlier lawyerly originalists, the recognition of that distinction clarified the magnitude of the political choice involved in abandoning the Constitution when its original intent was known. Whittington cleverly underscored this point by emphasizing that original intent could not always be known and therefore should be supplemented with what he called "construction," defined as "the method of elaborating constitutional meaning in [the] political realm" by "melding of the document with external interests and principles."[27] But part of what demanded and legitimated such a "construction" was that it stood as a political settlement necessitated *because* the original intent of the Constitution was consulted and did not address or decisively settle a particular issue.[28] Still, if the Constitution was an authoritative legal communication, then to interpret it was to be an originalist. When original meaning was exhausted, actors had two choices: participate in the politics of construction or forthrightly make the more heterodox argument that they conceived of the Constitution as merely a symbol or a set of practices or a conversation—but not as law.[29]

Increased theoretical justification for the equation of interpretation with the recovery of original intent tended to push the originalist debate toward more sustained reflection about historical inquiry. Originalists confronted the claim that both constitutional text and history were indeterminate, and typically they responded that this criticism was misplaced. Originalism did not depend on the fantasy of determinism. The originalist proposition was that empirical evidence of original intent could constrain the discretion of interpreters better than legal liberal theories, which simply assumed indeterminacy or abstraction without adequate historical investigation and which consequently depended upon the resulting judicial discretion.[30] If constitutional meaning were as unfathomable as the indeterminacy thesis claimed, it could not support the active use of judicial power.[31] Originalists insisted that law, to be law, must have at least some content that existed externally of, and prior to, application by an interpreter. If not there was "no identifiable constitution at all, merely a practice of constitutional interpretation."[32]

Nonetheless, there was a recognition of the need for better rules about what counted as evidence of original intent. Earl Maltz suggested using legal conventions analogous to those governing the interpretation of other authoritative documents, especially statutes, or the shared intent of a supermajority. Meeting the issue in a different way, Whittington denied that the intent of a collective body, such as a drafting or ratifying convention, was inherently indeterminate. "To the extent that a core of common principles can be found, the text has meaning, though the consequences of those principles may be in dispute," he wrote. The challenge of discovering the core of shared meaning was evidentiary and empirical. Indeed, Whittington and Kay emphasized that the very process of negotiating and approving the text demonstrated that it had some commonly recognized meaning, even if the motivations or expectations surrounding it differed for particular members of the authorizing group.[33] Kay argued further that in actual litigation judges were not asked to give a full account of the original meaning of a constitutional provision, but only to answer the binary question of whether original intent permitted or disallowed a challenged government action: "All [the judge] needs to do is decide which of the two possible answers in that case is *more likely* . . . consistent with original intentions."[34] H. Jefferson Powell, a critic of originalism, offered several rules for originalist historical inquiry. They were intended to discipline originalism by calling attention to the subjectivity involved in historical interpretation. Thus, Powell urged caution but also recognized that historical inquiry would always be part of American constitutionalism because consideration of the source and extent of legal authority was unavoidably historical.[35]

Saikrishna B. Prakash applied some of these arguments to Rakove's treatment of originalism, which he described as a "straw man" version of the theory because Rakove had equated it with determinate meaning. Additionally, Prakash argued that Rakove's own scholarship proved that such acts of historical recovery were possible and that Rakove improperly attempted to "salvage history while savaging originalism."[36] At a deeper level, Prakash accused Rakove of practicing "'history department law'" because he did not adequately appreciate what was required if the constitutional text was to be treated as law. Lawmaking, including the creation of the Constitution, was an act that set rules for the future, in this case by inscribing them in a text with a finite set of meanings. Echoing the philosophical arguments of the originalists influenced by speech-act theory, Prakash reminded historians that textually based law was impossible if "lawmakers codify words but not meaning," which would require recognizing some set of words as law while simultaneously supplying them with meaning of one's own choosing.[37] Prakash's fundamental point cleverly reversed the historian's dismissal of "law office history" by insisting that law, at its core, consisted of rules with limited content that were fixed prior to interpretation.

Coopting Originalism and Historical Argument

In the late 1980s and 1990s the persistence and theoretical refinement of originalism forced liberal defenders of modern judicial power to account more thoroughly for history and original intent in their own theories. Consequently, despite the academic popularity of hermeneutic claims of subjectivity and indeterminacy, many legal liberal theoreticians followed originalists in the "turn to history." They searched for a "useable past," in the words of one, because "for better or worse, the lawyer participates in a culture in which historical arguments are important, and it is therefore unhelpful to throw up one's hands."[38] From her engaged perspective as a historian and advocate of legal liberalism, Laura Kalman agreed that "we [legal liberals] are stuck with originalism." Consequently she counseled pragmatic use of originalist arguments to protect and advance liberal goals.[39]

Eighteenth-century republicanism was a prominent historical idea that defenders of judicial power found pragmatically useful for opposing originalism. Theorists such as Frank R. Michelman, Bruce A. Ackerman, and Cass R. Sunstein drew primarily on the work of historians Bernard Bailyn, Gordon Wood, and J. G. A. Pocock to emphasize the importance at the American founding of such republican ideals as civic virtue, deliberative democracy, political participation, and commitment to an objectively knowable common good. Originalism was rejected not only because of its recent alliance with political conservatism but also because it was rooted in the classical liberal element of American constitutionalism. Originalism was only capable of supporting a liberal constitutionalism containing only a discrete (not ever-expanding) body of natural rights and a conception of politics as nothing more than the pluralistic bargaining of interest groups.[40]

The "republican revival" in constitutional theory provided modern liberal jurisprudence with a historically derived counterattack on originalism, one that still encouraged and depended upon modern judicial power to achieve its goals.[41] For example, Michelman stated that in his theory the judiciary, and especially the Supreme Court, could "take on as one of their ascribed functions the modeling of active self-government that citizens find practically beyond reach." The nation was incapable of deliberative self-government, but the Court could be a *"representation* and trace of the People's absent self-government."[42]

Bruce A. Ackerman's anti-originalist, neo-republican use of history similarly relied on judicial power. In Ackerman's view judges should protect the informal constitutional amendment of the New Deal. Like the founding and the formal amendments of Reconstruction, it was an expression of constitution-making by the sovereign people, who remained the source of legitimate political authority in the republican scheme. By redefining the New Deal as the functional equivalent of an Article V amendment, Ackerman called upon a historical sensibility and a core element of republicanism to protect the regulatory-welfare state from the conservative political movement that had emerged since the 1960s. The Court truly spoke for "we the people" in periods of "normal politics," so it could preserve informal constitutional amendments achieved in "constitutional moments" such as the New Deal. In this way Ackerman's convoluted protection of the New Deal regulatory-welfare state attempted to erect a legal-theoretical bar to any legislative attempts at reform that were unsatisfactory to the Court as the new voice of "we the people."[43]

Cass R. Sunstein combated originalism by combining the republican idea of deliberative democracy with a common law approach to constitutional adjudication. He stated that deliberative democracy was best achieved by constitutional reforms pursued not in courts but in more democratic venues, such as state governments, administrative bodies, and Congress.[44] Nevertheless, he did not abandon a fundamental dependence on judicial power. Sunstein would have the Supreme Court take an even more skeptical approach to legislative classifications based on race, gender, sexual orientation, and poverty, in order to provide citizens with the political equality required for full participation in democratic deliberation. He also would have the Court substantially reformulate First Amendment law by abandoning some kinds of speech currently protected and extending protection to others. Such judicially imposed changes would advance the deliberative democracy he thought was required by historical appreciation of the importance of republicanism.[45]

Sunstein also met the originalist challenge in another way. Asserting that

the Constitution should be understood at a high level of abstraction to preserve its original meaning, he advocated a "soft originalism" that would be
created through the common law tools of analogical reasoning and *stare decisis*. By maintaining the modern position that constitutional language created
abstract standards that judges specified in adjudication, Sunstein would allow
them to revise or alter constitutional meaning by analogical and precedential
reasoning, or when they thought that social and political change required it.[46]

The work of Lawrence Lessig presented yet another variation on the continued influence of originalism in constitutional theory. Lessig proposed to
maintain "fidelity" to the Constitution through a process of "translation."[47]
But for him the meaning of the Constitution was derived mainly from context, not original intent, so its meaning changed with social and political developments. Changes in context required present-day judicial translation of
original constitutional "commitments" or "values" in ways that realized the
original meaning in new circumstances. Proffering concern that the relevance
and importance of original constitutional meaning be more fully recognized
in constitutional theory, Lessig developed criteria to guide the Court in its
duty of "translation." But the major burden of this theory was to show "the
sense in which translation can be used as a shield against a current crusade of
restoration organized under the banner of originalism and fidelity."[48] Thus,
translation could justify judicial activism in the area of individual rights, long
identified by originalists as a proper area for restraint.[49]

Each in his own way, Lessig, Ackerman, and Sunstein recognized the importance of the founding and original constitutional meaning. However, they
did so in ways that clearly divorced their projects from the originalist attempt
to limit judicial power through historical inquiry. The informal amendment
of Ackerman, the common law constitutional updating of Sunstein, and the
translation of Lessig were all forms of what Charles A. Miller had earlier called
"ongoing" history. This type of history did not see the text of the Constitution as having established commands that bound interpreters, as originalists
did, but consulted history as a demonstration of the "currents and lessons of
experience. Ongoing history does not say 'this is what was expected,' but 'this
is what the nation has become.'"[50] Such responses to originalism are best understood as calls for the continued use of modern judicial power in defense
of modern liberalism. They offered abstract versions of history that, like the
Dworkinian concept/conception distinction they mirrored, sought to justify

judicial domination of constitutional change through the updating of a "living Constitution." Such "liberal" or "soft" originalism, as it has come to be known, did reflect the success of originalists in continuing the debate about the relevance of history, the role of judicial review, and the nature of constitutional change. But, as one observer pointed out, the fundamental gap between the liberal originalists of the 1990s and the originalism that had emerged since the 1960s was the difference between "a Supreme Court that is *an agent* of social change and a Supreme Court that *takes account* of social changes only after they have already occurred."[51]

Increased Historical Research

While the theoretical and jurisprudential debates surrounding originalism developed, another notable development in the 1990s was a steady stream of new historical research. Recent work focused less on gainsaying the legitimacy of the Warren Court's rights or equal protection jurisprudence, as the lawyerly originalism of figures such as Berger and Bork often had, and more on providing a solid historical basis for the development of constitutional doctrine.[52] To some extent this work proceeded on a track independent of the theoretical arguments, but at a deeper level the rapid increase in scholarship designed to demonstrate the original meaning of the text illustrated the influence of the notion that this was in fact the proper object of interpretation. Additionally, some of this scholarship was in dialogue with important recent originalist Supreme Court decisions (examined below).

Michael McConnell's work well illustrated the tendencies of originalist historical scholarship in the 1990s. While active in the jurisprudential debate,[53] he also consulted the history of the founding and the early republic to argue that the free exercise clause of the First Amendment was originally intended to create judicially enforceable religious exemptions from secular laws of general application.[54] In another widely noted historical argument, McConnell offered an originalist defense of *Brown v. Board of Education* (1954), the famous school desegregation decision. Considering congressional debates on the civil rights acts of the 1870s as instances of constitutional interpretation by many of those who drafted the Fourteenth Amendment, McConnell argued that *Brown* was within the legitimate range of interpretations of the amendment held by its authors.[55] McConnell's work offered historical evidence as the basis for legal doctrine and typified the originalist view that the original under-standing of the text and structure of the Constitution could be known and should limit judicial interpretation.

Other new and equally detailed originalist historical arguments similarly supported or implied conservative positions in several areas that can only be mentioned here. In the wake of recent Supreme Court decisions the commerce clause and federalism received particular attention.[56] Executive power and the Second Amendment also were the subjects of close study.[57]

Many such recent originalist arguments were contested.[58] Likewise, there were abundant further examples of other scholars relying on actual histori-cal evidence and not merely the idea of it at the jurisprudential level. For ex-ample, Suzanna Sherry resurrected the logic of Justice Arthur Goldberg's *Gris-wold v. Connecticut* (1965) concurrence and argued that the original intent of the Ninth Amendment justified judicial protection of unenumerated rights, thereby rewarding "historically-minded nonoriginalists beyond their wildest dreams."[59] Others argued that support for race-based affirmative action, and hence justification for judicial protection of it, could be found in the original intent of Reconstruction-era poor relief legislation, Freedmen's Bureau poli-cies, civil rights laws, and constitutional amendments.[60]

Additionally, several noted liberal historians submitted an *amicus* brief to the Supreme Court in *Patterson v. McLean Credit Union* (1989), arguing that nondiscrimination provisions of the 1866 Civil Rights Act applied to private persons, not just state action, even though this claim was not supported by the scholarship of one of the brief's signatories.[61] In another brief, several noted critics of originalism argued on originalist grounds that President George H. W. Bush could not constitutionally commit American troops to combat in the Persian Gulf without congressional authorization.[62] The impeachment of Pres-ident Bill Clinton also induced longtime liberal critics of originalism to defend him with originalist arguments. Cass R. Sunstein, for example, consulted Eng-lish constitutional history and the framing, ratification, and interpretation of the impeachment clause of the Constitution, drawing conclusions about what "*the founders were thinking*" and the "general agreement" during the rati-fication period. Laurence Tribe also consulted historical sources to support his view of the original intent of the Constitution's impeachment provision.[63]

While we cannot adjudicate the myriad historical disputes involved in these examples, it is worth exploring another one in a bit more depth to appreciate the extent to which originalism reoriented the scholarly debate onto the terrain of history. Scholars recently have considered whether originalist jurisprudence could justify a claim of a "regulatory taking" under the Fifth Amendment, in which litigants challenge legislation that without physical expropriation diminishes property values or extracts from individuals the cost of public benefits. Investigations into this issue were prompted in part by Justice Scalia's majority opinion in *Lucas v. South Carolina Coastal Council* (1992), which said that strictly speaking the claim of a regulatory taking was not reconcilable to originalism but held that determination of a compensable taking could be based on the ancient harm-benefit distinction in the common law of nuisance. In a rather non-originalist fashion, Scalia noted that the bare language of the amendment, despite the limitation of its original intent to physical deprivations, also could be read more broadly to encompass regulatory deprivations.[64]

At one extreme, Richard Epstein, a prominent libertarian defender of property rights, advocated active judicial use of the takings clause in a fashion that mirrored legal liberal defenses of judicially created rights. Epstein appealed to the general principles underlying the clause and the Constitution as a whole rather than to the more limited meaning the clause had at the time of its adoption. He regarded the takings clause to have incorporated a classical liberal, Lockean conception of property. In the modern world, he argued, constitutionally protected Lockean property rights required compensation for regulatory takings. This protection was due even if the framers did not recognize that it was implied by the principle they adopted as fundamental law.[65]

Douglas W. Kmiec, a conservative originalist, argued that the original intent of the takings clause was to incorporate the established common law harm-benefit distinction, in which the right of private property did not include the right to commit nuisances. Accordingly, regulations that prevented nuisance-like harms did not require compensation, but those that extracted public benefits from private property were compensable. Kmiec defended *Lucas* and *Dolan v. Tigard* (1994) as a return to both the original meaning of the takings clause and federalism. Indeed, these decisions could be regarded as originalist because they resurrected federalism from its moribund status since the establishment of the New Deal regulatory state. Instead of having the Court dictate a solution to every local dispute, the decisions linked the requirement of compensation to an evolving state law of nuisance. And by requiring compensation for regulations not aimed at a nuisance-like use of property, they ensured that the costs of public policy were not unfairly borne by individual property owners.[66]

William Michael Treanor countered the originalist arguments of property rights advocates with an originalist argument of his own.[67] Treanor argued that the takings clause was originally intended to apply only to physical deprivations and that it reflected eighteenth-century republicanism, not Lockean-liberal individualism. The original intent, said Treanor, was that compensation was required only when the majoritarian political process inadequately protected physical possession of property, not when regulation diminished the value of property held by those who could defend themselves in the political process. Therefore, the takings clause allowed government to realize the public good even if the value of private property was diminished through regulation in the process. Consequently, Treanor would have denied compensation to the property owners in *Lucas* and *Dolan*.

As the work of Treanor and others showed, liberals clearly regarded historical research and originalist theory as too important to be left to conservative or libertarian critics of judicial power. It is for this reason that some recent suggestions of a "new originalism" on the scene have identified one of its major features as a liberal willingness to treat history in the broad or abstract way generally resisted by scholars who are more critical of judicial power.[68] It remains to be seen whether this development will encourage liberals to claim the mantle of originalism directly or to continue theorizing non-originalist uses of history that encourage judges to advance a preferred normative theory.[69] Likewise, as we have seen, recently originalists and others have produced more refined defenses of interpretation plus detailed historical research and have not been focused as much as was the originalism of the 1980s on attacking the rights and equal protection jurisprudence of the Warren and Burger Courts.[70] Furthermore, fruitful engagement with the question of whether originalism is necessarily tied to a morally skeptical legal positivism or a posture of majoritarian deference also has shown that the doctrine is not simply reactive or naysaying. Although these recent developments add nuance and sophistication to originalism, they also bespeak a certain fragmentation and diffusion of the originalist project into possibly incompatible versions. Careful historical recovery and philosophical grounding of originalism are more complicated and perhaps more divisive tasks than the critique that particular decisions or doctrines of the Warren and Burger Courts bore little readily discernible relationship to the original meaning of the Constitution.[71]

Originalism and the Supreme Court in the 1990s

Although it is clear that originalism substantially reoriented constitutional theory, its influence on the Court was not as deep. Here we will briefly survey some of the most notable originalist opinions of the 1990s, but we nonetheless observe that while originalism became more prominent, the Rehnquist Court still cannot be regarded as originalist in orientation.

Justice Antonin Scalia wrote notable originalist opinions denying rights claims that would have undermined legislative prerogatives. For example, in *Harmelin v. Michigan* (1991), Scalia's majority opinion upheld a state mandatory sentencing law against a claim that the Eighth Amendment's ban on "cruel and unusual punishments" created a right to "proportionate" punishment.[72] Scalia relied heavily on the pre-adoption history of the "cruel and unusual" formulation, the understanding of the concept at the time the amendment was adopted, and its early judicial interpretation. He wrote that the original meaning of a prohibition on "cruel and unusual punishments" did not require punishments to be proportionate to the individual crime, but only banned certain modes of punishment.

Scalia's opinion in *Harmelin* also reflected the originalist challenge to modern judicial power by rejecting the invitation to engage in the textually and historically unguided "balancing" test proposed by the statute's challengers. Guidelines for determining the proportionality of a punishment were not clear, unlike those for determining which modes of punishment were originally understood as "cruel and unusual." Consequently, if judges determined proportionality after the legislature had entered its judgment in the form of the statute at issue, they took up "an invitation to imposition of subjective values."[73]

Scalia also used originalist analysis to defend the separation of powers and federalism. For example, he dissented in *Morrison v. Olson* (1988), which upheld the post-Watergate independent counsel statute. He appealed to text and history (and secondarily to the Court's precedents) to defend what he understood as the originally intended unity of the executive branch and the constitutional structure of separation of powers. In addition to analyzing the text for what it revealed about the structure and relationship of the three branches,

Scalia cited historical sources such as the *Federalist*, the Massachusetts Constitution of 1780, and the records of the Philadelphia convention to argue that "the Founders conspicuously and very consciously declined to sap the Executive's strength . . . by dividing the executive power." Such a division was precisely what had been achieved in the independent counsel law, contrary to the originally intended design of the Constitution.[74] As in *Harmelin*, equally notable in *Morrison* was Scalia's pointed condemnation of the majority's balancing test as a threat to the rule of law.[75]

In *Plaut v. Spendthrift Farm* (1995) Scalia's majority opinion undertook another originalist defense of the separation of powers. Citing the *Federalist*, early judicial decisions, the historian Gordon Wood, and the early twentieth-century constitutional scholar Edward S. Corwin, Scalia analyzed the history of the separation concept and the nature of judicial power established in Article III of the Constitution. Understood according to their original meaning, these fundamental constitutional principles prohibited Congress from requiring federal courts to reopen final judgments in certain financial securities suits, which earlier had been held time-barred and dismissed.[76]

In *Printz v. United States* (1997) the issue was federalism. Scalia wrote the majority opinion holding unconstitutional a provision of a congressional act requiring local law enforcement officials to investigate the background of firearms purchasers. He found no constitutional text directly bearing on the issue but engaged the government's defense of the law, which adduced statues of the first Congress as contemporaneous evidence of the original meaning of the Constitution. Scalia found that "these early laws establish, at most, that the Constitution was originally understood to permit imposition on state *judges* to enforce federal prescriptions, insofar as those prescriptions related to matters appropriate for the judicial power."[77] Nor did Scalia find any support for the government's case in the *Federalist*.[78] Conceding that such historical materials did not conclusively settle the issue, Scalia turned to the structure of the Constitution for a principle that could help resolve the case. He found it in the "incontestible" idea that the Constitution created a system of "dual sovereignty," which prohibited the national government from commandeering the states for enforcement of national laws. In this way federalism, as an originally intended feature of the constitutional design, guided his resolution of the case.[79] Additionally, as in *Morrison* and *Harmelin*, Scalia explicitly declined to undertake a balancing analysis.[80]

Originalist thinking also was apparent in the opinions of Justice Clarence

Thomas. His most notable originalist opinions were his defenses of federalism in his concurrence in *United States v. Lopez* (1995) and his dissent in *United States Term Limits, Inc. v. Thornton* (1995).[81] In *Lopez* the Court overturned a federal statute based on the commerce clause for the first time since the New Deal, holding that possession of a firearm within one thousand feet of a school did not "substantially effect" interstate commerce. Thomas's concurrence offered a thorough originalist reevaluation of commerce clause jurisprudence. He argued that the "substantial effect" test was a New Deal innovation that had spawned case law "far from the original understanding of the Commerce Clause." He discussed the text, structure, and history of the clause and analyzed the Court's early decisions "to show how far [the Court had] departed from the original understanding and to demonstrate that the result we reach today is by no means 'radical.'" Notwithstanding the post–New Deal expansion of the commerce clause, Thomas argued that the Constitution was originally understood to grant Congress only limited power, not the general police power it now regularly exercised through the clause with the Court's approval. He concluded that "there was no question that activities wholly separate from business, such as gun possession, were beyond the reach of the commerce power."[82]

In *Thornton,* the term limits case, Justice Stevens's majority opinion relied in part on a historical argument to hold that the qualifications clauses of the Constitution (Article I, sections 2 and 3) were exclusive requirements for membership in Congress. The decision overturned a state constitutional amendment that limited the number of terms of service for members of the state's congressional delegation. Thomas's dissent, joined by Chief Justice Rehnquist and Justices Scalia and Sandra Day O'Connor, defended federalism as a critical feature of the original intent of the Constitution. Thomas argued that the express terms of the Constitution did not prohibit states from imposing additional qualifications on their delegates—the people had not consented to such a limitation on their power. The federalist principle of reserved powers in the Tenth Amendment allowed the states to add qualifications. Thomas supported this position with an analysis of the records of the Philadelphia convention, the ratification debates, the *Federalist,* and state government practices immediately after ratification. He concluded that such evidence proved that the original intent was only that Congress could not supplement the qualifications clauses; this in no way affected the states' power over the issue.[83]

Thomas also wrote an originalist concurrence in *McIntyre v. Ohio Elections*

Commission (1995), where the Court found a violation of the First Amendment in a state's prohibition of the distribution of anonymous literature during an election campaign. The majority relied on the Court's doctrines and precedents and secondarily on general historical evidence concerning the practice. Thomas argued that the law should be overturned because it violated the original intent of the First Amendment. Acknowledging the paucity of the historical record on the precise question of anonymous campaign literature, Thomas turned to "the practices and beliefs held by the Founders."[84] He cited modern historians, discussed the tradition of anonymous political writing exemplified by the *Federalist,* and analyzed the use of anonymous pamphlets in the famous Zenger trial (1735) and controversies involving the Continental Congress and the New Jersey state legislature. From these sources he concluded that "freedom of the press" was intended to include anonymous political writing and that later regulations such as the challenged statute were in error.

It is notable that in *McIntyre* Justice Scalia, joined by Chief Justice Rehnquist, dissented and specifically disagreed with Thomas's originalist concurrence. Scalia first affirmed his adherence to "the Court's (and the society's) traditional view that the Constitution bears its original meaning and is unchanging"[85] but argued that Thomas's historical evidence of anonymous political writing did not conclusively demonstrate that it was originally intended as a constitutional right in the electoral context. Absent conclusive historical evidence, Scalia would have deferred to the statute as a "governmental practice that has become general throughout the United States . . . [and] that has the validation of long, accepted usage."[86] Thus, while maintaining his loyalty to originalism, Scalia held that the proper judicial response to historical ambiguity was deference to the tradition embodied in the statute. The disagreement among the dissenters in *McIntyre* underscored the fact that the Court's originalists did not march in lockstep, nor did they always agree on the dictates of their method in a particular case.

In addition to Scalia, Thomas, and Rehnquist, Justices Kennedy and O'Connor occasionally wrote originalist opinions. Indeed, O'Connor's majority opinion in *New York v. United States* (1992) first announced what became a noticeable trend: the use of originalist arguments to reinvigorate federalism. *New York* overturned a portion of a federal statute requiring states to enact and enforce federal regulation of low-level radioactive waste. Analyzing evidence from the Philadelphia convention of 1787, O'Connor wrote that the core principle of federalism meant that "States are not mere political subdivisions of the

United States [nor] regional offices [or] administrative agencies of the Federal Government."[87]

The trend continued in *Alden v. Maine* (1999), in which Justice Kennedy wrote the majority opinion. The Court held that employees of the state of Maine could not recover overtime pay and damages under the Fair Labor Standards Act (1938). The act unconstitutionally violated Maine's sovereign immunity by providing for private actions against states in the state's own courts without the state's consent. Kennedy elucidated his view of the original understanding of sovereign immunity and federalism by historical analysis of the drafting and ratification of the Constitution, the famous case of *Chisholm v. Georgia* (1793), and the Eleventh Amendment, which overturned *Chisholm*. Kennedy wrote that the Eleventh Amendment retrieved the original understanding of federalism from the *Chisholm* misinterpretation by holding that a state could not be sued in federal court by a citizen of another state or by a citizen of a foreign state. Because the amendment confirmed rather than established sovereign immunity as a constitutional principle, Kennedy affirmed earlier cases indicating that the scope of the immunity was not limited to the bare text of the amendment. Rather, consistent with the reinvigorated federalism announced in *New York* and pursued in *Lopez* and *Printz*, the scope of the immunity was determined ultimately by the fundamental postulates of divided sovereignty that defined the federal system. Sovereign immunity and the originally intended constitutional design of federalism mandated that the state of Maine could not be sued for violation of a federal law in its own courts without its consent.[88]

Originalist opinions in the 1990s were not the exclusive preserve of the Court's conservative and centrist members.[89] For example, Justice David Souter turned to history in response to originalist opinions by Scalia, Thomas, and Kennedy. Concurring in *Lee v. Weisman* (1992), he responded to Scalia's originalist claim that the First Amendment permitted government accommodation of religion by arguing that the original intent of the establishment clause of the First Amendment was to ensure strict separation of church and state.[90] Souter elaborated this argument in *Rosenberger v. University of Virginia* (1995) by consulting James Madison's "Memorial and Remonstrance" (1785), insisting that it supported an originally intended "wall of separation" between church and state.[91] Consulting a wide range of historical sources, Souter also argued in originalist terms in his dissents from the Court's sovereign immunity-federalism cases.[92]

In addition to occasionally forcing other justices to argue in historical terms, another measure of the continuing relevance of originalism was that Justices Thomas and Scalia readily identified themselves with it, not only in some of their judicial opinions but also in scholarly writings and public speeches. For example, Scalia argued that originalism best protected the rule of law in a democratic system because it fostered a rule-based jurisprudence capable of constraining judicial discretion. In treating the Constitution as the source of legal rules he rejected the modern judicial practice, derived from the "common-law, discretion conferring approach," of balancing vague "values" and updating a "Living Constitution" with judges' views of contemporary needs. Substitution of *"current* meaning" for the *"original* meaning" of the text conferred ad hoc, discretionary power on judges and undermined the ability of more democratically legitimate legislatures to adapt the law to change.[93] While Scalia denied that recapturing the subjective mental state of individual historical actors was required, it was possible to comprehend the public understanding of the text of the Constitution by analysis of the ratification debates, the records of the first Congress, and early judicial opinions and commentary.[94] Justice Thomas likewise stated that basing interpretation on the original understanding could reduce judicial discretion and thereby sustain the limits on judges that allowed for the democratic formulation of policy decisions. Thomas also similarly stated that originalism encouraged the clarity, stability, and fairness of a rule-based jurisprudence, in contrast to the more discretionary modern balancing approach.[95]

Judicial opinions and other statements by Scalia and Thomas, plus the ongoing developments in academic theory, assured the continued importance of originalism in the 1990s. However, originalist jurisprudence remained contested among scholars and did not dominate Supreme Court decision-making. Indeed, despite usually voting the same way, even Scalia, Thomas, and Chief Justice Rehnquist did not understand or practice originalism in precisely the same way, nor did they adopt what some originalist theorists might consider the best version of the doctrine. Rehnquist usually relied on historical evidence and textual analysis to resist expansive or innovative rights claims, but in federalism and separation of powers cases he typically relied on more general arguments drawn from structure and principle.[96] Moreover, Scalia described himself as a "faint-hearted" originalist who might not always stick to original meaning in extreme cases (as in holding that the Eighth Amendment prohibition on "cruel and unusual punishments" outlawed "public lashing, or branding of the right hand" though, to be fair, he also doubted that such a case could ever arise).[97] Likewise, Scalia reviled the use of legislative history in statutory interpretation, which one might think would be permitted, if not required, by the logic of originalism.[98] Finally, reliance on tradition in the absence of a clear textual command has been as much a part of Scalia's jurisprudence as originalist arguments based on historical evidence of how the text was understood.[99] Consequently, two close studies of Scalia (from opposed perspectives) recently have concluded that for him originalism is merely one jurisprudential tool designed to achieve the overarching goal of constraining judicial discretion.[100]

Moreover, Scalia's (and Rehnquist's) modern, legal positivist approach was at odds with Justice Thomas's Straussian-inspired attempt to read the Constitution in light of the natural rights basis of the Declaration of Independence.[101] The clearest example of Thomas's approach was a concurrence in which the majority held that federal affirmative action programs were subject to the same strict scrutiny review previously applied only to the states. In a sentence immediately followed by a quotation of the Declaration of Independence, Thomas wrote that "there can be no doubt that the paternalism that appears to lie at the heart of this [affirmative action] program is at war with the principle of inherent equality that underlies and infuses our Constitution."[102] Still, as illustrated in some of Thomas's opinions analyzed above, the most extensive study of his jurisprudence to date has rightly concluded that the natural rights form of originalism is not the only one he has practiced. While Thomas typically subscribed to this version in cases concerning race, such as *Adarand,* in civil liberties and federalism cases he usually located the original meaning of the Constitution by methods that more closely tracked originalism as it had developed in previous decades—textual analysis supplemented by extrinsic evidence of how the text was originally understood.[103]

Beyond such methodological differences among the justices and within their own approaches, other factors revealed the limitations of originalism on the Court. Scholars (and non-originalist justices) began to argue that originalism, whatever its strengths and prominence in theory, has not constrained its practitioners on the Court any more than the legal liberalism it contested.[104] If self-described originalist judges manipulate or ignore historical facts, then the approach is no more judge-proof than the alternatives, and some scholars sympathetic to originalism have not hesitated from pointing out what they perceive as lapses.[105]

The most basic illustration of the limited influence of originalism on the Court was that the originalist opinions of the 1990s were only a fraction of its overall output. Accordingly, most recent observers of the Rehnquist Court agree that it encompasses several competing jurisprudential approaches, with many justices influenced as much or more by their "legal process" education as by originalism. The bulk of the Court's opinions cohere around a pragmatic, incremental centrism, not adherence to original intent at any cost. Moreover, although the innovations of the New Deal and the Warren and Burger years have not been wholly undisturbed, the Rehnquist Court, let alone originalism, has neither fundamentally undermined them nor decisively reoriented the law.[106] Modern judicial review, if not confidently reformist legal liberalism, is alive and well.[107]

Conclusion

The limitations of originalism on the Rehnquist Court form part of the conclusion about its place in American constitutional history after World War II. Notwithstanding the ongoing and substantial originalist influence on theory and commentary, its failure fundamentally to reorient Supreme Court decision-making supports the view that American constitutional jurisprudence is best described empirically as an amalgam of plural modalities of argument that depend on competing conceptions of legal authority, which are never able wholly to displace one another.[108] While, as we have seen, originalism to some extent cut across the modalities of text, structure, and doctrine, its practitioners most commonly called upon the historical mode of argument to contest the legal liberalism they perceived as motivated by controversial ethical or political commitments insufficiently grounded in the original Constitution.[109] In attacking legal liberalism, then, originalism returned the historical (and less directly the textual and structural) modes of argument to more prominence, but it did not establish itself as the primary legitimate jurisprudential method.

The history of the emergence and development of originalism presented here also bears upon an interpretive claim associated with the prominence of "historical institutionalism" in recent scholarly literature on law and courts.[110] While not wholly rejecting the legal realist–derived notion that political loyalties affect judicial behavior, historical institutionalists claim that legal change is best explained by regarding the interaction of law and politics as reciprocal and nonreductive. Legal principles and conceptions of judicial office have normative (if not determinative) force for commentators and judges who think about how to decide cases and develop doctrine in ways that can be regarded as legitimate and persuasive in the legal-political system they inhabit. The influence and attraction of various jurisprudential elements wax and wane as the law is affected by the intellectual developments and partisan shifts surrounding it. This process affects legal actors' perceptions of what counts as an available or persuasive mode of argument without necessarily determining how it might be used or misused in a particular case or doctrinal area. Likewise, changes in the context of the law also suggest the limitations or dangers of some approaches while pointing to the attractions of others that might have been neglected.

This is what happened as the New Deal coalition disintegrated and the new conservative political movement emerged. These changes created the political space for originalism to have influence again. Its traditional jurisprudential approach and conception of legal authority and legitimacy implied conservative policy results, at least when compared to recent liberal Supreme Court decisions and the modes of argument on which they often rested. Therefore the arrival of originalism, like the academic development of legal realism and process-restraint jurisprudence before it, shows that in a receptive political and intellectual context scholarly defense of one or another mode of argument can shift the boundaries of what is considered admissible or persuasive. In particular cases the Court may manipulate or ignore the requirements of originalism (or any other mode of argument) to achieve ideological ends, and thus the realist-derived, behavioralist approach to the study of law and courts cannot be wholly dismissed. But over the longer term standards and boundaries for judicial action are established by scholars' evaluations of the Court and their education of practitioners, as well as the effect they have on the justices' jurisprudence and conceptions of their own roles. In this way principled jurisprudential commitments affect what arguments get made and how opinions are written.[111]

Accordingly, despite the limitations of originalism in practice, which support at least some form of the realist-behavioralist position, a fundamental attraction of originalism remains its expression of the traditional liberal constitutionalist idea that law must have authoritative, foundational content before its application. From this perspective too much permeability to ethical argument or too much pragmatic instrumentalism threatens the regime's attempt to secure order and stability by using words to distinguish law from politics. Originalism, then, is perhaps best understood as an attempt to reassert this traditional liberal constitutionalist view as a normative standard for evaluation and direction of the Court, but one that in practice still demonstrates the inevitable inability of words wholly to separate law from politics.

Perhaps unsurprisingly, once originalist criticism helped curtail legal liberalism, some scholars attempted to make use of it for liberal ends, while others advanced theoretical justifications for the pluralist, pragmatic, and common law–oriented practice that often typifies contemporary judicial decision-making.[112] While the former development is more susceptible to judgment based on historical facts, the latter may offer a stronger rationale for consolidating legal liberal achievements. Of course, pragmatic, pluralist theories premise the ultimate unworkability of originalism, but they at least acknowledge the influence of the originalist conception of law in the American regime (though without according it any privileged normative status). What remains to be seen is whether incorporation of the originalist idea among the various ingredients of a pragmatic or pluralist theory, or the related view of constitutional law as a deliberative "process" or "conversation," can be made to cohere in a fashion capable of displacing the traditional liberal constitutionalist conception of legal authority and the "textualist-originalist interpretive presumption that written constitutionalism introduces into American government."[113] Indeed, the emergence and development of originalism show that a merely symbolic, pragmatic, or judicially adapted Constitution is in deep conflict with the basic American legal and political principles that derive from the writtenness and historical reality of the fundamental law. It is significant that in originalism the post–World War II political shift toward conservatism called out a longstanding form of jurisprudence related directly to the nature of the regime—not some mode or amalgam less readily found there. This confirms that in the American regime changes are bound, at least along one dimension, by a system of social contract and written fundamental law that in practice limits the jurisprudential concepts legal-political actors consider appealing and persuasive.

Even though the resonance and traction that originalism gains from the nature of the American regime presents a continuing obstacle to theorists of the legal liberal, pluralist, pragmatic, or common law Constitution, in a more concrete sense its own future also remains to be seen. Only the passage of time will permit judgment of whether the arrival of originalism on the scene is the first step toward returning to a more traditional conception of the American constitutional order. It is quite possible that instead it is the last gasp of that order before its final replacement by some version of the pragmatic, pluralist instrumentalism now gaining adherents, in which originalism is likely to be just one more tool as susceptible to manipulation as the others.

At another level, as we have seen above, contemporary theorists debate whether originalism is wed to the legal positivist, majoritarian restraintism characteristic of its earlier and more reactive attempt to refocus debate on the original meaning of the Constitutional text. This development highlights that American constitutionalism is concerned not only with the limitations imposed by foundational authority as expressed in a legal text but also strives to reconcile this vision of law with more abstract ethical imperatives, as well as critical evaluations of how well the polity lives up to the principles and limits it proclaims as foundational. But this point cuts both ways. The Warren Court demonstrated that the modern liberal ontology of rights (or autonomy) and equality are part of the constitutional order and will sometimes drive judicial decisions in spite of other conceptions of the regime, even if such decisions cannot be readily reconciled to either the original understanding of foundational texts or the conceptions of the regime held by the Court's critics. Accordingly, we do well to note that many of the Warren Court's far-reaching decisions had some plausible claim to roots in the constitutional order and established doctrine, and those now regarded as settled law would not have been so quickly accepted if the polity and Court observers had regarded them as so innovative as to be alien.[114]

From this perspective we should recognize forthrightly that as a defense of the written Constitution, originalism partakes of the conservatism inherent in the constitutionalist attempt to achieve order and stability by creating some distance between written law and political aspirations based on more direct appeals to justice, nature, rights, or class. The rules, procedures, and forms written into the American Constitution limit in advance what can be admitted to legal-political debate. That debate privileges legally educated elites who have the special knowledge required to participate in it. Accordingly, originalist maintenance of the written Constitution fences out more direct recourse to other political principles as the basis for reforms that might circumvent the constitutional process in favor of more profoundly redistributionist or emancipatory aims.[115] Yet it should always be recalled that modern constitutionalism, and modern politics more generally, was birthed in the desire to gain a measure of order and stability at the expense of continued direct and sometimes bloody confrontation with divisive questions of ultimate justice.[116] The value of modern written constitutionalism is its ability to justify on the bases of relatively spare ontological principles a "second best" regime that can provide peace and prosperity, even a haven for philosophy, while also permitting individuals to pursue life projects whose ultimate principles are often irreconcilable. Politics in this regime frequently features rather thin conceptions of the public good and human virtue—but ones that do not require more agreement on the nature of justice than we moderns seem able to generate.

Notes

Introduction

1. I do not claim that all originalists subscribe to every aspect of the following formulation, but compare Keith E. Whittington, *Constitutional Interpretation: Textual Meaning, Original Intent, and Judicial Review* (Lawrence: University Press of Kansas, 1999), 35–36; Richard S. Kay, "American Constitutionalism," in *Constitutionalism: Philosophical Foundations*, ed. Larry Alexander (Cambridge: Cambridge University Press, 1998), 16–63, 27–35; Earl M. Maltz, *Rethinking Constitutional Law: Originalism, Interventionism, and the Politics of Judicial Review* (Lawrence: University Press of Kansas, 1994), 20, 26–27, 34; Antonin Scalia, *A Matter of Interpretation* (Princeton, NJ: Princeton University Press, 1997), 37–41; id., "Originalism: The Lesser Evil," *University of Cincinnati Law Review* 57 (1989): 849–65, 854; Robert H. Bork, *The Tempting of America: The Political Seduction of the Law* (New York: Free Press, 1990), 5, 144, 218; Raoul Berger, *Federalism: The Founders' Design* (Norman: University of Oklahoma Press, 1987), 70–71; id., *Government by Judiciary: The Transformation of the Fourteenth Amendment* (Cambridge: Harvard University Press, 1977), 363.

2. For example, Maltz, *Rethinking*, 49–73; Whittington, *Interpretation*, 27–32, 37.

3. The following discussion draws on Andrew C. McLaughlin, *The Confederation and the Constitution, 1783–1789* (New York: Harper, 1905), 247–52; id., *A Constitutional History of the United States* (New York: Appleton, Century, Crofts, 1935), 91–105; Edward S. Corwin, *The "Higher Law" Background of American Constitutional Law* (1928; repr. Ithaca, NY: Cornell University Press, 1988); Charles McIlwain, *Constitutionalism: Ancient and Modern*, (1947; Ithaca, NY: Cornell University Press, 1987); Gordon Wood, *The Creation of the American Republic, 1776–1787* (1969; repr. New York: W. W. Norton, 1972), 259–305, 453–63, 600–602; Gerald Stourzh, "*Constitution*: Changing Meanings of the Term from the Early Seventeenth to the Late Eighteenth Century," in *Conceptual Change and the Constitution*, ed. Terrence Ball and J. G. A. Pocock (Lawrence: University Press of Kansas, 1987), 35–53; Donald S. Lutz, *The Origins of American Constitutionalism* (Baton Rouge: Louisiana State University Press, 1988); Herman Belz, "Constitutionalism and the American Founding," in *The Framing and Ratification of the Constitution*, ed. Leonard W. Levy and Dennis J. Mahoney (New York: Macmillan, 1987), 333–54; Kay, "American Constitutionalism."

4. Massachusetts Constitution of 1780, Article 30, in *The Federal and State Constitutions, Colonial Charters, and Other Organic Laws of the States, Territories, and Colonies*, ed. Francis Newton Thorpe, 7 vols. (Washington, DC: GPO, 1909), 3:1893; Jacob Cooke, ed., *The Federalist* (Middletown, CT: Wesleyan University Press, 1961), nos. 1, 3. See also McIlwain, *Constitutionalism*, 146.

5. For more detail, see Gary L. McDowell, "The Language of Law and the Foundations of American Constitutionalism," *William and Mary Quarterly* 3rd ser., 55 (1998): 375–98. See also Philip A. Hamburger, "The Constitution's Accommodation of Social Change," *Michigan Law Review* 88 (1989): 239–327; Walter Berns, "Judicial Review and the Rights and Laws of Nature," *Supreme Court Review 1982*, 49–83.

6. Compare Charles A. Miller, *The Supreme Court and the Uses of History* (Cambridge: Belknap Press of Harvard University Press, 1969), esp. 193, 149–61; Stephen M. Griffin, *American Constitutionalism: From Theory to Politics* (Princeton, NJ: Princeton University Press, 1996), 182.

7. The discussion in this and the following paragraph draws on Philip Bobbitt, *Constitutional Fate* (New York: Oxford University Press, 1982); id., *Constitutional Interpretation* (Oxford: Blackwell, 1991), 11–30; Walter F. Murphy, James E. Fleming, and Sotirios A. Barber, *American Constitutional Interpretation*, 2nd ed. (Westbury, NY: Foundation Press, 1995), 383–418. See also Robert Post, "Theories of Constitutional Interpretation," *Representations* 30 (1990): 13–41; Griffin, *Interpretation*, 143–52; Miller, *Uses*, 14–38.

8. Miller, *Uses*, 26. See also Murphy, Fleming, and Barber, *Interpretation*, 395–97.

9. Morton White, *Social Thought in America: The Revolt Against Formalism* (New York: Viking Press, 1949).

10. See Christopher Wolfe, *The Rise of Modern Judicial Review: From Constitutional Interpretation to Judge-Made Law*, rev. ed. (Lanham, MD: Rowman and Littlefield, 1994). See also William Wiecek, *The Lost World of Classical Legal Thought* (New York: Oxford University Press, 1998) and Morton Horwitz, *The Transformation of American Law, 1870–1960* (New York: Oxford University Press, 1992). For ease of expression I use interchangeably the phrases "modern judicial review" and "modern judicial power."

11. T. Alexander Aleinikoff, "Constitutional Law in the Age of Balancing," *Yale Law Journal* 96 (1987): 943–1005; Wolfe, *Rise*, 426 n1, 247, 258, 291, 293, 359, and chs. 9 and 10. As will be developed in more detail in chapter 1, I follow these scholars (and those in note 17 below) in treating balancing as a manifestation of the intellectual revolt against formalism that increasingly (but not immediately) became characteristic of many areas of constitutional law, and not merely in the First Amendment context as debated, for example, in *Barenblatt v. United States*, 360 U.S. 109 (1959). See also Murphy, Fleming, and Barber, *Interpretation*, 410–14.

12. Classic examples are Woodrow Wilson, *Constitutional Government in the United States* (New York: Columbia University Press, 1908; paper ed., 1961), 55–56, 165–69 and passim; Karl Llewellyn, "The Constitution as an Institution," *Columbia Law Review* 34 (1934): 1–40, esp. 22, 26, 32–33, 39. More generally, see Howard Gillman, "The Collapse of Constitutional Originalism and the Rise of the Notion of the 'Living Constitution' in the Course of American State-Building," *Studies in American Political Development* 11 (1997): 191–247.

13. *Brown v. Board of Education*, 347 U.S. 483 (1954).

14. See Laura Kalman, *The Strange Career of Legal Liberalism* (New Haven: Yale University Press, 1996). In deference to the contemporary usage established largely by Kalman, I adopt the label "legal liberalism." However, the developments outlined here (and in her book) are actually jurisprudential concomitants of liberalism in the version variously called "modern," "progressive," or "pragmatic," not earlier Enlightenment-derived "classical" liberalism. See, for example, Alan Ryan, "Liberalism," in Robert E. Goodin and Philip Pettit, eds., *A Companion to Contemporary Political Philosophy* (Oxford:

Blackwell, 1993), 291–311. I similarly defer to contemporary terminology by referring at various points to "conservatives" who might more punctiliously be labeled "classical liberals," "traditionalists," "natural lawyers," etc. Despite the cost to philosophical precision I cannot undertake discursive *mutatis mutandis* adjustments in every instance.

15. Kalman, *Legal Liberalism,* 13–17, 59, and passim.

16. To cite only a few outstanding examples, see A. Selwyn Miller, "Notes on the Concept of a Living Constitution," *George Washington Law Review* 31 (1963): 881–918; William Brennan, "The Constitution of the United States: Contemporary Ratification" [Georgetown University, October 12, 1985], in *Judges on Judging: Views from the Bench,* ed. David M. O'Brien (Chatham, NJ: Chatham House, 1997), 200–210; Paul Brest, "The Misconceived Quest for Original Understanding," *Boston University Law Review* 60 (1980): 204–54, 224–38. See also Ronald Dworkin, *A Matter of Principle* (1985; repr. Oxford: Clarendon, 1986), 48–50, 55–57.

17. Mark Tushnet, "Truth, Justice, and the American Way: An Interpretation of Public Law Scholarship in the Seventies," *Texas Law Review* 57 (1979): 1307–59, 1322, 1335; id., "Legal Scholarship in the United States: An Overview," *The Modern Law Review* 50 (1987): 804–17, 810; Ronald K. L. Collins and David M. Skover, "The Future of Liberal Legal Scholarship," *Michigan Law Review* 87 (1988): 189–239, 228–29. See also sources cited in note 11.

18. J. Skelly Wright, "Professor Bickel, the Scholarly Tradition, and the Supreme Court," *Harvard Law Review* 84 (1971): 769–805, 797, 804.

19. Ronald Dworkin, "The Jurisprudence of Richard Nixon," *New York Review of Books,* May 4, 1972, 27–35; repr. in id., *Taking Rights Seriously,* paper ed. (Cambridge: Harvard University Press, 1978), 131–49, 134–35.

20. John Hart Ely, *Democracy and Distrust: A Theory of Judicial Review* (Cambridge: Harvard University Press, 1980).

21. Mark Tushnet, "Legal Realism, Structural Review, and Prophecy," *University of Dayton Law Review* 8 (1983): 809–31, 811. This is a major theme of Kalman, *Legal Liberalism.*

22. Paul Brest, "The Fundamental Rights Controversy: The Essential Contradictions of Normative Constitutional Scholarship," *Yale Law Journal* 90 (1981): 1063–1109, 1109.

23. See Ronald Kahn, *The Supreme Court and Constitutional Theory, 1953–1993* (Lawrence: University Press of Kansas, 1994), 211–49; Paul W. Kahn, *Legitimacy and History: Self-Government in American Constitutional Theory* (New Haven: Yale University Press, 1992), 171–209.

24. For a history from this perspective, see Stephen M. Feldman, *American Legal Thought from Premodernism to Postmodernism: An Intellectual Voyage* (New York: Oxford University Press, 2000).

O N E : From Textual Originalism to Modern Judicial Power

1. Compare Morton Horwitz, *The Transformation of American Law, 1780–1860* (Cambridge: Harvard University Press, 1977), 255: "One cannot but be struck by the sharp contrast between the utilitarian and instrumentalist character of early nineteenth century private law and the equally emphatic antiutilitarian, formalist cast of public law." See also T. Alexander Aleinikoff, "Constitutional Law in the Age of Balancing," *Yale Law Journal* 96 (1987): 943–1005, 949–52.

2. William Blackstone, *Commentaries on the Laws of England,* facsimile of 1769 ed., 4 vols. (Chicago: University of Chicago Press, 1979) 1:91, 59, 61. My treatment draws on Christopher Wolfe, *The Rise of Modern Judicial Review: From Constitutional Interpretation to Judge-Made Law,* rev. ed. (Lanham, MD: Rowman and Littlefield, 1994), 18–19; Robert L. Clinton, *Marbury v. Madison and Judicial Review* (Lawrence: University Press of Kansas, 1989), 18–30. For a collection of pre-Blackstone appeals to intent, see Gregory Bassham, *Original Intent and the Constitution: A Philosophical Study* (Lanham, MD: Rowman and Littlefield, 1992), 2, 131–32 n3 and Raoul Berger, "'Original Intention' in Historical Perspective," *George Washington University Law Review* 54 (1986): 296–337, 298–308.

3. Blackstone, *Commentaries,* 1:59, 61. The mischief rule is often known as *Heydon's* rule because of its invocation in Heydon's Case, 3 *Coke's Reports* 7a (1584).

4. Blackstone, *Commentaries,* 1:60.

5. Ibid., 1:91. If parliament's "intent" was "evident and express" it could even make a local lord judge in his own cause.

6. Blackstone's accommodation of equity to judicial interpretation of sovereign parliamentary acts further emphasized that law derived from intent. Equity was the fulfillment of an enactment's intended purpose and never a power to correct a disfavored legislative enactment. Blackstone, *Commentaries,* 1:62.

7. Howard Gillman, "The Collapse of Constitutional Originalism and the Rise of the Notion of the 'Living Constitution' in the Course of American State-Building," *Studies in American Political Development* 11 (1997): 191–247, 203; Stephen M. Griffin, *American Constitutionalism: From Theory to Politics* (Princeton, NJ: Princeton University Press, 1996), 146. For analysis of originalism as constitutional "maintenance," see Paul W. Kahn, *Legitimacy and History: Self-Government in American Constitutional Theory* (New Haven: Yale University Press, 1992), ch. 2. Compare Caleb Nelson, "Originalism and Interpretive Conventions," *University of Chicago Law Review* 70 (2003): 519–98, 563.

8. "Natural justice review" was a temptation in this period, but as a justification for judicial power it was a decidedly minor theme, even in fugitive slave cases. Robert M. Cover, *Justice Accused: Antislavery and the Judicial Process* (New Haven: Yale University Press, 1975), 25–30, 174; Wolfe, *Rise,* 108–13. See also Matthew J. Franck, *Against the Imperial Judiciary: The Supreme Court vs. the Sovereignty of the People* (Lawrence: University Press of Kansas, 1996), 113–49.

9. Jacob E. Cooke, ed., *The Federalist* (Hanover, NH: Wesleyan University Press, 1961), no. 82, 556. Such terminology can be exhaustively traced using Thomas S. Engeman, Edward J. Erler, and Thomas B. Hofeller, eds., *The Federalist Concordance* (Chicago: University of Chicago Press, 1988). See also Wolfe, *Rise,* 20–24.

10. *Federalist,* no. 37, 235–37; Philip A. Hamburger, "The Constitution's Accommodation of Social Change," *Michigan Law Review* 88 (1989): 239–327, 303–10.

11. *Federalist,* no. 78, 525.

12. Ibid., 526, 529. See also Wolfe, *Rise,* 74–79. The anti-Federalist Brutus held the same conception of interpretation, though he feared it would not be honored. Brutus, "To the People of the State of New York" [December 13, 1787], in *The Anti-Federalist: Writings by Opponents of the Constitution,* ed. Herbert J. Storing (Chicago: University of Chicago Press, 1985), 134.

13. For a summary, see Jack Rakove, *Original Meanings: Politics and Ideas in the Making of the Constitution* (New York: Knopf, 1996), 339–65.

14. Morton Horwitz, "Foreword: The Constitution of Change: Legal Fundamentality without Fundamentalism," *Harvard Law Review* 107 (1993): 32–117, 51.

15. This is the general assessment of H. Jefferson Powell, "The Original Understanding of Original Intent," *Harvard Law Review* 98 (1985): 885–948. See also Charles A. Lofgren, "The Original Understanding of Original Intent?" *Constitutional Commentary* 5 (1988): 77–113; Rakove, *Original Meanings,* 341, 349.

16. Alexander Hamilton, "Opinion on the Constitutionality of an Act to Establish a Bank," February 23, 1791, in *The Papers of Alexander Hamilton,* ed. Harold C. Syrett and Jacob Ernest Cooke (New York: Columbia University Press, 1965), 8:97–134, 111. Elbridge Gerry made the same point by quoting Blackstone. Gerry, speech of February 7, 1791, in *Documentary History of the First Federal Congress,* ed. Charlene Bangs Bickford and Helen E. Veit (Baltimore: Johns Hopkins University Press, 1995), 14:453. Hamilton also invoked the "intent of the Convention" and the "sense" of the ratifying conventions. See Wolfe, *Rise,* 29–36, and Lofgren, "Original Understanding," 94 n58.

17. For example, Joseph M. Lynch, *Negotiating the Constitution: The Earliest Debates Over Original Intent* (Ithaca, NY: Cornell University Press, 1999); Kent Greenfield, "Original Penumbras: Constitutional Interpretation in the First Year of Congress," *Connecticut Law Review* 26 (1993): 79–144. See also Robert N. Clinton, "Original Understanding, Legal Realism, and the Interpretation of 'This Constitution,'" *Iowa Law Review* 72 (1987): 1177–1280, 1197–1208.

18. David P. Currie, *The Constitution in Congress: The Federalist Period, 1789–1801* (Chicago: University of Chicago Press, 1997), 122.

19. Greenfield, "Original Penumbras," 133.

20. Madison, speech of May 19, 1789, *Documentary History,* 10:735.

21. For a similar judgment, see Gillman, "Collapse," 204; Christopher Wolfe, *How to Read the Constitution* (Lanham, MD: Rowman and Littlefield, 1996), 82. See also Richard S. Kay, "Adherence to the Original Intentions in Constitutional Adjudication: Three Objections and Responses," *Northwestern University Law Review* 82 (1988): 226–92, 261–63, 273–79.

22. Compare Kay, "Adherence," 262–63 and Lofgren, "Original Understanding," 92–93. See also Rakove, *Original Meanings,* 18.

23. For examples from the founding period, see *Rutgers v. Waddington* (1784), in *The Law Practice of Alexander Hamilton,* ed. Julius Goebel Jr., 5 vols. (New York: Columbia University Press, 1964), 1:392–419; *Bayard v. Singleton,* 1 Mart. (N.C.) 42 (1787). See also Charles Grove Haines, *The American Doctrine of Judicial Supremacy,* 2nd ed. (Berkeley: University of California Press, 1932), 88–121; Clinton, *Marbury,* 48–54.

24. Kermit L. Hall, *The Supreme Court and Judicial Review in American History* (Washington, DC: American Historical Association, 1985), 13; Michael Zuckert, "Epistemology and Hermeneutics in the Constitutional Jurisprudence of John Marshall," in *John Marshall's Achievement: Law, Politics, and Constitutional Interpretations,* ed. Thomas C. Shevory (New York: Greenwood Press, 1989), 193–216; William E. Nelson, *Marbury v. Madison: The Origins and Legacy of Judicial Review* (Lawrence: University Press of Kansas, 2000), 59–71, 117; Wolfe, *Rise,* 381–84. See also Charles Hobson, *The Great Chief Justice: John Marshall and the Rule of Law* (Lawrence: University Press of Kansas, 1996). For a recent reading of the modern realist-pragmatist view back onto Marshall, see Richard A. Posner, *Law, Pragmatism, and Democracy* (Cambridge: Harvard University Press, 2003), 85–93.

25. *Marbury v. Madison,* 1 Cranch 137, 175 (1803). See also Wolfe, *Rise,* 80–89.
26. *Ogden v. Saunders,* 12 Wheat. 213, 332 (1827).
27. *McCulloch v. Maryland,* 4 Wheat. 316, 415 (emphasis in orig.) (1819); Gillman, "Collapse," 204–5; Frank, *Imperial,* 102, 96; Robert A. Burt, *The Constitution in Conflict* (Cambridge: Harvard University Press, 1992), 136–37. See also G. Edward White, *The American Judicial Tradition* (New York: Oxford University Press, 1976), 21–22.
28. For more detailed analysis of Marshall, see Wolfe, *Rise,* ch. 2, 381–97; Sylvia Snowiss, *Judicial Review and the Law of the Constitution* (New Haven: Yale University Press, 1990), ch. 5; Hobson, *John Marshall,* passim, and other sources cited in note 24 above.
29. Quoted in Gerald Gunther, ed., *John Marshall's Defense of McCulloch v. Maryland* (Stanford: Stanford University Press, 1969), 168–69.
30. Madison to Spencer Roane, September 2, 1819, in Gaillard Hunt, ed., *The Writings of James Madison* (New York: Putnam, 1908), 8:447, 448. See also Madison to Henry Lee, June 25, 1824, ibid. (1910), 9:191.
31. *Cooley v. Board of Wardens,* 12 How. 299 (1851). This case is emphasized in Aleinikoff, "Balancing," 950–51. See also Wolfe, *Rise,* 64–67.
32. *Dred Scott v. Sandford,* 19 How. 393, 405, 426 (1857); ibid., 621 (Curtis). See also *The Passenger Cases,* 7 How. 283, 478 (Taney) (1849).
33. *The Works of James Wilson,* ed. James DeWitt Andrews, 2 vols. (Chicago: Callaghan, 1896), 1:11; Nathan Dane, *A General Abridgement and Digest of American Law,* 9 vols. (Boston: Cummings, Hilliard, 1823, 1829), 6:596; James Kent, *Commentaries on American Law,* 2nd ed., 4 vols. (New York: O. Halsted, 1832), 1:468; Theodore Sedgwick, *A Treatise on the Rules which Govern the Interpretation and Application of Statutory and Constitutional Law* (New York: John S. Voorhies, 1857), 229, 231.
34. See Elizabeth Kelley Bauer, *Commentaries on the Constitution, 1790–1860* (New York: Columbia University Press, 1952).
35. John Taylor, *New Views of the Constitution of the United States,* ed. James McClellan (1823; repr. Washington, DC: Regnery, 2000), esp. 363, 3–4, 22, 46, 194, 273, 275, 292–93, 300, 325–27.
36. William Rawle, *A View of the Constitution of the United States* (Philadelphia: H. C. Carey and I. Lea, 1825), 27–28.
37. Joseph Story, *Commentaries on the Constitution of the United States,* 3 vols. (Boston: Hilliard, Gray, 1833), 1:383. Story's historical section drew heavily on Dane's *Digest;* see Bauer, *Commentaries,* 225.
38. Abel P. Upshur, *A Brief Enquiry into the True Nature and Character of Our Federal Government* (Philadelphia: John Campbell, 1863, repub. and repr. from the original Petersburg edition of 1840), 93, 94.
39. Henry Baldwin, *A General View of the Origin and Nature of the Constitution and Government of the United States* (Philadelphia: 1837), 37, as cited in Bauer, *Commentaries,* 243 n117; Frank Otto Gatell, "Henry Baldwin," in *The Justices of the United States Supreme Court, 1789–1969: Their Lives and Major Opinions,* ed. Leon Friedman and Fred L. Israel, 5 vols. (New York: Chelsea House and R. R. Bowker, 1969–78), 1:571–80, 578.
40. Francis Lieber, *Legal and Political Hermeneutics* (Boston: Little, Brown, 1839). The 1880 edition is reprinted in *Cardozo Law Review* 16 (1995): 1883–2105, 1900 (quote).
41. On Lieber's conception of the state, see James Farr, "The Americanization of Hermeneutics: Francis Lieber's *Legal and Political Hermeneutics,*" in *Legal Hermeneutics:*

History, Theory, and Practice, ed. Gregory Leyh (Berkeley: University of California Press, 1992), 83–102, 97.

42. Story, *Commentaries,* 1:390–92 n1.

43. For examples, see Clinton, "Original Understanding," 1216–19.

44. Wendell Phillips, *The Constitution a Pro-Slavery Compact, or Extractions from the Madison Papers,* 3rd enlarged ed. (1844; repr. New York: American Anti Slavery Society, 1856), 9. See also "Address of the Executive Committee of the American Anti-Slavery Society. . ." May 20, 1844, ibid., 150; Cover, *Justice Accused,* 149–58; William M. Wiecek, *The Sources of Antislavery Constitutionalism in America, 1760–1848* (Ithaca, NY: Cornell University Press, 1977), 240–48, 263–64.

45. *Dred Scott,* 520. See also ibid., 572 (Curtis).

46. *The Congressional Globe* (39th Cong., 1st sess., 1866), 677 (Sumner); Senate Report No. 21 (42nd Cong., 2nd sess., January 25, 1872), 2, repr. in Alfred Avins, ed., *The Reconstruction Amendments' Debates* (Richmond, VA: Virginia Commission on Constitutional Government, 1967), 571.

47. William Nelson, *The Fourteenth Amendment: From Political Principle to Judicial Doctrine* (Cambridge: Harvard University Press, 1988). See also Earl Maltz, *Civil Rights, The Constitution, and Congress, 1863–1869* (Lawrence: University Press of Kansas, 1990); Michael Les Benedict, *A Compromise of Principle: Conservative Republicans and Reconstruction, 1863–1869* (New York: Norton, 1975). But see Akhil Amar, *The Bill of Rights: Creation and Reconstruction* (New Haven: Yale University Press, 1998).

48. *The Slaughterhouse Cases,* 16 Wal. 36, 71, 72, 78 (1873).

49. Ibid., 89. See also Nelson, *Fourteenth,* 174–75, 181–82.

50. *The Legal Tender Cases,* 79 U.S. 457 (1871), overruling *Hepburn v. Griswold,* 75 U.S. 603 (1870). Much of the scholarship on this topic has concerned the circumstances of this rapid and controversial reversal. See Charles Fairman, *History of the Supreme Court of the United States, Volume Six: Reconstruction and Reunion, 1864–88* (New York: Macmillan, 1971), 677–775. The constitutional issues are treated succinctly in David P. Currie, *The Constitution in the Supreme Court: The First Hundred Years, 1789–1888* (Chicago: University of Chicago Press, 1985), 320–29. See also Kenneth W. Dam, "The Legal Tender Cases," *The Supreme Court Review 1981,* 367–412.

51. *Juilliard v. Greenman,* 110 U.S. 421 (1884).

52. *Legal Tender Cases,* 559–60 (Bradley, concurring); ibid., 585–87 (Chase, dissenting); ibid., 588–90, 605–7 (Clifford, dissenting); ibid., 651–56 (Field, dissenting); *Juilliard,* 443–44 (Gray, majority opinion); ibid., 451–54 (Field, dissenting).

53. George Ticknor Curtis, "An Argument Against the Constitutional Validity of the Legal Tender Clause Contained in the Act of Congress. . . " (New York: William C. Bryant 1862); George Bancroft, *A Plea for the Constitution of the United States, Wounded in the House of its Guardians* (1886; repr. Sewanee, TN: Spencer Judd, 1982).

54. George Ticknor Curtis, *Constitutional History of the United States,* 2 vols., ed. Joseph Culbertson Clayton (New York: Harper and Brothers, 1896), 2:18. See also Herman von Holst, *The Constitutional Law of the United States of America,* trans. Alfred Bishop Mason (Chicago: Callaghan, 1887), 38–55; Roger Foster, *Commentaries on the Constitution of the United States* (1895; repr. Toronto, Canada: Carswell, 1896), 80 and passim.

55. Thomas M. Cooley, *A Treatise on the Constitutional Limitations. . .* 4th ed. (Boston: Little, Brown, 1878), 68 (emphasis in orig.). See also id., *A Treatise. . .* (Boston: Little, Brown, 1868), 54–55 as quoted in Gillman, "Collapse," 209–10.

56. Henry Campbell Black, *Handbook on the Construction and Interpretation of the Laws* (St. Paul, MN: West Publishing, 1896), 1, 15, 8. Lesser-known commentators echoed these views. See John Alexander Jameson, *The Constitutional Convention; Its History, Powers, and Modes of Proceeding* (New York: Charles Scribner, 1867), 77–78; Joel Prentiss Bishop, *Commentaries on the Written Laws and Their Interpretation* (Boston: Little, Brown, 1882), 57–58, 80, 81.

57. Arthur W. Machen Jr., "The Elasticity of the Constitution," pts. I and II, *Harvard Law Review* 14 (1900–01): 200–216, 203 (quote), 204–205; ibid., 273–85.

58. William M. Wiecek, *The Lost World of Classical Legal Thought* (New York: Oxford University Press, 1998), esp. 4–7, 80–82, 89–94; Neil Duxbury, *Patterns of American Jurisprudence* (New York: Oxford University Press, 1995), 9–32; Morton Horwitz, *The Transformation of American Law, 1870–1960* (New York: Oxford University Press, 1992), 9–19; Thomas C. Grey, "Langdell's Orthodoxy," *University of Pittsburgh Law Review* 45 (1983): 1–53; Duncan Kennedy, "Toward an Historical Understanding of Legal Consciousness: The Case of Classical Legal Thought in America, 1850–1940," *Research in Law and Sociology* 3 (1980): 3–24; Horwitz, *Transformation I,* 253–66.

59. Horwitz, *Transformation II,* 19–31; Franck, *Imperial Judiciary,* 150–69; Michael Les Benedict, "Laissez-Faire and Liberty: A Re-Evaluation of the Meaning and Origins of Laissez-Faire Constitutionalism," *Law and History Review* 3 (1985): 293–331; Howard Gillman, *The Constitution Besieged: The Rise and Demise of Lochner Era Police Powers Jurisprudence* (Durham, NC: Duke University Press, 1993), for citations to scholars asserting the older view that the Court simply read social Darwinist, laissez-faire ideology into the Constitution, see ibid., 207–8 n8. See also Nelson, *Fourteenth,* 148–200.

60. For detailed discussion of the numerous cases, see David P. Currie, *The Constitution in the Supreme Court: The Second Century, 1888–1986* (Chicago: University of Chicago Press, 1990), 7–201 and, more briefly, Wiecek, *Lost World,* 124–26, 133–56.

61. G. Edward White, *The Constitution and the New Deal* (Cambridge: Harvard University Press, 2000), 4, 36–37, 233; Wiecek, *Lost World,* 19–27; Gillman, *Besieged,* 20, 10, 23–33. See also Howard Gillman, "More on the Origins of the Fuller Court's Jurisprudence," *Political Research Quarterly* 49 (1996): 415–37; Gillman, "Collapse," 225–26.

62. Kennedy, "Legal Consciousness," 8. See also White, *New Deal,* 272. This interpretation corresponds in a general way to the idea of originalism as the methodology for "maintenance" of a constitutional regime based on popular sovereignty. See Kahn, *Legitimacy,* 62–64, 46–50, although I see the existence of this approach extending farther into the early twentieth century than Kahn seems to.

63. *Pollock v. Farmers' Loan and Trust Co.,* 158 U.S. 601, 618, 619 (quote), 619–29 (1895); *Hylton v. United States* 3 U.S. 171 (1796).

64. *Gibbons v. Ogden,* 22 U.S. 1, 203 (1824); *United States v. E.C. Knight Co.,* 156 U.S. 1, 12 (quote) (1895). Noting that even Harlan's dissent did not dispute the distinction, Gillman concluded that "all of these justices shared a concern about maintaining originalist distinctions." Gillman, "Collapse," 226. See also ibid., 208.

65. *Lochner v. New York,* 198 U.S. 45, 56, 59 (quote) (1905); Kennedy, "Legal Consciousness," 9–14; Gillman, *Besieged,* 128–31; Horwitz, *Transformation II,* 29–30.

66. *Adkins v. Children's Hospital,* 261 U.S. 525 (1923). See Gillman, *Besieged,* 167–75; G. Edward White, "The 'Constitutional Revolution' as a Crisis in Adaptivity," *Hastings Law Journal* 48 (1997): 867–912, 890–93.

67. In addition to the decisions analyzed above, exemplars are *Adair v. United States,*

208 U.S. 161 (1908); *Coppage v. Kansas*, 236 U.S. 1 (1915) *Hammer v. Dagenhart*, 247 U.S. 251 (1918); *Schechter v. United States*, 295 U.S. 495 (1935); *Carter v. Carter Coal*, 298 U.S. 238 (1936); *United States v. Butler*, 297 U.S. 1 (1936); *Morehead v. New York ex. rel. Tipaldo*, 298 U.S. 587 (1936). Of course, the approach did not always prove fatal to regulations. For one of numerous counterexamples, see *Euclid v. Ambler Realty Co.*, 272 U.S. 365 (1926).

68. Morton White, *Social Thought in America: The Revolt Against Formalism* (New York: Viking Press, 1949). The best explanations of this development in the constitutional context are Wiecek, *Lost World*, and Edward A. Purcell Jr., *The Crisis of Democratic Theory: Scientific Naturalism and the Problem of Value* (Lexington: University Press of Kentucky, 1973), 74–94, 159–78. See also White, "Adaptivity," and Gillman, "Collapse." Duxbury has helpfully observed that the notion of a "revolt" connotes a quicker event than the cumulative criticism that actually developed over several decades. Duxbury, *Patterns*, 64.

69. Robert S. Summers, *Instrumentalism and American Legal Theory* (Ithaca, NY: Cornell University Press, 1982).

70. Horwitz, *Transformation II*, 109–43; Purcell, *Crisis*, 74–76, 82; White, *Revolt*, 59–75, 103–6.

71. Oliver Wendell Holmes Jr., *Collected Legal Papers* (New York: Harcourt, Brace, and Howe, 1920), 239.

72. The literature on legal thought in this period is abundant. I have benefitted from Horwitz, *Transformation II*, ch. 6; Laura Kalman, *Legal Realism at Yale* (Chapel Hill: University of North Carolina Press, 1986); Grant Gilmore, *The Ages of American Law* (New Haven: Yale University Press, 1977), 68–91; Wilfrid E. Rumble Jr., *American Legal Realism* (Ithaca, NY: Cornell University Press, 1968). See also Laura Kalman, *The Strange Career of Legal Liberalism* (New Haven: Yale University Press, 1996), 13–18; Alfred H. Kelly, Winfred A. Harbison, and Herman Belz, *The American Constitution: Its Origins and Development*, 7th ed. 2 vols. (New York: W. W. Norton, 1991), 2:453–56.

73. Brian Leiter, "Legal Realism" in *A Companion to Philosophy of Law and Legal Theory*, ed. Dennis Patterson (Cambridge: Harvard University Press, 1996), 261–79, 269–70 (quote). See, for example, Herman Oliphant, "A Return to Stare Decisis," *American Bar Association Journal* 14 (1928): 71–76, 107. For further illustrations from the realist literature, see Brian Leiter, "Rethinking Legal Realism: Toward a Naturalized Jurisprudence," *Texas Law Review* 76 (1997): 267–315, 275–79.

74. *Lochner*, 76. For a concise treatment of legal indeterminacy as the realists understood it, see Leiter, "Legal Realism," 265–69.

75. See, for example, Walter W. Cook, "Scientific Method and the Law," *American Bar Association Journal* 13 (1927): 303–9. Also influential in this regard was John Dewey, "Logical Method and the Law," *Cornell Law Quarterly* 10 (1924–25): 17–27. Llewellyn wrote that realism "fits into the pragmatic and instrumental developments in logic." Karl Llewellyn, "A Realistic Jurisprudence: The Next Step," *Columbia Law Review* 30 (1930): 431–65, 454. See also Rumble, *Legal Realism*, 60–63, 72–74, 194; Horwitz, *Transformation II*, 200, 202; William W. Fisher III, "The Development of Modern American Legal Theory and the Judicial Interpretation of the Bill of Rights," in *A Culture of Rights*, ed. Michael J. Lacey and Knud Haakonssen (Cambridge: Cambridge University Press, 1991), 266–365, 270.

76. Felix Cohen, *Ethical Systems and Legal Ideals* (New York: Harcourt, Brace, 1933), 244–45 (analogies); Karl Llewellyn, *The Bramble Bush* (New York: Oceana, 1951), 56–81 (precedents and analogies); Max Radin, "The Theory of Judicial Decision," *American Bar*

Association Journal 11 (1925): 357–362, 360–61 (statutes); Karl Llewellyn, "Remarks on the Rules or Canons About How Statutes are to be Construed," *Vanderbilt Law Review* 3 (1949): 395–406, 401–6 (statutes); Jerome Frank, *Law and the Modern Mind* (New York: Brentano, 1930), 106–11(facts). See also Rumble, *Legal Realism*, 55–60, 63–69, 107–26.

77. Purcell, *Crisis*, 77–90.

78. Joseph C. Hutcheson Jr., "The Judgement Intuitive: The Function of the Hunch in Judicial Decision," *Cornell Law Quarterly* 14 (1929): 274–88, 278; Frank, *Law and the Modern Mind*, 104, 110–11; see also Leiter, "Legal Realism," 271.

79. Prominent in this group were Llewellyn, Cohen, Underhill Moore, and Herman Oliphant. Realists' various nonlegal explanations for legal decisions are given in Rumble, *Legal Realism*, 145–67, and Leiter, "Legal Realism," 272–75. I refrain here from delving into the complex arguments about the relationship between legal realism and sociological jurisprudence. In general I agree that historians should treat them as "subcategories of pre- and post-World War I Progressive legal thought" and not look for "sharper distinctions between [them] than are justified." Horwitz, *Transformation II*, 171.

80. Realism was not wholly destructive in that it heavily influenced the behavioralist understanding of law typical of most modern political science. See Nancy Maveety, ed., *The Pioneers of Judicial Behavior* (Ann Arbor: University of Michigan Press, 2003). Likewise, the initial development of New Deal administrative agencies called upon the characteristic Progressive and realist confidence in social scientific expertise, and realists' support of and employment in the New Deal is well documented. See, Horwitz, *Transformation II*, 185, 213–16, 221–25, 230; Kahn, *Legitimacy*, 126–31; Rumble, *Legal Realism*, 76–77; Peter H. Irons, *The New Deal Lawyers* (Princeton, NJ: Princeton University Press, 1982), 6–10; Ronen Shamir, *Managing Legal Uncertainty: Elite Lawyers in the New Deal* (Durham, NC: Duke University Press, 1995), 131–57, 99–105.

81. Leiter, "Legal Realism," 277 (quote), 278; Rumble, *Legal Realism*, 198, 216, 220–22, 227–32; Fisher, "Legal Theory," 278–82.

82. Radin, "Theory," 360.

83. Purcell, *Crisis*, 11, 88–92, 94.

84. Fisher, "Legal Theory," 284–85; Horwitz, *Transformation II*, 5–6, 208–9, 247; Kalman, *Legal Liberalism*, 13–22; William Wiecek, *Liberty under Law: The Supreme Court in American Life* (Baltimore: Johns Hopkins University Press, 1988), 187–88; Gary Minda, *Postmodern Legal Movements* (New York: New York University Press, 1995), 32–33; Robert W. Gordon, "Legal Realism" in *A Companion to American Thought*, ed. Richard Wightman Fox and James T. Kloppenberg (Oxford: Blackwell, 1995), 393.

85. Brian Leiter, "Is There An 'American' Jurisprudence?" *Oxford Journal of Legal Studies* 17 (1997): 367–87, 374.

86. Purcell, *Crisis*, 93, 78. An adaptive, evolutionary tendency was always an aspect of the common law, even though in the formalist period jurisprudents understood themselves as discoverers of new rules that were immanent in the cases they examined. Herbert Hovenkamp, "Evolutionary Models in Jurisprudence," *Texas Law Review* 64 (1985): 645–85, 645; Grey, "Langdell's Orthodoxy," 31.

87. Rumble, *Legal Realism*, 4–8, 74–75, 195, 234; Horwitz, *Transformation II*, 187–90, 169–71; Purcell, *Crisis*, 78–79, 93; Wiecek, *Lost World*, 198.

88. The "living Constitution" approach was forecast in a seminal text of Progressive political science, Arthur F. Bentley, *The Process of Government* (1908; repr., Cambridge:

Belknap Press of Harvard University Press, 1967), 276–77, 295–96, 328–29. Classic examples are Woodrow Wilson, *Constitutional Government in the United States* (1908; New York: Columbia University Press, 1961), 55–56, 165–69, and passim; Howard Lee McBain, *The Living Constitution* (New York: Worker's Education Bureau, 1927); Karl Llewellyn, "The Constitution as an Institution," *Columbia Law Review* 34 (1934): 1–40, esp. 1 n1, 22, 26, 32–33, 39. More generally, see Herman Belz, "The Constitution in the Gilded Age: The Beginnings of Constitutional Realism in American Scholarship," *American Journal of Legal History* 13 (1969): 10–25; id., "The Realist Critique of Constitutionalism in the Era of Reform," *American Journal of Legal History* 15 (1971): 288–306; Gillman, "Collapse."

89. Aleinikoff, "Balancing," 962 (quote), 952–63. For a similar judgment, see Horwitz, *Transformation II*, 199–200, 17–18; Grey, "Langdell's Orthodoxy," 52.

90. *Missouri v. Holland*, 252 U.S. 416, 433 (1920); Oliver Wendell Holmes Jr., "The Path of the Law" *Harvard Law Review* 10 (1897): 457–78, 467.

91. Roscoe Pound, "Liberty of Contract," *Yale Law Journal* 18 (1909): 454–87, 457, 454.

92. Roscoe Pound, "Law in Books and Law in Action," *American Law Review* 44 (1910): 12–36, 30, 24.

93. Roscoe Pound, "A Survey of Social Interests" *Harvard Law Review* 57 (1943): 1–39, 39. This article was first delivered as a paper in 1921. See Aleinikoff, "Balancing," 959.

94. Benjamin N. Cardozo, *The Nature of the Judicial Process* (New Haven: Yale University Press, 1921), 102, 161 (quote), 162 (quote), 104 (quote).

95. Ibid., 17. See also ibid., 71; Wolfe, *Rise*, 230–40; Horwitz, *Transformation II*, 189–92; White, *American Judicial Tradition*, 254–60, 276–83; Bassham, *Original Intent*, 109–118; William Gangi, *Saving the Constitution from the Courts* (Norman: University of Oklahoma Press, 1995), 170–75.

96. Zechariah Chaffee Jr., "Freedom of Speech in Wartime," *Harvard Law Review* 32 (1919): 932–73; id., "Legislation Against Anarchy," *New Republic* 19 (July 23, 1919): 379–85; id., *Freedom of Speech* (New York: Harcourt, Brace, and Howe, 1920); *Olmstead v. U.S.*, 277 U.S. 438, 472 (1928). See also Wolfe, *Rise*, 181–202; White, *New Deal*, 128–63; Gillman, "Collapse," 220–23.

97. Scholars currently debate the relative influence of internal doctrinal development and external political pressure on the Court's validation of the New Deal. My treatment accords with the general revisionist notion that doctrinal development, and hence the Court's transformation, occurred gradually and reflected the broader intellectual shifts associated with the "revolt against formalism." For a summary and balanced assessment, see Edward A. Purcell Jr., "Rethinking Constitutional Change," *Virginia Law Review* 80 (1994): 277–90.

98. "A 'Fireside Chat' Discussing the Plan for Reorganization of the Judiciary, Washington, DC, March 9, 1937," in Franklin D. Roosevelt, *The Public Papers and Addresses of Franklin D. Roosevelt, 1937* (New York: Macmillan, 1941), 122–33, 132, 127, 130. On Roosevelt's preference for adaptation over amendment, see David E. Kyvig, *Explicit and Authentic Acts: Amending the U.S. Constitution, 1776–1995* (Lawrence: University Press of Kansas, 1996), 306.

99. Homer Cummings, "The American Constitutional Method," December 18, 1935, in *Selected Papers of Homer Cummings*, ed. Carl Brent Swisher (1939; repr. New York: Da Capo, 1972), 131–40, 140; "A statement on the decision sustaining state minimum wage

legislation, March 31, 1937," ibid., 155–56. See also "Change and the Constitution. . . July 4, 1936," ibid., 295–96; "Modern Tendencies in the Law. . . August 31, 1933," ibid., 97–99; "The Constitution as a Living Document. . . October 11, 1937," ibid., 176–78.

100. *Home Building and Loan Association v. Blaisdell*, 290 U.S. 398 (1934). See Charles A. Miller, *The Supreme Court and the Uses of History* (Cambridge: Belknap Press of Harvard University Press, 1969), 39–51, 198; Wolfe, *Rise*, 219–21; White, "Adaptivity," 881–87.

101. *Blaisdell*, 426, 428, 442.

102. *Blaisdell*, 443; *McCulloch v. Maryland*, 4 Wheat. 316, 415 (1819); *Missouri v. Holland*, 252 U.S. 416, 433 (1920). Although Marshall was referring to legislative adaptation, Cardozo made similar use of the *McCulloch* passage in *Judicial Process*, 82–84.

103. Edward S. Corwin, "Moratorium Over Minnesota," *University of Pennsylvania Law Review* 82 (1934): 311–16. Gillman notes similar expressions by other commentators in the period, "Collapse," 205, 234–38.

104. Wiecek, *Lost World*, 234. Cases are traced in ibid., 234–41.

105. *Nebbia v. New York*, 291 U.S. 502, 525, 537 (1934). The fundamental departure marked by this case is emphasized in Barry Cushman, *Rethinking the New Deal Court: The Structure of a Constitutional Revolution* (New York: Oxford University Press, 1998), 79–83.

106. *West Coast Hotel v. Parrish*, 300 U.S. 379, 391, 390 (1937); White "Adaptivity," 894–907.

107. *Wickard v. Filburn*, 317 U.S. 111 (1942).

108. Ibid., 124, 125.

109. White, "Adaptivity," 907 (quote), 900–907. Further examples are analyzed in Wolfe, *Rise*, 242–47.

110. Aleinikoff, "Balancing," 963 n116 (quote), 984 n243.

111. *U.S. v. Carolene Products Co.*, 304 U.S. 144, 152 n4 (1938); Martin M. Shapiro, "The Constitution and Economic Rights," in *Essays on the Constitution of the United States*, ed. M. Judd Harmon (Port Washington, NY: Kennikat Press, 1978), 74–98; Wiecek, *Liberty Under Law*, 156–57, 176; Wolfe, *Rise*, 248–56; Kelly, Harbison, and Belz, *Constitution*, 2:522, 613, 632–35.

112. *Palko v. Connecticut*, 302 U.S. 319, 325 (quoting *Snyder v. Massachusetts*, 291 U.S. 97, 105 (1933) (1937)); Melvin I. Urofsky, *A March of Liberty: A Constitutional History of the United States* (New York: Knopf, 1988), 708–9 (quotes); id., *Division and Discord: The Supreme Court Under Stone and Vinson, 1941–53* (Columbia: University of South Carolina Press, 1997), 85–86.

113. *South Carolina v. United States*, 199 U.S. 437, 448–49 (1905). The decision held that Congress was not forbidden by the Tenth Amendment to tax state-regulated liquor dispensaries.

114. Charles Warren, *The Supreme Court in United States History*, 3 vols. (Boston: Little, Brown, 1922), 3:470–71.

115. *Blaisdell*, 453, 449.

116. *West Coast Hotel*, 403.

117. Louis Boudin, "Government by Judiciary" *Political Science Quarterly* 26 (1911): 238–70; id., *Government By Judiciary*, 2 vols. (New York: Godwin, 1932); Charles A. Beard, *An Economic Interpretation of the Constitution* (New York: Macmillan, 1913); id., *The Supreme Court and the Constitution* (New York: Macmillan, 1912). More generally, see Clinton, *Marbury*, 211–16; Wolfe, *Rise*, 216–19.

118. *Santa Clara v. Southern Pacific Railroad,* 118 U.S. 394 (1886). See also Andrew C. McLaughlin, "The Court, The Corporation, and Conkling," *American Historical Review* 46 (1940): 45–63.

119. Charles A. Beard and Mary R. Beard, *The Rise of American Civilization,* 4 vols. (New York: Macmillan, 1927–42), 2:111–14, repr. in Howard Jay Graham, ed. *Everyman's Constitution: Historical Essays on the Fourteenth Amendment* (Madison: State Historical Society of Wisconsin, 1968), 27–30. For the influence of the conspiracy theory, see id., 17, 33–34, 64–67. See also Herman Belz, "The Civil War Amendments to the Constitution: The Relevance of Original Intent," *Constitutional Commentary* 5 (1988): 115–41, 118–19. But compare Horwitz, *Transformation II,* 65–107.

120. Howard Jay Graham, "'The Conspiracy Theory' of the Fourteenth Amendment, Part I," *Yale Law Journal* 47 (1938) 371–403; "Part II," ibid., 48 (1938): 171–94, repr. in Graham, ed. *Everyman,* 23–97. See also Louis Boudin, "Truth and Fiction About the Fourteenth Amendment" *New York University Law Review* 16 (1938): 19–82; Belz, "Relevance," 118–22.

121. Graham, *Everyman,* 45. Justice Hugo Black cited Graham and, in dissent, implored the Court to return to the "Negro freedom" theory of original intent. *Connecticut General Life Insurance Co. v. Johnson,* 303 U.S. 77, 87, 87 n11 (1938).

122. Jacobus tenBroek, "Admissibility and Use by the United States Supreme Court of Extrinsic Aids in Constitutional Construction," pt. 1, *California Law Review* 26 (1938): 287–308; pt. 2, ibid., 437–54; pt. 3, ibid., 664–81; pt. 4, *California Law Review* 27 (1939): 157–81; pt. 5, ibid., 399–421, 399 (quote).

123. Ibid., pt. 1, 287.

124. Ibid., pt. 5, 405–6.

125. See, for example, ibid., pt. 1, 308.

126. Ibid., pt. 2, 448.

127. TenBroek's career further illustrated the power and persistence of the originalist proposition, as he later helped advance the "Negro freedom" theory of the Fourteenth Amendment. See Belz, "Relevance," 121–22, and chapter four below.

128. *West Coast Hotel,* 391, 397.

129. Gillman, "Collapse," 238.

130. See for example, Kelly, Harbison, and Belz, *Constitution,* 2:612–13. See also additional sources cited in note 143 below.

131. Lucas A. Powe Jr., *The Warren Court and American Politics* (Cambridge: Belknap Press of Harvard University Press, 2000), 215 (quote), 214.

132. G. Edward White, "Earl Warren's Influence on the Warren Court," in *The Warren Court in Historical and Political Perspective,* ed. Mark Tushnet (Charlottesville: University Press of Virginia, 1993), 37–50, 39, 47, 43.

133. Melvin I. Urofsky, "William O. Douglas as Common Law Judge," ibid., 64–85, 65, 77.

134. Kalman, *Legal Liberalism,* 46. See also id., *Abe Fortas: A Biography* (New Haven: Yale University Press, 1990).

135. Robert C. Post, "William J. Brennan and the Warren Court," in *Warren Court,* ed. Tushnet, 123–36, 135; Mark V. Tushnet, *Making Constitutional Law: Thurgood Marshall and the Supreme Court, 1961–1991* (New York: Oxford University Press, 1997) 184, 181. Goldberg's biographer does not directly associate him with legal realism, but he notes that he held the "Yale" as opposed to the "Harvard" view of the Supreme Court and

rightly observes that Goldberg's replacement of Frankfurter in 1962 solidified a liberal activist majority. See David L. Stebenne, *Arthur J. Goldberg: New Deal Liberal* (New York: Oxford University Press, 1996), 319.

136. Morton J. Horwitz, *The Warren Court and the Pursuit of Justice* (New York: Hill and Wang, 1998), 114, 85. See also ibid., 113, 115, and id., "The Warren Court and the Pursuit of Justice," *Washington and Lee Law Review* 5 (1993): 5–13, 5–8.

137. Powe, *Warren Court*, 489–94; Martin Shapiro, "The Supreme Court: From Warren to Burger," in *The New American Political System*, ed. Anthony King (Washington, DC: AEI, 1978), 179–211, 188–94.

138. To cite only the leading cases, *Reynolds v. Sims*, 377 U.S. 533 (1964); *Miranda v. Arizona*, 384 U.S. 436 (1966); *Memoirs v. Massachusetts*, 383 U.S. 413 (1966); *Brown v. Board of Education*, 347 U.S. 483 (1954); *Engel v. Vitale*, 370 U.S. 421 (1962).

139. *Griswold v. Connecticut*, 381 U.S. 479 (1965); *Shapiro v. Thompson*, 394 U.S. 618 (1969). See also *Goldberg v. Kelly*, 397 U.S. 254 (1970).

140. Powe, *Warren Court*, 496.

141. *Brown*, 489, 492, 494.

142. *Harper v. Virginia Board of Elections*, 383 U.S. 663, 669 (1966). See also *Oregon v. Mitchell*, 400 U.S. 112, 274–75 (1970) (Brennan, Marshall, and White, dissenting in part).

143. For analysis of the Warren Court as the elaboration of the *Carolene* model, see Kelly, Harbison, and Belz, *Constitution*, 2:612–13, 632–34; Powe, *Warren Court*, 487–89; For criticism of "substantive equal protection" as the replacement for the old substantive due process and of the discretion in its balancing approach, see Wallace Mendelson, "From Warren to Burger: The Rise and Decline of Substantive Equal Protection," *American Political Science Review* 66 (1972): 1226–33; Shapiro, "From Warren to Burger," 206–7; Shapiro, "Constitution and Economic Rights," 88; Wolfe, *Rise*, 258–91. See also Aleinikoff, "Balancing," 964–72; Wiecek, *Liberty*, 156–76; Robert F. Nagel, *Constitutional Cultures: The Mentality and Consequences of Judicial Review* (Berkeley: University of California Press, 1989), 84–105.

144. *Reynolds* and *Engel*, cited above, note 138; *Bell v. Maryland*, 378 U.S. 226 (1964); *Jones v. Alfred H. Mayer Co.*, 392 U.S. 409 (1968). These cases are analyzed in chapter 3.

145. Kermit L. Hall, "The Warren Court in Historical Perspective," in *The Warren Court: A Retrospective*, ed. Bernard Schwartz (New York: Oxford University Press, 1996), 293–312, 303.

146. *Griswold; Miranda*.

147. *Swann v. Charlotte-Mecklenburg Board of Education*, 402 U.S. 1 (1971); *Griggs v. Duke Power Co.*, 401 U.S. 424 (1971).

148. *Roe v. Wade*, 410 U.S. 113 (1973); *Furman v. Georgia*, 408 U.S. 238 (1972); *University of California Regents v. Bakke*, 438 U.S. 265 (1978).

T W O : Modern Judicial Power and the
Process-Restraint Tradition

1. James B. Thayer, "The Origin and Scope of the American Doctrine of Constitutional Law," *Harvard Law Review* 7 (1893): 129–56, 148.

2. Ibid., 152, 138; Sylvia Snowiss, *Judicial Review and the Law of the Constitution* (New Haven: Yale University Press, 1990), 187–94. See also Sanford Byron Gabin, *Judicial Review and the Reasonable Doubt Test* (Port Washington, NY: Kennikat Press, 1980).

3. Most famously, *Lochner v. New York*, 198 U.S. 45, 74–76 (1905). See also Morton Horwitz, *The Transformation of American Law, 1870–1960* (New York: Oxford University Press, 1992), 142.

4. *United States v. Butler*, 297 U.S. 1, 79 (1936).

5. Compare Frankfurter's assertions of judicial discretion to discern and balance fundamental rights against legislation in *Malinski v. New York*, 324 U.S. 401 (1945); *Haley v. Ohio*, 332 U.S. 596 (1948); *Louisiana ex rel. Francis v. Resweber*, 329 U.S. 459 (1947); *Rochin v. California*, 342 U.S. 165 (1952); *Sweezy v. New Hampshire*, 354 U.S. 234 (1957); with his use of various jurisdictional or structural techniques of abstention or deference in *West Virginia State Board of Education v. Barnette*, 319 U.S. 624 (1943); *Colegrove v. Green*, 328 U.S. 549 (1946); *Poe v. Ullman*, 367 U.S. 497 (1961); *Baker v. Carr*, 369 U.S. 186 (1962). For a similar assessment, see Mark Silverstein, *Constitutional Faiths: Felix Frankfurter, Hugo Black, and the Process of Judicial Decision Making* (Ithaca, NY: Cornell University Press, 1984), ch. 2, 128–29, 143–48; Melvin I. Urofsky, *Division and Discord: The Supreme Court under Stone and Vinson, 1941–53* (Columbia: University of South Carolina Press, 1997), 88, 91–92, 216–18, 220–25; id., *Felix Frankfurter: Judicial Restraint and Individual Liberties* (Boston: Twayne, 1991), 148–57. See also Wallace Mendelson, "The Influence of James B. Thayer upon the Work of Holmes, Brandeis, and Frankfurter," *Vanderbilt Law Review* 31 (1978): 71–87.

6. The best historical treatment of process jurisprudence can be found in Neil Duxbury, *Patterns in American Jurisprudence* (Cambridge: Oxford University Press, 1995), 204–99. See also Richard H. Fallon Jr., "Reflections on the Hart and Wechsler Paradigm," *Vanderbilt Law Review* 47 (1994): 953–86; William Eskridge and Philip Frickey, "The Making of *The Legal Process*," *Harvard Law Review* 107 (1994): 2031–55; Norman Silber and Geoffrey Miller, "Toward 'Neutral Principles' in the Law: Selections from the Oral History of Herbert Wechsler," *Columbia Law Review* 93 (1993): 854–931; William N. Eskridge and Gary Peller, "The New Public Law Movement," *Michigan Law Review* 89 (1991): 707–791, 710; Gary Peller, "Neutral Principles in the 1950s," *University of Michigan Journal of Law Reform* 21 (1988): 561–622; G. Edward White, "The Evolution of Reasoned Elaboration: Jurisprudential Criticism and Social Change," *Virginia Law Review* 59 (1973): 279–302; Bruce A. Ackerman, "*Law and the Modern Mind* by Jerome Frank," *Daedalus* 103 (1974): 119–30.

7. Anthony J. Sebok, *Legal Positivism in American Jurisprudence* (New York: Cambridge University Press, 1998), 141–42 emphasizes that control of discretion was a major goal of the process school.

8. Process jurisprudence is contextualized with consensus thought in Duxbury, *Patterns*, 242–51; Horwitz, *The Transformation of American Law, 1870–1960*, 247–68; Sebok, *Legal Positivism*, 169–76; Peller, "Neutral Principles," 572–86. See also Edward A. Purcell Jr., *The Crisis of Democratic Theory* (Lexington: University of Kentucky Press, 1973), 235–66.

9. Purcell, *Crisis*, 238. See also Paul W. Kahn, *Legitimacy and History: Self-Government in American Constitutional Theory* (New Haven: Yale University Press, 1993), 136–47.

10. Duxbury, *Patterns*, 241.

11. See Felix Frankfurter and James Landis, *The Business of the Supreme Court* (New York: Macmillan, 1928).

12. Felix Frankfurter and Henry M. Hart Jr., "The Business of the Supreme Court at October Term, 1934," *Harvard Law Review* 49 (1935): 68–107, 90, 91. See also Duxbury, *Patterns*, 234.

13. Felix Frankfurter and Henry M. Hart Jr., "The Business of the Supreme Court at October Term, 1933," *Harvard Law Review* 48 (1934): 238–81, 277, 280. See also id., "Business, 1934," 94, 107. Compare Henry M. Hart Jr., "The Time Chart of the Justices," *Harvard Law Review* 73 (1959): 84–125.

14. See, for example, Felix Frankfurter and James M. Landis, "The Business of the Supreme Court at October Term, 1929," *Harvard Law Review* 44 (1930): 1–40; 38–40; Felix Frankfurter and Henry M. Hart Jr., "The Business of the Supreme Court at October Term, 1932," *Harvard Law Review* 47 (1933): 245–97, 285–83; id., "Business, 1934," 94, 98, 103; id., "Business, 1932," 260ff.; id., "Business, 1933," 246ff.; id., "Business, 1934," 77–79; Felix Frankfurter and Adrian S. Fisher, "The Business of the Supreme Court at the October Terms, 1935 and 1936," *Harvard Law Review* 51 (1938): 577–637, 623. Brandeis's influential restatement was in *Ashwander v. TVA*, 297 U.S. 288, 345–49 (1936).

15. Felix Frankfurter and Wilber G. Katz, *Cases and Other Authorities on Federal Jurisdiction and Procedure* (Chicago: Callaghan, 1931), vi, i (quoting Benjamin R. Curtis, "Proceedings . . . at the Time of Chief Justice Taney's Death," 30 F. Cas 1341, 1343 (1864)). See also Felix Frankfurter and Harry Shulman, ibid. (rev. ed.), 1937; Mary Brigid McManamon, "Felix Frankfurter: The Architect of 'Our Federalism,'" *Georgia Law Review* 27 (1993): 697–788.

16. Henry Hart and Herbert Wechsler, *The Federal Courts and the Federal System* (Brooklyn: The Foundation Press, 1953); Duxbury, *Patterns*, 233 (quote). Wechsler further highlighted the importance of federalism in "The Political Safeguards of Federalism," *Columbia Law Review* 54 (1954): 543–60.

17. Henry Hart and Albert Sacks, *The Legal Process* (tent. ed, mimeograph from Harvard Law School, 1958). See also Fallon, "Paradigm," 965.

18. Hart and Sacks, *Legal Process*, 4; Eskridge and Peller, "Public Law," 722.

19. Horwitz, *Transformation II*, 253. See also Hart and Sacks, *Legal Process*, 3. Sebok, *Positivism*, 133, 168–69 focuses on "institutional settlement" as important evidence of the legal positivism and majoritarianism of process jurisprudence.

20. Hart and Sacks, *Legal Process*, 1157.

21. Henry M. Hart Jr., "Holmes' Positivism: An Addendum," *Harvard Law Review* 64 (1951): 929–37, 933.

22. Philip Bobbitt, *Constitutional Fate* (New York: Oxford University Press, 1982), 42–43, 57. See also Hart and Sacks, *Legal Process*, 1156–57.

23. Henry M. Hart Jr., "Legislation Notes," January 4, 1950, n.p., ser. III, box 16, fol. 2; id., "Legislation Notes," n.d. (but filed with 1950), n.p., ser. III, box 16, fol. 3, Papers of Henry M. Hart Jr., Harvard Law School Library. See also Eskridge and Frickey, "Making," 2038.

24. James Landis, "A Note on 'Statutory Interpretation,'" *Harvard Law Review* 43 (1930): 886–93, 886.

25. Hart and Sacks, *Legal Process*, 161, 165–68, 170, 487. See also Duxbury, *Patterns*, 228ff.; Fallon, "Paradigm," 966; Sebok, *Positivism*, 120–28.

26. Hart and Sacks, *Legal Process*, 166, 1156 (quote).

27. Hart, "Legislation Notes," January 4, 1951, n.p., ser. III, box 17, fol. 2, Hart Papers. See also Eskridge and Frickey, "Making," 2038.

28. Felix Frankfurter, "Some Reflections on the Reading of Statutes," *Columbia Law Review* 47 (1947): 527–46, 538, 539.

29. Ibid., 534.

30. Hart and Sacks, *Legal Process,* 161.

31. Hart and Sacks, *Legal Process,* 160 (quote), 164 (quote); Frankfurter, "Reflections," 533. See also Edward H. Levi, *An Introduction to Legal Reasoning* (Chicago: University of Chicago Press, 1949). Ackerman, *"Law and the Modern Mind* by Jerome Frank," 128 n26 includes Levi in a list of process thinkers.

32. Levi, *Introduction,* 28. See also Hart and Sacks, *Legal Process,* 1156–57.

33. Duxbury, *Patterns,* 238, quoting Alexander M. Bickel and Harry H. Wellington, "Legislative Purpose and Judicial Process: The Lincoln Mills Case," *Harvard Law Review* 71 (1957): 1–39, 15, quoting Learned Hand in *United States v. Klinger,* 199 F. 2nd 645, 648 (2nd Cir. 1952). See also Archibald Cox, "Judge Learned Hand and the Interpretation of Statutes," *Harvard Law Review* 60 (1947): 370–93.

34. Hart, "Legislation Notes," January 4, 1950, n.p., ser. III, box 16, fol. 2, Hart Papers.

35. Frankfurter, "Reflections," 542 (quoting *U.S. v. Fisher,* 2 Cranch 358, 386 (1805)), 543–44.

36. Landis, "Interpretation," 891.

37. Frankfurter, "Reflections," 536–37, quoting *Henry v. United States,* 251 U.S. 393, 395 (1920). See also ibid., 541, 529. Compare Hart: "no view of actual intention ought to stray outside the bounds of language," "Legislation Notes," January 4, 1950, n.p., ser. III, box 16, fol. 2, Hart Papers. This thinking is also laid out with admirable clarity in Levi, *Introduction,* 27–33. See also Cox, "Learned Hand."

38. Frankfurter, "Reflections," 533, 539 (emphasis added).

39. Hart, "Legislation Notes," January 8, 1953, n.p., ser. III, box 17, fol. 2, Hart Papers.

40. Hart, "Legislation Notes," n.d. (but filed with 1950), n.p., ser. III, box 16, fol. 2, Hart Papers.

41. Bobbit, *Fate,* 57; Sebok, *Positivism,* 178 (quoting Hart and Sacks, *Legal Process,* 124).

42. Frankfurter, "Reflections," 533; id., "John Marshall and the Judicial Function," *Harvard Law Review* 69 (1955): 217–38, 218, 231.

43. For a similar point, see Eskridge and Peller, "Public Law," 729.

44. *Brown v. Board of Education,* 347 U.S. 483 (1954).

45. Herbert Wechsler, "Toward Neutral Principles of Constitutional Law," *Harvard Law Review* 73 (1959): 1–35; Silber and Miller, "Oral History," 855 n6.

46. Wechsler, "Neutral Principles," 12, 11, 15.

47. Ibid., 19–20, 22. This echoed the kind of criticism process theorists had been aiming at the Warren Court in the annual forewords to the *Harvard Law Review.* See "The Supreme Court, 1953 Term: Foreword," *Harvard Law Review* 68 (1954): 96–193 (unsigned); Hart, "Time Chart;" Bickel and Wellington, "The Lincoln Mills Case"; Duxbury, *Patterns,* 274–75.

48. Wechsler, "Neutral Principles," 31–35; compare M. P. Golding, "Principled Decision-making and the Supreme Court," *Columbia Law Review* 63 (1963): 35–58, 54.

49. Learned Hand, *The Bill of Rights* (Cambridge: Harvard University Press, 1958), 55.

50. Ibid.

51. Wechsler, "Neutral Principles," 6 (quoting Hand, *Bill,* 15), 9.

52. Remarks of Herbert Wechsler, Annual Judicial Conference, Second Judicial Circuit of the United States, *Federal Rules Decisions* 74:219, 294 (1976). See also Duxbury,

Patterns, 274–75; Wechsler, "The Courts and the Constitution," *Columbia Law Review* 65 (1965): 1001–14.

53. Jan G. Deutsch, "Neutrality, Legitimacy, and the Supreme Court: Some Intersections Between Law and Political Science," *Stanford Law Review* 20 (1968): 169–261, 188–90; Addison Mueller and Murray L. Schwartz, "The Principle of Neutral Principles," *UCLA Law Review* 7 (1960): 571–88, 580–84.

54. Wechsler, "Neutral Principles,"15; Louis H. Pollak, "Constitutional Adjudication: Relative or Absolute Neutrality," *Journal of Public Law* 11 (1962): 48–63, 55, 60–61. See also White, "Evolution," 288–89.

55. Mueller and Schwartz, "Principle," 586; Pollak, "Adjudication," 60–61; Golding, "Principled Decision-Making," 48–49; Duxbury, *Patterns,* 277.

56. Martin Shapiro, *Law and Politics in the Supreme Court: New Approaches to Political Jurisprudence* (New York: Free Press, 1964), 20–21, 337 n49. See also Sebok, *Positivism,* 183–84.

57. Duxbury, *Patterns,* 278.

58. Kent Greenawalt, "The Enduring Significance of Neutral Principles," *Columbia Law Review* 78 (1978): 982–1021, 985.

59. Ibid., 989, 991; Duxbury, *Patterns,* 276. Compare Silber and Miller, "Oral History," 927–28.

60. Shapiro, *Law and Politics,* 31, 46 (quote).

61. Arthur S. Miller and Roland F. Howell, "The Myth of Neutrality in Constitutional Adjudication," *University of Chicago Law Review* 27 (1960): 661–95, 689.

62. Mueller and Schwartz, "Principle," 588.

63. Mueller and Schwartz, "Principle," 588 (quote). Sebok argues that there was a "false choice" between morally confident Warren Court judicial activism and the morally skeptical legal positivism of the process, and later, originalist approaches. Sebok, *Positivism,* ch. 5. This claim is part of his own jurisprudential argument for an "incorporationist" positivism that can include some limited appeals to moral principles.

64. Charles E. Clark, "A Plea for the Unprincipled Decision," *Virginia Law Review* 49 (1963): 660–65.

65. Duxbury, *Patterns,* 276. See also Laura Kalman, *The Strange Career of Legal Liberalism* (New Haven: Yale University Press, 1996), 42–53.

66. Duxbury, *Patterns,* 266.

67. Alexander Bickel, "The Original Understanding and the Segregation Decision," *Harvard Law Review* 69 (1955): 1–65.

68. Bickel's initial memo to Frankfurter read, "It is impossible to conclude that the 39th Congress intended that segregation be abolished; impossible also to conclude that they foresaw it might be, under the language they were adopting." Quoted in Richard Kluger, *Simple Justice* (New York: Knopf, 1976), 654.

69. Bickel, "Original Understanding," 3, 4–5.

70. Ibid., 59, 63 (emphasis in orig.), 65.

71. Ibid., 61 (quote); Alexander M. Bickel, "Integration: The Second Year in Perspective," *The New Republic* 135 (October 8, 1956), 12, as quoted in Edward A. Purcell Jr., "Alexander Bickel and the Post-Realist Constitution," *Harvard Civil Rights–Civil Liberties Law Review* 11 (1976): 521–63, 533.

72. Alexander M. Bickel, *The Least Dangerous Branch: The Supreme Court at the Bar of Politics* (New York: Bobbs-Merrill, 1962), 71.

73. Ibid., 71, 132.

74. Alexander M. Bickel, "Foreword: The Passive Virtues," *Harvard Law Review* 75 (1961): 40–79, repr. in Bickel, *Least Dangerous*, 111–98.

75. Bickel, *Least Dangerous*, 113. See also James E. Radcliffe, *The Case or Controversy Provision* (University Park: Pennsylvania State University Press, 1978). Unlike Bickel, Herbert Wechsler and Henry Hart denied that the Court legitimately could decline to hear a case within its jurisdiction and insisted that the power of Congress to regulate appellate jurisdiction was the proper gatekeeping device, not the "passive virtues." Wechsler, "Neutral Principles," 10. See also Fallon, "Paradigm," 957–58, analyzing Henry M. Hart Jr., "The Power of Congress to Limit the Jurisdiction of the Federal Courts: An Exercise in Dialectic," *Harvard Law Review* 66 (1953): 1362–1402. Compare Bickel, *Least Dangerous*, 124–29.

76. *Poe v. Ullman*, 367 U.S. 497 (1961); Bickel, *Least Dangerous*, 146 (quote), 156 (quote), 143–56. See also "Comment: Threat of Enforcement: Prerequisite of a Justiciable Controversy," *Columbia Law Review* 62 (1962): 106–32. The line of cases that developed from *Poe*, where the American Civil Liberties Union first argued for a constitutional right of privacy, was central to later debates about judicial review and for the emergence of originalism. See chapter 7.

77. Bickel, *Least Dangerous*, 174; *Naim v. Naim*, 350 U.S. 985 (1956). Compare Kalman, *Legal Liberalism*, 33.

78. This point also has been noticed recently as part of an analysis of the "turn to history." See G. Edward White, "The Arrival of History in Constitutional Scholarship," *Virginia Law Review* 88 (2002): 485–633, 564–67.

79. Bickel, *Least Dangerous*, 15–19, 16 (quote), 91, 96, 103–4 (quotes), 104–110.

80. Ibid., quotes at 16, 24, 25–26, 26 quoting Eugene V. Rostow, "The Democratic Character of Judicial Review," *Harvard Law Review* 66 (1952): 193–224, 208.

81. Bickel, *Least Dangerous*, 43. For the influence of Thayer's reasonableness rule upon Frankfurter's judicial restraint position, see Urofsky, *Frankfurter*, 31; Mendelson, "Influence of Thayer;" *West Virginia Board of Education v. Barnette*, 319 U.S. 624, 646–71 (dissenting opinion) (1943).

82. Bickel, *Least Dangerous*, 56; Alfred H. Kelly, "Clio and the Court: An Illicit Love Affair," *Supreme Court Review 1965*, 119–58, 131.

83. Gerald Gunther, "The Subtle Vices of the 'Passive Virtues': A Comment on Principle and Expediency in Judicial Review," *Columbia Law Review* 64 (1964): 1–25, 3, 7.

84. Deutsch, "Some Intersections," 206, quoting Hand, *Bill of Rights*, 73: "For myself it would be most irksome to be ruled by a bevy of Platonic Guardians, even if I knew how to choose them, which I assuredly do not."

85. Purcell, "Bickel," 538 (quote).

86. Alexander M. Bickel, *The Supreme Court and the Idea of Progress* (New York: Harper and Row, 1970); Maurice J. Holland, "American Liberals and Judicial Activism: Alexander Bickel's Appeal from the New to the Old," *Indiana Law Journal* 51 (1976): 1025–50, esp. 1041; Purcell, "Bickel."

87. *Sweezy v. New Hampshire*, 354 U.S. 234, 267 (1957).

88. Bickel, *Idea*, 34.

89. Compare Kahn, *Legitimacy*, 169–70.

90. Bickel, *Idea*, 34.

91. Ibid., 99 (quote), 37, 82–85; Holland, "American Liberals," 1026.

92. Bickel, *Idea*, 177; Purcell, "Bickel," 555 (quote). For additional analyses of Bickel, see also Purcell, "Bickel"; Holland, "American Liberals"; Anne Prince Standley, "Alexander Bickel, Charles Black, and the Ambiguous Legacy of *Brown v. Board of Education*," Ph.D. dissertation, Yale University, 1993, esp. 126–29, 156–59; Duxbury, *Patterns*, 278–86.

93. Philip Kurland, *Politics, the Constitution, and the Warren Court* (Chicago: University of Chicago Press, 1970), 173, 204. See also Isidore Silver, "The Warren Court Critics: Where Are They Now that We Need Them?" *Hastings Constitutional Law Quarterly* 3 (1976): 373–452; Lane Sunderland, "Constitutional Theory and the Role of the Court: An Analysis of Contemporary Constitutional Commentators," *Wake Forest Law Review* 21 (1986): 855–900.

94. Both authors briefly criticized the Warren Court's use of history. For example, Bickel, *Idea*, 45–50; Kurland, *Politics*, 105–7, 153. But such analysis was quickly subordinated to the established focus of process criticism on legal reasoning, institutional competence, and jurisdiction.

THREE: The Return of Originalist Analysis in the Warren Court Era

1. Charles A. Miller, *The Supreme Court and the Uses of History* (Cambridge: Belknap Press of Harvard University Press, 1969), 115–118, 116 (quote).

2. Miller observed two opposed uses of history, "ongoing" history, in which generalized constitutional provisions support the logic of a judicially updated "living Constitution," and "intent" history, which ties interpretation to the meaning words in the text had for those who enacted them into law. Ibid., 25–26.

3. *Adamson v. California*, 332 U.S. 46 (1947).

4. See Mark Silverstein, *Constitutional Faiths: Felix Frankfurter, Hugo Black, and the Process of Constitutional Decision Making* (Ithaca, NY: Cornell University Press, 1984).

5. *Adamson*, 64, 68.

6. See chapter 2.

7. *Adamson*, 69, 71. Frankfurter's concurrence denied that incorporation was intended by the due process clause, refused to consider that it could have been accomplished through the privileges or immunities clause, and restated the holding of the *Slaughterhouse Cases*, 16 Wal. 36 (1873).

8. Charles Fairman, "Does the Fourteenth Amendment Incorporate the Bill of Rights? The Original Understanding," *Stanford Law Review* 2 (1949): 5–139, 68, 139; Richard L. Aynes, "Charles Fairman, Felix Frankfurter, and the Fourteenth Amendment," *Chicago-Kent Law Review* 70 (1997): 1197–1273. Frankfurter cited Fairman in *Bartkus v. Illinois*, 359 U.S. 121, 124 n3 (1959) and Black responded to Fairman directly in *Duncan v. Louisiana*, 391 U.S. 145, 165 (1968) (dissenting opinion).

9. William Winslow Crosskey, *Politics and the Constitution in the History of the United States*, 2 vols. (Chicago: University of Chicago Press, 1953). See also Philip Bobbitt, *Constitutional Fate: Theory of the Constitution* (New York: Oxford University Press, 1982), 14–20.

10. Several reviewers pilloried Crosskey's historical assertions as frequently unproven and sometimes wholly fabricated; for example, Irving Brant, "Mr. Crosskey and Mr. Madison," *Columbia Law Review* 54 (1954): 443–50; Julius Goebel Jr., "*Ex Parte* Clio,"

ibid., 450–83; Ernest J. Brown, "Book Review," *Harvard Law Review* 67 (1954): 1439–56. See also Henry M. Hart Jr., "Professor Crosskey and Judicial Review," ibid., 1456–86.

11. Charles Fairman, "The Supreme Court and Constitutional Limitations on State Governmental Authority," *University of Chicago Law Review* 21 (1953): 1–23; William Winslow Crosskey, "Charles Fairman, 'Legislative History,' and the Constitutional Limitations on State Authority," *University of Chicago Law Review* 22 (1954): 1–143; Charles Fairman, "A Reply to Professor Crosskey," *University of Chicago Law Review* 22 (1954): 144–56. See also Alfred Avins, "Incorporation of the Bill of Rights: The Crosskey-Fairman Debates Revisited," *Harvard Journal on Legislation* 6 (1968): 1–26; Aynes, "Fairman and Frankfurter," 1243–56.

12. Crosskey, "Fairman," 3–4, 117–19, 139–40; Fairman, "Reply," 154; see also Aynes, "Fairman and Frankfurter," 1255 n384.

13. A recent sociological study insists that history cannot be clear enough to control outcomes but nonetheless observes that Fairman and Crosskey "assumed the legitimacy of an originalist jurisprudence." Pamela Brandwein, *Reconstructing Reconstruction: The Supreme Court and the Production of Historical Truth* (Durham, NC: Duke University Press, 1999), 138.

14. *Everson v. Board of Education*, 330 U.S. 1 (1947); *McCollum v. Board of Education*, 333 U.S. 203 (1948).

15. Black used the metaphor in *Everson*, 16 (quoting *Reynolds v. United States*, 98 U.S. 145, 164 (1878)), which quoted Jefferson to the Danbury Baptist Association, January 1, 1802, *The Works of Thomas Jefferson*, 8:113. Supporting the wall metaphor in dissent, Justice Rutledge also canvassed the history of Virginia in the late eighteenth century and appended James Madison's "Memorial and Remonstrance Against Religious Assessments" (1785) to his opinion. *Everson*, 28–74.

16. *McCollum*, 211–12.

17. Ibid., 247, 256.

18. Ibid., 244; Edward S. Corwin, "The Supreme Court as a National School Board," *Law and Contemporary Problems* 14 (1949): 3–20, 20.

19. J. M. O'Neill, *Religion and Education Under the Constitution* (New York: Harper, 1949) xii, 48 (quote, emphasis removed), 1 (quote), 55–56, 11, 49 (quote, emphasis in orig.).

20. *Brown v. Board of Education*, 345 U.S. 972 (June 8, 1953). There were no ratification conventions; see Richard Kluger, *Simple Justice: The History of Brown v. Board of Education and Black America's Struggle for Equality* (New York: Knopf, 1976), 615.

21. *Brown* (1953), 972–73.

22. Howard Jay Graham, "The Early Anti-Slavery Backgrounds of the Fourteenth Amendment," *Wisconsin Law Review* (1950), 479–507, 810–61; id., "The Fourteenth Amendment and School Segregation," *Buffalo Law Review* 3 (1953): 1–24; id., "Our 'Declaratory' Fourteenth Amendment," *Stanford Law Review* 7 (1954): 3–39. The last two articles were drawn from the NAACP brief in *Brown* and are collected in id., *Everyman's Constitution* (Madison: State Historical Society of Wisconsin, 1968), 266–336; Jacobus tenBroek, *The Antislavery Origins of the Fourteenth Amendment* (Berkeley: University of California Press, 1951.) See also Jacobus tenBroek and Joseph Tussman, "The Equal Protection of the Laws," *California Law Review* 37 (1949): 341–81; John P. Frank and Robert F. Munro, "The Original Understanding of 'Equal Protection of the Laws,'" *Columbia Law Review* 50 (1950): 131–69; Kluger, *Simple Justice*, 623–26, 644; Herman Belz, "The Civil

War Amendments to the Constitution: The Relevance of Original Intent," *Constitutional Commentary* 5 (1988): 115–41, 120–27.

23. Graham, *Everyman*, 290–93, 269.

24. *Brown v. Board of Education*, 347 U.S. 483, 489, 492, 494 (1954).

25. Alfred H. Kelly, "The Fourteenth Amendment Reconsidered: The Segregation Question," *Michigan Law Review* 54 (1956): 1049–86; id., "The School Segregation Case," in *Quarrels That Have Shaped the Constitution*, ed. John A. Garraty (New York: Harper and Row, 1964), 243–68.

26. Kelly, "Segregation Question," 1086.

27. Id., "Segregation Case," 268 (quote); id., "When the Supreme Court Ordered Desegregation," *U.S. News and World Report*, February 5, 1962, 86–88, 88 (quote).

28. Kelly, "Segregation Case," 264, 265; Kelly, "Supreme Court," 88 (quote).

29. Norman Silber, "The Solicitor General's Office, Justice Frankfurter, and Civil Rights Litigation, 1946–60," *Harvard Law Review* 100 (1987): 817–52, 832–35, 843–44; "With All Deliberate Impropriety," editorial, *New York Times*, March 24, 1987, A30, col. 1; Philip Elman, "Letter to the Editor," *New York Times*, April 1, 1987, A30, col. 3. See also Alexander Bickel, *The Supreme Court and the Idea of Progress* (New York: Harper and Row, 1970), 33; Richard E. Morgan, "Coming Clean About *Brown*," *City Journal*, Summer 1996, 42–52; Kelly, "Supreme Court," 87.

30. Frankfurter quoted in Mark Tushnet and Katya Lezin, "What Really Happened in *Brown v. Board of Education*," *Columbia Law Review* 91 (1991): 1867–1930, 1906; and in Dennis J. Hutchinson, "Unanimity and Desegregation: Decisionmaking in the Supreme Court, 1948–1958," *Georgetown Law Journal* 68 (1979): 1–96, 24. See also Tushnet and Lezin, "Really," 1872–73, 1918–21. Frankfurter typically used history to argue in developmental or inferential terms, not to hew to the original intent of constitutional language. Miller, *Uses*, 198, 138–40, 163–65.

31. William Anderson, "The Intention of the Framers: A Note on Constitutional Interpretation," *American Political Science Review* 49 (1955): 340–52, 351 (quote). See also Edmond Cahn, "Jurisprudence," *New York University Law Review* 30 (1955): 150–69; Charles L. Black, "The Lawfulness of the Segregation Decisions," *Yale Law Journal* 69 (1960): 421–30; Charles Fairman, "Foreword: The Attack on the Segregation Cases," *Harvard Law Review* 70 (1956): 83–94.

32. L. Brent Bozell, *The Warren Revolution: Reflections on the Consensus Society* (New Rochelle, NY: Arlington House, 1966), 56–57.

33. Charles S. Hyneman, *The Supreme Court on Trial* (New York: Atherton/Prentice-Hall, 1964), 189–97.

34. Bozell, *Warren Revolution*, 29–35; Hyneman, *Supreme Court*, 198–99, 270–75.

35. Virginia Commission on Constitutional Government, *Did the Court Interpret or Amend?* (Richmond, VA: 1960), 43, 3–5. See also id., *A Question of Intent* (Richmond, VA: 1959). This is a reprint of the testimony of David J. Mays before a subcommittee of the United States Senate, May 14, 1959, which in turn drew on the brief Mays helped prepare for submission to the Supreme Court in desegregation litigation.

36. Quoted in Fairman, "Attack," 84.

37. James F. Byrnes, "The Supreme Court Must Be Curbed," *U.S. News and World Report*, May 18, 1956, 50–58. See also "What 36 State Chief Justices Said about the Supreme Court [text of Resolutions of the Committee on Federal-State Relationships as Affected by Judicial Decisions, Conference of State Chief Justices, Pasadena, California, August

23, 1958], *U.S. News and World Report,* October 3, 1958, 92–102; "How U.S. Judges Feel About the Supreme Court" [poll of federal judges], *U.S. News and World Report,* October 24, 1958, 36–37.

38. *Civil Rights Cases,* 109 U.S. 3 (1883). See also Alfred H. Kelly, Winfred A. Harbison, and Herman Belz, *The American Constitution: Its Origins and Development,* 7th ed., 2 vols. (New York: W. W. Norton, 1991), 2:357, 591–95. *Shelley v. Kramer,* 334 U.S. 1 (1948); Herbert Wechsler, "Toward Neutral Principles of Constitutional Law," *Harvard Law Review* 73 (1959): 1–35, 29–31.

39. *Bell v. Maryland,* 378 U.S. 226 (1964). The case was remanded after Maryland passed a law during the litigation that forbade restaurant owners and operators from denying service on the basis of race.

40. *Bell,* 289, 290. Ibid., 290 (citing Frank and Munro, "Original Understanding"); 315–16 (citing, among others, *McCulloch v. Maryland,* 4 Wheat. 316, 407, 415 (1819); *United States v. Classic,* 313 U.S. 299, 316 (1941); *Brown v. Board of Education,* 347 U.S. 483, 492–93 (1955); Bickel, "Original Understanding;" and Holmes in *Missouri v. Holland,* 252 U.S. 416, 433 (1920)).

41. *Bell,* 335–41.

42. Ibid., 339, 341–42.

43. Alexander M. Bickel, *Politics and the Warren Court* (New York: Harper and Row, 1965), 170; Alfred Avins, "'State Action' and the Fourteenth Amendment," *Mercer Law Review* 17 (1966): 352–63; id., "The Civil Rights Act of 1875: Some Reflected Light on the Fourteenth Amendment and Public Accommodations," *Columbia Law Review* 66 (1966): 873–915. For a similar assessment, see Alfred H. Kelly, "The Congressional Controversy Over School Segregation, 1867–1875," *American Historical Review* 64 (1959): 537–63.

44. Alfred H. Kelly, "Clio and the Court: An Illicit Love Affair," *Supreme Court Review 1965,* 119–58, 145–49; Miller, *Uses,* 105–112.

45. Monrad G. Paulsen, "The Sit-in Cases of 1964: But Answer There Came None," *Supreme Court Review 1964,* 137–70, 155.

46. *Jones v. Alfred H. Mayer Co.,* 392 U.S. 409 (1968); Kelly, Harbison, and Belz, *Constitution,* 2:604. See also Belz, "Relevance," 129–31.

47. *Jones,* 454–76.

48. Gerhard Casper, "*Jones v. Alfred H. Mayer Co.*: Clio, Bemused and Confused Muse," *Supreme Court Review 1968,* 89–132. See also Sam J. Ervin Jr., "Jones v. Alfred Mayer Co.: Judicial Activism Run Riot," *Vanderbilt Law Review* 22 (1969): 485–502.

49. Bickel, *Idea,* 45–49; Kurland, *Politics, the Constitution, and the Warren Court* (Chicago: University of Chicago Press, 1970), 152–55.

50. Paulsen, "Sit-in Cases," 151–59, 158 (quote), 148–49, 149 (quote).

51. Robert Kohl, "The Civil Rights Act of 1866: Its Hour Come Round at Last: *Jones v. Alfred H. Mayer Co.,*" *Virginia Law Review* 55 (1969): 272–300, 289, 300.

52. Arthur Kinoy, "The Constitutional Right of Negro Freedom," *Rutgers Law Review* 21 (1967): 387–441.

53. *Baker v. Carr,* 369 U.S. 186 (1962).

54. *Gray v. Sanders,* 372 U.S. 368, 381 (1963).

55. *Wesberry v. Sanders,* 376 U.S. 1, 7–8, 18 (citing *Gray v. Sanders,* 381) (1964).

56. *Reynolds v. Sims,* 377 U.S. 533, 568–76, 573 (quote) (1964).

57. *Lucas v. Forty-Fourth General Assembly of Colorado,* 377 U.S. 713 (1964).

58. *Baker,* 267, 268, 297, 269–70.

59. Phil C. Neal, "*Baker v. Carr*: Politics in Search of Law," *Supreme Court Review 1962*, 252–327, 327, quoting Nicholas Katzenbach, "Some Reflections on *Baker v. Carr*" *Vanderbilt Law Review* 15 (1962): 829–38, 836.

60. *Wesberry*, 48; *Reynolds*, 624–25.

61. *Gray*, 386 (quoting Justice Holmes in *Louisville and Nashville Railroad Co. v. Barber Asphalt Co.*, 197 U.S. 430, 434 (1905)). Harlan reiterated this point in *Reynolds*, 621; remaining quotes from *Reynolds*, 590–91, 615, 624–25.

62. *Wesberry*, 20–50.

63. Miller, *Uses*, 128–35, 129 n28 (quote); Kelly, "Clio," 135; Bozell, *Warren Revolution*, 80–112, 341–50, 112 (quote). See also Paul G. Kauper, "Some Comments on the Reapportionment Cases," *Michigan Law Review* 63 (1964): 243–52, 248, 254.

64. Kelly, "Clio," 136, 136–37; William Van Alstyne, "The Fourteenth Amendment, the Right to Vote, and the Understanding of the Thirty-Ninth Congress," *Supreme Court Review 1965*, 33–86.

65. See, for example, Edward M. Goldberg, "Mr. Justice Harlan, the Uses of History, and the Congressional Globe" *Journal of Public Law* 15 (1966): 181–86.

66. Carl A. Auerbach, "The Reapportionment Cases: One Person, One Vote—One Vote, One Value," *Supreme Court Review 1964*, 1–87, 85 (quote), 74–78, 66 (quote).

67. Alfred Avins, "The Equal 'Protection' of the Laws: The Original Understanding," *New York Law Forum* 12 (1966): 385–429. Avins argued *Katzenbach v. Morgan*, 384 U.S. 641 (1966) for the state of New York and helped write an *amicus* brief for the state of Louisiana in support of the plaintiff in *South Carolina v. Katzenbach*, 383 U.S. 301 (1966).

68. Alfred Avins, "The Right to Bring Suit under the Fourteenth Amendment: The Original Understanding," *Oklahoma Law Review* 20 (1967): 284–300.

69. Avins, "Equal 'Protection,'" 427.

70. Ibid., 428.

71. Robert G. Dixon Jr., "Reapportionment in the Supreme Court and Congress," *Michigan Law Review* 63 (1964): 209–42; 212, 214. See also id., *Democratic Representation: Reapportionment in Law and Politics* (New York: Oxford University Press, 1968), 277–86.

72. H.R. 11926, 88th Cong., 2nd sess. (1964). The bill raised fundamental questions of constitutional theory that will be treated in more detail in the next chapter.

73. For example, *Congressional Record* 110 (August 19, 1964): 20218, 20220, 20233, 20234, 20240, 20247, 20259.

74. *Congressional Redistricting: Hearings Before a Subcommittee of the Committee on the Judiciary*, House of Representatives, Committee on the Judiciary, 88th Cong., 2nd sess. (1964), 7–10, 9 (quote).

75. *Engel v. Vitale*, 370 U.S. 421 (1962); *Abington v. Schempp*, 374 U.S. 203 (1963).

76. In *Zorach v. Clausen*, 343 U.S. 306 (1952) the Court upheld a "dismissed time" statute, which allowed students to leave school for religious instruction, and in *McGowan v. Maryland*, 366 U.S. 420 (1961) it upheld Sunday closing laws because they had come to serve the secular purpose of a day of rest.

77. *Schempp*, 222 (quote), 216.

78. Ibid., 215–16.

79. Richard E. Morgan, *The Supreme Court and Religion* (New York: Free Press, 1972), 21.

80. Leo Pfeffer, *Church, State, and Freedom*, rev. ed. (1953; repr. Boston: Beacon Press, 1967), 128, 127, 728.

81. John Herbert Laubach, *School Prayers: Congress, the Courts, and the Public* (Washington, DC: Public Affairs Press, 1969), 22 (quote), 24.

82. Chester James Antieau, Arthur T. Downey, and Edward C. Roberts, *Freedom from Federal Establishment: Formation and Early History of the First Amendment Religion Clauses* (Milwaukee: Bruce Publishing, 1964), viii, 208–9.

83. Robert G. McCloskey, "Principles, Powers, and Values: The Establishment Clause and the Supreme Court," in *Religion and the Public Order 1964,* ed. Donald A. Gianella (Chicago: University of Chicago Press, 1965): 3–32, 5 (quote), 7.

84. Ibid., 11.

85. Ibid., 12; *Schempp,* 237, 236.

86. McCloskey, "Principles," 15.

87. Charles E. Rice, *The Supreme Court and Public Prayer: The Need for Restraint* (New York: Fordham University Press, 1964), 94, xiii.

88. *School Prayers, Bible Reading, Etc.: Hearings Before the Committee on the Judiciary,* House of Representatives, Committee on the Judiciary, 88th Cong., 2nd sess. (1964). Senator Everett Dirksen also introduced amendments to allow voluntary school prayer in 1966 and 1967.

89. For example, *Hearings,* 348–51, 370–73, 1658. See also Laubach, *School Prayers,* 57–59, 63–67.

90. *Hearings,* 363. For the text of the Becker amendment, see ibid., 22. See also Laubach, *School Prayers,* 66.

91. *Hearings,* 349–50.

92. Ibid., 1658.

93. For an overview, see Laubach, *School Prayers,* 70–97. See also *Hearings,* for example, 1668–89 (remarks of Paul Freund).

94. *Hearings,* 2483–84 (quote); Laubach, *School Prayers,* 66, 69 (quote).

95. *Griswold v. Connecticut,* 381 U.S. 479, 484 (1965). The significance of the Douglas opinion as a spur to the originalism of Robert Bork will be considered in chapter 7.

96. Ibid., 493 (quoting Cardozo in *Snyder v. Massachusetts,* 291 U.S. 97, 105 (1933)).

97. *Griswold,* 489–93.

98. Ibid., 529 (quote), 530 (quote), 507–27.

99. Ibid., 490–91 n6, citing Bennett B. Patterson, *The Forgotten Ninth Amendment* (Indianapolis: Bobbs-Merrill, 1955); Norman Redlich, "Are There 'Certain Rights. . . Retained by the People?'" *New York University Law Review* 37 (1962): 787–812; Knowlton H. Kelsey, "The Ninth Amendment of the Federal Constitution," *Indiana Law Journal* 11 (1936): 309–23.

100. Redlich, "Certain Rights," 810.

101. For a listing of articles on the Ninth Amendment prompted by *Griswold,* see David J. Garrow, *Liberty and Sexuality: The Right to Privacy and the Making of Roe v. Wade* (New York: Macmillan, 1994), 785–87 n90.

102. For Goldberg's influence, see David K. Sutelan, "The Ninth Amendment: Guidepost to Fundamental Rights," *William and Mary Law Review* 8 (1966): 101–20. For Black's influence, see James F. Kelley, "The Uncertain Renaissance of the Ninth Amendment," *University of Chicago Law Review* 33 (1966): 814–36.

103. Kelly, "Clio," 150.

104. Ibid., 155.

105. Hugo Black, *A Constitutional Faith* (New York: Alfred A. Knopf, 1969), 11. See also *Griswold*, 514–15, 520–24.

106. Leonard W. Levy, "The Right against Self-Incrimination: History and Judicial History," *Political Science Quarterly* 84 (1969): 1–29, 1.

107. Roger J. Traynor, "Chief Justice Warren's Fair Question," *Georgetown Law Journal* 58 (1969): 1–5; Laura Kalman, *The Strange Career of Legal Liberalism* (New Haven: Yale University Press, 1996), 70 (quote).

F O U R : At the Crossroads

1. For an overview, see Allen J. Matusow, *The Unravelling of America: A History of Liberalism in the 1960s* (New York: Harper and Row, 1984).

2. Literature on party realignment and polarization is summarized in Arthur Paulson, *Realignment and Party Revival: Understanding American Electoral Politics at the Turn of the Twenty-First Century* (Westport, CT: Praeger, 2000), xv–xxiv, 96–123. Compare Everett Carll Ladd, "Like Waiting for Godot: The Uselessness of 'Realignment' for Understanding Change in Contemporary American Politics," in *The End of Realignment? Interpreting American Electoral Eras*, ed. Byron E. Shafer (Madison: University of Wisconsin Press, 1991), 24–36, 33–34. See also Ronald Radosh, *Divided They Fell: The Demise of the Democratic Party, 1964–1996* (New York: Free Press, 1996).

3. Mary C. Brennan, *Turning Right in the Sixties: The Conservative Capture of the GOP* (Chapel Hill: University of North Carolina Press, 1995); Paulson, *Realignment*, 14–20. See also Lee Edwards, *The Conservative Revolution: The Movement That Remade America* (New York: Free Press, 1999); William C. Berman, *America's Right Turn: From Nixon to Clinton*, 2nd ed. (Baltimore: Johns Hopkins University Press, 1998); Godfrey Hodgson, *The World Turned Right Side Up: A History of the Conservative Ascendancy in America* (New York: Houghton Mifflin, 1996); Jonathan Rieder, "The Rise of the 'Silent Majority,'" in *The Rise and Fall of the New Deal Order*, ed. Steve Fraser and Gary Gerstle (Princeton, NJ: Princeton University Press, 1989), 243–68. The seminal blueprint for how conservative populism could fragment the New Deal coalition and put Republicans in the majority was Kevin Phillips, *The Emerging Republican Majority* (New Rochelle, NY: Arlington House, 1969).

4. Laura Kalman, *The Strange Career of Legal Liberalism* (New Haven: Yale University Press, 1996), 57, 43.

5. Alfred H. Kelly, Winfred A. Harbison, and Herman Belz, *The American Constitution: Its Origins and Development*, 7th ed. 2 vols. (New York: W. W. Norton, 1991), 2:637.

6. Quoted in Homer Bigart, "Nominee is Heard on TV in the South," *New York Times*, October 4, 1968, 50; and Lewis Chester, Godfrey Hodgson, and Bruce Page, *An American Melodrama: The Presidential Campaign of 1968* (New York: Viking Press, 1969), 462.

7. Bernard Schwartz, *Super Chief: Earl Warren and His Supreme Court* (New York: New York University Press, 1983), 680–83, 723–24; G. Edward White, *Earl Warren: A Public Life* (New York: Oxford University Press, 1982), 307–13. See also Bruce Allen Murphy, *Fortas: The Rise and Ruin of a Supreme Court Justice* (New York: Morrow, 1988), 270–73, 438.

8. Sue Davis, *Justice Rehnquist and the Constitution* (Princeton, NJ: Princeton University Press, 1989), 9–10.

9. Earl M. Maltz, *The Chief Justiceship of Warren Burger, 1969–1986* (Columbia: University of South Carolina Press, 2000), 22–23, 264, 267–69. See also Bernard Schwartz, *The Ascent of Pragmatism: The Burger Court in Action* (New York: Addison-Wesley, 1990).

10. David E. Kyvig, *Explicit and Authentic Acts: Amending the U.S. Constitution, 1776–1995* (Lawrence: University Press of Kansas, 1996), 378; Kenneth M. Dolbeare and Phillip E. Hammond, *The School Prayer Decisions: From Court Policy to Local Practice* (Chicago: University of Chicago Press, 1971).

11. *Shapiro v. Thompson*, 394 U.S. 618, 630 (1969).

12. *Swann v. Charlotte-Mecklenburg Board of Education*, 402 U.S. 1 (1971); *Griggs v. Duke Power Co.*, 401 U.S. 424 (1971).

13. *Roe v. Wade*, 410 U.S. 113 (1973); *Griswold v. Connecticut*, 381 U.S. 479 (1965); *Furman v. Georgia*, 408 U.S. 238 (1972); *University of California Regents v. Bakke*, 438 U.S. 265 (1978).

14. See Thomas Byrne Edsall with Mary D. Edsall, *Chain Reaction: The Impact of Race, Rights, and Taxes on American Politics* (New York: W. W. Norton, 1991), 13–14, 45–46, 87–90, 107–112, 122–25; Berman, *Right Turn*, 10–11, 43. See also George H. Nash, *The Conservative Intellectual Movement in America Since 1945* (Wilmington, DE: ISI, 1996), 320–21; Michael Kazin, *The Populist Persuasion* (New York: Basic Books, 1995), 245–66; Byron E. Shafer, "The Notion of an Electoral Order," in *End of Realignment*, ed. Shafer, 37–84, 47; Rieder, "'Silent Majority,'" 261–62, 255; Ronald P. Formisano, *Boston Against Busing: Race, Class, and Ethnic Identity in the 1960s and 1970s* (Chapel Hill: University of North Carolina Press, 1991), 3, 66–69, 235–37.

15. Nathan Glazer, "Towards an Imperial Judiciary?" *The Public Interest* 41 (1975): 104–23, 106; Richard Y. Funston, *Constitutional Counterrevolution?* (New York: John Wiley and Sons, 1977); Vincent Blasi, ed., *The Burger Court: The Counter-Revolution That Wasn't* (New Haven: Yale University Press, 1983).

16. Martin Shapiro, "The Supreme Court: From Warren to Burger," in *The New American Political System*, ed. Anthony King (Washington, DC: American Enterprise Institute, 1978), 179–211, 202–11, 210 (quote); Ralph K. Winter Jr., "Poverty, Economic Equality, and the Equal Protection Clause," *Supreme Court Review 1972*, 41–102; Robert McCloskey, "Economic Due Process: An Exhumation and Re-burial," *Supreme Court Review 1962*, 34–62. For an important discussion of the relation between the Warren and Burger Courts, see Ronald Kahn, *The Supreme Court and Constitutional Theory, 1953–1993* (Lawrence: University Press of Kansas, 1994). See also Maltz, *Burger*, 2–3.

17. Donald L. Horowitz, *The Courts and Social Policy* (Washington, DC: Brookings Institution, 1977), 5. See also Glazer, "Imperial Judiciary." Some established process critics agreed that the Court had come to exercise essentially legislative power. See Philip Kurland, "Government By Judiciary," *Modern Age* 20 (1976): 358–71; Wallace Mendelson, "Mr. Justice Douglas and Government By Judiciary," *Journal of Politics* 38 (1976): 918–37.

18. Many agreed with Fred Rodell, an early legal realist and avid defender of the Warren Court, that Bickel's *The Supreme Court and the Idea of Progress* (1969), "might far better have been titled *Justice Frankfurter and the Idea of Standing Still.*" Process jurisprudence yielded "judicial inertia, a deliberate ducking of the big issues on whatever excuse [Frankfurter or Bickel] could fish up." Charles Clark too thought that the "Harvard" or "ostrich" approach "weight[ed] the dice in favor of the conservative or do-nothing judge or decision." Quoted in Laura Kalman, *Legal Realism at Yale, 1927–1960* (Chapel Hill: University of North Carolina Press, 1986), 203, 223.

19. The phrase is from Richard Kluger, *Simple Justice: The History of Brown v. Board of Education and Black America's Struggle for Equality* (New York: Knopf, 1976).

20. J. Skelly Wright, "Professor Bickel, the Scholarly Tradition, and the Supreme Court," *Harvard Law Review* 84 (1971): 769–805, 797, 804.

21. Kalman, *Legal Liberalism*, 52, 57. See also Martin Shapiro, "Fathers and Sons: The Court, the Commentators, and the Search for Values," in *Burger Court*, ed. Blasi, 218–38, 220–21; Mary Ann Glendon, *A Nation under Lawyers: How the Crisis in the Legal Profession is Transforming American Society* (New York: Farrar, Straus, and Giroux, 1994), 140–41, 169–70, 270.

22. Kalman, *Legal Liberalism*, 59; Stephen M. Griffin, *American Constitutionalism: From Theory to Politics* (Princeton, NJ: Princeton University Press, 1996), 141–42.

23. John Hart Ely, "The Wages of Crying Wolf: A Comment on *Roe v. Wade*," *Yale Law Journal* 82 (1973): 920–49, 927, 949.

24. Thomas Grey, "Do We Have an Unwritten Constitution?" *Stanford Law Review* 27 (1975): 703–18, 705.

25. Kalman defines "legal liberalism" as "trust in the potential of courts, particularly the Supreme Court, to bring about 'those specific social reforms that affect large groups of people such as blacks, or workers, or women, or partisans of a particular persuasion; in other words, *policy change with nationwide impact.*'" Kalman, *Legal Liberalism*, 2, quoting Gerald Rosenberg, *The Hollow Hope: Can Courts Bring About Social Change* (Chicago: University of Chicago Press, 1991), 4 (emphasis Rosenberg's). Compare above, introduction, notes 14 and 15 and accompanying text.

26. See G. Edward White, "The Arrival of History in Constitutional Scholarship," *Virginia Law Review* 88 (2002): 485–633, 558–60, 567–87, and chapter 2 of this book.

27. Ronald Dworkin, "The Jurisprudence of Richard Nixon," *New York Review of Books*, May 4, 1972, 27–35; repr. in id., *Taking Rights Seriously*, paper ed. (Cambridge: Harvard University Press, 1978), 131–49, 133, 134–35, 149.

28. For further analysis, see Mark Tushnet, "Truth, Justice, and the American Way: An Interpretation of Public Law Scholarship in the Seventies," *Texas Law Review* 57 (1979): 1307–59, esp. 1316. See also Lawrence Wiseman, "The New Supreme Court Commentators: The Principled, the Political, and the Philosophical," *Hastings Constitutional Law Quarterly* 10 (1983): 315–431.

29. John Hart Ely, *Democracy and Distrust: A Theory of Judicial Review* (Cambridge: Harvard University Press, 1980); White, "Arrival," 569.

30. Tushnet, "Public Law Scholarship," 1322, 1335; Ronald K. L. Collins and David M. Skover, "The Future of Liberal Legal Scholarship," *Michigan Law Review* 87 (1988): 189–239, 228–29. See also T. Alexander Aleinikoff, "Constitutional Law in the Age of Balancing," *Yale Law Journal* 96 (1987): 943–1005. Ely, "Wages," 948–49, argued that balancing should not be treated as a substitute for reasoning rooted in the Constitution.

31. Wright, "Bickel," 797, 804.

32. Dworkin, *Taking Rights Seriously*, 134–35.

33. Ely, *Democracy and Distrust*.

34. Kalman, *Legal Liberalism*, 92.

35. Mark V. Tushnet, "Legal Realism, Structural Review, and Prophecy," *University of Dayton Law Review* 8 (1983): 809–31, 811. This is a major theme of Kalman, *Legal Liberalism*.

36. Paul Brest, "The Fundamental Rights Controversy: The Essential Contradictions of Normative Constitutional Scholarship," *Yale Law Journal* 90 (1981): 1063–1109, 1109.

37. Crime Control and Safe Streets Act of 1968, 90th Cong., 2nd sess. (1968), repr. in *Hearings on the Supreme Court Before the Subcommittee on Separation of Powers of the Senate Committee on the Judiciary,* 90th Cong., 2nd sess. (June 1968), 639–40. See also Paul Bator, Paul Mishkin, David Shapiro, and Herbert Wechsler, eds., *Hart and Wechsler's The Federal Courts and the Federal System,* 2nd ed. (Mineola, NY: Foundation Press, 1973), 361–62.

38. *Miranda v. Arizona,* 384 U.S. 436 (1966).

39. Ervin quoted in "Supreme Court 'Goes on Trial' Before Senators," *National Observer,* June 10, 1968, repr. in *Hearings,* 642–45, 644; *Hearings,* 6 (remarks of Dirksen).

40. Ibid., 55, 61 (remarks of Gerald Gunther). See also ibid., 60, 65ff. (remarks of Alexander M. Bickel and Alfred H. Kelly).

41. Ibid., 84–85.

42. Ibid., 73. This statement expanded upon Kelly, "Clio and the Court."

43. *Hearings,* 74 (Kurland), 194 (Ervin).

44. *Katzenbach v. Morgan,* 384 U.S. 641 (1966). The disagreement over the use of the exceptions clause and section V of the Fourteenth Amendment can be traced in *Hearings,* 35ff., 43ff., 121ff., 136ff., 164ff., 196ff. See also chapter 3.

45. Alfred H. Kelly, "Clio and the Court: An Illicit Love Affair," *Supreme Court Review 1965,* 119–58, 135, 141, 157, 144. On Kelly's involvement in *Brown,* see chapter 3.

46. Charles A. Miller, *The Supreme Court and the Uses of History* (Cambridge: Belknap Press of Harvard University Press, 1969), 51, 169, 193, 200–201.

47. Ibid., 25–26, 191 (quoting Holmes in *Missouri v. Holland,* 252 U.S. 416, 434 (1920)), 196.

48. Jacobus tenBroek, *Equal Under Law,* enl. ed. (New York: Collier Books, 1965), 25. Originally published as *The Antislavery Origins of the Fourteenth Amendment* (Berkeley: University of California Press, 1951).

49. *Wells v. Rockefeller,* 394 U.S. 542, 549–50 (1969); *Oregon v. Mitchell,* 400 U.S. 112, 203 (1970); *Flast v. Cohen,* 392 U.S. 83, 130 (1968).

50. *Furman v. Georgia,* 408 U.S. 238, 468, 470 (1972). See also the dissenting opinion of Justice Powell, ibid., 418–20, 431–33.

51. *Roe v. Wade,* 410 U.S. 113, 174 (1973).

52. *Trimble v. Gordon,* 430 U.S. 762 (1977).

53. Ibid., 786, 784, 785 (Rehnquist, dissenting).

54. Wright, "Bickel," 803; Charles Black, *Structure and Relationship in Constitutional Law* (Baton Rouge: Louisiana State University Press, 1969), 72 (quote) and passim; Vince Blasi, "Creativity and Legitimacy in Constitutional Law" [review of Black, *Structure and Relationship*], *Yale Law Journal* 80 (1970): 176–94, 192 (quote), 191 (quote, emphasis in orig.), 194.

55. Hans A. Linde, "Judges, Critics, and the Realist Tradition," *Yale Law Journal* 82 (1972): 227–56, 256, 254.

56. Ibid., 253, 254, 256.

57. Grey, "Unwritten."

58. Ely, "Wages;" Richard A. Epstein, "Substantive Due Process By Any Other Name: The Abortion Cases," *Supreme Court Review 1973,* 159–85; Winter, "Equal Protection Clause"; Robert Bork, "Neutral Principles and Some First Amendment Problems," *Indiana Law Journal* 47 (1971): 1–35.

59. Grey, "Unwritten," 705, 718. Somewhat paradoxically, Grey used history as the major part of his justification for "noninterpretivism." Ibid., 715–17.

60. Ibid., 707, 709, 705, 718.

61. William Rehnquist, "The Notion of a Living Constitution," *Texas Law Review* 54 (1976): 693–706, 695.

62. Ibid., 696, 704.

63. Ibid., 706.

FIVE: Raoul Berger and the Restoration of Originalism

1. For a bibliography, see Berger, *Government by Judiciary: The Transformation of the Fourteenth Amendment,* 2nd ed. (Indianapolis: Liberty Fund, 1997), 485–91.

2. Raoul Berger, *Selected Writings on the Constitution* (Cumberland, VA: James River Press, 1987), 7.

3. Raoul Berger, "Natural Law and Judicial Review: Reflections of an Earthbound Lawyer," *University of Cincinnati Law Review* 61 (1992): 5–28. See also id., "The Constitution and the Rule of Law," *Western New England Law Review* 1 (1978): 261–75.

4. See, for example, Raoul Berger, "From Hostage to Contract," *Illinois Law Review* 35 (1940): 154–74; ibid., 281–92.

5. Raoul Berger, "Constructive Contempt: A Post Mortem," *University of Chicago Law Review* 9 (1942): 602–42, repr. id., *Selected Writings,* 8–35, 35, 10 (quote, notes omitted). The case, *Bridges v. California,* 314 U.S. 252 (1941), held that the First Amendment, incorporated by the Fourteenth, barred a court's contempt citation of a publication that it deemed an obstruction of justice in a pending case. Berger argued that neither the First Amendment nor the Fourteenth had been intended to displace the traditional judicial power over contemptuous publications.

6. Raoul Berger, *Congress v. The Supreme Court* (Cambridge: Harvard University Press, 1969).

7. For Berger's statement of his method, see for example, ibid., 71, 114–16.

8. Ibid., 285–89.

9. Ibid., 289–96, 336–37.

10. Ibid., 194–95, 286 (quoting Henry M. Hart, "The Power of Congress to Limit the Jurisdiction of Federal Courts: An Exercise in Dialectic, " *Harvard Law Review* 66 (1953): 1362, 1365).

11. Raoul Berger to Scott H. Bice, October 10, 1970, [6pp.], 4 (quote), ser. I, box 1, fol. 4, Raoul Berger Papers, Harvard Law School Archives; Raoul Berger to Henry M. Hart Jr., March 13, 1967, box 1, fol. 7, Papers of Henry M. Hart Jr., Harvard Law School Archives; Berger to Hart, August 17, 1967, ibid.; Berger to Hart, September 19, 1967, ibid.

12. Berger, *Congress,* 188–96, 241–44, 346.

13. Ibid., 170–76, 337–38, 341.

14. Ibid., 339–46, 346 (quote); James Bradley Thayer, "The Origin and Scope of the American Doctrine of Judicial Review," *Harvard Law Review* 7 (1893): 129–52.

15. Raoul Berger, "Executive Privilege v. Congressional Inquiry," parts I and II, *UCLA Law Review* 12 (1965): 1044–1120, 1288–1364; id., "Impeachment of Judges and 'Good Behavior Tenure,'" *Yale Law Journal* 79 (1970): 1475–1531; id., "Impeachment for 'High Crimes and Misdemeanors,'" *Southern California Law Review* 44 (1971): 395–460. These articles were included as chapters in Berger's *Impeachment: The Constitutional Problems* (Cambridge: Harvard University Press, 1973). See also Berger's testimony in *Hearings on Executive Privilege Before the Subcommittee on the Separation of Powers of the Senate Commit-*

tee on the Judiciary, 92nd Cong., 1st sess. (July 1971); Raoul Berger, *Executive Privilege: A Constitutional Myth* (Cambridge: Harvard University Press, 1974).

16. Berger, "Impeachment for 'High Crimes and Misdemeanors'" is reprinted in *Impeachment: Selected Materials,* Committee on the Judiciary, House of Representatives, 93rd Cong., 1st sess. (October 1973), 617–62. Berger's *Impeachment* was cited in *Constitutional Grounds for Presidential Impeachment: Report by the Staff of the Impeachment Inquiry,* Committee on the Judiciary, House of Representatives, 93rd Cong., 1st sess., 5 n5, 7 n20, 12 n50; Warren Weaver Jr., "St. Clair Rebuked on Legal Defense," *New York Times,* May 15, 1974, 1; Raoul Berger, "The President, Congress, and the Courts," *Yale Law Journal* 83 (1974): 1111–55; Garry Wills, "The Impeachment Man," *Atlantic Monthly* 233 (May, 1974): 79–84; Berger, "Executive Privilege in Light of *United States v. Nixon,*" address delivered to the Organization of American Historians Annual Convention, Boston, Mass., April 17, 1975, repr. in *The Maryland Historian* (1975): 67–78; *United States v. Nixon,* 418 U.S. 683 (1974). See also Raoul Berger, "Impeachment: An Instrument of Regeneration," *Harper's* 248 (January 1974): 14; id., "To the Editor," *New York Times,* March 6, 1974, 36; id., "Mr. Nixon's Refusal of Subpoenas: 'A Confrontation With the Nation,'" *New York Times,* July 8, 1974, 29; R. W. Apple Jr., "Mansfield Backs 6-Day Trial Week," *New York Times,* July 24, 1974, 23.

17. See, for example, Berger, "Executive Privilege," 1111, 1332; id., *Congress,* 170–76; id., *Impeachment,* 94–102; id., *Executive Privilege,* 3–4, 45–47, 89ff. See also *Hearings,* 277–78, 288, 290–92, 301–3.

18. See, for example, Berger, "Executive Privilege," 1046–47, 1060, 1070–74; id., *Impeachment,* 5–6, 71, 87, 138ff., 164, 178–79, 203–4, 213; id., *Executive Privilege* 10–11, 42–43, 88–100. See also *Hearings,* 279.

19. Berger, "Executive Privilege," 1078, 1325, 1358–60; id., *Congress,* 177–97, 343–46; id., *Impeachment,* 116–21, 202, 213, 291, 297–301; id., "To the Editor," *New York Times,* January 14, 1974, 26. See also id., *Executive Privilege,* 304–9, 338–41; *Hearings,* 285–86, 290, 295.

20. Berger, *Impeachment,* 213; id., *Executive Privilege,* 97, quoting Jonathan Elliot, ed., *Debates in the Several State Conventions on the Adoption of the Federal Constitution,* 2nd ed. (Washington, 1836) 4:446 and Galliard Hunt, ed., *The Writings of James Madison* (New York, 1900–1910) 9:191, 372. See also Berger, *Congress,* 340–46.

21. *Baker v. Carr,* 369 U.S. 186 (1962); *Reynolds v. Sims,* 377 U.S. 533 (1964); *Wesberry v. Sanders,* 376 U.S. 1 (1964).

22. Berger, *Government by Judiciary,* 18–19, 37–51, 166–220.

23. Ibid., 363–72, 363 (quote).

24. For an overview of Berger's use of common law canons of construction in the book and some of the initial academic debate it inspired, see William Gangi, "Judicial Expansionism: An Evaluation of the Ongoing Debate," *Ohio Northern University Law Review* 8 (1981): 1–68, 5–10.

25. For example, Berger, *Government by Judiciary,* 157, 189, 7; Gangi, "Evaluation," 6.

26. Berger, *Government by Judiciary,* 76, 18–36, 171–72, 427.

27. Ibid., 124, 155, 300–311, 353–54.

28. Ibid., 9–10, 99–116, 230–45, 373–96.

29. Berger, *Government by Judiciary,* 105–16, 57–68, 70–84. Here Berger relied heavily on Michael Les Benedict, *A Compromise of Principle: Conservative Republicans and Reconstruction, 1863–1869* (New York: W. W. Norton, 1975).

30. Berger, *Government by Judiciary,* 134–56. Berger subsequently defended this position in more detail; see *The Fourteenth Amendment and the Bill of Rights* (Norman: University of Oklahoma Press, 1989).

31. *Palko v. Connecticut,* 302 U.S. 319 (1937).

32. *U.S. v. Carolene Products Co.,* 304 U.S. 144 (1938).

33. Gerald Gunther, ed., *John Marshall's Defense of McCulloch v. Maryland* (Stanford: Stanford University Press, 1969), 185. *McCulloch v. Maryland,* 4 Wheat. 316, 415 (1819); *Missouri v. Holland,* 252 U.S. 416, 433 (1920).

34. Berger, *Government by Judiciary,* 269–82; 373–86. See also Berger, *Executive Privilege,* 88–100.

35. Berger to Ward Elliott, April 24, 1976, [4 pp.], 2, ser. I, box 1, fol. 13, Berger Papers.

36. Berger to Sanford Byron Gabin, September 14, 1977, [3pp.], 3, ser. I, box 1, fol. 13, Berger Papers.

37. Berger to Ward Elliott, May 21, 1976, ser. I, box 1, fol. 13, Berger Papers.

38. Berger, *Government by Judiciary,* 129–33, 259–62, 385–86. Berger further pointedly criticized Frankfurter's due process jurisprudence in id., *Death Penalties: The Supreme Court's Obstacle Course* (Cambridge: Harvard University Press, 1982), 99–103.

39. Berger, *Government by Judiciary,* chs. 14 and 17.

40. Ibid., 52–116, 419–27; 117–33.

41. Ibid., 407.

42. Forrest McDonald, "Foreword," *Government by Judiciary,* 2nd ed., xviii; Richard B. Saphire, "Judicial Review in the Name of the Constitution," *University of Dayton Law Review* 8 (1983): 745–808, 753.

43. Paul Brest, "Berger v. *Brown,* et al.," *New York Times Book Review,* December 11, 1977, 10–11, 44 (quotes at 10, 44); Leonard W. Levy quoted in "Fie on the Fourteenth: Berger Barks Again," *Time,* November 14, 1977, 101–2, (quote at 102).

44. Arthur S. Miller, "Do the Founding Fathers Know Best?" *Washington Post,* November 13, 1977, E3; Robert Cover, "Books Considered," *New Republic,* January 14, 1978, 26–28, 27. See also Bernard Schwartz, "'A Third Chamber'?" *Chronicle of Higher Education,* November 21, 1977, 13.

45. Michael Perry, "Book Review," *Columbia Law Review* 78 (1978): 685–705, 687–88; Donald P. Kommers, "The Role of the Supreme Court," *Review of Politics* 40 (1978): 409–15, 413–14; Randall Bridwell, "Book Review," *Duke Law Journal* (1978): 907–20, 913, 913 n32; Henry J. Abraham, "'Equal Justice Under Law' or 'Justice At Any Cost'?" *Hastings Constitutional Law Quarterly* 6 (1979): 467–86, 467; Wallace Mendelson, "Raoul Berger's Fourteenth Amendment," ibid., 452–53; Dean Alfange Jr., "On Judicial Policymaking and Constitutional Change," *Hastings Constitutional Law Quarterly* 5 (1978): 603–38, 606–7; 622; Nathaniel Nathanson, "Constitutional Interpretation and the Democratic Process," *Texas Law Review* 56 (1978): 579–85, 580–81.

46. Louis Fisher, "Raoul Berger on Public Law," *The Political Science Reviewer* 8 (1978): 173–203; Walter Murphy, "Constitutional Interpretation: The Art of Historian, Magician, or Statesman?" *Yale Law Journal* 87 (1978): 1752–71; Aviam Soifer, "Protecting Civil Rights: A Critique of Raoul Berger's History," *New York University Law Review* 54 (1979): 651–706; Paul Dimond, "Strict Construction and Judicial Review of Racial Discrimination under the Equal Protection Clause: Meeting Raoul Berger on Interpretivist Grounds," *Michigan Law Review* 80 (1982): 462–511; Michael Kent Curtis, "The Bill of

Rights as a Limit on State Authority: A Reply to Professor Berger," *Wake Forest Law Review* 16 (1980): 45–101.

47. Paul Brest, "The Misconceived Quest for Original Understanding," *Boston University Law Review* 60 (1980): 204–38; Ronald Dworkin, "The Forum of Principle," *New York University Law Review* 56 (1981): 469–518.

48. Dworkin, "Forum," 478.

49. Henry Paul Monaghan, "The Constitution Goes to Harvard," *Harvard Civil Rights–Civil Liberties Law Review* 13 (1978):117–31, 127–29; Richard Kay, "Book Review," *Connecticut Law Review* 10 (1978): 801–10, 808–9; James Ely Jr., "Book Review," *Villanova Law Review* 23 (1977–78): 1187–96, 1194; John Hart Ely, "Constitutional Interpretivism: Its Allure and Impossibility," *Indiana Law Journal* 53 (1978): 399–448, 433–35 n128, n129, 436 n132, n133; Perry, "Book Review," 691, 695, 703–5; Gangi, "An Evaluation," 18–22.

50. See, for example, Perry, "Book Review," 698–703; Miller, "Elusive Quest," 498–509; Alfange, "On Judicial Policymaking," 611, 615–16, 623–24, 627–28, 635; Stanley I. Kutler, "Raoul Berger's Fourteenth Amendment: A History or Ahistorical?" *Hastings Constitutional Law Quarterly* 6 (1979): 511–26, 523, 525; Ely, "Constitutional Interpretivism," 413–15, 433–40. See also sources cited in note 47.

51. See, for example, Raoul Berger, "A Political Scientist as Constitutional Lawyer: A Reply to Louis Fisher," *Ohio State Law Journal* 41 (1980): 147–175; id., "The Scope of Judicial Review and Walter Murphy," *Wisconsin Law Review* (1979): 341–71; id., "Soifer to the Rescue of History," *South Carolina Law Review* 32 (1981): 427–69; id., "Paul Dimond Fails to 'Meet Raoul Berger on Interpretivist Grounds,'" *Ohio State Law Journal* 43 (1982): 284–315; id., "Incorporation of the Bill of Rights: A Reply to Michael Curtis," *Ohio State Law Journal* 44 (1983): 1–19.

52. Berger, "Reply to Murphy," 354 (quote); id., "The Scope of Judicial Review: An Ongoing Debate," *Hastings Constitutional Law Quarterly* 6 (1979): 527–633, 570, 548–49, 593ff.; 625–26; id., "Reply to Fisher," 167–68; id., "Dimond Fails," 311–14; id., "Government by Judiciary: Some Countercriticism," *Texas Law Review* 56 (1978): 1125–45, 1129–32; id., "Mark Tushnet's Critique of Interpretivism," *George Washington University Law Review* 51 (1983): 532–50, 545, 545 n114; id., "The Activist Legacy of the New Deal Court," *Washington Law Review* 59 (1984): 751–93, in id., *Selected Writings*, 263–91, 284–86.

53. Raoul Berger, "The Fourteenth Amendment: Light from the Fifteenth," *Northwestern University Law Review* 74 (1979): 311–71, 370 (quote). See also, for example, id., "Ongoing Debate," 618, 625–26, 590; id., "Reply to Murphy," 353; id., "Government by Judiciary: John Hart Ely's 'Invitation,'" *Indiana Law Journal* 54 (1979): 277–312, 302, 304–8; id., "The Role of the Supreme Court," *University of Arkansas at Little Rock Law Journal* 3 (1980): 1–12, 10–11.

54. Raoul Berger, "Michael Perry's Functional Justification for Judicial Activism," *University of Dayton Law Review* 8 (1983): 465–532, 468–90, 520–27; id., "Lawyering vs. Philosophizing: Facts or Fancies," *University of Dayton Law Review* 9 (1984): 171–217, 190–91, 208–14; id., "Ongoing Debate," 628–29. See also id., *Government by Judiciary*, 320ff., 369–70, 387–91.

55. Randall Bridwell, "The Scope of Judicial Review: A Dirge for the Theorists of Majority Rule?" *South Carolina Law Review* 31 (1980): 617–60, 631 (quote); see also Gangi, "An Evaluation," 22–26, 33–37. Berger also made this point in, for example, "Ongoing Debate," 546, 634.

56. Berger, "Rule of Law," 274; id., "Lawyering vs. Philosophizing," 188–89, 199, 201; id., "Ongoing Debate," 532, 605, 610–12, 634–35; id., "The Scope of Judicial Review: A Continuing Dialogue," *South Carolina Law Review* 31 (1980): 171–99, 193–94; id., "Perry's Justification," 529–30; id., "Role of the Court," 11–12; id., "Against an Activist Court," *Catholic University Law Review* 31 (1982): 173–80; id., "Tushnet's Critique," 533, 536, 548–50; id., "Light from the Fifteenth," 369–71; id., "Paul Brest's Brief for an Imperial Judiciary," *Maryland Law Review* 40 (1981): 1–38, 24–26, 37–38; id., "Some Countercriticism," 1143–44.

57. Berger, *Government by Judiciary*, 366 (quote); id., "Reply to Murphy," 348–49, 354–56, 354 (quote); id., "'Government by Judiciary': Judge Gibbons' Argument Ad Hominem," *Boston University Law Review* 59 (1979): 783–809; id., "Ongoing Debate," 543–44, 558 n91, 561, 561 n113, 616–18; id., "Light from the Fifteenth," 356–58; id., "Activist Legacy," 276–78, id., "Brest's Brief," 29–30; id., "Ely's 'Invitation,'" 291, 295–96; id., "Role of the Supreme Court," 9; id., "Lawyering vs. Philosophizing," 191–92, 205; id., "Some Countercriticism," 1132–33, 1142; id., "The Fourteenth Amendment: Facts vs. Generalities," *Arkansas Law Review* (1978): 280–92; id., "Tushnet's Critique," 542–44.

58. Berger, "Light from the Fifteenth," 368 (quote, emphasis in orig.). See also id., "Reply to Murphy" 351–52; id., "Some Countercriticism," 1139–40; id., "Reply to Gibbons," 807; id., "Ongoing Debate," 623; id., "Tushnet's Critique," 547; id., "Ely's 'Invitation,'" 284, 298; id., "Ely's 'Theory of Judicial Review,'" *Ohio State Law Journal* 42 (1981): 87–130, 110–11. Berger's position was central to a dispute about the intent of the founders on the topic of interpretation itself, including the relevance of extrinsic evidence and ratification. This debate was adumbrated in Brest, "Misconceived Quest," 214–16 and was joined by H. Jefferson Powell, "The Original Understanding of Original Intent," *Harvard Law Review* 98 (1985): 885–948. Berger responded in "'Original Intention' in Historical Perspective," *George Washington University Law Review* 54 (1986): 296–337. See also Charles A. Lofgren, "The Original Understanding of Original Intent," *Constitutional Commentary* 5 (1988): 77–113; Raoul Berger, "The Founders' Views—According to Jefferson Powell," *Texas Law Review* 67 (1989): 1033–95. The debate is analyzed in Christopher Wolfe, *How to Read the Constitution: Originalism, Constitutional Interpretation, and Judicial Power* (Lanham, MD: Rowman and Littlefield, 1996), 43–82. See also Gregory Bassham, *Original Intent and the Constitution: A Philosophical Study* (Lanham, MD: Rowman and Littlefield, 1992), 67–71.

59. See, for example, Berger, "Brest's Brief," 37–38; id., "Lawyering vs. Philosophizing," 208–15; id., "Reply to Murphy," 358–60; id., "Tushnet's Critique," 543–44; id., "Ely's 'Invitation,'" 284–88; id., "Facts vs. Generalities," 281–82, 289–92. Berger subsequently stated that both the framers' and ratifiers' intent was binding, but the ratifiers' intent should take precedence if cases of conflict could be demonstrated. Id., *Federalism: The Founders' Design* (Norman: University of Oklahoma Press, 1987), 70–71.

60. Berger, "Tushnet's Critique," 544. See also id., "Activist Court," 178; id., "Facts vs. Generalities," 285, 287; id., "Role of the Court," 12; id., "Some Countercriticism," 1135; id., "Ely's 'Invitation,'" 304–5 n215; id., "Continuing Dialogue," 191–92.

61. See, for example, id., "Constitutional Law and the Constitution," *Suffolk University Law Review* 19 (1985): 1–14; id., "Rule of Law," 262–63. See also id., *Government by Judiciary*, 288–99.

62. Berger, *Government by Judiciary*, chs. 17, 14; id., "Ongoing Debate," 573–75; id., "Activist Court," 180; id., "Ely's 'Invitation,'" 278; id., "Rule of Law," 263 (quote).

63. Berger, "Ongoing Debate," 531 (quote). See also, for example, id., "Ely's 'Invi-

tation,'" 311; id., "Activist Legacy," 263–65; id., "Dimond Fails," 314–15; id., "Rule of Law," 270; id., "Role of the Court," 1–2; id., "Perry's Justification," 489; id., "Constitutional Law and the Constitution," 2–3. Berger also frequently cited to legal liberals his own longstanding criticism of what he regarded as overreaching judicial power in "Constructive Contempt: A Post Mortem." See also note 5 above and accompanying text.

64. Robert Bork, "Neutral Principles and Some First Amendment Problems," *Indiana Law Journal* 47 (1971): 1–35. See chapter 7.

65. Patrick B. McGuigan and Claudia A. Keiper, eds., *A Conference on Judicial Reform: The Proceedings* (Washington, DC: Free Congress Research and Education Foundation, 1982), 127–31, 128 (quote).

66. Charles J. Cooper [assistant attorney general, Office of Legal Counsel, U.S. Department of Justice], "Raoul Berger, Constitutionalist," *Benchmark* 3 (July–October 1987): 183–85; James Willard Hurst, "Raoul Berger: An Appreciation and Qualification," ibid., 187–88; William Gangi, "Raoul Berger's Impact on Constitutional Law," ibid., 189–96; Gary McDowell, "The Intellectual Achievement of Raoul Berger," ibid., 197–204, 203 (quote); Wallace Mendelson, "Raoul Berger on the Fourteenth Amendment Corno Copia [*sic*]," ibid., 205–12.

67. Berger, *Congress.*

68. Berger, *Death Penalties,* 158–72, 161–62 n31; quotes at 162, 164, 172. See also id., "Light from the Fifteenth," 350–55; id., "Congressional Contraction of Federal Jurisdiction," *Wisconsin Law Review* (1980): 801–10; id., "Insulation of Judicial Usurpation: A Comment on Lawrence Sager's 'Court Stripping' Polemic," *Ohio State Law Journal* 44 (1983): 611–47.

69. McGuigan and Keiper, *Judicial Reform,* 129. Berger also identified himself as a liberal and disagreed with conservative policy preferences in Berger, "Some Countercriticism," 1144 ; id., "Constitutional Law and the Constitution," 4; Berger, "Benno Schmidt vs. Rehnquist and Scalia," *Ohio State Law Journal* 47 (1986): 709–12, 709–10.

70. Herman Belz, *A Living Constitution or Fundamental Law? American Constitutionalism in Historical Perspective* (Lanham, MD: Rowman and Littlefield, 1998), 226.

71. Gary L. McDowell, *Curbing the Courts: The Constitution and the Limits of Judicial Power* (Baton Rouge: Louisiana State University Press, 1988) xiv; William Gangi, *Saving the Constitution from the Courts* (Norman: Oklahoma University Press 1995), xi.

72. Kay, "Book Review," 803 (footnote omitted).

73. Richard Kay to Berger, May 28, 1981, ser. I, box 2, fol. 1, Berger Papers. The symposium was "Judicial Review versus Democracy," *Ohio State Law Journal* 42 (1981). For Kay's later originalism, see Richard S. Kay, "Adherence to the Original Intention in Constitutional Adjudication: Three Objections and Responses," *Northwestern University Law Review* 82 (1988): 228–92; id., "American Constitutionalism" in *Constitutionalism: Philosophical Foundations,* ed. Larry Alexander (Cambridge: Cambridge University Press, 1998), 16–63.

74. Larry A. Alexander, "Modern Equal Protection Theories: A Metatheoretical Taxonomy and Critique," *Ohio State Law Journal* 42 (1981): 3–68, 4 (footnote omitted).

75. Alexander to Berger, June 4, 1981, ser. I, box 1, fol. 1, Berger Papers. For his later defense of originalist interpretation, see Larry Alexander, "All or Nothing at All? The Intentions of Authorities and the Authority of Intentions," in *Law and Interpretation: Essays in Legal Philosophy,* ed. Andrei Marmor (New York: Oxford University Press, 1995), 357–404.

76. Michael W. Mcconnell, "Federalism: Evaluating the Founders' Design," *University of Chicago Law Review* 54 (1987): 1484–1512, 1484. While elaborating different versions of originalism, other scholars acknowledged Berger's influence on the doctrine. See Keith E. Whittington, "The New Originalism," 2, paper presented at the American Association of Law Schools Conference on Constitutional Law, Washington, DC, June 2002, available at http://www.princeton.edu/~kewhitt/new_originalism.pdf; Christopher Wolfe, *The Rise of Modern Judicial Review: From Constitutional Interpretation to Judge-Made Law*, rev. ed. (Lanham, MD: Rowman and Littlefield 1994), ix.

77. Perry, "Book Review," 703–4 (footnote omitted). This idea was reiterated in Perry to Berger, February 4, 1979 [2 pp.], ser. I, box 2, fol. 8, Berger Papers. Perry's initial theoretical effort was *The Constitution, The Courts, and Human Rights: An Inquiry into the Legitimacy of Constitutional Policymaking by the Judiciary* (New Haven: Yale University Press, 1982).

78. Dworkin, "Forum of Principle"; Ely, "Constitutional Interpretivism."

s I X : Originalism in the Era of Ronald Reagan

1. Of course this major development has generated a massive literature. For a good overview, see William C. Berman, *America's Right Turn: From Nixon to Reagan*, 2nd ed. (Baltimore: Johns Hopkins University Press, 1998), 60–84, 111–18.

2. Thomas Grey, "Do We Have an Unwritten Constitution?" *Stanford Law Review* 27 (1975): 703–18. See chapter 4.

3. John Hart Ely, *Democracy and Distrust: A Theory of Judicial Review* (Cambridge: Harvard University Press, 1980).

4. Paul Brest, "The Misconceived Quest for Original Understanding," *Boston University Law Review* 60 (1980): 204–38, 204.

5. Ibid., 232 n108.

6. For examples of scholars observing this theme of liberal scholarship, see Vincent Blasi, ed., *Law and Liberalism in the 1980s* (New York: Columbia University Press, 1991), xi; Bruce Fein, "Legal Education and Moral Conscience," *Harvard Journal of Law and Public Policy* 8 (1985): 313–15.

7. Ronald Kahn, *The Supreme Court and Constitutional Theory, 1953–1993* (Lawrence: University Press of Kansas, 1994), 186.

8. Ronald K. L. Collins and David M. Skover, "The Future of Liberal Legal Scholarship," *Michigan Law Review* 87 (1988): 189–239, 196–97.

9. Laura Kalman, *The Strange Career of Legal Liberalism* (New Haven: Yale University Press, 1996), 62–68, 88–93, 240 (quote).

10. William Brennan, "The Constitution of the United States: Contemporary Ratification" [Georgetown University, October 12, 1985], in *Judges on Judging: Views from the Bench*, ed. David M. O'Brien (Chatham, NJ: Chatham House, 1997), 200–210, 205, 210, 208. See also Brest, "Misconceived Quest, 224–38; Ronald Dworkin, *A Matter of Principle* (1985; repr. Oxford: Clarendon, 1986), 48–50, 55–57; A. Selwyn Miller, "Notes on the Concept of a Living Constitution," *George Washington Law Review* 31 (1963): 881–918.

11. For frequently noted hermeneutic critiques of the period, see Ronald Dworkin, "The Forum of Principle," *New York University Law Review* 56 (1981): 469–518; Paul Brest, "The Fundamental Rights Controversy: The Essential Contradictions of Normative Con-

stitutional Scholarship," *Yale Law Journal* 90 (1981): 1063–1109, 1091 (quote); Mark Tushnet, "Following the Rules Laid Down: A Critique of Interpretivism and Neutral Principles," *Harvard Law Review* 96 (1983): 781–827; Sanford Levinson, "Law as Literature," *Texas Law Review* 60 (1982): 373–403. See also H. Jefferson Powell, "The Original Understanding of Original Intent," *Harvard Law Review* 98 (1985): 885–948. For further explication and contextualization, see Kalman, *Legal Liberalism,* 108–18, 137.

12. See Kahn, *Constitutional Theory,* 211–49; Paul W. Kahn, *Legitimacy and History: Self-Government in American Constitutional Theory* (New Haven: Yale University Press, 1992), 171–209.

13. Two sympathetic surveys that contextualize these developments are Gary Minda, *Postmodern Legal Movements: Law and Jurisprudence at Century's End* (New York: New York University Press, 1995); and Stephen M. Feldman, *American Legal Thought from Premodernism to Postmodernism: An Intellectual Voyage* (New York: Oxford University Press, 2000). See also Pierre Schlag, Paul F. Campos, and Stephen D. Smith, *Against the Law* (Durham, NC: Duke University Press, 1996).

14. Michael Perry, "Noninterpretive Review in Human Rights Cases: A Functional Justification," *New York University Law Review* 56 (1981): 278–352, 279–83. See also Joseph Grano, "Judicial Review and a Written Constitution in a Democratic Society," *Wayne Law Review* 28 (1981): 1–75, 63–64; Henry Monaghan, "Our Perfect Constitution," *New York University Law Review* 56 (1981): 353–96, 353–55; William Gangi, "The Supreme Court: An Intentionist's Critique of Non-Interpretive Review," *The Catholic Lawyer* 28 (1983): 253–314, 273–84.

15. William Van Alstyne, "Interpreting *This* Constitution: The Unhelpful Contribution of Special Theories of Judicial Review," *University of Florida Law Review* 35 (1983): 209–35, 217 n27. Van Alstyne was not an originalist, but his arguments in this article echoed the originalist criticisms of the period. Gary McDowell, "The Moral Wish as Father to the Constitutional Thought" [review of Philip Bobbitt, *Constitutional Fate*], *Louisiana Law Review* 45 (1985): 831–36, 832.

16. Robert Bork, Remarks on "Constitutional Courts and Democratic Government," in *A Conference on Judicial Reform: The Proceedings* [June 14, 1982], ed. Patrick B. McGuigan and Claudia A. Keiper (Washington, DC: Free Congress Foundation, 1982), 132, 133; Grano, "Judicial Review," 59; Robert Bork, "Styles in Constitutional Theory," *Supreme Court Historical Society Yearbook 1984,* 53–60, 58; id., *Tradition and Morality in Constitutional Law* (Washington, DC: AEI, 1984), 11, 10. See also J. Clifford Wallace, "The Jurisprudence of Judicial Restraint: A Return to the Moorings," *George Washington Law Review* 50 (1981): 1–16, 16; John McArthur, "Abandoning the Constitution: The New Wave in Constitutional Theory," *Tulane Law Review* 59 (1984): 280–334, 313, 320–23; Monaghan, "Perfect Constitution," 358–60; William Gangi, "The Exclusionary Rule: A Case Study in Judicial Usurpation," *Drake Law Review* 34 (1984–85): 33–134, 119.

17. Frank Michelman, "Welfare Rights in a Constitutional Democracy," *Washington University Law Quarterly* (1979): 659–93; Robert Bork, "The Impossibility of Finding Welfare Rights in the Constitution," *Washington University Law Quarterly* (1979): 695–701, 696.

18. Bork, "Impossibility," 697. Bork responded to articles by Ely that were the basis of Ely's *Democracy and Distrust,* which Ely claimed could be seen as "the ultimate interpretivism." Ibid., 88. Bork later stated that Ely was "a non-interpretivist whether he

knows it or not." Bork, "Styles," 56. For further analysis of Ely, see Kalman, *Legal Liberalism*, 88–89.

19. Christopher Wolfe, "A Theory of U.S. Constitutional History," *The Journal of Politics* 43 (1981): 292–316. See also id., *The Rise of Modern Judicial Review: From Constitutional Interpretation to Judge-Made Law* (Lanham, MD: Rowman and Littlefield, 1986); and Monaghan, "Perfect Constitution," 378, 363; Raoul Berger, "New Theories of 'Interpretation': The Activist Flight from the Constitution," *Ohio State Law Journal* 47 (1986): 1–45, 26–27; id., "Lawyering vs. Philosophizing: Facts or Fancies," *University of Dayton Law Review* 9 (1984): 171–217, 193–94; Lino A. Graglia, "Judicial Review on the Basis of 'Regime Principles': A Prescription for Government by Judges," *South Texas Law Journal* 26 (1985): 435–52, 445; id., "Would the Court Get 'Procedural Due Process' Cases Right If It Knew What 'Liberty' Really Means?" *Journal of Law, Ethics, and Public Policy* 1 (1985): 813–28, 817; Gangi, "An Intentionist's Critique," 269–71.

20. Robert Bork, "The Constitution, Original Intent, and Economic Rights" [speech delivered November 18, 1985], *San Diego Law Review* 23 (1986): 823–32, 827, 828, 826. See also Robert Bork, "Foreword" in Gary L. McDowell, *The Constitution and Contemporary Constitutional Theory* (Cumberland, VA: Center for Judicial Studies, 1985), x–xi.

21. Bork, "The Constitution," 826–27, 829; *Griswold v. Connecticut*, 381 U.S. 479 (1965). Bork also criticized the right to privacy while he was a federal judge in *Dronenberg v. Zech*, 741 F.2nd 1388 (D.C. Cir. 1984); see chapter 7. See also Raoul Berger, "Some Reflections on Interpretivism," *George Washington Law Review* 55 (1986): 1–16, 7; id., "Mark Tushnet's Critique of Interpretivism," *George Washington Law Review* 51 (1983): 532–50, 536.

22. See, for example, Earl Maltz, "The Concept of Equal Protection of the Laws—An Historical Inquiry," *San Diego Law Review:* 22 (1985): 499–540 (federalism). Raoul Berger's work in the early 1980s also consistently contained both themes, see the bibliography in *Government By Judiciary: The Transformation of the Fourteenth Amendment,* 2nd ed. (Indianapolis: Liberty Fund, 1997), 485–91.

23. McDowell, *The Constitution,* 41; Earl M. Maltz, "Federalism and the Fourteenth Amendment: A Comment on *Democracy and Distrust,*" *Ohio State Law Journal* 42 (1981): 209–21; id., "Murder in the Cathedral: The Supreme Court as Moral Prophet," *University of Dayton Law Review* 8 (1983): 623–31, 626–27.

24. See, for example, Monaghan, "Perfect Constitution," 364; Gangi, "An Intentionist's Critique;" 299–301 and passim; Graglia, "Judicial Review," 436–38.

25. Bork, "The Constitution," 824–25; Monaghan, "Perfect Constitution," 363, 363 n67; Berger, "New Theories of 'Interpretation,'" 10 (quoting Larry Simon, "The Authority of the Constitution and Its Meaning," *Southern California Law Review* 58 (1985): 603–46, 620); Bork, *Tradition and Morality,* 11. See also Wallace, "Jurisprudence of Judicial Restraint," 11–12; Gangi, "An Intentionist's Critique," 299, 313; McDowell, *The Constitution,* 12–13.

26. Compare, Kalman, *Legal Liberalism,* 92.

27. Van Alstyne, *"This* Constitution," 229 (quote); McDowell, *The Constitution,* 3 (quote), 40, 7, 21, 23, 24, 29, 32, 33. See also Lino Graglia, "In Defense of Judicial Restraint," in *Supreme Court Activism and Restraint,* ed. Stephen C. Halpern and Charles M. Lamb (Lexington, MA: Lexington Books, 1982), 135–66, 143; id., "Judicial Review," 443, 446–47, 449; Stanley C. Brubaker, "From Incompetent Imperialism to Principled Prudence: The Role of Courts in Restoring 'the State,'" *Hastings Constitutional Law Quar-*

terly 10 (1982): 82–143, 113–14; McArthur, "Abandoning the Constitution," 330; Bork, "Styles," 56; Earl Maltz,"Some New Thoughts on An Old Problem—The Role of Intent of the Framers in Constitutional Theory," *Boston University Law Review* 63 (1983): 811–51; Gangi, "An Intentionist's Critique," 264, 281ff.

28. Gangi, "An Intentionist's Critique," 253–57, which expands on Gangi, "Judicial Expansionism: An Evaluation of the Ongoing Debate," *Ohio Northern University Law Review* 8 (1981): 1–68. A similar categorization is offered in Van Alstyne, "*This* Constitution," 215–18. For Gangi's recent work, see *Saving the Constitution from the Courts* (Norman: University of Oklahoma Press, 1995).

29. William Rehnquist, "The Notion of a Living Constitution," *Texas Law Review* 54 (1976): 693–706, 695. See chapter 4.

30. Wallace, "Jurisprudence of Judicial Restraint," 2; McDowell, *The Constitution,* 21, 28; Berger, "New Theories of 'Interpretation,'" 44; Bork, "The Constitution," 827; Gangi, "An Intentionist's Critique," 253, 268.

31. Robert H. Bork, "Neutral Principles and Some First Amendment Problems," *Indiana Law Journal* 47 (1971): 1–35, 14. See chapter 7.

32. Maltz, "Some New Thoughts," 846–50; 850 (quote).

33. Ibid., 847.

34. See, for example, Bruce Fein, "Selecting a Supreme Court Justice Devoted to Judicial Restraint," *Benchmark* 1 (November–December 1984): 1–12, 11; Stephen J. Markman [assistant attorney general, Office of Legal Policy], "On Interpretation and Non-Interpretation," *Benchmark* 3 (July–October 1987): 219–28, 220–21; Dallin H. Oaks, "Judicial Activism," *Harvard Journal of Law and Public Policy* 7 (1984): 1–11; Monaghan, "Perfect Constitution," 360.

35. McArthur, "Abandoning the Constitution," 319, 320. See also Paul M. Bator, "Legal Methodology and the Academy," *Harvard Journal of Law and Public Policy* 8 (1985): 335–39, 337.

36. Scholars have recognized how fundamental principles aided originalism. See, for example, Grey, "Unwritten Constitution," 705; William Nelson, "History and Neutrality in Constitutional Adjudication," *Virginia Law Review* 72 (1986): 1237–96, 1260–61; Herman Belz, "History, Theory, and the Constitution," *Constitutional Commentary* 11 (1994): 45–64, 51.

37. Collins and Skover, "Liberal Legal Scholarship," 199 (emphasis in orig.).

38. For a related observation, see Kalman, *Legal Liberalism,* 138.

39. Maltz, "Federalism and the Fourteenth Amendment," 210. See also Bork, "The Constitution," 825–26; Bork, "Styles," 59.

40. See, for example, Graglia, "Judicial Restraint," 162.

41. Graglia, "Judicial Restraint," 155–56; id., "Judicial Review," 444, 451 and passim; Grano, "Judicial Review," 55ff.; Wallace "Jurisprudence of Judicial Restraint," 13; Gangi, "An Intentionist's Critique," 264ff., 308, 311, 312–13; Bork, "The Constitution" 827; id., "Styles," 56. See also United States Department of Justice, Office of Legal Policy, *Original Meaning Jurisprudence: A Sourcebook* (Washington, DC, March 12, 1987); Erwin Chemerinsky, "The Price of Asking the Wrong Questions: An Essay on Constitutional Scholarship and Judicial Review," *Texas Law Review* 62 (1984): 1207–61; John Philip Reid, "Originalism and Subjectivism in the Bicentennial Year," *Social Science Quarterly* 68 (1987): 687–702.

42. Monaghan, "Perfect Constitution," 370–72, 396 (quote); Bork, "Styles," 60. Maltz was careful to point out that originalist judicial review would not always serve majoritarianism. Maltz, "Some New Thoughts," 820–24.

43. The best scholarly treatment of the history of the Department of Justice and its growing importance to separation of powers issues is Cornell W. Clayton, *The Politics of Justice: The Attorney General and the Making of Legal Policy* (Armonk, NY: M. E. Sharpe, 1992); for the 1980s, see 146–58. See also Elder Witt, *A Different Justice: Reagan and the Supreme Court* (Washington, DC: Congressional Quarterly, 1986). An informative but frequently partisan and tendentious journalistic account is Lincoln Caplan, *The Tenth Justice: The Solicitor General and the Rule of Law* (New York: Knopf, 1987); see also Douglas W. Kmiec, *The Attorney General's Lawyer: Inside the Meese Justice Department* (New York: Praeger, 1992).

44. William French Smith [attorney general], "Urging Judicial Restraint," *American Bar Association Journal* 68 (1982): 59–61; id., "Federal Courts Have Gone Beyond Their Abilities," *Judges Journal* 21 (1982): 4–7, 59. See also William Bradford Reynolds [assistant attorney general for civil rights], "Renewing the American Constitutional Heritage," *Harvard Journal of Law and Public Policy* 8 (1984): 225–37. For a retrospective view, see Terry Eastland [director of public affairs, Department of Justice], "Reagan Justice: Combating Excess, Strengthening the Rule of Law," *Policy Review* (Fall 1988): 16–23.

45. Judicial selection in the Reagan years was a contested issue prior to the Bork nomination in 1987; see Sheldon Goldman, *Picking Federal Judges: Lower Court Selection From Roosevelt Through Reagan* (New Haven: Yale University Press, 1997), 285–345. See also Douglas W. Kmiec, "Judicial Selection and the Pursuit of Justice," *Catholic University Law Review* 39 (1989): 1–27; David M. O'Brien, "The Reagan Judges: His Most Enduring Legacy?" in *The Reagan Legacy: Promise and Performance*, ed. Charles O. Jones (Chatham, NJ: Chatham House, 1988), 60–101.

46. A list of measures in committee in the early 1980s can be found in Paul Bator [deputy solicitor general], "Withdrawing Jurisdiction from the Federal Courts," *Harvard Journal of Law and Public Policy* 7 (1984): 31–34, 31 n2; Judicial Reform Act of 1982, S.3018, 97th Cong., 2nd sess., October 1, 1982. See also Gary L. McDowell, *Curbing the Courts: The Constitution and the Limits of Judicial Power* (Baton Rouge: Louisiana State University Press, 1988), 154–67; David E. Kyvig, *Explicit and Authentic Acts: Amending the U.S. Constitution, 1776–1995* (Lawrence: University Press of Kansas, 1996), 449–53. On the Human Life Bill, see Susan Burgess, *Contest for Constitutional Authority* (Lawrence: University Press of Kansas, 1992), 30–48.

47. Grover Rees III, "Methods of Constitutional Interpretation," *Harvard Journal of Law and Public Policy* 7 (1984): 81–86, 84. For Goldwater's position, see Robert Alan Goldberg, *Barry Goldwater* (New Haven: Yale University Press, 1995), 315–16. Raoul Berger, "Congressional Contraction of Federal Jurisdiction," *Wisconsin Law Review* (1980): 801–10; id., "Lawrence Sager's 'Court Stripping' Polemic," *Ohio State Law Journal* 44 (1983): 611–47. See also Lino A. Graglia, "The Power of Congress to Limit Supreme Court Jurisdiction," *Harvard Journal of Law and Public Policy* 7 (1984): 23–29; and the articles by Charles Rice, Patrick McGuigan, and Paul Bator, all titled "Withdrawing Jurisdiction from the Federal Courts," in ibid., 13–15, 17–21, 31–34.

48. *Report of the Subcommittee on the Separation of Powers on the Human Life Bill, S. 158*, 97th Cong., 1st sess. (1981), partially repr. in *Hearings on the Nomination of Robert H. Bork to be Associate Justice of the Supreme Court*, U.S. Senate, Committee on the Judiciary,

100th Cong., 1st sess. (1987), 1380; Bork, "Styles," 57; "Constitutionality of Legislation Limiting the Remedial Powers of the Inferior Federal Courts in School Desegregation Litigation," *Opinions of the Attorney General* 43 (May 6, 1982): 334–49; "Constitutionality of Legislation Withdrawing Supreme Court Jurisdiction to Consider Cases Relating to Voluntary Prayer," ibid., 350–68. See also Lawrence Sager, "Constitutional Limitations on Congress's Authority to Regulate the Jurisdiction of the Federal Courts," *Harvard Law Review* 95 (1981): 17–89; Ralph Rossum, "Congress, the Constitution, and the Appellate Jurisdiction of the Supreme Court," *William and Mary Law Review* 24 (1983): 385–428; "Symposium: Congressional Limits on Federal Court Jurisdiction," *Villanova Law Review* 27 (1981–82): 893–1076.

49. Jonathan Mahler, "The Federalist Capers," *Lingua Franca* (September 1998), 38–47.

50. For example, Reynolds, "Constitutional Heritage."

51. Charles Cooper, personal interview, Washington, DC, June 2003; Edward Lazarus, *Closed Chambers: The First Eyewitness Account of the Epic Struggles inside the Supreme Court* (New York: Random House, 1998), 264.

52. James McClellan, "Editor's Brief," *Benchmark* 1 (Fall 1983): 1–2; id., "Editor's Brief: Kicking the Amendment Habit," ibid., 1 (January–February 1984): 1–3, 2 (quote); Gary L. McDowell, "On Meddling with the Constitution," *Journal of Contemporary Studies* 5 (1982): 3–17. See also James McClellan, "Congressional Retraction of Federal Court Jurisdiction to Protect the Reserved Powers of the States: The Helms Prayer Bill and a Return to First Principles," *Villanova Law Review* 27 (1981–82): 1019–29; id., "Ghost of Jefferson Haunts Roscoe Pound Conference on Separation of Powers," *Benchmark* (Fall 1983): 41–45; Al Kamen and Howard Kurtz, "Theorists on Right Find Fertile Ground: Conservative Legal Activists Exert Influence on Justice Department," *Washington Post*, August 9, 1985, A–1.

53. James McClellan, "Editor's Brief: A Lawyer Looks at Rex Lee," *Benchmark* 1 (March–April 1984): 1–16, quotes at 4, 5, 11, 12; *City of Akron v. Akron Center for Reproductive Health*, 462 U.S. 416 (1983); "Brief of United States as *Amicus Curiae* in Support of Petitioners," in *Landmark Briefs and Arguments of the Supreme Court*, ed. Philip Kurland and Gerhard Caspar (Frederick, MD: University Publishers of America, 1984), 138:340–59; *Lynch v. Donnelly*, 465 U.S. 668 (1984). Lee's "Brief of United States as *Amicus Curiae* Supporting Reversal," in *Lynch v. Donnelly, Landmark Briefs* 151:181–91, appealed to the original meaning of the establishment clause and also echoed Chief Justice Burger's recent opinion in *Marsh v. Chambers*, 463 U.S. 783 (1983), which relied heavily on history and custom (not the Court's precedents) to uphold prayer in a state legislature by a chaplain at taxpayer's expense.

54. *Jaffree v. Board of School Commissioners of Mobile County*, 554 F. Supp. 1104, 1113 n5 (S.D. Ala., 1983); "Other Litigation of Interest," *Benchmark* 1 (Fall 1983): 37–38; *Jaffree v. Wallace*, 705 F.2nd 1526 (11th Cir., 1983). Citing an interview of March 17, 1987, with Forrest McDonald, a renowned constitutional historian at the University of Alabama who followed the case, Lincoln Caplan has written that "McClellan also drafted Hand's opinion." Caplan, *Tenth Justice*, 99, 300 n75.

55. "Brief *Amicus Curiae* of the Center for Judicial Studies in Support of Appellants [signed by Charles Rice]," in Kurland and Caspar, eds., *Landmark Briefs* 155:524–58. See also Charles Rice, "The *Jaffree* Case," *Benchmark* 1 (May–June 1984): 15–21.

56. *Wallace v. Jaffree*, 472 U.S. 38 (1985), Rehnquist dissenting, 91–114; quotes at 107, 108, 113, 100, 98. On the history of the "wall" metaphor, see chapter 3.

57. *Roe v. Wade,* 410 U.S. 113 (1973); "Brief of United States as Amicus Curiae in Support of Appellants," No. 84-495, Thornburgh v. American College of Obstetricians and Gynecologists, July 1985, 1–30, quotes at 20, 27, 24 in Transcripts of Records and File Copies of Briefs, United States Supreme Court; *Thornburgh v. American College of Obstetricians and Gynecologists,* 476 U.S. 747 (1986).

58. For a detailed recent treatment of the Burger Court, see Earl M. Maltz, *The Chief Justiceship of Warren Burger, 1969–1986* (Columbia: University of South Carolina Press, 2000). See also Bernard Schwartz, ed., *The Burger Court: Counter-Revolution or Confirmation?* (New York: Oxford University Press, 1998).

59. Compare Alfred Kelly, Winfred Harbison, and Herman Belz, *The American Constitution: Its Origins and Development,* 7th ed., 2 vols. (New York: W. W. Norton, 1991), 2:729.

60. *Valley Forge Christian College v. Americans United for Separation of Church and State,* 454 U.S. 464, 487 (1982); *Flast v. Cohen,* 392 U.S. 83 (1968); *INS v. Chada,* 462 U.S. 919 (1983).

61. On *Chada,* see, for example, Michael Wallace "Ad Astra Aspera: *Chada* Transcends Adversity," *Benchmark* 1 (Fall 1983): 13–15; and Kelly, Harbison, and Belz, *American Constitution,* 2:750–51.

62. *Original Meaning Jurisprudence,* 56–57; Bruce Fein, "October Term 1983: Hinge Year in Constitutional Jurisprudence," *Benchmark* 1 (1984): 1–13, 1 (quote).

63. *Firefighters v. Stotts,* 467 U.S. 561 (1984); *Wygant v. Jackson,* 476 U.S. 267 (1986). See Witt, *A Different Justice,* 126, 141–42; Wolfe, *Rise,* 302; Kelly, Harbison and Belz, *American Constitution,* 2:743–44.

64. *United States v. Leon,* 468 U.S. 897 (1984); John S. Baker Jr., "Rights, Remedies, and the Exclusionary Rule After *U.S. v. Leon,*" *Benchmark* 1 (1984): 23–29, 23.

65. Wolfe, *Rise,* ix–x, 292–322; Martin Shapiro, "The Supreme Court: From Warren to Burger," in *The New American Political System,* ed. Anthony King (Washington, DC: AEI, 1978), 179–211; Maltz, *Burger,* 268–69, 23. See also Mark Tushnet, "Legal Scholarship in the United States: An Overview," *The Modern Law Review* 50 (1987): 804–17, 810, 817.

66. For example, Bruce Fein, as quoted in "Judging the Judges," *Newsweek,* October 14, 1985, 73.

67. Edwin Meese III, "Address Before the American Bar Association," July 9, 1985, in *Major Policy Statements of the Attorney General* (Washington, DC: GPO, 1989), 1–8, 1, 3, 6, 7; id., "Address Before the D.C. Chapter of the Federalist Society Lawyers Division," November 15, 1985, in *Original Meaning Jurisprudence,* 91–100, 95. *Garcia v. San Antonio Metropolitan Transit Authority,* 469 U.S. 528 (1985).

68. Edwin Meese III, "Address Before the American Bar Association," July 17, 1985, in Witt, *A Different Justice,* 178–82, 179, 182; Meese, "Address Before the American Bar Association," July 9, 1985, 7.

69. Meese, "Federalist Society," 94, 98, 99 (quoting *Baker v. Carr,* 369 U.S. 186, 270 (1962)). On other occasions Meese carefully pointed out that "unfettered majority rule would be an abomination to liberty," id., "Speech Before the Economic Liberties Conference," June 14, 1986, *Major Policy Statements,* 138–42, 140. He thus recognized the importance of the natural rights tradition to American constitutionalism, but even when making such acknowledgments he emphasized that the modern Supreme Court threatened the concept of government by consent that was rooted in this same theory. See also

id., "The Moral Foundations of Republican Government," in *Still the Law of the Land? Essays on Changing Interpretations of the Constitution*, ed. Joseph F. McNamara (Hillsdale, MI: Hillsdale College Press, 1987), 63–77.

70. Edwin Meese III, "Address Before the St. Louis School of Law," September 12, 1986, *Major Policy Statements*, 31–37, 34–35; id., "American Bar Association," July 17, 1985, 182; *Griswold v. Connecticut*, 381 U.S. 479 (1965).

71. Meese, "Federalist Society," 97. *Brown v. Board of Education*, 347 U.S. 483 (1954); *Plessy v. Ferguson*, 163 U.S. 537 (1896); see also *Original Meaning Jurisprudence*, 46.

72. Edwin Meese III, "The Law of the Constitution," [New Orleans, October 10, 1986] repr. *Tulane Law Review* 61 (1987): 979–90, quotes at 981, 983. Ibid., 987 n28 (citing Philip Kurland, *Politics, The Constitution, and the Warren Court*, 116, 185); *Cooper v. Aaron*, 358 U.S. 1, 18 (1958).

73. See, for example, Lino A. Graglia, "How the Constitution Disappeared," *Commentary*, February 1986, 19–27; Jack N. Rakove, "Mr. Meese, Meet Mr. Madison," *Atlantic Monthly*, December 1986, 77–86. Citations of the widespread news coverage of Meese's challenge to judicial supremacy are collated and summarized by several authors in a symposium inspired by the speech in *Tulane Law Review* 61 (1987).

74. John Paul Stevens, "[Remarks] Before the Federal Bar Association, October 23, 1985," repr. in *The Great Debate: Interpreting Our Written Constitution*, ed. Paul G. Cassell (Washington, DC: Federalist Society, 1986), 27–30, quotes at 28, 29; William Bradford Reynolds, "Securing Equal Liberty in an Egalitarian Age" [University of Missouri, Columbia, September 12, 1986], repr. in *Missouri Law Review* 52 (1987): 585–606.

75. Meese "Foreword," in Kmiec, *Attorney General's Lawyer*, xi. See also Reynolds, "Securing Equal Liberty"; Graglia, "How the Constitution Disappeared"; Terry Eastland, "Ultra-Wrong About the 'Ultra-Right'" [review of Herman Schwartz, *Packing the Courts: The Conservative Campaign to Rewrite the Constitution*], *Michigan Law Review* 87 (1989): 1450–63.

76. Brennan, "Contemporary Ratification," 202. On Meese's Tulane speech, see the citations collected and analyzed in Mark Tushnet, "The Supreme Court, the Supreme Law of the Land, and Attorney General Meese: A Comment," *Tulane Law Review* 61 (1987): 1017–25, 1017–18. See also, for example, Ramsey Clark, "Enduring Constitutional Issues," ibid., 1093–95; Burt Neuborne, "The Binding Quality of Supreme Court Precedent," ibid., 991–1002, 1002.

77. Tushnet, "The Supreme Court," 1019–25; Mark Tushnet, "The U.S. Constitution and the Intent of the Framers," *Buffalo Law Review* 36 (1987): 217–226, 218 (quote); Sanford Levinson, "Could Meese Be Right This Time?" *Tulane Law Review* 61 (1987): 1071–78, 1078.

78. William F. Harris II, "Bonding Word and Polity: The Logic of American Constitutionalism," *American Political Science Review* 76 (1982): 34–45, 44 (quote); Schwartz, *Packing the Courts*, 34 (quote); Brennan, "Contemporary Ratification," 202.

79. *Original Meaning Jurisprudence*, 1, 14–23; Antonin Scalia, "Address Before the Attorney General's Conference on Economic Liberties" [Washington, DC, June 14, 1986], in ibid., 101–6; Working Group on Federalism of the Domestic Policy Counsel, "The Status of Federalism in America" [November 1986], repr. in *Benchmark* 5 (Winter 1991), 5–38, 29–30 n168; Markman, "On Interpretation," 219 n1; Charles Lofgren, "The Original Understanding of Original Intent," *Constitutional Commentary* 5 (1988): 77–113.

80. For example, see Henry Paul Monaghan, "Stare Decisis and Constitutional Adjudication," *Columbia Law Review* 88 (1988): 723–73, 723 n2; Robert N. Clinton, "Original Understanding, Legal Realism, and the Interpretation of 'This Constitution,'" *Iowa Law Review* 72 (1987): 1177–1279, 1180–82 n4; Richard Kay, "Adherence to the Original Intentions in Constitutional Adjudication: Three Objections and Responses," *Northwestern University Law Review* 82 (1988): 226–292, 229 n15; Daniel A. Farber, "The Originalism Debate: A Guide for the Perplexed," *Ohio State Law Journal* 49 (1989): 1085–1100, 1085–87.

81. Meese, "Federalist Society," 96. See also Bork, "The Constitution," 824–26.

82. For a similar and nearly contemporaneous judgment by legal liberals, see Collins and Skover, "Liberal Legal Scholarship," 198–99.

83. *Bowers v. Hardwick*, 478 U.S. 186, 194, 195 (1986).

SEVEN: Robert Bork and the Trial of Originalism

1. On this movement, see Neil Duxbury, *Patterns of American Jurisprudence* (Oxford: Oxford University Press, 1995), 301–419.

2. Robert Bork, "Legislative Intent and the Policy of the Sherman Act," *Journal of Law and Economics* 9 (1966): 7–48. Bork's fuller treatment of antitrust, *The Antitrust Paradox: A Policy at War with Itself* (New York: Free Press, 1978), was based partly on work from the 1960s but appeared later because Bork was solicitor general of the United States, 1973–77.

3. *Nomination of Robert H. Bork to be Associate Justice of the Supreme Court of the United States: Hearings before the Senate Committee on the Judiciary*, 100th Cong., 1st sess. (September 1987), 3313–48 (testimony and prepared statements of Phillip Areeda, Thomas E. Kauper, James T. Halverson, and Donald I. Baker); ibid., 388–90 (letter in support of Bork from fifteen past chairmen of the American Bar Association Section on Antitrust Law); William E. Kovacic, "*The Antitrust Paradox* Revisited: Robert Bork and the Transformation of Modern Antitrust Policy," *Wayne Law Review* 36 (1990): 1413–71.

4. Kovacic, "Bork and Transformation," 1451, 1461–64, 1469. See also Bork, "The Crisis in Constitutional Theory: Back to the Future" [speech before the Philadelphia Society, April 3, 1987], in *Hearings*, 653–62.

5. Alexander M. Bickel, *The Morality of Consent* (New Haven: Yale University Press, 1975).

6. Robert H. Bork, "We Suddenly Feel That Law Is Vulnerable," *Fortune*, December 1971, 115; Bickel to Richard G. Kleindienst, May 25, 1972, ser. I, box 10, fol. 223, Alexander Mordecai Bickel Papers, Manuscripts and Archives, Yale University Library. Seeking to secure for Bork an interview with Chief Justice Warren E. Burger, Bickel described the article as addressing "what [Bork] views as the current malaise of the legal order in this country, including our tendency to over use law and repose a naive and exaggerated faith in it as the sovereign instrument for altering social ills." Bickel to Burger, August 12, 1971, ser. I, box 10, fol. 218, Bickel Papers.

7. Bork, "Vulnerable," 117.

8. Ibid., 143 (all quotes).

9. Ibid.

10. "Proposal for an Institute of Legal Theory" [6pp., unpaginated], n.d., ser. I, box 1, fol. 22, Bickel Papers. This document lists no author, but its first page bears the holograph notation "Bork" and is filed with correspondence from him, the purport of which

suggests that it reflected the views of both men. See, for example, Bork to Bickel, February 17, 1969, ser. I, box 1, fol. 22, Bickel Papers; Bork to Bickel, January 15, 1969, ibid. A similar inference is suggested by the proposal's use of the plural voice.

11. "Proposal," 3, ser. I, box 1, fol. 22, Bickel Papers.

12. Bork to Bickel, October 14, 1968, [2pp.], 1, ser. I, box 1, Fol. 22, Bickel Papers. This venture was Robert H. Bork, "The Supreme Court Needs a New Philosophy," *Fortune,* December 1968, 138.

13. Bickel to Bork, October 9, 1968 [3pp.], 3, ser. I, box 10, fol. 193.

14. Bork, "New Philosophy," 177.

15. Robert H. Bork, "Neutral Principles and Some First Amendment Problems," *Indiana Law Journal* 47 (1971): 1–35, 1.

16. Bork, "Vulnerable," 143.

17. Bork "New Philosophy," 141.

18. Ibid.

19. Ibid., 166. Bork referred to Bickel's "passive virtues" theory in *The Least Dangerous Branch* as the one most able to force the political branches "to face up to hard choices and their consequences." Ibid., 168.

20. *Griswold v. Connecticut,* 381 U.S. 479 (1965).

21. Bork, "New Philosophy," 170.

22. Ibid.

23. Ibid., 170. See also ibid., 177.

24. Bork, "Neutral Principles," 8.

25. Fred M. Shapiro, "The Most-Cited Law Review Articles Revisited," *Chicago-Kent Law Review* 71 (1996): 751–779, 767. Bork's "Neutral Principles" is seventh on Shapiro's "most-cited" list.

26. Bork, "Neutral Principles," 8, 9, 11.

27. Ibid., 6–7, quoting Alexander M. Bickel, *The Supreme Court and the Idea of Progress* (New York: Harper and Row, 1970), 34.

28. Ibid., 7.

29. Ibid., 5 n10 (quote), 4–6.

30. Ibid., 3.

31. Ibid., 7.

32. Ibid., 7 (emphasis in orig.), 16, 8.

33. Ibid., 21.

34. Ibid., 14–15.

35. Ibid., 14, 13, 11–12.

36. Ibid., 10–11.

37. Bork has been read by others as extending the process concern with generality and neutrality. See Earl M. Maltz, *Rethinking Constitutional Law: Originalism, Interventionism, and the Politics of Judicial Review* (Lawrence: University Press of Kansas, 1996), 49.

38. See for example, Bork, "Neutral Principles," 10.

39. Ibid. See also ibid., 12, 20–21, 30.

40. Robert Bork, "The Struggle Over the Role of the Court," *National Review,* September 17, 1982, 1137–39; id., *Tradition and Morality in Constitutional Law* (Washington, DC: AEI, 1984).

41. Bork, "Struggle," 1139. See also Bork *Tradition,* 6, 1–2.

42. Bork, *Tradition,* 6, 8, 3.

43. Ibid., 5, 10, 11.

44. *Barnes v. Kline*, 759 F.2nd 21, 56–59 (D.C. Cir. 1985), held moot, 479 U.S. 361 (1987).

45. *Dronenberg v. Zech*, 741 F.2nd 1388, 1395, 1397 (D.C. Cir. 1984).

46. Henry J. Abraham, *Justices and Presidents: A Political History of Appointments to the Supreme Court*, 3rd ed. (New York: Oxford University Press, 1992), 350–54.

47. Herman Schwartz, *Packing the Courts: The Conservative Campaign to Rewrite the Constitution* (New York: Charles Scribner's Sons, 1988), 74–118; Patrick B. McGuigan and Jeffrey P. O'Connell, *The Judges War* (Washington, DC: Free Congress Foundation, 1987).

48. Stephen M. Griffin, "Politics and the Supreme Court: The Case of the Bork Nomination," *Journal of Law and Politics* 5 (1989): 551–604, 594–96. See also David M. O'Brien, "The Reagan Judges: His Most Enduring Legacy?" in *The Reagan Legacy: Promise and Performance*, ed. Charles O. Jones (Chatham, NJ: Chatham House, 1988), 60–101.

49. Griffin, "Bork Nomination," 555–56.

50. The campaign against Bork is treated in a fine journalistic account, Ethan Bronner, *Battle for Justice: How the Bork Nomination Shook America* (New York: Norton, 1989). A revealing memoir is Mark Gitenstein [chief counsel, Senate Judiciary Committee], *Matters of Principle: An Insider's Account of America's Rejection of Robert Bork's Nomination to the Supreme Court* (New York: Simon and Schuster, 1992); accounts by opposed activists are Patrick B. McGuigan and Dawn M. Weyrich, *Ninth Justice: The Fight for Bork* (Washington, DC: Free Congress Foundation, 1990); and Michael Pertschuk and Wendy Schaetzel, *The People Rising: The Campaign against the Bork Nomination* (New York: Thunder's Mouth Press, 1989).

51. *Congressional Record* 133, S9188 (daily ed., July 1, 1987). Similarly, the president of the National Organization for Women called Bork a "neanderthal," quoted in Pertschuk and Schaetzel, *People Rising*, 124.

52. Public Citizen Litigation Group, "The Judicial Record of Judge Robert H. Bork," in "The Bork Nomination: Essays and Reports," *Cardozo Law Review* 9 (1987): 297–371; for a rebuttal, see United States Department of Justice, "A Response to the Critics of Judge Robert H. Bork," ibid., 373–508. See also Bronner, *Battle*, 150–51.

53. ACLU Foundation Priority Letter, August 31, 1987, in *Hearings*, 4444; National Abortion Rights Action League, "What women have to fear from Robert Bork," *New York Times*, September 13, 1987, E7, ibid., 4452.

54. See Jeffrey K. Tulis, "Constitutional Abdication: the Senate, the President, and Appointments to the Supreme Court," *Case Western Reserve Law Review* 47 (1997): 1331–57; and John Massaro, *Supremely Political: The Role of Ideology and Presidential Management in Unsuccessful Supreme Court Nominations* (Albany: State University of New York Press, 1990), 177–82. See also Martin Shapiro, "Interest Groups and Supreme Court Appointments," *Northwestern University Law Review* 84 (1990): 935–61.

55. *Congressional Record* 133 (July 23, 1987), 10524 (remarks of Senator Biden). See also McGuigan and Weyrich, *Ninth Justice*, 58 (quoting statements supporting examination of the nominee's philosophy and ideology by Terry Sanford (D-NC) and Wyche Fowler Jr. (D-GA)).

56. "The White House Report: Information on Judge Bork's Qualifications, Judicial Record and Related Subjects," *Cardozo Law Review* 9 (1987): 187–217, 214.

57. Quoted in Bronner, *Battle*, 198.

58. Joseph D. Grano, "The 'Response Prepared to White House Analysis of Judge Bork's Record': A Critical Appraisal," in *Hearings*, 1596–1629, 1597 (emphasis in orig.); Viguerie quoted in Gitenstein, *Matters*, 88; Justice Department, "Response to Critics."

59. Bork's firing of Special Prosecutor Archibald Cox during the Watergate affair in 1973 was reexamined, but with little effect. Norma Vieira and Leonard Gross, *Supreme Court Appointments: Judge Bork and the Politicization of Senate Confirmations* (Carbondale: Southern Illinois University Press, 1998), 106–115. See also Stanley Kutler, *The Wars of Watergate: The Last Crisis of Richard Nixon* (New York: Knopf, 1990), 409. Bork also was accused of changing the rationale of a draft decision on the D.C. Circuit in 1983 without informing his colleagues. The issue was fully investigated in the hearings, and the American Bar Association found no ethical or professional violation. Stephen L. Carter, "The Confirmation Mess Revisited," *Northwestern University Law Review* 84 (1990): 962–75, 969, describes this attack on Bork as "truly weird" and "silly." See also Vieira and Gross, *Appointments*, 146–50.

60. Harold R. Tyler Jr., chairman, ABA Standing Committee on the Federal Judiciary, to The Honorable Joseph R. Biden Jr., September 21, 1987, in *Hearings*, 1228–34, 1233 (quote). See also Vieira and Gross, *Appointments*, 116–30; Bronner, *Battle*, 205–6; Gitenstein, *Matters*, 203–4; Sheldon Goldman, *Picking Federal Judges: Lower Court Selection from Roosevelt through Reagan* (New Haven: Yale University Press, 1997), 323–27; O'Brien, "The Reagan Judges," *Reagan Legacy*, ed. Charles O. Jones, 67–71.

61. Bronner, *Battle*, 285–96; Vieira and Gross, *Appointments*, 86–87, 158, 168–69; Griffin, "Bork Nomination," 574. Bronner, Vieira and Gross, and Griffin present detailed overviews of the nomination that expose some of the more overt distortions of Bork's record. See also Ronald D. Rotunda, "The Confirmation Process for Supreme Court Justices in the Modern Era," *Emory Law Journal* 37 (1988): 559–86; Grano, "Critical Appraisal," in *Hearings*, 1596–1629; U.S. Congress, Senate, Committee on the Judiciary, *Nomination of Robert H. Bork to be an Associate Justice of the United States Supreme Court: Report of the Committee on the Judiciary, United States Senate, together with Additional, Minority, and Supplemental Views*, Executive Report 100-7 (100th Cong., 1st sess.), October 13, 1987, 215–310 (*Minority Report*); Committee for a Fair Confirmation Process, "A Response to the Majority Report in the Senate Confirmation Hearings of Judge Robert H. Bork," November 2, 1987, *Hearings*, 4339–4456.

62. Massaro, *Supremely Political*, 176–93. See also Vieira and Gross, *Appointments*, 22–36; Gitenstein, *Matters*, 83–88, 175–85, 194–201; McGuigan and Weyrich, *Ninth*, 53–61, 75–77, 92–93; Bronner, *Battle*, 106–9, 147–53, 188–207; Pertschuk and Schaetzel, *Campaign*, 62–73, 117–45. See also below, text accompanying note 106.

63. For example, *Hearings*, 104–5, 180–84, 262–63; 441–42, 449, 715–16.

64. Ibid., 817, 819, 402, 129.

65. *Ollman v. Evans*, 750 F.2nd 970, 995 (D.C. Cir. 1984); *Hearings*, for example, 316, 715–16.

66. *Hearings*, 115, 262–63, 316, 441, 466, 715–16.

67. Ibid., 150, 248–50, 265, 290; Bork to Joseph R. Biden, October 1, 1987, repr. in ibid., 3896–3910, 3903–9. *Griswold v. Connecticut*, 381 U.S. 479 (1965).

68. *Hearings*, 183, 115, 242. See also ibid., 250; *Minority Report*, 253–62; Bork to Biden, *Hearings*, 3903.

69. Vieira and Gross, *Appointments*, 71–77; Gitenstein, *Matters*, 112–17; Bronner, *Battle*, 159–60; Pertschuk and Schaetzel, *Campaign*, 256–58, 129. *Roe v. Wade*, 410 U.S. 113 (1973).

70. *Hearings*, 862. See also ibid., 701 (remarks of Senator Biden); ibid., 721 (remarks of Senator Arlen Specter (R-PA); ibid., 469–70, (remarks of Senator Metzenbaum); ibid., 733 (remarks of Senator DeConcini); ibid., 1283, 1306 (prepared statement and testimony of Laurence Tribe); ibid., 2833–34, 2844–47, 2851, 2860 (prepared statement and testimony of Philip Kurland).

71. Gitenstein, *Matters*, 249.

72. See Alfred H. Kelly, Winfred A. Harbison, and Herman Belz, *The American Constitution: Its Origins and Development*, 7th ed. 2 vols. (New York: W. W. Norton, 1991) 2:632–33, 691–92, 613.

73. Bork, "Neutral Principles," 11, 17; id., "'Worldnet' Broadcast," June 10, 1987, excerpted in *New York Times*, September 21, 1987, B14.

74. *Hearings*, 160–61, 254–57, 316, 330–34, 392–96, 434–38, 699–706; Bork to Biden, October 1, 1987, in ibid., 3896–3902.

75. Citing confidential interviews, Ethan Bronner has written that the position on equal protection Bork articulated at the hearings was "largely cobbled together for him" by supporters in the Justice Department in response to the opposition to the nomination. Bronner, *Battle*, 255. There is no suggestion of this in Bork's memoir, *The Tempting of America: The Political Seduction of the Law* (New York: Free Press, 1990), 329–30.

76. *Hearings*, 254, 703, 705–6, 160–61, 255, 330–31, 333, 436; Bork to Biden, October 1, 1987, in ibid., 3899.

77. *City of Cleburne v. Cleburne Living Center*, 473 U.S. 432, 452–54 (1985).

78. *Hearings*, 256. See also Bork to Biden, October 1, 1987, ibid., 3900–3902.

79. For example, as solicitor general, Bork submitted an amicus brief arguing that the equal protection clause applied to women, *Vorcheimer v. School District to Philadelphia*, 430 U.S. 703 (1977), and one arguing that under Title VII of the Civil Rights Act of 1964 discrimination based on pregnancy was illegal, *General Electric Co. v. Gilbert*, 429 U.S. 125 (1976). Additionally, he joined in opinions on the D.C. circuit that enforced the Equal Pay Act amendments to the Fair Labor Standards Act and applied Title VII of the 1964 Act to the State Department. *Laffey v. Northwest Airlines*, 740 F. 2nd 1071 (D.C. Cir., 1984); *Ososky v. Wick*, 704 F.2nd 1264 (D.C. Cir., 1983); *Palmer v. Schultz*, 815 F.2nd 84 (D.C. Cir., 1987).

80. *Hearings*, 160. See also ibid., 257, 733–34 (remarks of Senator DeConcini); ibid., *Majority Report*, 214 (additional views of Senator Specter); *Majority Report*, 46–50; *Hearings*, 1269–70, 1284–86, 1301 (prepared statement and testimony of Laurence Tribe). But see also Committee for a Fair Confirmation Process, "Response to the Majority Report," ibid., 4384–92.

81. Another issue Bork's opponents sensationalized was his unanimous opinion in *Oil Chemical and Atomic Workers v. American Cyanamid Co.*, 741 F. 2nd 444 (D.C. Cir. 1984), which arose from an employer's exposure of employees to ambient lead levels that might harm a fetus. Rather then simply firing women, the company allowed them the option of sterilization and retention of their employment but was fined under the Occupational Health and Safety Act on the ground that informing the women of the sterilization option was a "workplace hazard." The court rejected this interpretation, and Bork's opinion was offered as proof that he was a dangerous reactionary bent on

destroying human rights and sterilizing women. See, for example, *Hearings,* 467–70 (colloquy of Bork and Senator Howard Metzenbaum (D-OH)). Scholars have routinely condemned the treatment Bork received on this issue; see Vieira and Gross, *Appointments,* 77–79; Lawrence C. Marshall, "Intellectual Feasts and Intellectual Responsibility," *Northwestern University Law Review* 84 (1990): 832–50, 845–47; Bronner, *Battle,* 160, 177–79; Stephen Carter, *The Confirmation Mess: Cleaning Up the Federal Appointments Process* (New York: Basic Books, 1994), 45–48.

82. *Skinner v. Oklahoma,* 316 U.S. 535 (1942). Like many of the other themes in the hearings, Bork first made the observation about *Skinner* in "Neutral Principles," 12.

83. *Hearings,* 405. See also ibid., 117–20 (colloquy of Bork and Chairman Biden); ibid., 149 (remarks of Senator Kennedy); Vieira and Gross, *Appointments,* 71, 78–79; Bronner, *Battle,* 179–80. See also Marshall, "Intellectual Feasts," 837–38 and Robert F. Nagel, "Advice, Consent, and Influence," *Northwestern University Law Review* 84 (1990): 858–75, 872–73.

84. For a collection of citations to "many other scholars—some considered much more to the left" than Bork, see Rotunda, "Confirmation Process," 573 n71. The cases were *Shelley v. Kramer,* 334 U.S. 1 (1948); *Harper v. Virginia State Board of Election,* 383 U.S. 663 (1966); *Katzenbach v. Morgan,* 384 U.S. 641 (1966); *Bolling v. Sharpe,* 347 U.S. 497 (1954); *Reynolds v. Sims,* 377 U.S. 533 (1964).

85. Bronner, *Battle,* 159 (quote, emphasis in orig.); Vieira and Gross, *Appointments,* 80–83, 86–87; Rotunda, "Confirmation Process," 573–77.

86. *Hearings,* 327, 351, 405, 428, 465, 666, 855–56.

87. Ibid., 335 (quote), 420. Bork's willingness to accept as a judge cases or doctrines he had criticized as a scholar, especially in the area of free speech, was used by his opponents to suggest that he was merely attempting to win confirmation. See Vieira and Gross, *Appointments,* 99–105. *Brandenburg v. Ohio,* 393 U.S. 948 (1969).

88. *Hearings,* 430, 292.

89. Ibid., 753–54, 438, 710–11.

90. *Majority Report,* 28–29, 8–14; *Hearings,* 841 (remarks of Senator Specter).

91. This aspect of originalism in the hearings is highlighted in Philip Bobbitt, *Constitutional Interpretation* (London: Blackwell, 1991), 93–101. See also Richard S. Kay, "The Bork Nomination and the Definition of 'The Constitution,'" *Northwestern University Law Review* 84 (1990): 1190–1202, 1199–1200.

92. Bobbitt, *Interpretation,* 102.

93. *Hearings,* 435–36 (remarks of Senator Specter). See also *Majority Report,* 213–14 (additional views of Senator Specter).

94. Bobbitt, *Interpretation,* 100–103.

95. Vieira and Gross, *Appointments,* 99–105, 177; Bronner, *Battle,* 242–51, 248 (quote), 251 (quote).

96. *Hearings,* 132, 285–86.

97. Ibid., 104.

98. Dworkin criticized Bork's attempt to reconcile *Brown v. Board of Education* (1954) to originalism and also his opinion in *Dronenberg v. Zech* (1984) in "Reagan's Justice," *New York Review of Books,* November 8, 1984, 27–31. See also Dworkin, "The Bork Nomination," *New York Review of Books,* August 13, 1987, 3, 6, 8, 10.

99. Dworkin, "Bork Nomination," 6.

100. *Hearings,* 3297, 3299–3300, 3302, 3303 (prepared statement of Terrance San-

dalow). See also ibid., 3242–43 (August 25, 1987, letter of Gerhard Casper and Robert H. Mundheim to the Senate Judiciary Committee); ibid., 2415–19 (prepared statement of Forrest McDonald); ibid., 2425–27 (prepared statement of Daniel J. Meador).

101. *Minority Report,* 227–31; *Congressional Record* 133 (October 9, 1987), 27250 (remarks of Senator Nickles); ibid. (October 22, 1987), 28858–59 (remarks of Senator Roth); ibid. (October 21, 1987), 28702–3 (remarks of Senator Hatch); ibid. (October 21, 1987), 28705–6 (remarks of Senator Grassley); ibid. (October 22, 1987), 28971–72 (remarks of Senator Hatch).

102. Griffin, "Bork Nomination," 583, 600. See also Erwin Chemerinsky, "The Constitution is Not 'Hard Law': The Bork Rejection and the Future of Constitutional Jurisprudence," *Constitutional Commentary* 6 (1989): 29–38, 36.

103. *Hearings,* 313 (remarks of Senator Paul Simon); *Congressional Record* 133 (October 8, 1987), S13824 (remarks of Senator Brock Adams) as quoted in Griffin, "Bork Nomination," 577–78.

104. Griffin, "Bork Nomination," 575, 581.

105. Bruce A. Ackerman, "Transformative Appointments," *Harvard Law Review* 101 (1988): 1164–84, 1178 (emphasis removed).

106. Quoted in Vieira and Gross, *Appointments,* 168.

107. Rader and Bork quoted in Bronner, *Battle,* 238; *Hearings,* 854 (quote). See also *Majority Report,* 96–99. Many Senators also suggested Bork did not appear adequately concerned with rights. See Griffin, "Bork Nomination," 575–78. See also Morton J. Horwitz, "The Bork Nomination and American Constitutional History," *Syracuse Law Review* 39 (1988): 1029–39, 1036–37.

108. Terry Eastland, "What Next for Justice Department?" *Legal Times,* October 31, 1988, as quoted in McGuigan and Weyrich, *Ninth Justice,* 213. The neologism was also defined as the process in which opponents "painted [a nominee] as a dangerous radical" based on "snippets of the [the nominee's] writings." Carter, *Confirmation Mess,* 9.

109. Bork, *Tempting,* 2, 5.

110. Ibid., 143, 145, 173–74, 176, 262, 155 (quote).

111. Ibid., 144 (quote), 218.

112. Ibid., 149 (quote), 213–14.

113. Ibid., 157–59.

114. Ibid., 223–40, 131, 264 (quote), 2, 131–32, 153.

115. Ibid., 66, 258–59.

116. Robert H. Bork, *Slouching Towards Gomorrah: Modern Liberalism and American Decline* (New York: HarperCollins, 1996), xiii (quote), 96, ch. 6 passim, 319–21; Robert H. Bork, *Coercing Virtue: The Worldwide Rule of Judges* (Toronto, Canada: Vintage Canada, 2002). See also Bork, *Tempting,* 7, 9, 130, 241–48.

117. Bork, *Tempting,* 163, 257, 242, 249–59, 352–54; Robert H. Bork, "Natural Law and the Constitution," *First Things* 21 (March 1992), 16–20; Robert H. Bork, "The Challenges of Biology for Law," *Texas Review of Law and Politics* 4 (1999–2000): 1–6.

118. Bork, *Slouching,* 117; Robert H. Bork, "Federalist Society Tenth Anniversary Banquet Speech," *Journal of Law and Politics* 13 (1997): 513–23, 518 (quote). See also Bork, *Coercing,* 61–66.

119. Nathan Schlueter and Robert H. Bork, "Constitutional Persons: An Exchange on Abortion," *First Things* 129 (January 2003): 28–36, 34 (quote); Nathan Schlueter, Robert

H. Bork, and Their Critics, "Abortion and the Constitution: An Exchange Continued," *First Things* 132 (April 2003): 15–22, 22 (quote).

120. Bork, "Natural Law," 19–20. See also Bork, *Tempting*, 258–59.

EIGHT: Originalism in the 1990s

1. Richard S. Kay, "American Constitutionalism," in *Constitutionalism: Philosophical Foundations*, ed. Larry Alexander (Cambridge: Cambridge University Press, 1998), 16–63, 31 (quote). See also id., "Adherence to the Original Intentions in Constitutional Adjudication: Three Objections and Responses," *Northwestern University Law Review* 82 (1988): 226–92, esp. 261–62, 289–90, 255–57; id., "'Originalist' Values and Constitutional Interpretation," *Harvard Journal of Law and Public Policy* 19 (1996): 335–41; Earl M. Maltz, *Rethinking Constitutional Law: Originalism, Interventionism, and the Politics of Judicial Review* (Lawrence: University Press of Kansas, 1996) 20, 26–27, 73.

2. Keith E. Whittington, *Constitutional Interpretation: Textual Meaning, Original Intent, and Judicial Review* (Lawrence: University Press of Kansas, 1999), 47–61, 152–59, 217. For similar emphasis on the fundamental or deeply rooted character of originalist claims, see also Ronald Rotunda, "Original Intent, the View of the Framers, and the Role of the Ratifiers," *Vanderbilt Law Review* 41 (1988): 507–16, 515, 516; Lillian R. BeVier, "The Moment and the Millennium: A Question of Time, or Law?" *The George Washington Law Review* 66 (1998): 1112–18; id., "The Integrity and Impersonality of Originalism," *Harvard Journal of Law and Public Policy* 19 (1996): 283–91, 284–85; Jonathan R. Macey, "Originalism as an 'ism,'" ibid., 301–09, 308; Frank H. Easterbrook, "Alternatives to Originalism?" ibid., 479–86, 486; Earl M. Maltz, "The Failure of Attacks on Constitutional Originalism," *Constitutional Commentary* 4 (1987): 43–56, 55.

3. For example, Robert N. Clinton, "Original Understanding, Legal Realism, and the Interpretation of 'This Constitution,'" *Iowa Law Review* 72 (1987): 1177–1279, 1263; Michael J. Perry, "The Legitimacy of Particular Conceptions of Constitutional Interpretation," *Virginia Law Review* 77 (1991): 669–719, 687–88; Stephen Macedo, "The Rule of Law, Justice, and the Politics of Moderation," in *Nomos 36: The Rule of Law*, ed. Ian Shapiro (New York: New York University Press, 1994), 148–77, 163–72.

4. For such advocacy in the context of the originalist debate, see Daniel A. Farber, "The Originalism Debate: A Guide for the Perplexed," *Ohio State Law Journal* 49 (1989): 1085–1100, 1104–5; Gregory Bassham, *Original Intent and the Constitution: A Philosophical Study* (Lanham, MD: Rowman and Littlefield, 1992), 100–127; Bret Boyce, "Originalism and the Fourteenth Amendment," *Wake Forest Law Review* 33 (1998): 909–1034, 1029–34; Leonard W. Levy, *Original Intent and the Framers' Constitution* (New York: Macmillan, 1988), 334–44, 349, 392; Ronald Dworkin, *Freedom's Law: The Moral Reading of the American Constitution* (Cambridge: Harvard University Press, 1996), 1–38.

5. Whittington, *Interpretation*, esp. 17–46; Michael McConnell, "The Importance of Humility in Judicial Review: A Comment on Ronald Dworkin's 'Moral Reading' of the Constitution," *Fordham Law Review*: 65 (1997): 1269–93, esp. 1289–93. See also Christopher Wolfe, *The Rise of Modern Judicial Review: From Constitutional Interpretation to Judge-Made Law*, rev.ed. (Lanham, MD: Rowman and Littlefield, 1994); id., *How to Read the Constitution: Originalism, Constitutional Interpretation, and Judicial Power* (Lanham, MD: Rowman and Littlefield, 1996); William Gangi, *Saving the Constitution from the Courts*

(Norman: University of Oklahoma Press, 1995); Matthew J. Franck, *Against the Imperial Judiciary: The Supreme Court vs. the Sovereignty of the People* (Lawrence: University Press of Kansas, 1996).

6. On Bork's recent work, see chapter 7. Lino Graglia, "Constitutional Theory: The Attempted Justification for the Supreme Court's Liberal Program," *Texas Law Review* 65 (1987): 789–98; id., "'Interpreting' the Constitution: Posner on Bork," *Stanford Law Review* 44 (1992): 1019–50; Raoul Berger, "Jack Rakove's Rendition of Original Meaning," *Indiana Law Journal* 72 (1997): 619–49; id., "Ronald Dworkin's *The Moral Reading of the Constitution:* A Critique," *Indiana Law Journal* 72 (1997): 1099–1114.

7. Keith E. Whittington, "The New Originalism," 8, paper presented at the American Association of Law Schools Conference on Constitutional Law, Washington, D.C., June 2002, available at http://www.princeton.edu/~kewhitt/new_originalism.pdf; Whittington, *Interpretation,* 45–46. Whittington also rejected recourse to moral realism in the practice of judicial review. Ibid., 30–32, 185.

8. Maltz, *Rethinking,* passim.

9. See Harry Jaffa, *Original Intent and the Framers of the Constitution: A Disputed Question* (Chicago: Regnery Gateway, 1994); compare Robert Bork, "Mr. Jaffa's Constitution" [review], *National Review,* February 7, 1994, 61–62, 64; Harry Jaffa, *Storm Over the Constitution* (Lanham, MD: Lexington, 1999); id., "Graglia's Quarrel with God: Atheism and Nihilism Masquerading as Constitutional Argument," *Southern California Interdisciplinary Law Journal* 4 (1995): 715–38. See also Hadley Arkes, *Beyond the Constitution* (Princeton, NJ: Princeton University Press, 1990), 14–15, 154; Graham Walker, *Moral Foundations of Constitutional Thought: Current Problems, Augustinian Prospects* (Princeton, NJ; Princeton University Press, 1990), 14–15, 36, 115, 118, 124; Sotirios A. Barber, *The Constitution of Judicial Power* (Baltimore: Johns Hopkins University Press, 1993), 2–10, 79, 103, 238–39 n29, 250 n34; Scott Douglas Gerber, *To Secure These Rights: The Declaration of Independence and Constitutional Interpretation* (New York: New York University Press, 1995), 4, 124n, 163.

10. Robert P. George, *In Defense of Natural Law* (Oxford: Clarendon, 1999), 108–11, 110 (quote); id., "Natural Law and the Constitution Revisited," *Fordham Law Review* 70 (2001): 273–82, 280. See also Russell Hittinger, in "Natural Law and the Law: An Exchange," *First Things* 23 (May 1992), 48–50; id., "Natural Law in the Positive Laws: A Legislative or Adjudicative Issue?" *Review of Politics* 55 (1993): 5–34.

11. Compare Howard Gillman, "The Collapse of Constitutional Originalism and the Rise of the Notion of the 'Living Constitution' in the Course of American State-Building," *Studies in American Political Development* 11 (1997): 191–247, 242–44.

12. For example, David Lyons, "Constitutional Interpretation and Original Meaning," *Social Philosophy and Policy* 4 (1986): 75–101, esp. 77–82, 101; David Couzens Hoy, "A Hermeneutical Critique of the Originalism/Nonoriginalism Distinction," *Northern Kentucky Law Review* 15 (1988): 479–98; Eric J. Segall, "A Century Lost: The End of the Originalism Debate," *Constitutional Commentary* 15 (1998): 411–39, 432–33; Perry, "Constitutional Interpretation," 695, 718, elaborated in id., *The Constitution in the Courts: Law or Politics?* (New York: Oxford University Press, 1994). See also Sanford Levinson and Steven Mailloux, eds., *Interpreting Law and Literature: A Hermeneutic Reader* (Evanston, IL: Northwestern University Press, 1988); Stephen M. Feldman, *American Legal Thought from Premodernism to Postmodernism: An Intellectual Voyage* (New York: Oxford University

Press, 2000), 149–87; Laura Kalman, *The Strange Career of Legal Liberalism* (New Haven: Yale University Press, 1996), 112–21.

13. Ronald Dworkin, *A Matter of Principle* (Cambridge: Harvard University Press, 1985), 57.

14. Ronald Dworkin, "Comment," in Antonin Scalia, *A Matter of Interpretation: Federal Courts and the Law* (Princeton, NJ: Princeton University Press, 1997), 116 (quote), 119.

15. Dworkin, *Freedom's Law*, 13.

16. For a helpful overview arguing that Dworkin is properly understood as an origi-nalist, see Jeffrey Goldsworthy, "Dworkin as an Originalist," *Constitutional Commentary* 17 (2000): 49–78.

17. Jack N. Rakove, *Original Meanings: Politics and Ideas in the Making of the Constitu-tion* (New York: Knopf, 1996).

18. Jack N. Rakove, "Fidelity Through History (Or to It)," *Fordham Law Review* 65 (1997): 1587–1609, 1591 (quote). Compare ibid., 1604, 1607.

19. This literature is extensive, but among the major works called upon by legal scholars are P. F. Strawson, "Intention and Convention in Speech Acts," *Philosophical Review* 73 (1964): 439–60; E. D. Hirsch Jr., *Validity in Interpretation* (New Haven: Yale University Press, 1967); H. P. Grice, "Utterer's Meaning and Intentions," *Philosophical Review* 78 (1969): 147–77; P. F. Strawson, *Logico-Linguistic Papers* (London: Methuen, 1971); Steven Knapp and Walter Benn Michaels, "Against Theory," *Critical Inquiry* 8 (1982): 723–42; Donald Davidson, "A Nice Derangement of Epitaphs," in *Truth and In-terpretation: Perspectives on the Philosophy of Donald Davidson,* ed. Ernest LePore (Oxford: Blackwell, 1986), 433–46. One of the first extensions of these ideas to the legal debate was Walter Benn Michaels, "The Fate of the Constitution" *Texas Law Review* 61 (1982): 765–76.

20. For use of these ideas by originalists, see Kay, "Adherence," esp. 230–32, 241; id., "Original Intentions, Standard Meanings, and the Legal Character of the Constitution," *Constitutional Commentary* 6 (1989): 39–50, esp. 40–42; id., "American Constitution-alism," esp. 29–33; Whittington, *Interpretation,* 59–60, 89–109; id., "Dworkin's 'Origi-nalism': The Role of Intentions in Constitutional Interpretation," *Review of Politics* 62 (2000): 197–229, 211–13, 219–20. See also Randy E. Barnett, "An Originalism for Non-originalists," *Loyola Law Review* 45 (1999): 611–54, 629–36.

21. Kay, "Original Intentions," 40–41.

22. Paul Campos, "A Text is Just a Text," *Harvard Journal of Law and Public Policy* 19 (1996): 327–33, 327. See also Whittington, "New Originalism," 9.

23. For example, Paul Campos, "Against Constitutional Theory," *Yale Journal of Law and the Humanities* 4 (1992): 279–310; Larry Alexander, "All or Nothing at All? The Inten-tions of Authorities and the Authority of Intentions," in *Law and Interpretation: Essays in Legal Philosophy,* ed. Andrei Marmor (Oxford: Oxford University Press 1995), 357–404; Joseph Raz, "Intention in Interpretation," in *The Autonomy of Law: Essays on Legal Posi-tivism,* ed. Robert P. George (Oxford: Clarendon Press, 1996), 249–86; Aileen Kavanagh, "Original Intention, Enacted Text, and Constitutional Interpretation," *American Journal of Jurisprudence* 47 (2002): 255–98.

24. Whittington, "Dworkin," 222. See also ibid., 219, 221; Whittington, *Interpreta-tion,* 182–87; Alexander, "All or Nothing," 389–90; Kay, "Constitutionalism," 35–36.

25. Richard S. Kay, "Preconstitutional Rules," *Ohio State Law Journal* 42 (1981): 187–

207; Kay, "Constitutionalism," 34; Whittington, *Interpretation,* 49; Campos, "Just a Text," 329; Alexander, "All or Nothing," 398–404, 358, 360; Larry Alexander, "Originalism, or Who is Fred?" *Harvard Journal of Law and Public Policy* 19 (1996): 321–26.

    26. Joseph Raz, "On the Authority and Interpretation of Constitutions: Some Preliminaries," in *Constitutionalism,* ed. Larry Alexander, 152–93; Aileen Kavanagh, "The Idea of a Living Constitution," *Canadian Journal of Jurisprudence* 16 (2003): 55–89, esp. 63–69. Compare Kay, "Constitutionalism," 24–25.

    27. Keith E. Whittington, *Constitutional Construction: Divided Powers and Constitutional Meaning* (Cambridge, MA: Harvard University Press, 1999), 1 (quote), 1–15. See also id., "Extrajudicial Constitutional Interpretation: Three Objections and Responses," *North Carolina Law Review* 80 (2002): 773–851.

    28. Whittington, *Interpretation,* 209–15.

    29. Whittington, "New Originalism," 11. See also Alexander, "All or Nothing," 398.

    30. Whittington, *Interpretation,* 61, 89–90. See also Kay, "Adherence to Original Intentions," 236–43; id., "Constitutionalism," 35–39, id., "Original Intentions," passim; Macey, "Originalism," 302, 306; Rotunda, "Original Intent," 514–15; Earl Maltz, "Foreword: The Appeal of Originalism," *Utah Law Review* (1987): 773–805, 795–800; Thomas B. McAffee, "Originalism and Indeterminacy," *Harvard Journal of Law and Public Policy* 19 (1996): 429–36.

    31. For example, Whittington, *Interpretation,* 89.

    32. Kay, "Constitutionalism," 25.

    33. Maltz, "Appeal," 800ff.; id., "A Minimalist Approach to the Fourteenth Amendment," *Harvard Journal of Law and Public Policy* 19 (1996): 451–55, 454–55; id., *Rethinking,* 22–23; id., "Failure of Attacks," 55. For Maltz's own historical effort, see *Civil Rights, the Constitution, and Congress, 1863–1869* (Lawrence: University Press of Kansas, 1990). Whittington, *Interpretation,* 96–97, 97 (quote); Kay, "Original Intentions," 245–51. See also Gary Lawson, "Legal Indeterminacy: Its Causes and Cure," *Harvard Journal of Law and Public Policy* 19 (1996): 411–28.

    34. Kay, "Original Intentions," 244 (emphasis in orig.); Kay, "Constitutionalism," 36. See also Campos, "Just a Text," 329.

    35. H. Jefferson Powell, "Rules for Originalists," *Virginia Law Review* 73 (1987): 659–99. See also Clinton, "Original Understanding," esp. 1273, 1264ff., 1279.

    36. Saikrishna B. Prakash, "Unoriginalism's Law Without Meaning," review of *Original Meanings,* by Jack N. Rakove, *Constitutional Commentary* 15 (1998): 529–46, 535.

    37. Ibid., 534 (quote), 531 (quote), 542–44.

    38. Cass Sunstein, "The Idea of a Useable Past," *Columbia Law Review* 95 (1995): 601–8, 604 n17.

    39. Kalman, *Legal Liberalism,* 238 (quote); id., "Border Patrol: Reflections on the Turn to History in Legal Scholarship," *Fordham Law Review* 66 (1997):87–124, 120–24.

    40. For an overview see Kalman, *Legal Liberalism,* 147–63; Neil M. Richards, "Clio and the Court: A Reassessment of the Supreme Court's Uses of History," *Journal of Law and Politics* 13 (1997): 809–91, 828–30; J. David Hoeveler Jr., "Original Intent and the Politics of Republicanism," *Marquette Law Review* 75 (1992): 863–901; "Symposium: The Republican Civic Tradition," *Yale Law Journal* 97 (1988): 1493–1723.

    41. Scott D. Gerber, "The Republican Revival in American Constitutional Theory," *Political Research Quarterly* 47(1994): 985–97, 991. See also Hoeveler, "Politics of Republicanism," 888.

42. Frank R. Michelman, "Traces of Self-Government," *Harvard Law Review* 100 (1986): 4–77, 74, 65 (emphasis in orig.).

43. Bruce A. Ackerman, *We the People: Foundations* (Cambridge: Harvard University Press, 1991). See also Herman Belz, *A Living Constitution or Fundamental Law? American Constitutionalism in Historical Perspective* (Lanham, MD: Rowman and Littlefield, 1998), 240–42.

44. Cass R. Sunstein, *The Partial Constitution* (Cambridge: Harvard University Press, 1993), 9–10; id., "What Judge Bork Should Have Said," *Connecticut Law Review* 23 (1991): 205–28, 221–28.

45. Gerber, "Republican Revival," 989, 992–93.

46. Cass R. Sunstein, "Five Theses on Originalism," *Harvard Journal of Law and Public Policy* 19 (1996): 311–15; id., *Legal Reasoning and Political Conflict* (New York: Oxford University Press, 1996), 178–82; id., "Making Amends," *New Republic*, March 3, 1997, 38–43, 42–43. See also Belz, *Fundamental Law,* 246–47.

47. Lawrence Lessig, "Fidelity in Translation," *Texas Law Review* 71 (1993): 1165–1268; id., "Understanding Changed Readings: Fidelity and Theory," *Stanford Law Review* 47 (1995): 395–472; id., "Fidelity and Constraint," *Fordham Law Review* 65 (1997): 1365–1433.

48. Lessig, "Fidelity in Translation," 1266.

49. As with the legal rights of homosexuals, Lessig, "Fidelity and Constraint," 1415–29.

50. Charles A. Miller, *The Supreme Court and the Uses of History* (Cambridge: Belknap Press of Harvard University Press, 1969), 26. See also Larry Kramer, "Fidelity to History—and Through It," *Fordham Law Review* 65 (1997): 1627–55.

51. Steven G. Calabresi, "The Tradition of the Written Constitution: A Comment on Professor Lessig's Theory of Translation," *Fordham Law Review* 65 (1997): 1435–56, 1450 (emphasis in orig.).

52. Whittington, "New Originalism," 7, 5.

53. Michael W. McConnell, "A Moral Realist Defense of Constitutional Democracy," in *The Rights Retained by the People: The History and Meaning of the Ninth Amendment,* ed. Randy E. Barnett, 2 vols. (Fairfax, VA: George Mason University Press, 1993), 2:71–93; id., "Importance of Humility"; id., "Textualism and the Dead Hand of the Past," *George Washington Law Review* 66 (1998): 1127–40.

54. Michael W. McConnell, "The Origins and Historical Understanding of the Free Exercise of Religion," *Harvard Law Review* 103 (1990): 1410–1517. A major new contribution to the literature in this area is Philip Hamburger, *Separation of Church and State* (Cambridge: Harvard University Press, 2002).

55. Michael W. McConnell, "Originalism and the Desegregation Decisions," *Virginia Law Review* 81 (1995): 947–1140; id., "The Originalist Case for *Brown v. Board of Education,*" *Harvard Journal of Law and Public Policy* 19 (1996): 457–64.

56. Randy E. Barnett, "The Original Meaning of the Commerce Clause," *University of Chicago Law Review* 68 (2001): 101–47; id., "New Evidence of the Original Meaning of the Commerce Clause," *Arkansas Law Review* 55 (2003): 847–99; Robert H. Bork and Daniel E. Troy, "Locating the Boundaries: The Scope of Congress's Power to Regulate Commerce," *Harvard Journal of Law and Public Policy* 25 (2002): 849–93; John Choon Yoo, "Federalism and Judicial Review," in *The Tenth Amendment and State Sovereignty: Constitutional History and Contemporary Issues,* ed. Mark R. Killenbeck (Lanham, MD: Rowman and Littlefield, 2002), 131–79.

57. John C. Yoo, "The Continuation of Politics by Other Means: The Original Understanding of War Powers," *California Law Review* 84 (1996): 167–305; Steven G. Calabresi and Christopher S. Yoo, "The Unitary Executive During the First Half-Century," *Case Western Reserve Law Review* 47 (1997): 1451–1561; John C. Yoo, "Treaties and Public Lawmaking: A Textual and Structural Defense of Non-Self-Execution," *Columbia Law Review* 99 (1999): 2218–2258; Randy E. Barnett and Don B. Kates, "Under Fire: The New Consensus on the Second Amendment," *Emory Law Journal* 45 (1996): 1139–1259. See also "Symposium on the Second Amendment: Fresh Looks," *Chicago-Kent Law Review* 76 (2000): 3–600.

58. For example, Michael J. Klarman, "*Brown*, Originalism, and Constitutional Theory: A Response to Professor McConnell," *Virginia Law Review* 81 (1995): 1881–1936; Joseph Biancalana, "Originalism and the Commerce Clause," *University of Cincinnati Law Review* 71 (2003): 383–404; Kenneth Lasson, "Blunderbuss Scholarship: Perverting the Original Intent and Plain Meaning of the Second Amendment," *University of Baltimore Law Review* 32 (2003): 127–68.

59. Suzanna Sherry, "The Ninth Amendment: Righting an Unwritten Constitution," in *Rights Retained,* ed. Randy E. Barnett, 2:283–96, 284. Barnett argued similarly in "Introduction: Implementing the Ninth Amendment," ibid., 1–46. For the originalist response, see Earl M. Maltz, "Unenumerated Rights and Originalist Methodology," ibid., 261–66; Raoul Berger, "The Ninth Amendment: The Beckoning Mirage," ibid., 297–326; Thomas B. McAffee, "The Bill of Rights, Social Contract Theory, and the Rights 'Retained' by the People," ibid., 327–65; id., "The Original Meaning of the Ninth Amendment," *Columbia Law Review* 90 (1990): 1215–1320.

60. Stephen A. Siegel, "The Federal Government's Power to Enact Color-Conscious Laws: An Originalist Inquiry," *Northwestern University Law Review* 92 (1998): 477–590; Jed Rubenfeld, "Affirmative Action," *Yale Law Journal* 107 (1997): 427–72; Eric Schnapper, "Affirmative Action and the Legislative History of the Fourteenth Amendment," *Virginia Law Review* 71 (1985): 753–98. But see Andrew Kull, *The Color Blind Constitution* (Cambridge: Harvard University Press, 1992).

61. Brief Amicus Curiae of Eric Foner et al., *Patterson v. McLean Credit Union,* 491 U.S. 164 (1989), Supreme Court of the United States, October term, 1987. For comparison of this document to Foner's historical monograph, *Reconstruction: America's Unfinished Revolution, 1863–1877* (New York: Harper and Row, 1988), see Randall Kennedy, "Reconstruction and the Politics of Scholarship," *Yale Law Journal* 98 (1989): 521–39, 537–39; Kalman, *Legal Liberalism,* 205–6.

62. Memorandum Amicus Curiae of Law Professors, *Dellums v. Bush,* 752 F. Supp. 1141 (D.D.C. 1990) (No. 90-2866), repr. in *Stanford Journal of International Law* 27 (1991): 257–64. The signatories of this brief were Bruce A. Ackerman, Abram Chayes, Lori Fisler Damrosch, John Hart Ely, Erwin N. Griswold, Gerald Gunther, Louis Henkin, Harold Hongju Koh, Philip B. Kurland, Laurence H. Tribe, and William W. Van Alstyne. See also McAffee, "Originalism and Indeterminacy," 432–34.

63. Prepared Statement of Cass R. Sunstein, in *The Impeachment of William Jefferson Clinton, Volume XX: Background and History of Impeachment,* House of Representatives, Committee on the Judiciary, Subcommittee on the Constitution, 105th Cong., 2nd sess., November 9, 1998, 83–91, 85 (emphasis in orig.), 86. Prepared Statement of Laurence H. Tribe, ibid., 221–30, 225–27. The arguments of Sunstein and Tribe were rebutted; see Prepared Statement of Charles J. Cooper, ibid., 184–94; Prepared Statement of Gary L.

McDowell, ibid., 31–44; Prepared Statement of John O. McGinnis, ibid., 106–11; Prepared Statement of Stephen B. Presser, ibid., 119–28.

64. *Lucas v. South Carolina Coastal Council,* 505 U.S. 1003 (1992).

65. Richard A. Epstein, *Takings: Private Property and the Power of Eminent Domain* (Cambridge: Harvard University Press, 1985). On behalf of the Institute for Justice in *Lucas* Epstein helped formulate an *amicus* brief urging reversal.

66. Douglas W. Kmiec, "The Original Understanding of the Taking Clause is Neither Weak Nor Obtuse," *Columbia Law Review* 88 (1988): 1630–66; id., "At Last, The Supreme Court Solves the Takings Puzzle," *Harvard Journal of Law and Public Policy* 19 (1995): 147–59; id., "Inserting the Last Remaining Pieces into the Takings Puzzle," *William and Mary Law Review* 38 (1997): 995–1046; *Dolan v. Tigard,* 512 U.S. 374 (1994). See also Daniel A. Ippolito, "An Originalist's Evaluation of Modern Takings Jurisprudence," *Seton Hall Law Review* 26 (1995): 317–47.

67. William Michael Treanor, "The Original Understanding of the Takings Clause and the Political Process," *Columbia Law Review* 95 (1995): 782–887.

68. Barnett, "For Nonoriginalists," 617–22; G. Edward White, "The Arrival of History in Constitutional Scholarship," *Virginia Law Review* 88 (2002): 485–633, 629–30.

69. See James E. Fleming, "Are We All Originalists Now? I Hope Not!" Alpheus T. Mason Lecture, Princeton University, September 19, 2002, available at http://web.princeton.edu/sites/jmadison/events/archives/FlemingTalk.pdf.

70. For similar observations, see Barnett, "For Nonoriginalists," 650; Whittington, "New Originalism," 5, 7; White, "Arrival," 623–31.

71. Compare John Harrison, "Forms of Originalism and the Study of History," *Harvard Journal of Law and Public Policy* 26 (2003): 83–94, 85–87; Whittington, "New Originalism," 4.

72. *Harmelin v. Michigan,* 501 U.S. 957 (1991).

73. Ibid., 966–75, 986 (quote).

74. *Morrison v. Olson,* 487 U.S. 654, 697–99, 698–99 (quote), 720–21 (1988).

75. Ibid., 711–12.

76. *Plaut v. Spendthrift Farm, Inc.,* 514 U.S. 211, 219–25 (1995).

77. *Printz v. United States,* 521 U.S. 898, 907 (1997).

78. Ibid., 910–15.

79. Ibid., 918–22, 918 (quotes).

80. Ibid., 932–33.

81. *United States v. Lopez,* 514 U.S. 549 (1995); *United States Term Limits, Inc. v. Thornton,* 514 U.S. 779 (1995). In addition to *McIntyre v. Ohio Elections Commission,* 514 U.S. 334 (1995), discussed below, Thomas also wrote an originalist dissent on the Eighth Amendment in *Helling v. McKinney,* 509 U.S. 25, 37–40 (1993) and an originalist concurrence on the First Amendment in *Rosenberger v. Rector and Visitors of the University of Virginia,* 515 U.S. 819, 852–63 (1995).

82. *Lopez,* 584, 585, 599.

83. *Thornton,* 845–926.

84. *McIntyre,* 360. See also Richards, "Clio," 841–49.

85. *McIntyre,* 371–72.

86. Ibid., 375.

87. *New York v. United States,* 505 U.S. 144, 163–66, 188 (quote) (1992).

88. *Alden v. Maine,* 527 U.S. 706 (1999). See also *Lopez,* 575–78 (Kennedy, concurring).

89. For more detailed development of this point, see Richards, "Clio."

90. *Lee v. Weisman,* 505 U.S. 577, 612–16, 622–26 (1992).

91. *Rosenberger v. Rector and Visitors of the University of Virginia,* 515 U.S. 819, 868–73 (1995).

92. *Seminole Tribe of Florida v. Florida,* 517 U.S. 44, 100–185 (1996); *Alden,* 760–814.

93. Antonin Scalia, "The Rule of Law as a Law of Rules," *University of Chicago Law Review* 56 (1989):1175–88, 1178; id., *A Matter of Interpretation: Federal Courts and the Law* (Princeton, NJ: Princeton University Press, 1997), 38–47, 38 (emphasis in orig.).

94. Scalia, *Matter of Interpretation,* 38.

95. Clarence Thomas, "Judging," *Kansas Law Review* 45 (1996): 1–8, 6–7. See also Clarence Thomas, "Be Not Afraid," Francis Boyer Lecture, American Enterprise Institute, Washington, DC, February 13, 2001; http://www.aei.org/boyer/thomas.htm.

96. This is a major finding in Sue Davis, *Justice Rehnquist and the Constitution* (Princeton, NJ: Princeton University Press, 1989), who nonetheless notes that Rehnquist understood this as an originalist position. Ibid., 152. See also Keith E. Whittington, "William H. Rehnquist: Nixon's Strict Constructionist, Reagan's Chief Justice," in *Rehnquist Justice: Understanding the Court Dynamic,* ed. Earl M. Maltz (Lawrence: University Press of Kansas, 2003), 8–33.

97. Antonin Scalia, "Originalism: The Lesser Evil," *University of Cincinnati Law Review* 57 (1989): 849–65, 864, 861.

98. Scalia has rebelled against the modern practice of "planting" legislative history in the record because it usually attempts to impress on courts the favored views of special interests rather than an unbiased interpretation of the statutory language that was actually made law by the legislature. See Ralph A. Rossum, "Text and Tradition: The Originalist Jurisprudence of Antonin Scalia," in *Rehnquist Justice,* ed. Earl M. Maltz, 34–69, 43–46.

99. The clearest statement of this position is Scalia's plurality opinion in *Michael H. v. Gerald D.,* 491 U.S. 110, 124–28 (1989).

100. Rossum, "Scalia," 35 and passim; Daniel A. Farber and Suzanna Sherry, *Desperately Seeking Certainty: The Misguided Quest for Constitutional Foundations* (Chicago: University of Chicago Press, 2002), 49, 42, 44. See also Richard A. Brisbin Jr., *Justice Antonin Scalia and the Conservative Revival* (Baltimore: Johns Hopkins University Press, 1997).

101. Rossum, "Scalia," in *Rehnquist Justice,* ed. Earl M. Maltz, 58, 42–43; Brisbin, *Scalia,* 332–37.

102. *Adarand Constructors, Inc. v. Pena,* 515 U.S. 200, 240 (1995).

103. Scott Gerber, *First Principles: The Jurisprudence of Clarence Thomas* (New York: New York University Press, 1999), 193, 162, and passim.

104. Robert M. Howard and Jeffrey A. Segal, "An Original Look at Originalism," *Law and Social Inquiry* 36 (2002): 113–37; Mark A. Graber, "Clarence Thomas and the Perils of Amateur History," in *Rehnquist Justice,* ed. Earl M. Maltz, 70–102, 87–90; Gerber, *First Principles,* 194–98; Erwin Chemerinsky, "The Constitutional Jurisprudence of the Rehnquist Court" in *The Rehnquist Court: A Retrospective* ed. Martin H. Belsky (New York: Oxford University Press, 2002), 195–216, 207–12; Farber and Sherry, *Desperately,* 44–54. See also Richards, "Clio."

105. Rossum, "Scalia," 39; Earl M. Maltz, "Introduction," in *Rehnquist Justice,* ed. Earl M. Maltz, 5; Christopher Wolfe, *The Rise of Modern Judicial Review,* rev.ed. (Lanham, MD: Rowman and Littlefield, 1994), 372–74; id., "The Rehnquist Court and 'Conservative

Judicial Activism,'" in *That Eminent Tribunal: Judicial Supremacy and the Constitution,* ed. Christopher Wolfe (forthcoming, Princeton University Press).

106. Tinsley E. Yarbrough, *The Rehnquist Court and the Constitution* (New York: Oxford University Press, 2000), xi, 267–69; Cornell Clayton, "Law, Politics, and the Rehnquist Court: Structural Influences on Supreme Court Decision Making," in *The Supreme Court in American Politics: New Institutionalist Interpretations,* ed. Howard Gillman and Cornell Clayton (Lawrence: University Press of Kansas, 1999), 151–77; Cass R. Sunstein, "Foreword: Leaving Things Undecided," *Harvard Law Review* 110 (1996): 6–101; Maltz, "Introduction," in *Rehnquist Justice,* ed. Earl M. Maltz, 1, 6–7. On the continued influence of legal process jurisprudence, see Brisbin, *Scalia,* passim; and Ken I. Kersch, "The Synthetic Progressivism of Stephen G. Breyer," in *Rehnquist Justice,* ed. Earl M. Maltz, 241–76, esp. 246–47, 257.

107. Wolfe, "Rehnquist Court"; Lawrence M. Friedman, "The Rehnquist Court: Some More or Less Historical Comments," in *Rehnquist Court,* ed. Martin H. Belsky, 143–58.

108. Philip Bobbitt, *Constitutional Fate* (New York: Oxford University Press, 1982); id., *Constitutional Interpretation* (Oxford: Blackwell, 1991), 11–30; Richard H. Fallon Jr. "A Constructivist Coherence Theory of Constitutional Interpretation," *Harvard Law Review* 100 (1987): 1189–1286; Robert Post, "Theories of Constitutional Interpretation," *Representations* 30 (1990): 13–41; Stephen M. Griffin, "Pluralism in Constitutional Interpretation," *Texas Law Review* 72 (1993–94): 1753–69; id., *American Constitutionalism: From Theory to Practice* (Princeton, NJ: Princeton University Press, 1996), 143–52.

109. The point about originalism cutting across the modalities of text, structure, and doctrine was also noted recently by Whittington, "New Originalism," 10 n55.

110. For recent collections containing historical institutionalist work, see Gillman and Clayton, eds., *New Institutionalist Interpretations;* Cornell W. Clayton and Howard Gillman, eds., *Supreme Court Decision-Making: New Institutionalist Approaches* (Chicago: University of Chicago Press, 1999). See also Keith E. Whittington, "Once More Unto the Breach: PostBehavioralist Approaches to Judicial Politics," *Law and Social Inquiry* 25 (2000): 601–34; Howard Gillman, "What's Law Got to Do with It? Judicial Behavioralists Test the 'Legal Model' of Judicial Decision Making," *Law and Social Inquiry* 26 (2001): 465–504. A major influence on this literature was Rogers M. Smith, "Political Jurisprudence, the 'New Institutionalism' and the Future of Public Law," *American Political Science Review* 82 (1988): 89–108.

111. Recent works that have informed my articulation of these ideas are Ronald Kahn, *The Supreme Court and Constitutional Theory, 1953–1993* (Lawrence: University Press of Kansas, 1994), esp. 206–7, 262–63, 112, 136–37; Griffin, *American Constitutionalism,* 38–39.

112. Daniel A. Farber, "Legal Pragmatism and the Constitution," *Minnesota Law Review* 72 (1988): 1331–78; Farber and Sherry, *Desperately,* 152–56; David A. Strauss, "Common Law Constitutional Interpretation," *University of Chicago Law Review* 63 (1996): 877–935; Bassham, *Original Intent,* 109–27; Cass R. Sunstein, *Legal Reasoning and Political Conflict* (New York: Oxford University Press, 1996). Another pragmatic approach, but one more oriented to economics, has long been defended by Richard Posner. His latest effort integrates legal pragmatism with its philosophic roots and related conception of democracy more deeply than previous work. Posner, *Law, Pragmatism, and Democracy* (Cambridge: Harvard University Press, 2003). It is notable that the scholars cited here, like Holmes and Cardozo before them, read the common law as a form of modern prag-

matism, not as the more Aristotelian edifice of practical reason that confronted modern liberal notions of sovereignty and written law. See James R. Stoner Jr., *Common Law and Liberal Theory: Coke, Hobbes, and the Origins of American Constitutionalism* (Lawrence: University Press of Kansas, 1992).

113. Belz, *Fundamental Law,* 255 (quote), 262. For analysis of recent theories positing that law is a "deliberative" "process" or "conversation" and the challenge they face from other theories, such as originalism, that regard law as rooted in foundational authority, see Paul Kahn, *Legitimacy and History: Self-Government in American Constitutional Theory* (New Haven: Yale University Press, 1992), 171–209, 221–23; Ronald Kahn, *The Supreme Court and Constitutional Theory, 1953–1993,* 245–49.

114. For a similar interpretation see Ronald Kahn, *The Supreme Court and Constitutional Theory, 1953–1993,* 36–53, 101–4, 250–52, 265.

115. A recent clear-eyed view of the limits of legal discourse in the context of recent constitutional jurisprudence is Brisbin, *Scalia,* 337–47. See also Ronald Kahn, *The Supreme Court and Constitutional Theory, 1953–1993,* 263–64.

116. Harvey C. Mansfield Jr., "Hobbes and the Science of Indirect Government," *American Political Science Review* 65 (1971): 97–110. See also Charles H. McIlwain, *Constitutionalism: Ancient and Modern,* rev. ed. (Ithaca, NY: Cornell University Press, 1947) (1987), 30–31.

Index

Rakove, Jack N., 194
Rawle, William, 21
reapportionment decisions, 81–86
Rehnquist, William, 9, 210; on abortion, 106; dissent in *Wallace v. Jaffree*, 151; on equal protection, 106; on living Constitution, 109, 142
republican revival, 198–99
revolt against formalism, 5, 28, 225n68; and New Deal, 227n97
Reynolds, William Bradford, 156
Reynolds v. Sims (1964), 81, 83
Rice, Charles E., 88
Roe v. Wade (1973), 42, 97, 99, 151
Roosevelt, Franklin D., 32
Rosenberger v. University of Virginia (1995), 209
rule of law: and Berger, 128; and Bork, 186; at founding, 3

Sacks, Albert, 49
Santa Clara County v. Southern Pacific Railroad Company (1886), 38
Scalia, Antonin, 205–6, 208; on originalism, 210, 211; on statutory interpretation, 274n98
Shapiro v. Thompson (1969), 1, 97
Shelley v. Kraemer (1948), 77
Sherman Antitrust Act (1890), 27, 162
Sherry, Suzanna, 202
Slaughterhouse Cases (1873), 23–24
Souter, David, 209
state action, 76–80
Story, Joseph, 21, 22
Sumner, Charles, 23
Sunstein, Cass R., 198, 199–200, 202
Sutherland, George, 37

Taney, Roger B., 20
Taylor, John, 21
tenBroek, Jacobus, 38–39; in *Brown* litigation, 73
Thayer, James Bradley, 44–45; and Berger, 114–15; and Bickel, 62
Thomas, Clarence, 206–8; on originalism, 210, 211

Treanor, William Michael, 204
Tribe, Laurence, 135, 202
Trimble v. Gordon (1977), 106
Tuck, William, 85
Tushnet, Mark, 157

United States Term Limits, Inc. v. Thornton (1995), 207
United States v. Carolene Products (1938), 35–36, 41, 121
United States v. E.C. Knight Co. (1895), 27
United States v. Leon (1984), 153
United States v. Lopez (1995), 207
United States v. Nixon (1974), 116
Upshur, Abel P., 22

Van Alstyne, William, 84, 142
Valley Forge Christian College v. Americans United (1982), 152

Wallace v. Jaffree (1985), 150–51
wall of separation, metaphor in First Amendment decisions, 72, 86–87, 150–51, 209
Warren, Charles, 37
Warren, Earl, retirement of, 96
Warren Court, 215; criticism of: —by Berger, 123; —by Bork, 163; as elaboration of legal realism, 40; major decisions, 40–41; and New Deal coalition, 40–41
Wechsler, Herbert, 49; on *Brown* and neutral principles, 55–59; criticized by contemporaries, 58–59; on jurisdiction, 235n75
Wesberry v. Sanders (1964), 81, 83
West Coast Hotel v. Parrish (1937), 34, 37, 39
Whittington, Keith E., 191, 192, 196, 197
Wickard v. Filburn (1942), 34–35
Winter, Ralph K., cited by Grey as interpretivist, 108
Wolfe, Christopher, 139
Wright, J. Skelly, 99, 106; criticized by Linde, 108
Wygant v. Jackson (1986), 153

Yates, Robert, 21